Well
Worth
Saving

Well
Worth
Saving

American Universities'
Life-and-Death
Decisions on Refugees
from Nazi Europe

LAUREL LEFF

Yale UNIVERSITY PRESS/NEW HAVEN & LONDON

Yale University Press books may be purchased in quantity
for educational, business, or promotional use. For information,
please e-mail sales.press@yale.edu (U.S. office) or
sales@yaleup.co.uk (U.K. office).

Set in Minion type by Integrated Publishing Solutions,
Grand Rapids, Michigan.
Printed in the United States of America.

Library of Congress Control Number: 2019941098
ISBN 978-0-300-24387-1 (hardcover : alk. paper)

A catalogue record for this book is available from the
British Library.

This paper meets the requirements of ANSI/NISO
Z39.48-1992 (Permanence of Paper).

10 9 8 7 6 5 4 3 2 1

To the refugees, then and now
and
To the memory of my father, Ernest Leff,
a World War II combat veteran who
was proudest of his fights for justice and for peace

Contents

Illustrations

Introduction

The telegram that landed on Princeton professor Rudolf Ladenburg's desk on May 7, 1940, was short and to the point. If an American university did not agree to hire Hedwig Kohn right away, the former University of Breslau physics professor would be loaded onto a train and shipped to Poland. "Deportation Poland a question of weeks," the telegram said. It came from a Swedish economist who, along with a German exile physicist, had arranged for Kohn to be able to enter neutral Sweden but only if her stay was temporary. Swedish authorities needed proof that Kohn had a job waiting for her in the United States.[1]

For six years, Ladenburg, who was himself a German émigré, had been working to find faculty positions for Kohn, his former student, and other physicists dismissed under the Nazi regime. So far he had not had any success finding a place for Kohn. The fifty-two-year-old Kohn was still in Breslau, without any means of support. Ladenburg knew he had until mid-June or Kohn would be sent to Poland, "and that means practically death."[2]

Princeton would not hire Kohn, for many reasons, starting with the fact that the university appointed only men to its faculty. So Ladenburg turned to the American Association of University Women (AAUW), whose contacts at women's colleges seemed the best hope. As soon as she received Ladenburg's warning, Esther Caukin Brunauer of the AAUW wrote to the presidents of seven colleges, explaining Kohn's "urgent, if not desperate . . . problem," asking for a "letter of invitation for next June," and insisting "the time is very short." If one of the presidents agreed to hire Kohn for the following academic year, she would be able to get an entry visa to Sweden and escape before she could be deported. On May 25, Brunauer dispatched the letters to Sweet Briar, Goucher, Connecticut College, New Jersey College for Women, Wellesley, Vassar, and Sarah Lawrence. She and Ladenburg then waited to see whether any American university would offer Kohn a faculty job, put it in writing, and save her life.[3]

Throughout the Nazi era, American universities made many choices similar to the one that faced the seven women's college presidents in May 1940. Should they hire scholars trying to escape Nazi-dominated Europe and thus restore their careers and ease their path to immigrating to the United States? Or should universities during a decade of economic depression allow budget and other concerns to lead them to reject the thousands of applicants banging on their doors? Those who received positions at American institutions of higher education could obtain non-quota visas that would spare them the long waiting lines, both literal and metaphoric, emerging all over Europe. Some universities made the choice to hire refugee scholars, knowing what those scholars were suffering in Europe. Immediate deportation was not always in the offing, but a life of privation and persecution certainly was. Many universities, however, did not.

This book examines the American academy's response to the immense moral, practical, and scholarly challenges posed by the decimation of Europe's academic elite during the 1930s and early 1940s. From 1933 until the end of World War II, desperate scholars besieged American universities. They had been fired from university posts for being Jewish or politically suspect or had been forced to flee when Germany overran their newfound havens. Some Americans helped in their quest— individual professors acting out of friendship, a sense of morality, or professional pride; and academic organizations seeking to preserve science, scholarship, and universal principles. Others stood in the way: faculties who feared competition from foreigners and Jews; administrators who worried about budgets, bureaucracy, and negative publicity; and State Department officials who sought to limit immigration, including of people with distinguished academic pedigrees. Ultimately, universities decided which scholars were "worth saving," in the unfortunate phrase of the time, and the State Department decided whether they were to be saved.

The promise of a non-quota visa exerted a powerful pull on those seeking to escape Hitler's Europe. Immigration law in the United States allowed scholars or clergy and their wives (wives did indeed mean wives, not spouses, as will be discussed later) and minor children to immigrate outside limited country-by-country quotas. During the 1930s, just 25,957 people could immigrate annually to the United States from Germany, when hundreds of thousands sought to leave. Those who qualified for a non-quota visa did not need to wait for a place within the quota. In addition, no limit existed on the overall number of non-quota visas that could be issued, while a 150,000 annual limit applied to quota visas. Close relatives of U.S. citizens and residents of countries in the Western Hemisphere could receive a non-quota visa, as could students who were at least fifteen years old and studying at a school approved by the secretary of labor.

For professors the key provision was Section 4(d) of the Immigration Act of 1924. It provided a non-quota visa to "an immigrant who continuously for at least two years immediately preceding the application for admission to the United States has been, and who seeks to enter the United States solely for the purpose of, carrying on the vocation of minister of any religious denomination, or professor of a college, academy, seminary, or university; and his wife, and his unmarried children under 18 years of age; if accompanying or following to join him." To qualify under the provision, immigrants had to establish that they *had been* professors in a higher education institution and that they *would be* professors in such an institution in the United States. Refugee scholars therefore needed American universities to offer them jobs to establish that their purpose in immigrating to the United States was to carry on the vocation of professor. Significantly, the provision also enabled professors' wives and minor children to receive non-quota visas.

Professors and clergy enjoyed the only professional privilege available under the restrictive immigration laws of the 1930s and 1940s, putting universities in the rare position of being able to extend a lifeline to imperiled refugees. Yet non-quota visas were rarely used. Relatives of U.S. citizens were far and away the largest group to receive non-quota visas. For the year ending June 30, 1938, 9,719 relatives received them, compared with just 493 ministers and professors, only 67 of whom were from Germany. All told, only 944 professors and 451 wives and 348 children received non-quota visas between 1933 and 1941, when most emigration from Europe ended.[4]

The State Department's stinginess in interpreting the law partly explains the small number of professors to receive non-quota visas. So does the reluctance of U.S. universities to make the offers in the first place. The decision to hire a refugee scholar was an individualized one, just like any other hiring decision. The faculty of a particular academic department would assess the candidate's qualifications in terms of teaching, publication, and service. The university administration would weigh in. An offer would be made—or not. Yet certain forces pushed these decisions in similar directions. The State Department defined who qualified as a professor under the Section 4(d) provision. Outside funding organizations set standards, and networks of professors backed or blackballed particular hires. It therefore is possible to detect hiring patterns that spanned departments, disciplines, and institutions. Overall, to be hired by American universities, refugee scholars had to be world class and well connected and working in disciplines for which the American academy had a recognizable need. They could not be too old or too young, too right or too left, or, most important, too Jewish. Having money helped; being a woman did not.

Thousands more scholars sought university jobs than received them; for instance, the primary committee in the United States that helped rescue European scholars—the Emergency Committee in Aid of Displaced Foreign Scholars—received more than 6,000 appeals and ended up placing just 335 scholars. The Exile University of the New School for Social Research, which was started to provide a haven for refugee scholars, estimated in late 1938 that "at least a thousand refugee scholars are looking for the ten jobs that are likely to turn up." Two and half years later, the ratios had improved but still were not encouraging. The school's director, Alvin Johnson, explained that "a thousand names [had] been submitted" in the previous year, and "we have invited almost 100," with twenty-five in the United States and "at work." Not surprisingly, the foundations and other committees that engaged in rescue work did not trumpet their failures in postwar accountings. In 1955, the Rockefeller Foundation, which helped just over three hundred scholars immigrate to the United States (there is considerable overlap with the list of 335 grantees of the Emergency Committee), noted simply that several "failed to reach America."[5]

Yet in a moment of candor, a Rockefeller Foundation vice president, Thomas Appleget, summarized in 1946 the academic community's wartime experience:

> The displacement of scholars for political and racial reasons began in Germany with the advent of Hitler. Subsequently, it spread to Spain, Italy, Austria, Czechoslovakia, and then, country by country, marched with the advancing armies until nearly all Europe was affected. Thousands of universities and research teachers were displaced, among them the most distinguished in the world; not merely debarred from teaching and research, they were not allowed to make a living at all. As the fury grew these men found themselves frequently in peril of their lives. Many eminent scholars, indeed, did die for no cause but their race, their religion, or their intellectual integrity.[6]*

The European scholars who failed to obtain a university appointment and a non-quota visa were not all thrust into the maw of the Final

---

* Two points about language. First, the term "refugees" will be used throughout this book with the understanding that a special category for those escaping political or religious persecution did not exist in the 1930s and 1940s under U.S. immigration law. Still, "refugee scholar" is a commonly used term, including at the time, and others, such as "exile scholar" or "foreign scholar" or "émigré scholar," assume a degree of volition in migration not appropriate to the circumstances. Second, contemporaneous documents almost always refer to "men" such as Appleget's comment "these men found themselves frequently in peril," even though female scholars are likely to be under discussion as well. This usage will not be noted again, but it is worth remembering as reflective of the attitude toward female academics.

Solution. Some managed to immigrate through the regular visa system (though in the process they might have deprived a nonscholar of a chance to emigrate), including dozens who ultimately received university appointments. Some went to other countries; Great Britain, Turkey, Palestine, and South Africa were common destinations, particularly for academics. Others managed to escape to neutral countries, such as Switzerland or Sweden, and wait out the war there. But many—perhaps thousands, certainly hundreds—were forced into hiding, imprisoned in concentration camps and ghettos, and deported to extermination centers.[7]

This book tells some of their stories and those of the universities that turned them down. It follows eight refugee scholars in particular, from their dismissals from European universities as Jews or non-Aryans, through their first attempts to obtain university jobs in the United States, to their last desperate pleas to escape. *Well Worth Saving* chronicles the lives of Max Fleischmann, dean of the law faculty at the University of Konigsberg and the University of Halle and director of Halle's newspaper institute; Hedwig Hintze, a historian of the French Revolution and the first woman to assume a faculty position at the University of Berlin; Leonore Brecher, a Rumanian-born zoologist who conducted research in Berlin, Rostock, Cambridge, Hamburg, and ultimately Vienna; Michel Gorlin, a St. Petersburg–born scholar of Russian literature and linguistics in Berlin and Paris; Mieczyslaw Kolinski, a Berlin-based musicologist and anthropologist who fled to Prague and Brussels; Marie Anna Schirmann, a researcher at the University of Vienna's Institute of Physics; Käthe Spiegel, an archivist and medieval historian in Prague; and Hedwig Kohn, the physicist trying to reach Stockholm from Breslau weeks ahead of her scheduled deportation to Poland.

The experiences of these refugee scholars add to what is a vast and worthy literature on the intellectual migration of the 1930s and 1940s. But their lives, and in some cases deaths, sound discordant notes in what has been presented as a triumphal symphony. In the familiar score, the United States welcomes Albert Einstein and Enrico Fermi, Hannah Arendt and Herbert Marcuse, Rudolf Carnap and Richard Courant, along with hundreds of other physicists, philosophers, mathematicians, historians, chemists, and linguists. They in turn transform the American academy through pathbreaking contributions to their disciplines. This version, composed over decades by both scholars and popularizers, is apt and important. Yet it slights significant undertones.[8]

The literature has tended to concentrate on famous, or at least successful, refugees and fixate on what the United States gained and Germany lost in pushing them into exile. Those who succeeded can be identified relatively easily, and their accomplishments can be summarized, synthesized, and analyzed. Not so for the many more whose lives flowed in disparate and often invisible directions. Yet the preoccupation with prominent refugees has led "the literature on emigration to become a literature of celebration." This literature of celebration also is one of self-congratulation, crediting the American academy for making possible the exiles' achievements. The scholars' contributions have been noted, but so too has the environment that seemingly recognized and fostered their talents.[9]

In addition, an obvious truth has distorted the understanding of the intellectual migration: those who survive calamitous events shape the history of the period, while the dead too often are forgotten. This phenomenon is magnified in the case of scholars who survived the Nazi conflagration by escaping to the United States. Many were writers and teachers, and they and their students have written about this migration to an extraordinary degree. At least four hundred autobiographies have been published. If the refugees themselves were not recounting and deconstructing their experiences, their colleagues and students were—"in other words . . . the very people least able or likely to provide a disinterested assessment."[10]

Although preoccupied by immigration while going through it, the refugees tended to overlook the bedeviling process in their accounts of exile. One minute the scholars are undergoing the savagery of the Nazi regime in Berlin, and the next they are in Princeton writing about totalitarianism or inventing the atomic bomb. *Escape to Life,* a contemporaneous account by Erika and Klaus Mann, for example, devoted a single paragraph to the topic in a book longer than three hundred pages. The Manns, novelist Thomas Mann's children and refugees themselves, acknowledged the difficulties of emigrating, yet they did not dwell upon them. "Of course, only a fraction of those who *want* to come, have actually arrived," the Manns point out, and "the emigration conditions in the

'totalitarian states' as well as the immigration regulations into America
are becoming increasingly stringent. In New York one meets a certain
literary man from Vienna and one knows all his colleagues would prefer
to be here also." Yet the Manns did not delve into why those colleagues
could not be here. Grateful to their new nation for saving their lives, the
refugees who escaped understandably did not highlight the difficulties
of gaining entry to the United States. Their scholarly successors initially
ignored the actual process of who came, and how and why as well, perhaps taking a cue from the refugees' accounts. A separate literature
chronicling the difficulties that all refugees faced when immigrating to
the United States during the 1930s and early 1940s barely mentions scholars' unique circumstances.[11]

During the past two decades, scholars of the intellectual migration
have begun to deepen and darken their ebullient depiction. They have
tackled the immigration and hiring problems scholars faced within specific disciplines, such as mathematics and physics. They have increasingly recognized the bias toward successful émigrés and tried to compensate for it. In examining a broader range of refugees who made it to
the United States, scholars have found great disappointment amid the
overall record of success. Even this reckoning, however, assumes a central fact—that all of those who wanted to come to the United States did.
It overlooks those who tried but could not come to this country; those
who not only did not achieve prominence, but did not even survive or
survived only after undergoing the horrors of the Holocaust. Without
their stories, the overriding myth of a welcoming American academy
remains largely intact.[12]

Well Worth Saving shifts the focus from those who arrived in the
United States to those who did not and in the process reveals the crushing
choices professors, administrators, foundation officials, and rescue advocates made along the way. It depicts American universities that never
fully acknowledged the crisis befalling the global community of scholars
nor rose to the challenges the Nazi era presented to intellectual life.

Of the seven college presidents to whom Esther Caukin Brunauer
had written in late May 1940 on behalf of physicist Hedwig Kohn, two
rose to the challenge: Meta Glass of Sweet Briar College and Mildred
McAfee of Wellesley College—though the latter required considerable

prodding. The day after Glass received Brunauer's letter, she expressed her willingness to invite Kohn for the 1941–1942 academic year. "In the years I have known Miss Glass I have appreciated increasingly her combination of wisdom and human sympathy," Brunauer wrote to Professor Ladenburg to tell him of her offer. "It is good to know that there are still people like that in the world."[13]

Ladenburg and Brunauer had overcome the first obstacle to saving Kohn's life. Many more would emerge in the coming months.

O • N • E

The Nazi University

s 1933 dawned in Germany, Hedwig Kohn was still a physics professor in Breslau, a city of about six hundred thousand people in Lower Silesia. Max Fleischmann was leading the University of Halle's law faculty and developing its newspaper institute. Hedwig Hintze was lecturing at the University of Berlin and caring for her ill husband, himself a prominent historian. Leonore Brecher was settling in at the University of Kiel's physiology institute, her fourth and last stop as part of a prestigious three-year Yarrow Research Fellowship. Michel Gorlin and Mieczyslaw Kolinski were beginning their careers in Berlin—Gorlin studying for a Ph.D. in Slavic studies and Kolinski working at an archives that collected traditional music from around the world. On January 30, 1933, Adolf Hitler became chancellor of Germany.

A little more than a month later, Daniel O'Brien, who worked for the Rockefeller Foundation in Paris, embarked upon his regular round of visits to German researchers funded by the foundation. Hoping to rebuild German scholarship after the Great War, the foundation supported many academic programs in Germany, where the universities were among the best in the world. O'Brien, who had received his M.D. from Johns Hopkins and had worked for the foundation for seven years, had many stops planned on his Germany trip. Yet from day one, he en-

(1) Daniel O'Brien, Rockefeller Foundation official based
in Paris. Courtesy of the Rockefeller Archive Center.

countered the disruption and distress caused by Hitler's accession to
power. Even before the law banning Jews and non-Aryans from being
employed by the government went into effect, German universities had
begun their purge.[1]

The Nazis had targeted Jewish influence in German universities
for years. National Socialist racial ideology required that academic life
be cleansed of Jewish teachers and students and that the state and universities coordinate in espousing Nazi tenets. Since the late 1920s, Nazi
and nationalist supporters had agitated against Jewish professors on many
German and Austrian university campuses. The promotion of Jewish

professors, or even their continued presence, led nationalist students and professors to protest, cheered on by the right-wing press. They also attacked Jewish students, often violently. These deliberate attempts at creating havoc succeeded, prompting the demotion or firing of Jewish professors and the expulsion of Jewish students. The victories demonstrated both the potency of antisemitism as a way to stir up social and political unrest and the vulnerability of German universities. Individual campus controversies spilled over into wider calls for the purification of the German academy. Upon assuming power with Hitler's accession to the chancellorship, the Nazis naturally turned their immediate attention to purifying German universities.

O'Brien saw the results during his stay in Berlin from March 23 to March 26, 1933. He discussed the "present situation" with August Wilhelm Fehling, the Rockefeller Foundation's German representative for the social sciences. Fehling warned O'Brien against sending letters that might be considered "anti-Party or involving Jews" and noted that many Jews were trying to obtain fellowships abroad. "The general situation is bad for science. It may get worse," O'Brien noted in the official diary that foundation representatives were required to keep. "The Jews have already been and are being put out of positions." As he continued his visits in Germany, O'Brien encountered many Jews who were "being put out."[2]

In Frankfurt, O'Brien found chaos when he visited Franz Volhard at the university's medical clinic. "Prof. V. does not know whether Prof. [Gustav] Embden will be able to stay," O'Brien recorded in his diary. Embden, a physiologist who had a Jewish grandfather, was "almost inarticulate because of emotional stress," O'Brien noted. A colleague of Embden's sat weeping during the interview. Embden did not know his future, but his pupil, Gerhard Schmidt, knew his. A few minutes after learning that his physician father had died of cerebral apoplexy upon receiving news of his dismissal, Schmidt got a telephone call that he too had been dismissed. In Munich, neuropathologist Walther Spielmeyer "was terribly upset" at the loss of two pathology colleagues and feared for his own future because he was "of partial Jewish ancestry," O'Brien also noted.[3]

In Freiburg, Siegfried Thannhauser, who headed the university's medical faculty, had watched the dismissal of his two Jewish assistants.

"I feel like a father who has been deprived of his children," Thannhauser, who was Jewish but whose service in the Great War meant he was not imperiled immediately, wrote a few days later to a Rockefeller Foundation official. "On the whole," O'Brien recorded in his diary, "the Jews are being put out everywhere and without justice." On April 11, he summarized the situation for his predecessor in Paris who now headed the medical division in New York: "The Nazi party here is in complete power; opposition is practically non-existent. The party has shown its inclination to follow its prescribed program, namely to oust the Jews, Communists and foreigners from posts and from business; to purify the race, to build up Nationalism. They have already gone a long way along these lines."[4]

As O'Brien made his rounds, the German government turned into law the policy the universities had anticipated in their preemptive dismissals. On April 7, the German government decreed that all members of the Jewish race were to be dismissed from civil service positions, meaning anyone who worked for the Reich, states, municipalities, or public corporations. Four days later another law defined Jews as those who had one Jewish grandparent, regardless of whether they or their parents or their grandparents had converted to another religion. Because all German universities were state run, that meant about twelve hundred Jews holding academic posts were dismissed immediately from German universities as a result of the 1933 legislation.[5]

Students at many universities demanded that their institutions fire more professors than the government required. At the University of Kiel, where Brecher was conducting research, students pushed the rector to fire twenty-eight professors immediately, including some who were not on the official list of those to be dismissed and some who would not resign voluntarily. The students planned to remove the twenty-eight professors' publications from the library and threatened to disrupt their lectures were they not removed. At the University of Berlin, where Gorlin studied and Kolinski worked at an affiliated institute, students insisted the rector resign unless he posted on all university buildings "12 theses against the un-German spirit" that included "Our most dangerous enemy is the Jew and those in bondage to him"; "Jews can only have Jewish thoughts. If a Jew writes in German he is a liar"; and "We demand that a selection be had of students and professors based upon surety of thought and the German spirit."[6]

By May 1933, the Rockefeller Foundation had assembled from official Prussian Press Service reports a list of thirty-nine people dismissed from six universities (and other reports of an additional thirty-seven dismissed) and unofficial reports on fourteen dismissed from seven other universities. The foundation received in July further confirmation of dismissals by the minister of education, as well as newspaper reports on those fired. Famed New York neurologist Bernard Sachs, who had studied under Germany's most prominent physicians, traveled to Germany in August 1933. "German conditions are as bad and as damnable as they could possibly be," Sachs wrote to Columbia anthropologist Franz Boas from the Grand Hotel in St. Moritz, "and no one dares to say a word!"[7]

Despite their firsthand perspective, Rockefeller Foundation staff members were not entirely sympathetic to the professors losing their jobs. Program director Robert Lambert initially noted a difference in reaction between the Paris and New York groups. "Difference is due undoubtedly to [the] fact that we here are in closer contact with the situation, and are meeting daily people who have suffered from the persecution," Lambert recorded in his diary on May 8, 1933. "The same Westerner who promptly forgets a newspaper headline reporting a million more Chinese dead from starvation, would be quite upset at seeing a single famished Oriental on his door step."[8]

Yet O'Brien, in the medical services division, and John Van Sickle, the assistant director for social sciences, both of whom were in the Paris office and traveled frequently to Germany, blamed the Jews at least partially for what was happening. As a result, they urged the foundation not to move too precipitously to cut funding in Germany. During his April 1933 visits to Germany, O'Brien echoed the views of University of Freiburg pathologist Ludwig Aschoff that "there is no doubt about the injustice of having such a large percentage of Jews—as many as 95–98% in some instances—in various city hospitals and . . . among the legal profession." O'Brien previously used a similar figure—98 percent of Berlin city hospital doctors were Jews—to conclude that "the Jews probably unwisely monopolized the situations and, consequently, there is some justification of the attitude of the Nazi party." (O'Brien's, or Aschoff's, numbers were exaggerated; about 16 percent of all physicians were non-Aryans and about one-third in the larger cities.) O'Brien advocated that the foundation "sit by and wait for [a] period of weeks or months to see what the eventual outcome is or where the base-line will be established." The following month Van Sickle noted that during his recent German tour four German-Jewish social scientists called on foundation officials one morning for help. "The individual cases are extraordinarily depressing," Van Sickle wrote, and then added, "We should not forget, however, that during the past fifteen years the Jewish liberal element has been definitely favored in Germany, and that they have, as a result, attained to a situation which inevitably produced a reaction."[9]

The foundation thus hesitated to withdraw its support of German scholars and projects in Germany in 1933, with the Paris office expressing concerns that "such action would be tantamount to our saying that the Jewish scholar and the Weimar Republicans alone had our confidence." Fehling, a foundation advisory board member, warned that the foundation reducing its support in the country would both harm the more liberal elements and discredit the foundation's work as "motivated by political and racial considerations." Even Lambert, who is often credited with being among the foundation officials most sympathetic to refugee scholars, wanted to make clear that the foundation was not going out of its way to help Jews. After Rockefeller Foundation president Max Mason visited the German education ministry, Lambert wrote in his July 3, 1933, diary entry: "I feel obliged . . . to correct MM's impression that we have been listening largely to the weepy tales of persecuted Jews. As a matter of fact, all of us have seen more Aryans in Germany than Jews." By this time, Lambert, who had initially insisted that it is "inevitable that the decrees will be modified," was no longer convinced. "The restrictions on Jews are, if anything being tightened," he wrote.[10]

Interrupted Research

Hedwig Kohn was not a Rockefeller fellow so O'Brien had not visited her department, though he had stopped at Breslau's Institute of Physiology to see Prof. Hans Winterstein. Winterstein's assistant had been fired, and Winterstein "was living on a grill and does not know whether his

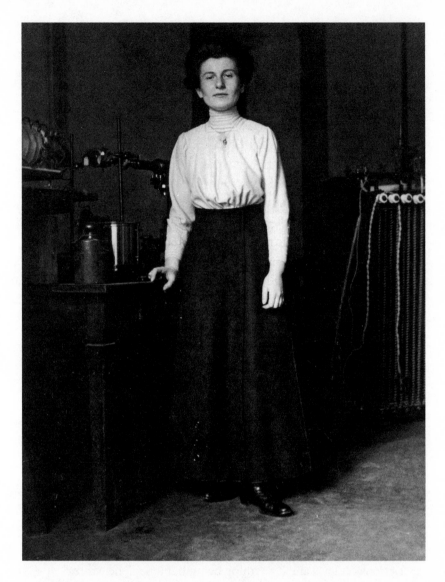

(2) Hedwig Kohn, University of Breslau Physics Institute, 1912. Courtesy of the Emilio Segre Visual Archives of the American Institute of Physics.

position is secure." (It was not; he was dismissed and took a position at the University of Istanbul.) Kohn's dismissal notice came to her at the Physics Institute in December 1933. Born in 1887, the daughter of a whole-sale merchant of fine cloth, Kohn had lived her whole life in Breslau and spent her entire professional and academic career at the university there. She later described herself as being "of Jewish descent and confession" (meaning that she considered herself part of the Jewish community) "and of German nationality." Breslau's Jewish community, at about thirty thousand people, was the third largest in Germany and was well integrated, particularly in scientific and academic circles.[11]

Kohn received her degrees at the University of Breslau, including a doctorate in experimental physics in 1913. She went to work at the university the following year as an assistant in the physics laboratory as well as working with another professor on heat radiation and illuminating engineering. During the Great War, she had replaced all five of the lab's male assistants in preparing professors' lectures, instructing students in practical exercises, and performing administrative work. In her research, she studied the quantitative measurement of the intensity of radiation and contributed to atomic and molecular spectroscopy. In 1930, she received habilitation, an additional degree that qualified the holder to teach certain subjects. (Only two other women received habilitation in physics before the war.) Kohn was given the title of *privatdozent*, enabling her to lecture without being on the full-time faculty and to conduct research. As a privatdozent at the University of Breslau, she taught atomic physics, heat radiation, and special optical subjects until being fired. Her father died the year before her dismissal; her mother had died in 1926. Kohn depended upon the small pension she, at least at first, received.

Historian Hedwig Hintze had just gotten her career back on track when she was fired from the University of Berlin. Born Hedwig Guggenheimer in 1884 of Jewish parents, she attended a higher girls' school while also being tutored in history and philology. Her parents' wealth— her father was a successful banker and influential member of the Munich community—enabled her to complete her education and pursue an academic career. She studied at the University of Munich, even though women were not yet able to receive degrees from there. Moving to Berlin in 1908, she continued her studies in German language and literature, history, and political economy. She participated in seminars taught by eminent University of Berlin historian Otto Hintze, who described her as his best student. They married in 1912, when he was fifty-one and she was twenty-eight.

She spent the next two decades nursing her ill husband and studying for an advanced degree in history. Although she participated in the
elite academic circles of which her husband was a part, Hedwig Hintze
was something of an outsider—as a woman, as a liberal, and as someone
of Jewish descent, though she had converted to Protestantism. In 1924,
when she was forty years old, she received her doctorate with a specialty
in the French Revolution. In 1928, she became the first woman at the
University of Berlin to receive habilitation and to become a privatdozent. She also published a major book on French constitutionalism that
year. Hintze edited *Historische Zeitschrift,* a respected historical journal,
and published essays and reviews in the press on French-German relations, a controversial topic during the decades after the Great War. In
May 1933, the journal's editors, including her thesis advisor, Friedrich
Meinecke, fired her, primarily for political reasons. On September 2,
1933, the University of Berlin expelled her, primarily for "racial" reasons.
University of Tubingen historian Adalbert Wahl referred to Hintze as "a
disgusting Jewess." She fled to Paris, leaving her husband in Germany.
She worked there for the French Center for the Study of the Revolution
of 1789; but, as she later explained, her husband was "aryan" and "aged"
so she had not emigrated "definitely" at that point. She might need to
return to Germany.[12]

Biologist Leonore Brecher also lost her position in September 1933.
She was a researcher at the University of Kiel's Physiological Institute
when its director, Rudolf Hober, was dismissed for being Jewish. Brecher
had had a peripatetic life and career until that point. Born in 1886, she
had lived in three Rumanian cities until she left the country in 1907 to
attend the University of Vienna. She earned her doctorate there in 1916
under the tutelage of Hans Przibram with a thesis on the color adaptation
of chrysalids. Throughout her career, her research focused on whether
and how the environment and heredity conditioned color changes in an-
imals, particularly the chrysalises of cabbage white butterflies. She became a researcher at Przibram's famed Institute for Experimental Biology
at the Austrian Academy of Sciences, publishing twenty articles, fifteen
in two leading journals, by October 1923. That year, with Przibram's backing, Brecher applied for the degree of habilitation at the University of
Vienna, which would have allowed her to teach. For three years, her ap-

(3) Scientists at Vienna's Institute of Experimental Biology, 1923,
including researcher Leonore Brecher, sitting in the front row,
with institute director Hans Przibram to her left and researcher
Auguste Jellinek standing behind Przibram. Courtesy of Barbara Eisert.

plication sat without being reviewed. One of the university's earliest and
most rabid Nazis headed the committee that finally reviewed it in 1926.
Along with two other future members of the Nazi Party, he rejected her
application, concluding that Brecher was "unsuited to maintain the authority required of a lecturer over students." (The same year, the university denied habilitation to Paul Weiss, her institute colleague, who was
also Jewish. He immigrated to the United States in 1927 and became one
of the most influential neurobiologists of his generation, winning the
National Medal of Science.)[13]

In 1928, Brecher received a Yarrow Research Fellowship from Girton
College, one of Cambridge University's female colleges. Her fellowship
took her to Cambridge, Vienna, and Hamburg to conduct research on
caterpillars and to assist the head of each laboratory where she worked.

She had previously worked in the labs of Hans Winterstein (who was then at the University of Rostock) and Rhoda Erdmann in Berlin. Brecher arrived in Kiel at the end of 1931, by which time her fellowship had expired. A cousin supported Brecher, whose parents both had died before she turned twenty, so she could work under Hober researching the permeability of membranes as well as her own caterpillar studies. Hober had been one of the Nazis' prime targets before the party assumed power in 1933. As the University of Kiel's rector, Hober had punished Nazi students who were violent and disruptive, leading to protests directed at him. On September 28, 1933, Hober received the notice that he was dismissed, and his laboratory was shut down. "It is therefore no more possible to continue research under Professor Hober at the Physiological Institute at Kiel," Brecher wrote to a colleague, "and I had to interrupt my research although it was going so well and gave such interesting results." She continued: "I liked so much to work under Professor Hober. He is wonderful." On November 1, 1933, Brecher returned to Vienna and to Przibram's biology institute.[14]

Poet and doctoral candidate Michel Gorlin also knew he had no future in Germany. Born in St. Petersburg in 1909, Gorlin, like many intellectuals, was drawn to study in Germany and went to the University of Berlin for Slavic studies. There he met Raissa Bloch, a graduate student who was also a Jew from St. Petersburg and eleven years his senior. In Berlin, Gorlin studied Russian literature of the nineteenth century and wrote and defended a thesis on Nikolai Gogol and Ernst Theodore Hoffman. Bloch received a doctorate in medieval history and wrote poetry. Together, they started a poetry club that included another Russian exile, Vladimir Nabokov; organized literary evenings; translated scholarly works; and coauthored a dozen children's books in German. Bloch began a serious study of a pioneering female German poet. When the Nazis assumed power in 1933, Gorlin went to Paris and Bloch followed soon after.[15]

"The Time of Objective Knowledge Is Past"

As the Nazi regime was dismissing professors, it was transforming German universities in other ways. On May 17, 1933, Rockefeller Foundation official John Van Sickle spoke by phone with a German economist who told him "objective work in the social sciences is greatly compromised," not only in teaching but in research as well. The economist further explained that "a professor, for example, would risk his position, however pure his Aryan stock," if he argued that Germany could pay more in reparations. The economist also described "the uncertainty of life in Germany," recounting what had happened in his own home while he and his wife were out of town. "Two brown-shirts" had ransacked his house from garret to cellar and pointed a pistol at his grandmother and young daughter who were there.[16]

In June 1933, the Rockefeller Foundation explained in a widely circulated memo the "revolution" in German universities: "The official watchword is: 'The time of objective knowledge is past'; the universities have now only the task of arousing and promoting the national consciousness of the people. . . . Natural sciences and mathematics are justifiable only in so far as they can serve national purposes." Ministry of Education officials had been dismissed, the memo stated, replaced by "impassioned but amateurish National-Socialists" who were often motivated by "resentment against the exact sciences which have been so successful in recent years." The ministers relied upon "confidential men" within the universities who informed them about "unreliable individuals, that is, individuals who in the opinion of the confidential men or National-Socialist student leaders are not prepared to serve the National-Socialist State with all their power." Even mathematics was endangered. In April 1934, the foundation circulated an article, "The New Mathematics," that described a lecture by University of Berlin's Ludwig Bieberbach, who argued that German and Jewish mathematics are "separated by an unbridgeable chasm."[17]

The dismissals of Jewish professors and the revolution in the universities' approach were connected. As historian and natural security specialist Karen Greenberg explains:

> The application of "Aryan" methods often entailed deletions from the accepted body of modern scholarship. Aryan physics rejected the name of Einstein as well as the theories of relativity and quantum mechanics on the grounds that "exces-

sive mathematical calculation," typically Jewish, was "inimical to the proper spirit of natural research." For similar reasons, advocates of "mathematical apartheid" encouraged discrimination against algebra scholars such as Emmy Noether. In psychology, the field of psychoanalysis, the brainchild of a Jew, was deemed anathema to the purposes of the Nazi state. In place of non-Aryan scholarship, Nazi scholars attempted to create "Aryan studies."[18]

German universities also delved into the "Jewish question" as a subject of study to validate antisemitic ideology. Anti-Jewish studies programs, dedicated to proving the danger Jews posed, replaced nascent Jewish studies programs such as the one led by Martin Buber at the University of Frankfurt. As Horst Junginger describes in *The Scientification of the "Jewish Question" in Nazi Germany,* longstanding antipathies toward Jews within the German academy made antisemitism, along with nationalism and antibolshevism, "a mutual point of reference between the universities and National Socialism making it possible for two worlds of thought, formerly not particularly compatible, to reach some kind of understanding."[19]

Mieczyslaw Kolinski, a Berlin-based musicologist and anthropologist who was thirty-two years old in 1933, fell victim to the ideological, as well as the "racial," change in German universities. Born in Warsaw in 1901, he moved with his family to Hamburg and became a pianist, performing his own compositions as well as Tchaikovsky's concertos with the Oldenburg Philharmonic Orchestra. Kolinski went to Berlin to continue studying piano and to embark on a Ph.D. in musicology and anthropology. His 1930 doctoral thesis was on the Malaka tribes and their relationship to Samoan music. He then worked as an assistant to Eric von Hornbostel, head of Berlin's Staatliches Phonogramm-Archiv, which collected traditional music. Hornbostel was considered the foremost scholar of what was then referred to as "primitive music," and he accepted very few students.[20]

Hornbostel recommended his best student, Kolinski, to two American anthropologists, the legendary Franz Boas of Columbia University and Melville Herskovits of Northwestern University, who had been Boas's student. Boas and Herskovits needed someone to transcribe music they had recorded as part of their fieldwork. Kolinski first transcribed Boas's Indian songs from Vancouver Island made in the late 1920s and then turned to Herskovits's work. During 1928 and 1929, Herskovits and his wife, Frances, also an anthropologist, had traveled to Suriname and recorded "the songs of Bush Negroes." Herskovits wanted Kolinski to transcribe and analyze the songs, being particularly attentive to what was derived from African sources and what from European sources. Beginning in April 1932, Northwestern paid Kolinski $75 a month. When Kolinski finished the music from Suriname, Herskovits obtained a grant from the American Council of Learned Societies for the musicologist to move on to the Dahomean religious songs that Herskovits had recorded in West Africa (in the country now known as Benin). Kolinski continued to work for Hornbostel, helping run the institute as his assistant and making several field trips to the Bavarian Alps and the Sudeten.[21]

In 1933, the newly installed Nazi regime began to dismantle the Phonogramm-Archiv and suppress comparative musicology as a field not worthy of study. Hornbostel, whose mother was Jewish, was fired from the archive in 1933 and moved first to Switzerland and then settled in England, where he died in 1935. Knowing what lay ahead, the Jewish Kolinski did not waste any time. In April, he took a previously planned trip to the Sudeten, sent the recordings he made there back to the archive, and stayed in Czechoslovakia. With its relatively open borders and large German-speaking population, Czechoslovakia was a popular destination for German Jews in the early years of the Nazi regime. Kolinski let Herskovits know immediately that he was in Prague, where Kolinski's brother lived.

"I am greatly distressed at the news that you have felt it necessary to leave Germany," Herskovits wrote in May 1933. "I hope that you will be able to find a safe and permanent refuge. I am very glad that you will be able to go on with the work on Dahomean records in spite of the necessity of leaving." Herskovits even managed to get Kolinski a raise to $100 a month to reflect the dollar's depreciation. Herskovits was beginning to realize how much his own search to find the African origins of American Negro spirituals depended on the work of the young German musicologist.[22]

More Dismissals

Herbert A. Strauss concluded that some two thousand German academics were dismissed from their positions between 1933 and 1935, about two-thirds of whom were of the Jewish religion or of Jewish descent. The remaining third either publicly supported their Jewish colleagues (a relatively small number that included the theologian Paul Tillich) or opposed the Nazi regime in other ways. As the Rockefeller Foundation's O'Brien made the rounds in 1934, the effects of the dismissals became clearer. In Berlin, for example, he encountered Frédéric Roulet and Robert Rössle, pathologists at Charité Hospital, who declared that their department "has been greatly injured, scientifically," and in teaching "by the loss of practically all of the assistants." The assistants had been replaced by "rather second rate men." O'Brien noted that Rössle was "very much disturbed but little can be done."[23]

A series of supplemental laws removed the exemption from dismissal for those who had served in or lost a father or son in the Great War and added people married to Jews to the list of those who could be banned from teaching positions. Another round of dismissals followed the adoption of the Nuremberg Laws in 1935. Max Fleischmann was dismissed in that wave. A former dean of the law faculty at the University of Konigsberg, Fleischmann was the current law dean and director of the newspaper institute at the University of Halle. He was generally recognized as one of the top international lawyers in Germany, having represented Prussia in its property dispute with the remnants of the Hohenzollern dynasty in the 1920s and the Weimar Republic at the Hague Conference on International Law in 1930. A Protestant convert with a Catholic wife, Fleischmann managed to hold onto his position at the University of Halle, where he had also been rector, until 1935.

Of the 247 people teaching at the University of Heidelberg in the 1932–1933 winter semester, 60—a quarter of the faculty—were gone by 1936. The University of Berlin and the University of Frankfurt each lost 32 percent of their faculty. Individual departments were even harder hit. At Heidelberg, for example, almost a third of the law, medicine, and philosophy faculty disappeared, replaced by younger, inexperienced adherents of Nazi ideology.[24]

Rockefeller Foundation officials continued to visit their grantees and record their circumstances. On December 6, 1935, for example, O'Brien visited the Munich home of psychiatrist Felix Plaut, who had just been fired from Deutsche Forschungsanstalt für Psychiatrie. "P., while philosophical, is deeply moved and upset about his dismissal as he is eager to continue his scientific work," O'Brien wrote in his diary. O'Brien noted Plaut's observation that "activities against Jews are increasingly severe and that it is probably only a question of time when life in general for any Jew will become quite insupportable in Germany." Plaut said he and his wife had not gone to a restaurant in more than a year. "Bathing establishments are completely closed to Jews," O'Brien continued, "as are clubs, municipal activities, etc., etc." As sympathetic as he might have been to Plaut's predicament, O'Brien mostly tried to figure out how to maintain Plaut's research in his absence.[25]

O'Brien was still making the rounds in September 1936 and finding the remaining professors adjusting to their circumstances. Medical professor Bernhard Fischer-Wasels at the Goethe University Frankfurt, whom O'Brien visited on September 16, had refused to join the Nazi Party. Yet Fischer-Wasels seemed relatively satisfied with the state of affairs, describing the Nazi regime as "doing sound and important nationalistic work." Despite "disturbances in the curriculum of the medical faculties which hamper teaching and also research," Fischer-Wasels considered the younger medical students, who were mostly interested in military camps and sports, to be "excellent" and thought they would "counteract the present disrupted state of medicine and teaching in Germany." Visiting another medical professor, Franz Volhard, whom he had met with in early 1933, O'Brien reported being surprised that "a man of V's capacity and knowledge" had been "completely swayed by the anti-communistic propaganda" in Germany.[26]

In November 1937, an organization to aid the displaced scholars reported that the dismissals, mostly of scholars who had "non-Aryan female relations" or who "could not tolerate the Nazi theories," showed "no signs of having come to an end." Earlier in the year, the group had estimated that 250 Aryan professors with wives who were Jewish or partly Jewish were being fired. Herman Hoepke, for example, was fired from his position at the Anatomical Institute of the University of Heidelberg in 1938 because his wife was half Jewish. He lived out the war practicing medicine in Heidelberg.[27]

By the end of 1938, German university faculties had shrunk by nearly 40 percent, with the percentage dismissed higher in certain disciplines, particularly the social sciences.[28]

Americans Learn of Germany's Change

As Americans confronted 1933, the fourth year of economic collapse at home, they learned of the transformation of universities and the dismissal of non-Aryan professors in Germany. Articles appeared in newspapers; analyses surfaced in scholarly publications; letters arrived in mailboxes. American academics often had professional ties to those in Europe and thus learned directly of the dismissals. Ross Gortner, chief of the division of agricultural biochemistry at the University of Minnesota, for example, learned in May 1933 that Prof. Herbert Freundlich, whose father was Jewish, had lost his post at Kaiser Wilhelm Institut für Elektrochemie in Berlin. Gortner wanted to bring Freundlich and other "outstanding" scientists to the United States in the hope of opening "the eyes of the German people to a fatal mistake which will have a profound influence on the scientific and cultural life of the German nation."[29]

Gortner's Minnesota colleague economist Alvin Hansen also learned of the dismissals directly. "I have received several letters from friends in Germany who have been discharged from academic positions under the Hitler regime and who are in serious distress," he wrote in 1933. Hansen, who became a Harvard faculty member four years later, ticked off the names of those who had been discharged, noting that "all of these men are known to me personally and they are very able in their respective fields." Henry R. Spencer of Ohio State University wrote on April 28, 1933: "The news has just reached me that Doctor Otto Lowenstein . . . has because of his race been just now eliminated from his position and is therefore ready to consider new opportunities; in short would like to come to America." As a political science professor, Spencer did not "presume to make a judgment" on the "scientific standing" of Lowenstein, a Bonn neuropsychiatrist, but considered him a "man of high character" and "sensitive conscience." Lowenstein fled immediately to Switzerland.[30]

As the decade progressed, American professors also learned about the transformation of German universities firsthand by attending Nazi-controlled academic conferences in Germany or by encountering Nazi-controlled German professors at conferences outside Germany. Walter Kotschnig, who had been director of the League of Nations' High Commission for Refugees from Germany, visited thirty-eight American universities in early 1936 as the commission's office disbanded. He sought to make people aware of the changes in German universities, delivering an address titled "The Dangers of Fascist Education." He simultaneously tried to assess the host university's likelihood of hiring refugee scholars. While in Chicago in February and in Boston and western Massachusetts in March, he spoke to groups of professors at faculty homes. He also reported speaking in April to about three hundred students and faculty at the University of Colorado, nine hundred at Colorado State University, and six hundred at the University of Nebraska.[31]

Kotschnig's message about the corruption of German universities, however, did not always get through. He spoke personally to the University of Nebraska chancellor, Edgar Allen Burnett, who seemed "mildly interested in the fate of the displaced German scholars" yet then bragged that a Nebraska philosophy professor, William Werkmeister, would be at the University of Berlin the next academic year. In exchange, Frederick Schonemann, a German professor of American literature and art history, would be at the University of Nebraska. Schonemann was a member of the Nazi Party and a steward of the Reich Propaganda Ministry who in 1933–1934 had been on a U.S. lecture tour to promote German-American relations. The exchange did indeed take place.[32]

Press accounts often reinforced what American academics discovered personally. In May 1933, Columbia anthropologist Franz Boas wrote to his university's president, Nicholas Murray Butler, informing him of the persecution of Jews and those opposed to the Nazi government. Boas explained that he had just talked to Danish physicist Niels Bohr, who had told him that "practically all the mathematicians in Gottingen have been ousted." But, Boas wrote Butler, "there is no need of dwelling

on the details because they are well known through our newspapers."
Throughout the 1930s and into the 1940s, American newspapers reported fairly routinely on what was going on in Germany and Jews' efforts to emigrate. Even the particularized problems of academics and
professionals were reported widely in the press. Indeed, many European
scholars learned about aid efforts by reading U.S. newspapers. The coverage picked up considerably in 1938 after the annexation of Austria,
referred to as the Anschluss, and then Germany's November nationwide
pogrom known as Kristallnacht.[33]

The topic also became a matter of academic study. Scholarly articles were published in journals including *Science,* the *University of Pennsylvania Law Review,* and the *Annals of the American Academy of Political and Social Sciences.* In 1937, Harvard tutor Edward Yarnall Harshorne,
who had spent a year studying the effects of Reich policies, published a
definitive account of the state of the German university. It was not possible to claim ignorance; as Karen Greenberg has concluded, "Scholars
in the United States . . . had ample information at their disposal about
German universities. Educators around the country acknowledged . . .
that the 'free German university is done for.'"[34]

Rescue Efforts

Back in Vienna in December 1933, Leonore Brecher wrote to Leslie C. Dunn, a Columbia University zoologist with whom she had worked in a Berlin laboratory six years earlier. Dunn had even invited her in 1930 to spend part of her Yarrow fellowship in his Columbia lab working on pigment production with the possibility of permanent employment there. The forty-year-old Dunn was building Columbia's zoology department into one of the country's best. Brecher never made it to the States, however, because of a "very unfriendly" Hamburg consul who had denied her a visitor visa. Brecher apparently had suggested to the consul that she might stay in the United States. Instead, she had headed to Kiel.[1]

But just for a year and a half. When the University of Kiel fired Rudolf Hober and shut the lab in which Brecher was working, she turned to Dunn. "On 1 November I had to leave Kiel and to return to Vienna because I had no more to live," Brecher wrote, noting that she was staying in a room in Vienna's Institute for Experimental Biology. Its director, Hans Przibram, allowed her to live there and gave her some administrative work so she would not be completely destitute. "I wish very much to go to the United States and continue there research," Brecher wrote Dunn, "and I beg you, if possible, to help me to a research place in the United States."[2]

(4) Columbia University geneticist Leslie C. Dunn,
1932. Courtesy of the Sixth International Congress
of Genetics, Ithaca, NY, Milislav Demerec
Papers, American Philosophical Society.

Across the continent, European scholars took up pens and turned
to typewriters to compose pleading letters to dispatch to the States.
Concerned American academics realized immediately that they had a
special obligation and a unique opportunity to help German scholars by
facilitating their hiring at U.S. universities. Hiring efforts took place at
three levels: through individual faculty members assisting friends and
acquaintances, through disciplines organizing to help colleagues in their
respective fields, and through national and international organizations
dedicated to helping scholars escape. These three levels often interacted.

As happened with Columbia zoologist Dunn, individual faculty
members would hear about friends or colleagues who had lost jobs, first
at German universities and then at Austrian, Czech, Polish, Italian, Danish, Dutch, Belgian, and French ones. American professors would start
writing to other academics to discover whether any university was able
to hire the displaced scholar. The efforts of Arthur Compton, a Nobel

Prize-winning physicist at the University of Chicago, were typical. In November 1938, he appealed on behalf of Bruno Rossi, an Italian physicist who had lost his position at the University of Padua because he was Jewish. Compton described the then-thirty-five-year-old Rossi as "the leading investigator of cosmic rays in Europe, perhaps in the world." Compton acknowledged that "bringing additional Jews into this country" could "promote serious antagonisms," yet it "would really be a world tragedy to have his abilities go to waste." Rossi did not immigrate to the United States immediately, going first to Denmark and then to Great Britain. He arrived in the United States in time to participate in the Manhattan Project through his work at the Radiation Laboratory at the Massachusetts Institute of Technology (MIT). Similarly, Northwestern's Melville Herskovits helped Mieczyslaw Kolinski, Yale Law School's Edwin Borchard helped Max Fleischmann, and Princeton's Rudolf Ladenburg helped Hedwig Kohn.[3]

At some universities, faculty members started funds to pay the salaries of displaced scholars. Columbia University was one of the most active. In 1933, 125 Columbia faculty members contributed a total of almost $4,000, or almost $80,000 in contemporary dollars, for temporary fellowships. Dunn, a committed refugee advocate even apart from his interactions with Brecher, was secretary of the Faculty Fellowship Fund, which John Dewey chaired. The fund supported five visiting professors, including theologian Paul Tillich and mathematician Felix Bernstein, without any university contribution. A few professors went beyond their initial contributions. Anthropologist Franz Boas, for example, instructed Columbia's secretary to withdraw $104.70 from his monthly pay during the 1935–1936 academic year to support sociologist Julius Lips.[4]

Some American professors devoted extraordinary amounts of time and effort to the refugee cause as well as to individual refugees. Among them were astronomer Harlow Shapley and government professor Carl Friedrich at Harvard; David Riesman, then at the University of Buffalo law school; Max Radin at the University of California law school in Berkeley; Borchard at the Yale Law School; Boas, Dunn, and law professor Joseph Chamberlain at Columbia; and mathematicians Oswald Veblen and Hermann Weyl at the Institute for Advanced Study. "God knows I would retreat from the nervous burden of worrying about academic ref-

ugees if my conscience would let me and anyone else would carry on—
anyone with academic connections and efficient machinery comparable
with those at my disposal," wrote Shapley, who directed the Harvard College Observatory. During his two decades of leadership, Shapley had
turned the Cambridge observatory into an essential destination for every
major astronomer. In a somewhat more optimistic tone, Shapley wrote,
"These refugee scholars, to be sure, take some of my time from the stars,
but the stars will not be of much good to us if we do not preserve the
minds with which to comprehend them."[5]

The refugee work often came at the expense of the Americans' own
academic duties. Chamberlain, who became chairman of the umbrella
refugee organization the National Coordinating Committee, acknowledged as much. "My time has been so taken up with meetings and conferences and handling cases that I have had little chance to see anybody
in these last twelve months, or indeed to do very much work in the university," he wrote in January 1939. "The need, however, is so great and the
conditions so terrible that I am glad to be able to do what I can to cooperate with those who are doing so much."[6]

That the faculty members assisting the scholars were feeling pres-
sured is evident from Chamberlain's response to John J. White, a Park
Avenue physician, who complained to Columbia University president
Nicholas Murray Butler. Chamberlain passed over White's "violent references to me" and insisted that his work on behalf of refugee scholars
"is but another application of the maxim that 'charity begins at home,'
for I am quite confident that American colleges and universities of the
future will be better for the bringing in of these few eminent teachers
from abroad." Riesman faced repeated complaints that the Buffalo law
school was getting the reputation that it cared more "about refugees than
about its duty to its unemployed graduates or its students." The then-
untenured Riesman was told that the refugee work was "taking too much
of my time for the good of the school" and that it "exposed me to criticism, which the school could ill afford." (Riesman recovered from any
career setback, becoming a sociologist, author of the classic of cultural
criticism *The Lonely Crowd*, and a Harvard professor.) Anthropologist
Boas's activism ultimately did not sit well with Columbia University and
probably brought a premature end to his distinguished career. He retired

with emeritus status in June 1936 and found his pay reduced and his office reassigned, which Boas considered a response to his criticisms of the university, particularly in a letter to the *New York Times*.[7]

Some professors, such as Chamberlain and Shapley, led or worked through existing organizations. Others, such as Phoebus Levene of the Rockefeller Institute for Medical Research, seemed to be one-man placement agencies, in Levene's case for chemists and physicians. (Norbert Wiener, an MIT mathematician, took a similar approach to helping mathematicians.) Levene received pleading letters, often from strangers. "It is the first time in my life, that I apply to people, I don't know personally, for support," Victor Egon Fleischmann wrote Levene sometime after November 1938, explaining that he had "neither friends nor relatives in U.S.A." Fleischmann described himself as being fifty-one and single, with degrees in medicine, law, and history from the University of Vienna. Levene apparently did not help Fleischmann, who was deported to the Dachau concentration camp on August 31, 1940, and died there four months later. Levene also received an entreaty from Gustav Kollmann, a forty-four-year-old Viennese biochemist whom Levene knew only because Levene had placed nucleic acids in Kollmann's lab. Still, Kollmann asked Levene to pay his fare to the United States from Utrecht, Holland, where he had fled after the Anschluss "with small luggage" and no money. "I am sure you will believe me, if I say, it is the most impleasant [*sic*] thing for a man of my social position to be forced to write such a letter as this," Kollmann wrote. Levene sent him $30. Kollmann's fate could not be discovered.[8]

Regine Kapeller-Adler, who headed a medical diagnostics laboratory in Vienna and developed a widely used pregnancy test, acknowledged immediately her discomfort in writing to Levene. "I should be extraordinary obliged to you, if you could procure me any call even very modest, that I may come with my husband and my girl of four years to your country as quickly as possible," the thirty-eight-year-old physician wrote after the Anschluss. "I am aware of my request, but I dare make it because of the actual situation in my country. I entreat you to do your possible." Levene declined, noting that he had "already given out all the affidavits I can possibly afford" and that the possibilities of obtaining a medical position were "practically negligible." Kapeller-Adler and her family immigrated to Great Britain, and she obtained a position at the University of Edinburgh. Levene claimed that he had "good luck" in placing about five of the forty scholars who had contacted him.[9]

Sometimes entire disciplines rallied around hiring refugee scholars, or even one individual scholar. Mitchell Ash noted the "many aid committees organized within individual disciplines, for example in mathematics, psychology and psychoanalysis." The American Philosophical Society prepared and circulated digests of exiled scholars in philosophy, which its exile committee described as "so variously gifted and [an] interesting group of scholars." In early 1939, the American Psychological Association sent a statement to all psychology departments in the United States, listing the roughly one hundred psychologists in need. The association's Committee on Displaced Foreign Psychologists had assembled the list and planned to hold a conference at Bryn Mawr at the end of March on placing psychologists. At that time, six psychologists had been placed. By the end of April, the list of those in need had grown to 150. The committee had corresponded with and had curricula vitae for a majority of those on the list, a third of whom were in the United States. By the end of the year, the Committee on Displaced Foreign Psychologists took credit for a total of twelve placements.[10]

American mathematicians provide another example. Although antiforeign, antisemitic, and protectionist sentiments were prevalent in U.S. mathematics departments, the discipline still managed to bring 120 to 150 mathematicians to the United States. The reason: prominent mathematicians—including Max Mason, president of the Rockefeller Foundation from 1929 to 1936; Oswald Veblen of the Institute for Advanced Study in Princeton; and Roland Richardson, a math professor at Brown University and dean of its graduate school—pushed for their hiring to fill gaps in the U.S. curriculum. American geographers raised enough money so that Alfred Philippson, a seventy-seven-year-old geography professor at the University of Bonn and his family could be transported to and supported in Switzerland. The plan failed, however, when the Swiss Finance Ministry would not issue a license to allow the funds to be deposited in a Swiss bank. Philippson and his family were sent to the Theresienstadt ghetto. He spent three years imprisoned there not too far from Prague and survived the war. By contrast, American historians did very little to help their European colleagues, as evidenced by the fact that almost no historians came on non-quota visas after being invited to join American institutions. The success of refugee historians in the States resulted from their own efforts to help one another and their strong professional profile.[11]

"This Has to Be Done Very Tactfully"

As impressive as these efforts were, they tended to be individualized and somewhat haphazard. The main impetus for saving European scholars came not from within the academy but from private organizations dedicated to that purpose that set the tone for university hiring. There were three broad categories of organizational assistance: organizations that sprang up to deal with the problem of refugee scholars, existing academic organizations that adapted to the new circumstances, and general refugee organizations that also assisted scholars. The two most significant of the new organizations were the University in Exile of the New School for Social Research and the Emergency Committee in Aid of Displaced German Scholars, which eventually changed to "Displaced Foreign Scholars" to acknowledge the problem's spread to countries throughout Europe.

The Emergency Committee started in May 1933 when Alfred E. Cohn, Bernard Flexner, and Fred M. Stein contacted Stephen Duggan, head of the Institute of International Education, a student exchange program. Cohn was a physician at the Rockefeller Institute for Medical Research; Flexner was a lawyer and a committed Zionist; and Stein was a retired businessman and philanthropist. All three were Jewish and lived in New York. Duggan, who had been a professor of diplomatic history at City College of New York and was an ardent internationalist, recognized immediately that Nazi control of German universities presented a problem for his group's exchange programs in Germany as well as for all of academia. Duggan agreed to be secretary of the Emergency Committee—the name indicated that he thought the problem would not last long—and assigned the young, ambitious assistant director of the Institute of International Education, Edward R. Murrow, to run the committee during his spare time. (Murrow went on to a legendary career as a broadcaster with CBS News.) The Emergency Committee assembled an executive committee to set policy, made up of the founders and several other members, including Leslie Dunn.

Demand for the committee's services was immediate. Elijah Bagster-Collins, an author representing the Emergency Committee, was in Berlin in November 1933 interviewing scholars about immigrating to the United States. "I am the lighthouse towards which the night birds fly!" Bagster-Collins wrote Duggan. (Bagster-Collins proved to be, as Felix Frankfurter put it, "a complete bust," ending his committee work in 1935.) After New York neurologist Bernard Sachs visited Germany in August 1933, he wrote to Duggan: "During my brief stay in Europe I have been besieged by cries for help from German university and other medical men. I have referred the university men to your committee. . . . I do not wish to add to the burdens of your Committee but I hadn't choice in the matter."[12]

As Sachs observed, a significant proportion of the academics would be "medical men." One of the first lists that circulated among American academics in May 1933 included the names of seventy-four people who had lost their academic posts in Germany—eighteen were medical researchers. Sachs soon formed an offshoot of the Emergency Committee to help medical academics, along with the Rockefeller Institute's Cohn. As a cardiologist and clinical researcher, Cohn took special responsibility for medical personnel. He had also served on the executive board of its parent and regularly communicated with other refugee organizations; Cohn probably took on more roles in trying to help refugee scholars than anyone else.[13]

The Emergency Committee sought to encourage universities to hire displaced scholars so they could receive a non-quota visa, emigrate from Germany, and resume their academic careers. The committee knew it was not going to be easy. American universities were undergoing serious financial distress as a result of the Great Depression, so, as Stein explained, "This, of course, has to be done very tactfully so as not to arouse resentment among the great number of professors here whose salaries have been cut or who have been dismissed because of the financial situation." More than two thousand American professors lost their jobs between 1930 and 1933—almost 10 percent of all academics. In 1933,

(5) Alfred E. Cohn, cardiologist,
Rockefeller Institute for Medical
Research. Courtesy of Rockefeller
Archive Center.

one hundred fewer people would be teaching math in colleges and universities and one hundred more would be looking for jobs than in the
previous year, Brown University's Richardson estimated. As a sign of the
decline, expenditures of U.S. law schools fell from $5.6 million in 1932 to
$4.6 million in 1933, with research budgets and professors' salaries tak-
ing a particular blow. In another example, Columbia University did not
increase the rank or salary of any of its junior faculty in the years following the 1929 stock market crash. The Emergency Committee at first
thought universities might ultimately fund the positions, but by 1935 the
realization had sunk in that that was not going to happen; it would be
necessary to continue to rely on outside money.[14]

The Emergency Committee developed a strategy to minimize objections among the American professoriate. First, the committee believed
it could lessen antagonism by having the request for scholars come from
universities themselves. Rather than send the names of available schol-

ars to universities, the committee would wait for a request to hire a particular professor to come from an institution. The committee stuck to this policy so strictly that it initially was not even willing to circulate names of scholars looking for jobs. The Emergency Committee's executive secretary, Betty Drury, sent her stock response to Helmut Guggenheimer, who had written about his father, Hans, a medical researcher and lecturer at the University of Berlin: "As it happens the Emergency Committee cannot because of its regulations bring the availability of displaced scholars to the notice of colleges and universities unless asked to do so by such institutions. Upon receiving such a request from a college or university the Committee will suggest candidates suitable for the position to be filled." Hans Guggenheimer escaped to Sweden in April 1939.[15]

At a 1938 meeting, several committee members declared that the committee was not "an employment service" and refused again to provide lists of displaced scholars because it might imply endorsement. As the problem grew, and more refugees reached out to the committee, it decided in 1940 to enlarge its staff "to develop our active but unobtrusive study of the field and promotion of candidates." The committee thus started a "cautious program of cultivation and persuasion—nationwide—on our part." It hired Laurens Seelye to "cultivate" possible openings, a process that could be a bit ghoulish. Committee staff seemingly scanned the obituary pages for the deaths of professors. Having learned of the demise of a University of Michigan mathematics professor in August 1942, for example, Seelye followed up by suggesting to Michigan "two or three very able people in this field." Seelye also noticed the death of a Michigan international law professor: "I wonder whether you would like to know more about a very able scholar by the name of Dr. Leo Gross." (The Fletcher School of Law and Diplomacy at Tufts University two years later hired Gross, who had been fired from his position at the University of Cologne in 1933.) This more aggressive approach came only quite late in the game.[16]

The second part of the strategy to lessen antagonism was to push temporary appointments and fund half the refugee's salary of $2,000, with other organizations picking up the remaining half. Universities thus were at least temporarily off the hook for paying for refugee scholars.

(The average salary for a full professor was $4,000 in 1935–1936, or the equivalent of about $76,000 in contemporary dollars.) The Emergency Committee's funds came primarily from Jewish institutions or individuals; as Stephen Duggan acknowledged in a letter, "As I said on Friday I leave all matters of finance to our Jewish members." In 1936, for example, the bulk of the Emergency Committee's money, $67,000, came from the New York Foundation, whose donors were primarily Jewish, and donations of between $500 and $2,000 from wealthy individual Jews. Other supporters over the years were the Nathan Hofheimer Foundation, the American Jewish Joint Distribution Committee, and the Rosenwald Family Association. In the spring of 1939, the committee was running out of money and cut its grants to $1,500 from $2,000 for a one-year, not two-year period.[17]

Ultimately, the committee spent $800,000 from 1934 to 1945 on refugee salaries and placed 335 scholars between 1933 and 1945. An affiliated organization, the Emergency Committee in Aid of Displaced Foreign Medical Scientists, made grants to 129 medical scientists, including four who were abroad and could not take advantage of the grants. Like its parent committee, the medical committee insisted that the universities themselves offer to hire the researchers with funds provided by the committee and other outside sources, usually the Rockefeller Foundation.[18]

The New School for Social Research started its University in Exile to provide academic positions for displaced scholars. American intellectuals and progressive educators founded the New School in 1919 to offer a new type of higher education where ordinary citizens and distinguished scholars could exchange ideas. In the 1920s, Alvin Johnson, the school's director and an economist by training, became a coeditor of the *Encyclopedia of Social Sciences* and collaborated with many German scholars. When the Nazis assumed power, Johnson realized immediately the implications for non-Aryan scholars. In 1934, the University in Exile received state authorization to offer master's and doctoral programs. It changed its name to the Graduate Faculty of Political and Social Science, which became the New School's graduate faculty populated entirely by displaced scholars. The sixty-year-old Johnson raised the money and chose the faculty among those he knew and considered creative, particularly in the social sciences.

When the Emergency Committee, which had formed around the same time, considered merging, Johnson resisted, primarily because his resources "were extremely mobile." As he described it in his memoir:

> I put the case of a scholar just one lap ahead of Hitler's hounds. What would the Emergency Committee be able to do for him? Recommend him to a college, where he would have to be approved by department, dean, college president, perhaps a committee of the board. In the meantime, Hitler's hounds would have got him. My institution could make up its mind in an hour and send off a cable carrying the privilege of non-quota immigration for the professor, his wife, and minor children. In such an emergency an Emergency Committee would have to turn to the University in Exile. We would always be ready to cooperate, but we could not merge.

Altogether, the New School hired about 180 scholars, including 23 after the fall of France when the Emergency Committee approach proved too slow.[19]

Unlike the New School's University in Exile, the Institute for Advanced Study in Princeton, New Jersey, was not started to help refugee scholars, yet its timing was fortuitous. Founded with money from Jewish philanthropists, the private, independent institute opened in 1933, just as German universities began dismissing their Jewish and non-Aryan scholars. The Institute, located in Princeton, New Jersey, though not officially affiliated with the university, welcomed a few dozen displaced scholars, most notably Albert Einstein. Hermann Weyl, who was a colleague of Einstein's in Zurich, joined the new Institute after leaving the University of Göttingen in 1933 because his wife was Jewish. Weyl, along with Einstein and math professor Oswald Veblen, also personally worked to place scholars at other institutions. Veblen and the Institute's two directors during this era, Abraham Flexner and Frank Aydelotte, both served on the Emergency Committee's executive board. Similarly, the founding of Black Mountain College outside Asheville, North Carolina, coincided with the rise of Hitler and the expulsion of German scholars. The experimental school thus hired several refugee scholars, including

(6) Mathematician Oswald Veblen of the Institute for Advanced
Study. Photograph by Alfred Eisenstaedt/Getty Images.

artists Joseph and Anni Albers, and taught many refugee students. Historically black colleges also had a particular need for talented professors willing to teach "Negroes" and therefore hired a number of refugee
scholars.[20]

Smaller organizations cropped up to deal with specific emergencies. For instance, the private Emergency Rescue Committee helped
scholars trapped in France after Germany invaded in 1940, including
many from Germany, Austria, and Czechoslovakia who had sought refuge there. Through its emissary in France, Varian Fry, this group helped
particular political and intellectual refugees whom the U.S. government
had recommended for emergency visas. The group assisted the escapes

of roughly two thousand refugees, including artists Marc Chagall and Max Ernst.

"To Maintain Standards of Intellectual Life"

Several other organizations extended their original mission to adapt to the emergency, most significantly the Rockefeller Foundation, which became a primary funder of refugee scholars' salaries. The Emergency Committee typically paid half a scholar's salary, and the Rockefeller Foundation paid the other half. As described previously, the foundation's extensive support of German scholars meant that it received an early and strong signal of the debasement of German universities. Yet the foundation initially hesitated to pull its support of scholars in Germany and to help Jewish scholars emigrate. From the start, the Emergency Committee tried to get the foundation to "come in our scheme." Alan Gregg, who headed the foundation's medical services division and had been in Paris until 1930, attended most committee meetings even though he was not on the board. Yet as of the end of 1934, the committee could not get "any clear statement" from the foundation on helping refugee scholars and considered some of the foundation department heads unwilling to change their rules to do so.[21]

Given the internal differences, the foundation's New York headquarters eventually commissioned international scholars, including economist Gunnar Myrdal from Stockholm, to evaluate German universities. The scholars' negative assessment of German higher education decided the matter. The foundation withdrew from Germany in 1936, thus freeing up funds for émigré scholars "without burdening the budget in any considerable way." From 1933 to 1939, the foundation allocated $730,000 to support displaced scholars, $500,000 to support 120 individuals in sixty-five American institutions and the rest to British ones. The German invasion of Western Europe in the spring of 1940 pushed the foundation into emergency mode, trying to save scholars in the Netherlands, Belgium, and France, among other countries. Overall, the Rockefeller Foundation spent $1.4 million on 303 refugee scholars between 1933 and 1945.[22]

The Emergency Committee also turned to a few other foundations to fill in its funding of university positions, including the Carnegie Foundation, which contributed a total of $100,000. The Oberlaender Trust, whose primary mission was to further German-American cultural relations, paid out $317,000 to support refugee scholars until they found other positions, even ones outside academia. Its contributions tended to be small, no more than $1,000 a year, and usually about $50 a month, for "maintenance," not even living expenses. The trust supported a number of scholars at smaller institutions, such as the Central College in Iowa and the Nebraska Central College, until the scholars moved on to more established research institutions.[23]

The American Association of University Women (AAUW) made a smaller contribution than the Rockefeller Foundation, though also significant, maintaining files on 152 university women and their families in Nazi-occupied countries. Like the Rockefeller Foundation, the AAUW's refugee work emerged from its prewar mission and its on-the-ground perspective, as it was part of an international federation that included organizations in Germany, Austria, the Netherlands, and other European countries. The German Federation of University Women expelled its non-Aryan members beginning in 1933. "We see this war not only as a war against brutality and aggression, but a war to maintain standards of culture and intellectual [sic] life and freedom," Jessie M. Bowie, the treasurer of the international federation, based in London, wrote in March 1940. "For us women this is particularly of importance knowing as we do, the way university women are treated in Germany in the years preceding the war, and what has been done to university men and women and all cultural life in Poland and Czecho-Slovakia since those countries were over-run."[24]

As soon as women in Germany and allied and occupied countries began losing their university positions, they turned to the international federation for help in emigrating. Marta Navarra Bernstein wrote the American group in January 1939, for example, noting her role as a founding member of the Italian branch of the international federation and the recent loss of her position teaching French and English literature "as a consequence of the last racial laws." The AAUW could not help the forty-three-year-old Navarra, however, who remained in wartime Italy, survived, and headed the Association of Italian Jewish Women in the postwar years.[25]

The AAUW's international connections often gave the group unusual insights into what was happening in Europe. For example, Karin
Kock of the group's Stockholm affiliate and vice president of the international federation told her fellow university women of the arrival in October 1943 of five thousand to six thousand Jewish refugees from Denmark. The Jews had escaped to Sweden as they were about to be deported
to Poland. Within days of the Jewish refugees having crossed the Ore-
sund "in bad weather or in moonlight nights," Kock described the extraordinary event. "Some have come without anything, literally without
clothes since they have had to swim," Kock wrote on October 20, 1943.
"Some have come in rowing-boats taking in water because of the heavy
loads and others in big sailing boats with several hundred passengers. . . .
The new Gestapo men who have come for this special purpose are beasts."
Kock noted that three university women were among those who had
arrived in Sweden, including one who is "working in my Institute." Kock
was the Swedish economist who had helped Hedwig Kohn three years
earlier.[26]

Esther Caukin Brunauer joined the AAUW in 1927 just after receiving her doctorate from Stanford University and headed its international relations program. During the 1932–1933 academic year, she took
a sabbatical in Berlin to revise her thesis on German World War I peace
proposals. After witnessing firsthand Hitler's rise and the initial dismissals from German universities, she switched her research interests to the
Nazi Party, interviewing its leaders and even conversing briefly with Hitler. When she returned to the AAUW, Brunauer took it upon herself to
spearhead the American organization's response. She informed American members about conditions in Germany through lectures and newsletter articles and helped European university women through placement
and immigration efforts.[27]

Unlike the Emergency Committee, the AAUW made direct appeals to university presidents. The group's general director routinely approached "colleges on our accredited list concerning university women
who have sought help from us finding a position in this country." In the
summer of 1938, for example, AAUW general director Kathryn McHale
inquired of those universities whether they might be making changes in
their faculty and enclosed descriptions of "some outstanding displaced

(7) Esther Caukin Brunauer, head of the American Association
of University Women's international relations program.
Courtesy of AAUW Archives, Washington, DC.

women scholars." As previously described, Brunauer in 1940 contacted
directly the presidents of women's colleges to see whether any of them
would be willing to hire physicist Kohn.[28]

Although scholars turned to organizations with connections to the
academic world, they also sought out any group that might help them
escape Europe. The refugees mostly wanted assistance finding U.S. citizens willing to sign affidavits promising to support them financially. At
the beginning of the Depression, the Hoover Administration decided to
use a provision of the immigration act, referred to as the "likely to become a public charge" clause, to keep immigration well below the quota
numbers. At first, the consuls turned away everyone who did not immigrate with substantial resources; eventually they modified their position

to allow in some immigrants who produced affidavits from U.S. citizens promising to support them so they would not become public charges. That set off a desperate hunt for Americans willing to provide such statements. (The State Department still managed throughout the Nazi era to keep immigration at about 15 percent of those allowable under quotas.)

Scholars who thought they might have to immigrate under the regular quota system thus sought assistance with affidavits from groups that aided refugees generally. Scholars who were offered university positions without credible salaries provided by the Emergency Committee, the Rockefeller Foundation, or the institution itself also needed to provide affidavits to prove they would not become a public charge. Among the organizations helping to find affidavits were the National Refugee Service, an umbrella organization that began life as the National Coordinating Committee; and the American Friends Service Committee, the Quaker organization that helped refugees who were not being helped by other organizations. The American Jewish Joint Distribution Committee and the Hebrew Immigrant Aid Society also provided assistance, as did smaller organizations such as the American Committee for Christian German Refugees and the American Guild for German Cultural Freedom.[29]

Scholars also turned to organizations outside the United States. The Academic Assistance Council, which renamed itself the Society for the Protection of Science and Learning in 1936, helped European scholars find positions in British universities. As a general rule, British universities accepted more readily the fact that German universities were no longer free intellectual enterprises. No British university sent a representative to celebrate the 550th anniversary of the University of Heidelberg in April 1936, for example, while many U.S. universities did, including Harvard, Yale, and Columbia. To the Emergency Committee's Cohn this exemplified a difference that also manifested itself in the willingness to accept refugee scholars. In fact, the Emergency Committee initially asked its chairman, Livingston Farrand, president of Cornell University, to resign after he agreed to send a Cornell representative to the Heidelberg celebration. Executive committee members pointed to statements from Oxford and Cambridge refusing to attend, which noted the contradiction between congratulating Heidelberg and attempting to aid the thousands of scholars Heidelberg and other German universities had sacked. The Emergency Committee's head, Duggan, who had been out of town when Farrand's resignation was sought, disapproved, insisting the committee stay out of such controversies. Farrand remained chair of the committee until his death in November 1939.[30]

The Emergency Committee's British counterpart also operated differently in significant respects. For one, it was far more involved in the hiring of scholars than the American group. Unlike the Emergency Committee, the British group compiled extensive lists of scholars by discipline. The Emergency Committee often found itself relying on the British list, which by 1938 included almost two thousand names and was considered a reliable guide. The Academic Assistance Council also differed from the American group in that it chose the scholars to be hired and paid part of their salary. Funding came from a type of self-taxation of British scholars. In fewer than two years, the British group raised $1,232,000.[31]

Columbia zoologist and Emergency Committee executive committee member Leslie Dunn tried to get American professors to contribute to the support of refugee scholars. He noted that Columbia had started such a fund in 1933, but no new appeals had been made in three years. "Conditions abroad are so bad, I'd be inclined to risk whatever repercussions might follow from renewed appeals," Dunn wrote in November 1938. "I've always been in favor of a broader base of support for refugee scholars—the dollars may not be important in amount but American professors will want to identify themselves with something that is of extreme importance to the future of our country as well as of Europe, and take a little share of a burden that has been borne almost entirely by the Jewish Community." American professors never established such a fund. These differences led Claus-Dieter Krohn to conclude that the British academy "demonstrated a much greater commitment and solidarity than their American colleagues." (The British Federation of University Women also had a better track record than the AAUW, which despite all its efforts placed just five women in American universities.)[32]

Although the groups aiding refugee scholars cooperated to a large extent, they also tended to engage in turf wars. The Emergency Committee and the Academic Assistance Council worried that greater resources for one group might diminish resources for the other. Emergency Committee members grew particularly enraged when their British counterparts toured U.S. universities, as happened in 1936, 1937, and 1939. Committee members expressed fears that the trips would stir up antisemitism, but they also assumed their British counterparts were poaching on their territory. The British group responded that its representatives were trying to learn about conditions in the States to better advise refugee scholars in Great Britain, not to find specific openings for particular scholars. The Emergency Committee also did not like the fact that the group, by then renamed the Society for the Protection of Science and Learning, made grants in the spring of 1938 for scholars to travel to the United States in the hopes of finding a position. When the Emergency Committee complained, the society stopped for a while and then resumed funding the travel. "Experience has taught us that when refugee scholars arrive from Germany without a position they naturally go shopping among institutions (naturally the same institutions) seeking a position," Duggan complained almost a year later.[33]

A few other international organizations were involved in refugee scholar work. The Comité International pour le Placement des Intellectuels Réfugiés specialized in the emigration of professionals primarily to France before the German invasion. German scholars founded the Notgemeinschaft Deutscher Wissenschaftler im Ausland, which was first headquartered in Zurich and then moved to London, with an office in New York and one in Istanbul. Directed by German economist and émigré Fritz Demuth, the Notgemeinschaft worked with the Turkish government to bring German professors in political science, law, medicine, and philosophy to Istanbul University. In the United States, the Notgemeinschaft primarily served as a resource for refugees; until the late 1930s, the New York office was basically a one-man operation with a budget of around $1,000. The Emergency Committee seemed satisfied that the Notgemeinschaft would act only as a directory, referring refugees to the appropriate agency, and therefore would not impede upon its work. It did worry, however, that the organization was foundering in 1939 just as the refugee crisis was growing. The Emergency Committee's Cohn even wrote to Felix Frankfurter to see whether he would be willing to help solicit funds to maintain the Notgemeinschaft as a clearinghouse.[34]

"Help in Finding a New Position"

All these organizations worked together to try to find jobs for refugee academics. Typically, a scholar who had lost his or her job would write to a friend, or an acquaintance, or even a stranger in the United States seeking help. The American then would write to one of the organizations involved in helping scholars, or even groups that helped refugees more generally such as the National Refugee Service. A staff member might then write to American professors in the scholar's field to determine his or her reputation and to perhaps prod the American professor to find a possible placement for the scholar. That might trigger a general hunt for a job, which, if successful, would prompt another round of inquiries to funding organizations and American professors to write recommendations. A funded university position would culminate in a request to the State Department for a non-quota visa, which, if the State Department had concerns, as it often did, might set off another round of inquiries about the scholar's qualifications and background.

Physicist Hedwig Kohn, after she was fired from her position at the University of Breslau in December 1933, thus contacted the British Academic Assistance Council. A November 1934 council note described Kohn as being forty-seven, single, formerly a privatdozent at Breslau University, and an assistant at Physikalisches Institut with a specialty in "atomic, optics, rays, light." Kohn also wrote Rudolf Ladenburg in Princeton, who spearheaded German physicists' emigration efforts from his lofty perch at the Palmer Physics Laboratory. Ladenburg passed her name to the Emergency Committee along with that of twelve other "German scientists who have lost their positions and who have written to me asking if I could help them in finding a new position." (Ladenburg mentioned that another professor had given him the information on five of the physicists and had asked him "to bring them to your attention.") Ladenburg wrote that Kohn, whom he listed second among the twelve professors, had worked with him when he was a professor at Breslau. "She did some very good research work and had quite a number of young physicists working under her direction," he wrote to the Emergency Committee. "She gets no salary now. I can recommend her very heartily as a teacher as well as a research worker." Ladenburg enclosed a detailed

curriculum vitae that included a list of publications, reviews of publications, and testimonials from five professors with whom she worked. But
neither a British nor an American university offered Kohn a position in
1934, or the year after that or the year after that. In 1935, she spent three
months at a Swiss observatory, researching "spectral distribution of the
intensity of sky radiation." She then returned to Breslau. For the next
three years, Kohn used space in the back of a university laboratory to
supervise students' research and to do research for industrial concerns.[35]

Max Fleischmann held onto his position at the University of Halle,
where he had also been rector, until 1935. Individual professors became
interested in his case, including Edwin Borchard, who had joined the
Yale law faculty in 1917 and was the Sterling Professor of International
Law. Although Borchard and Fleischmann both practiced international
law, Borchard knew Fleishmann only by reputation. Yet Borchard, the
son of a prosperous and distinguished New York Jewish merchant family, took up Fleischmann's cause and that of at least fifteen other refugee
scholars, including fourteen law professors from Germany, Austria, Italy,
and Czechoslovakia and one journalist from Germany. Borchard's ded-
ication is somewhat surprising because he was a committed isolationist,
even going so far as to write admiringly of Charles Lindbergh and the
America First movement. Ultimately, other professors, the Emergency
Committee itself, the Rockefeller Foundation, and the New School all
tried to find a U.S. teaching position for Fleischmann. At the same time
his brother, his nephew, and his cousins in the United States tried to
obtain a regular visa for him with the help of the American Friends Service Committee.[36]

Leonore Brecher also turned to the Emergency Committee and the
British Academic Assistance Council along with Columbia's Leslie Dunn.
Brecher was delighted to discover that Dunn served on the board of the
Emergency Committee. When she wrote him in 1933 seeking the committee's help, however, Dunn put her off. He explained that the committee assisted only in cases in which a university had extended an offer to
a scholar, and so far that had occurred only with "older and established
scientists." He advised that she try to obtain a position in a European lab
and then seek Rockefeller Foundation funding. Chances of employment
in the United States "are extremely bad just now," he wrote. Dunn also

may not have gotten over Brecher's imprudent interaction with the Hamburg counsel in 1930 because he warned that she would "again have the difficulty of convincing consular authorities that you do not intend to seek employment in the United States."[37]

In February 1934, Brecher complained to Dunn that her present situation was not sustainable because she could not do any research. Her work in Vienna's biology institute "consists mostly in technical help like order of the library, histological technique etc. and little time would be left for research work." What she wanted, she finally stated directly, was to work in Dunn's laboratory.[38]

A few months later, Brecher wrote to the Academic Assistance Council, but it sent her back to Dunn and the Emergency Committee. "It is becoming increasingly difficult to obtain invitations and temporary grants in the European universities," the council wrote her. It would be better if Dunn could secure an invitation from Columbia supported by an Emergency Committee grant. But Dunn seemed to have lost patience with Brecher, who had a tendency to write long, meandering letters (one went on for twenty-seven handwritten pages) and to commit to paper whatever thought popped into her head, from her need to see a physician, to her reluctance to transport her caterpillars on an ocean liner, to the amount of luggage to take with her on a trip. In responding, Dunn made clear that working at Columbia was not an option. He also had discussed her letter with the Emergency Committee and with two local university committees. All three indicated that very few openings existed. Dunn promised to keep looking but closed, "I am not very hopeful."[39]

Unsympathetic Administrators

W hile individual professors, entire disciplines, and national and international organizations were all trying to help refugee scholars, one group was conspicuously absent from the effort—university administrators. "Far from extending a concerted welcome to the scholars, the American academic establishment—represented primarily by the nation's universities and their spokesmen, the university presidents, greeted the scholars with marked hesitation," Karen Greenberg has written. A few university presidents did take part in the effort. Cornell president Livingston Farrand chaired the Emergency Committee from its inception until his death in 1939, although he mostly deferred to the committee staff. Carnegie Institute of Technology president Thomas Stockham Baker hired three "German Geniuses" after a 1933 trip to Germany, and he served on the Emergency Committee's board. Baker grew ill soon after his first hires—two of whom had bad experiences at the Carnegie Institute—and did not make any more. Johns Hopkins president Isaiah Bowman was one of the committee's go-to's for advice on a refugee's scholarly standing, though he did not have a good reputation among Jewish professors at that university or among refugee advocates. Alfred Cohn, who was on the Emergency Committee's executive board, seemed to think Bowman was better at lamenting the refugee problem than at taking action to help solve it. "Bowman made me tired; there's no good telling people who are wet that it's raining," Cohn wrote the New School's Alvin Johnson in 1936. "But then he's young at his game and I guess he has not got a lot of money and perhaps not a lot of bowels either." No university president was a leader in the effort.[1]

This reluctance was on display when the Emergency Committee first organized in 1933 and many prominent university presidents would not associate themselves publicly with it. At least fifteen of them came around once the committee announced it would provide funds to help hire scholars. But the misgivings did not go away, as the Emergency Committee's Edward Murrow noted when he made a trip to the western United States at the very end of 1934 and into 1935. Murrow visited many universities en route to California to try to raise funds and found that "all administrators are anxious to avoid a public statement of policy concerning the Germans now placed here" for fear of stirring up opposition in local communities. Murrow summarized the American attitude to his counterpart in Great Britain: "A general indifference of the [American] university world and a smug complacency in the face of what has happened to Germany . . . a tendency to consider the matter as a Jewish problem and a failure to realize that it represents a threat to academic freedom in this country as well as in Europe. Part of this attitude undoubtedly has its roots in a latent anti-Semitism which in my judgment is increasing very rapidly."[2]

Ruth Pope, educational counselor for the American Friends Service Committee, explained the administrators' attitude after she visited fifty-six Southern colleges in the spring of 1940. After noting that college presidents were "kindly and dominated largely by Christian zeal for the development of their students," Pope wrote:

> College presidents are concerned with educational efficiency. . . . They have their own ideas of what they need in selecting their faculty. They have heavy responsibility for administering their funds wisely. Pressure is irritating to them, largely because they long to be humanitarian and meet the need of refugees but they cannot afford to be emotional in spending other people's money. As one president was quoted, "I have

to maintain a college and should not be expected to stand as a philanthropist." While another said, "No sentiment can enter into my administration. I select for an opening the person who has the best qualifications. I can take no chances."[3]

Some university presidents were just at a loss. Irving Maurer, president of Beloit College in Wisconsin, wrote a plaintive letter to the Emergency Committee in December 1938, noting the "large number of personal applications we are receiving from professors in Germany and in Italy." Maurer explained: "When one faces the actual single representation of this evil situation naturally he feels particularly each appeal. At the same time, I feel very helpless, first in methods of appraisal and in the laying down of principles which should guide our actions." Maurer also expressed reluctance to assist the foreign scholars when "there are so many splendid teachers in America still looking for jobs."[4]

Alvin Johnson explained in 1940 the approach he and his fellow refugee advocates adopted toward university administrators: "It is very undesirable to approach presidents or deans directly. . . . It is, I think a good rule with respect to presidents and deans—let sleeping dogs lie."[5]

A few university presidents, however, could not be ignored. Karen Greenberg singled out as particularly obstructionist Harvard's James Conant, whom she says "demonstrated a more actively negative attitude," and Columbia's Nicholas Murray Butler, whom she credited with "a startling unconcern for the refugee scholars." She suggests that both men were far more interested in maintaining ties with German universities than in helping refugee scholars. Both Harvard and Columbia refused to be on the list of the Emergency Committee's initial advisors, which included the presidents of Princeton, Stanford, the University of Chicago, and twelve other schools. As already noted, both universities sent emissaries to the University of Heidelberg's 550th anniversary even though the entire British university system declined to do so. Although both presidents became more critical of German universities in 1937 and 1938, Greenberg considered this change to be "late and ineffectual."[6]

Columbia did hire several refugee scholars, including Paul Tillich and Max Horkheimer, but not at the initiative of its president. Like most American academics, President Butler received a steady stream of in-

(8) Columbia University president Nicholas Murray
Butler, 1924. Courtesy of National Photo Company
Collection (Library of Congress).

quiries about hiring foreign scholars. In 1940, he wrote that he was "receiving several requests a day to give aid to more or less distinguished
foreigners who have come to our shores." Yet, Butler explained, Columbia could not help them; instead, he would occasionally make inquiries
about establishing "relationships between them and other institutions."
Butler did make inquiries on behalf of a few select individuals, usually at
the behest of another prominent individual. For example, he requested
that "our fine arts people" look into a French art professor and determine
what organizations Butler could contact to help him "make a living." The
wife of a writer and member of the Bohemian Club prompted Butler's

inquiry. The following month, October 1940, Butler sent Rockefeller Foundation president Raymond Fosdick a list of six men for whom he was "doing [his] best to secure opportunities . . . to do university work of one sort or another somewhere in the United States." He asked Fosdick, who became the foundation's head in 1936, if he could "find it possible to give assistance to any of them." Only one of these six men—leftist French politician Pierre Cot—received a position at an American university, Yale, before the end of the war. It is not clear whether Butler helped Cot obtain the position. It was later revealed that Cot had been working for the Soviets.[7]

Butler's lack of concern for refugees may have stemmed from his abundance of concern about another issue that had a spillover effect: the large number of Jews in the vicinity of New York City who were attending Columbia University. Butler seemed to initiate what became the widespread policy of recruiting students from prep schools and from outside the New York metropolitan area so as to minimize the number of Jewish applicants. He explained to Columbia's secretary, Frank Fackenthal, the rationale for the policy: "It is particularly important that we use every effort to counterbalance the effect of the American tendency to go to a college in the immediate vicinity, since in the case of a college in the modern city of New York, this tendency if not held in check means the domination of the college in whole, or in part, by an undesirable element of the population." Dissatisfied with Columbia's law school in 1937, Butler used coded language to describe what was wrong. The "present student body is largely composed of those who lack many of the personal qualifications and equipment" necessary to attract college graduates "of the better class," Butler explained. To investigate the problem, Butler assembled a group of nine distinguished law school graduates, all seemingly WASPs.[8]

Columbia history professor Fritz Stern, who first encountered Butler as a Columbia undergraduate not long after Stern's arrival from Germany, considered Butler a "closet anti-Semite." At least some members of the Emergency Committee suspected that Columbia's reluctance to hire and retain too many refugee scholars resulted from antisemitism. When in the summer of 1938 the university balked at retaining legal scholar Arthur Nussbaum, who had been fired from his position at the

University of Berlin and was described as "somewhat semitic in appearance," Charles Liebman, a committee executive board member long involved in Jewish aid organizations, surmised the reason: "There is only one answer, and I do not want to give it." Columbia retained Nussbaum, who remained on the law school faculty until shortly before his death in 1964.[9]

"Medium Men of the Jewish Race Would Do a Lot of Harm"

Harvard's rocky relationship with the Emergency Committee and discomfort with the refugee issue began even before James Conant became president in 1933. His predecessor, A. Lawrence Lowell, did not have much use for Jews at Harvard. Upon assuming the Harvard presidency in the teens, Lowell had dismantled the university's once strong Semitics department and disassociated from the department's chief patron, financier Jacob Schiff, largely for antisemitic reasons. Lowell believed that "where Jews become numerous they drive off other people and then leave themselves." Lowell also tried in the 1920s to impose a formal quota on the number of Jewish students admitted to Harvard. He abandoned the plan, opting for an informal, albeit just as effective limit, only when the announcement caused an uproar.[10]

Not surprisingly, Lowell, who was Harvard president when Hitler became chancellor, took a dim view of the university hiring refugee scholars. He never responded to a request from Harvard Medical School dean David Edsall on behalf of several faculty members to establish a fund for German-Jewish professors. Edsall suspected Lowell was avoiding him. Lowell refused to serve on the Emergency Committee's general board as it was being formed in 1933. He would not commit to Harvard hiring a refugee scholar with the $2,000 the Emergency Committee promised to provide. Lowell at first suggested that as his presidency was ending he simply had not gotten around to the issue of hiring a scholar with Emergency Committee funds. In fact, the Harvard Corporation (Harvard's board of trustees) took up the issue in May, months before Lowell's departure, and had decided against becoming involved with the Emergency Committee. Lowell explained privately that he had not found the committee correspondence "sufficiently compelling" and had worried

(9) Harvard University president James Conant, 1933.
Old Paper Studios/Alamy Stock Photo.

that the proposal "appeared to be an attempt to use the College for purposes of propaganda." He echoed that concern in a memo he wrote upon
leaving the presidency, noting that New York Jews were trying to get the
Germanic Museum at Harvard to take "a professor of their race who had
been ejected from German universities." Lowell did not like the idea at
all: "This seemed to me an attempt at using Harvard for purposes of
propaganda, to which we would not want to lend ourselves; that if we
invited anyone it would be trumpeted all over the country by Jewish
organizations that Harvard was calling one of these expelled Jews and
that other places ought to do the same."[11]

Conant, who assumed the Harvard presidency on September 1,
1933, shared Lowell's attitude and for some of the same reasons—he

tended not to like Jews. When DuPont Corporation asked Conant, a chemist, to assess Max Bergmann, for a possible position with the company, Conant wrote in September 1933: "He is certainly very definitely of the Jewish type—rather heavy, as I recall." (Bergmann got a position at the Rockefeller Institute for Medical Research.) Conant then explained what he thought of hiring refugee scholars:

> We shall not help the cause of American science any by filling up the good positions in this country by imported foreigners. There was a time when it was essential to bring over some good men, but I think this time has passed, and I think a deluge of medium and good men of the Jewish race in scientific positions (age 40 or thereabouts) would do a lot of harm. Needless to say, do not quote me too widely on any of this.[12]

A month later, Conant received a letter from Selig Hecht, a distinguished Columbia biophysics professor who had received his doctorate from Harvard. "Since coming back from abroad a few weeks ago," Hecht wrote the Harvard president, "it has become painfully apparent to me that Harvard has taken no part in the effort of American learned institutions to provide places for those German scholars (Jewish or otherwise) who have been deprived of their posts by the Nazi government. I am puzzled by this because the two obviously possible reasons—lack of knowledge and lack of funds—do not apply." Conant ducked the issue, claiming to have "no information as to what attitude the Harvard administration took on many matters before September 1st of this year" when he became president. Conant was somewhat more forthright with the British political theorist and economist Harold Laski, who wanted Harvard to hire "an eminent international lawyer" dismissed from the University of Hamburg. To explain why Harvard would not hire the lawyer, Conant wrote: "I feel that any temporary measures in such a case can lead only to misunderstandings and do more harm than good. We are therefore not following the lead of other universities in this regard." The "misunderstanding" seemed to be that a temporary appointment would lead to a permanent place on the Harvard faculty. In another letter, Conant explained that should Harvard decide to hire "a distinguished

German scholar," the university would insist on paying an annual salary of $8,000 and commit to a lifetime appointment so it was not interested in the Emergency Committee's supplemented two-year positions.[13]

Conant did not publicly oppose the placement effort because of the influence of important Jewish alumni, such as Julian Mack, a federal appeals court judge involved in Jewish philanthropy. "I feel that people outside the University like Judge Mack are very apt to mix up charity and education, but of course I should be the last person to tell him this bluntly," Conant explained in a November 1933 letter to Grenville Clark, a Wall Street lawyer and a member of the Harvard Corporation. "A large number of the distinguished German chemists were Jews and have been displaced. I have not heard of any displaced one whom we could use satisfactorily in the Chemistry Department." Yet Conant indicated he would not stand too much in the way of departments that wanted individual scholars. In the same letter in which he wrote that not many of these men would fit at Harvard, he added, "If any of our departments recommends my calling one of these men, I shall be very glad to do so."[14]

Conant apparently did not stand in the way of Medical School dean Edsall as long as Edsall was in the role. When the Emergency Committee's medical offshoot in December 1933 wrote Harvard along with seventy other medical schools about their willingness to accept refugee professors, Edsall immediately put the question to his department heads. He received fifteen replies within the week, most saying they would hire foreign physicians. Until Edsall retired in 1935, the medical school considered many foreign researchers and hired about five.[15]

It did seem easier to get the university's acquiescence if the candidate was not Jewish. In writing that he wouldn't stop a department from hiring refugees, Conant noted that he had two such recommendations on his desk, "although they are not Jews." He added: "There may be a scrap of comfort in the fact that Yale is taking exactly the same attitude as we are." A few years later, Conant made extraordinary efforts to hire a non-Jewish German scholar whose life and career were not endangered. In 1936, Conant instructed dean of the Arts and Sciences Faculty George D. Birkhoff to induce University of Leipzig physicist and physical chemist Peter Debye to join the Harvard faculty. Birkhoff offered Debye a $12,000 annual salary (almost $220,000 in contemporary dollars), an annual research budget of $5,000, a very light teaching load, and the possibility of additional foundation support. It apparently was not enough; Debye continued to hold top positions at the Kaiser Wilhelm Institute and the University of Berlin during the Nazi regime. As chairman of the Deutsche Physikalische Gesellschaft, the German organization of physicists, he sought the resignation of all the group's Jewish members. In the past decade, critics have accused Debye of being a Nazi sympathizer, though the consensus seems to be that he was more of an opportunist than a believer. Debye left Germany in 1940 to become a professor at Cornell University.[16]

"Are Not We Doing Enough?"

Harvard's delicate dance—not helping the refugee effort, yet not looking as if it was blocking it—continued in 1934. The Emergency Committee made its first grants to American universities to hire refugee scholars that year, and Harvard was the only one to turn down the money. On page 23 of its January 28, 1934, issue, the *New York Times* declared, "Thirty-one American universities, including all the leading institutions of learning in the United States, with the exception of Harvard University, have made room on their teaching staffs for scholars who lost their places through Nazi persecution, it is revealed in the first report of the Emergency Committee in Aid of Displaced German Scholars." Harvard took umbrage. Conant's secretary complained that the Emergency Committee representation was unfair because Harvard had hired three scholars on its own, without committee funding. The Emergency Committee did not agree. It did not consider itself "responsible for the Times emphasizing the fact that Harvard did not participate. . . . the Times arrived at its own conclusion." The committee also was not convinced that Harvard had taken a bold stand in hiring three scholars: one was being financed by the Carl Schurz Memorial Foundation, another was receiving no salary, and a third was a former exchange student working with a Harvard professor.[17]

Although Emergency Committee members clearly considered Conant an adversary, they did not want to alienate the university any more. The frantic correspondence among committee members and sympathetic Harvard faculty illustrates the university's importance to the committee. After the committee discussed the issue at "great length" and "finally agreed unanimously" to respond, assistant director Murrow wrote to Conant in a letter he tried to phrase "as diplomatically as possible." Murrow explained that Harvard had put the committee in "an unfortunate position" by suggesting that the committee, rather than the *Times,* had emphasized the university's nonparticipation. In responding to Murrow, Conant did not explain why Harvard had not accepted any committee grants, focusing instead on the fact that the university did not intend to criticize the committee for leaving Harvard off its list. Duggan then weighed in to put an end to the back-and-forth. "Despite the poor light in which Harvard appears in this whole matter, I do not believe that anything will be gained by the Emergency Committee entering into a controversy with Harvard," he wrote. "My own belief is that the best thing to do is to drop the matter entirely." Harvard refused to take Emergency Committee funds to support scholars during the next academic year as well.[18]

A few Harvard faculty members, particularly Harlow Shapley in astronomy and Carl Friedrich in government, tried to push the administration to take more refugee scholars. Others, such as law professor and future U.S. Supreme Court justice Felix Frankfurter, seemed to profess great concern but demurred when it came to taking on the administration. Duggan had sought Frankfurter's help in getting then President Lowell to accept committee money to fund a refugee scholar, which was not forthcoming. Asked in 1935 to "take . . . up confidentially with President Conant" the possibility of finding a position for economist Moritz Bonn, Frankfurter bounced it back to Duggan "to bring the matter to President Conant's attention . . . in view of your general relation to these problems and your intimate personal knowledge of Bonn." Bonn, who had lost his position as rector of the Berlin Business School, immigrated to Great Britain. Frankfurter similarly declined to help Georg Wunderlich, an international lawyer. Wunderlich's sister, Frieda, an economist at the New School, had asked Frankfurter to meet with her brother at an international law conference. "Of course one wants to be of every possible help to a person like your brother, and it is more devastating than I can put into words that one is capable of being little help," Frankfurter wrote her. He then referred her to the Emergency Committee. The committee of course depended on university faculties to hire displaced scholars, which Frankfurter presumably knew. Georg Wunderlich immigrated to the United States and became an important human rights lawyer here.[19]

Still others aligned with Conant in opposing refugee hires. In May 1940, the possibility arose of hiring Harald Bohr, brother of Niels Bohr and himself a distinguished mathematics professor at the University of Copenhagen. The Institute for Advanced Study's Oswald Veblen was trying to find a position for Bohr. When Bohr's name was suggested to Conant, the president reportedly snapped, "'My God. . . . are not we doing enough in that field?" Harvard dean and mathematician Birkhoff passed along Conant's remarks to Shapley, who in turn, and as intended, passed them to Veblen. "I take it from George David's [Birkhoff's] remarks that Mr. Conant would like to have me pass on to you the conviction that we are not too much interested in Harald Bohr, and his future," Shapley wrote to Veblen. "How much of this is Conant—how much George David—you are as good a guesser as I am." Either way, Harvard was not interested. Bohr was trapped in German-occupied Demark. When the Germans began deporting Jews to Poland in the fall of 1943, Bohr fled with almost all the Danish Jews to Sweden. He survived the war, as did the vast majority of Danish Jews.[20]

Harvard had hired a number of foreign research fellows in the mid-1930s, but Conant, convinced that Harvard was "already doing enough," pushed at the end of the decade to limit their numbers. He told a meeting of fellows of Harvard College in October 1939 that he would not expand the current number of research associates and would consider only "exceptional cases." The president's position had an immediate impact. At the medical school, Sidney Burwell, who had replaced Edsall as dean, noted twelve days later, "I still have on my desk a large number of requests for refugee appointments for this year." The medical school had applications from forty-six refugees. Burwell formed a committee to screen for "exceptional cases" to present to the president. "Thus a somewhat conservative policy is in effect," he wrote the next month, "but the door is not closed to possible action in particularly urgent or important cases."[21]

Yet the medical school committee recommended very few hires, and even then the university administration turned them down. Despite the faculty's recommendation, for example, the medical school did not make an offer to Ludwig Pick, a world-renowned bone pathologist. Pick was deported from Berlin to Theresienstadt on June 16, 1943, and died there in 1944. The new standards were so tough that Harvard turned down Nobel laureate Otto Loewi when the Jewish physician and pharmacologist needed to escape first Austria and then Belgium in 1939. (Before leaving Austria, Loewi had been forced to transfer his Nobel Prize money to a prescribed German-controlled bank.) New York University found a position for Loewi, and he arrived in the United States in 1940.[22]

What Conant meant by "exceptional" became clearer in 1940. Harvard should hire only a refugee who was "preeminent and outstanding in his field" and not "simply the equal of some similar authority in this country" and only if Harvard could cover the person "financially for life." In other words, Harvard had to be willing to pay the refugee scholar's full salary for an indefinite number of years of service or the university would not hire the person, even if other sources of temporary funding were available. In October, Harvard's governing body officially adopted the policy of hiring only the most preeminent scholars to be supported for the rest of their lives. Harvard Corporation secretary Jerome Greene explained Harvard's unwillingness to take on more scholars in a letter to Duggan. He explained that Harvard already had seven or eight "Research Fellows by Special Appointment" and would not take on more because of the "grave danger of a quasi moral commitment" to keep "the men" on if funds were not available in the future; because of an inability to provide more facilities; and because Harvard had already taken on "a very large number of foreigners" and should not take on any more. "Apart from the scholarly competence and personal acceptability of the refugee scholars," Greene wrote, "the reasonable limitation on their number as members of the University community would have to be considered." The New School's Johnson placed the blame squarely on Conant: "I have been informed that President Conant in the last few days has notified departments that they should not take additional refugees as this would be unfair to the refugees they have already."[23]

Asked in January 1942 to issue a statement on the contributions to

American life of displaced foreign scholars, Harvard dean George Chase declined on Conant's behalf. Noting that Conant had not ever "touched on the subject," Chase wrote Duggan, "I have not the heart in the present rush in which he is to ask him to make a special statement." Even in January 1943 when the school was experiencing a staffing shortage because of the war, Conant would not budge. Medical school dean Burwell had written to Greene asking to hire refugee scholars, including one in the anatomy department. Sensing an opening, Greene wrote an encouraging letter to Burwell, but then added a postscript: "Since dictating the above, I have consulted President Conant whose answer is to the effect that the proposed appointment would be contrary to a policy emphatically declared by the Corporation some time ago and still in effect. I am sorry."[24]

Conant never shed his reluctance to support publicly the refugee scholar cause. Ultimately, Harvard hired forty-five scholars—some to the faculty, some in research positions—more than any other American university, yet not so many given the university's size and wealth. By May 1940, the California Institute of Technology, with 850 students, had hired fourteen refugee scholars, half as many as Harvard, which had ten times the enrollment.[25]

F • O • U • R

World Class and Well Connected

Whether it was Harvard, Cal Tech, Black Mountain College, or Southern Illinois State Normal University hiring refugee scholars, two potentially conflicting goals loomed over the process. One objective was to rescue the best scholars for the sake of intellectual advancement. The other was to save the most scholars for humanitarian reasons. A Rockefeller Foundation memo laid out the dilemma: "Are we trying to improve the quality of scholarly work in the USA, trying to do a dignified and humanitarian job from the standpoint of scholarship, or trying to do purely emergency relief to people with whom we have had previous relationships?" As Robin Rider put it in an article on mathematicians and physicists, "The crisis in German universities presented the rest of the academic world with both obligations and opportunities."[1]

The obligation to save fellow scholars and the opportunity to hire them often without paying their salaries played out throughout the period. Saving scholarship not scholars tended to be the dominant motivation, the one even the most ardent refugee advocates felt should be animating their decisions. "Much as I wish to alleviate the lot of scholars thrust out of their institutions by bigotry and tyranny," Alvin Johnson of the New School explained, "I could not wish to bring them to American institutions if I did not believe, as I do, that the cross fertilization of

66

American and European scholarship will raise the American intellectual life to a higher level." After visiting thirty-eight U.S. institutions of higher learning in early 1936, Walter Kotschnig, former director of the High Commission for Refugees from Germany, concluded that the Emergency Committee was succeeding largely because the committee had made sure the problem was "everywhere being viewed as an academic problem." He explained: "I found that those responsible for appointments are very eager to contemplate a possible appointment of German scholars as long as the candidature of these scholars is being made on an academic basis and not one of charity or an action prompted by humanitarian motives." Brown University mathematician and dean Roland Richardson explicitly rejected allowing "humanitarian considerations" into the selection process, arguing he would have "no adequate information for discrimination."[2]

There were exceptions. Harvard Medical School dean David Edsall, who had responded more enthusiastically to the idea of hiring refugee scholars than did his university's presidents, did not consider them like any other faculty hire. Harvard should hire, he wrote, "as many as possible of the men, who are of anywhere from good to excellent quality," and not just those who were exceptional and fit the university's needs. Edsall recognized that the university administration might think differently, and indeed it did, as we have seen.[3]

Academics went into hiring mode in some ways no different from any other hiring decision made then or now, though a bit more constrained by the lingering effects of the Great Depression; departments would assess scholars on the basis of scholarship, teaching, and the ability to fit into the existing faculty. Most universities maintained those standards even though the faculty making the decisions understood the consequences. In the 1930s, refusing to hire a scholar meant he or she probably could not emigrate and thus would have to face a life of privation and intense suffering in Europe. In the 1940s, rejection often meant death. Yale law professor Edwin Borchard recognized that possibility: "I believe it is pretty nearly a matter of life and death" for at least two of the three international law professors for whom he was seeking positions.[4]

Americans knew of the deplorable conditions under which Jews lived during the Third Reich: fired from jobs, subject to random violence,

arrests, and imprisonment; stripped of businesses and possessions; forced
to live in crowded, unsanitary conditions; denied entry to parks and
public transportation; and allowed to buy necessities and appear outside
only during designated hours. They also knew when state-imposed discrimination and destitution turned into decimation. So Americans knew
when the scholars they were trying to help were in concentration camps.
A summary of Ernst Emil Schweitzer's curriculum vitae described him
as a "recognized scholar in his field," having published several books on
jurisprudence. It then detailed his languages, his references, and his
present address: Camp de Gurs (Basses Pyrenees) France, Ilot C, Barque
XII, followed by this, under additional remarks: "His life is in danger on
account of enormous loss of weight through under-nourishment." His
American cousin tried to send him food, or money to buy food, but by
then, as will be seen, it was too late.[5]

Americans knew when the scholars were in hiding. In October
1940, the Rockefeller Foundation was considering assisting Gottfried
Salomon, who had been a sociologist at the University of Frankfurt.
Foundation officials knew Salomon was "hiding near Gard in the Rhone
Valley where he is living with friends under an assumed name." The New
School hired Salomon with Rockefeller Foundation funding. He escaped
France and arrived in the United States in September 1941.[6]

Americans knew generally that deportations were happening. In
advising Harvard Observatory head Harlow Shapley, who was trying to
get an astronomer out of France, the Rockefeller Foundation's Alexander
Makinsky explained that it was easier for a French Jew than a foreigner
to obtain an exit permit from the Vichy government. Foreign Jews "as
you may know," Makinsky added, "are now being deported en masse to
Eastern Poland."[7]

They knew when individual scholars were deported, including
specific information about their journey. The geographers trying to save
University of Bonn professor Alfred Philippson learned in November
1941 that he and his family were in a Catholic monastery outside Bonn
awaiting deportation to Poland. The Philippsons had been evacuated
from Bonn along with Jews from Berlin and the Rhineland. Else Bauer,
who knew Philippson's niece, wrote to his nephew in the United States,
who passed the information along to American geographers: "Unless it be

possible to obtain financial assistance, Prof. Alfred Philippson of Bonn—75 years old, will be transported to Poland,—the fate of the Jews there is so well known to us all—can you, or rather have you any possible way of averting such a tragedy?" Alvin Johnson, who was trying to determine whether Philippson was of "sufficient importance" to merit the New School's help, wrote fellow geographer and Johns Hopkins president Isaiah Bowman, informing him of the Philippson family's imminent deportation, "the worst thing that can happen to him."[8]

The Institute for Advanced Study recorded in a short memo dated February 6, 1942, the whereabouts of Ludwig Berwald, formerly head of the mathematics department at the German University in Prague, and his wife, Hedwig. "Our information of April 4, 1940, that Professor Berwald was in England was a mistake," Hermann Weyl wrote, noting that Berwald was a "mathematician of high distinction." "He stayed on in Prague, and he and his wife have now been deported to Poland." Helpfully, perhaps hopefully, the memo listed the Berwalds' transport information and new address: An den Altestenrat der Juden Prager Transport C., Nr. 816 und 817 Warthegau/Franziskanerstrasse 21 Litzmannstradt [Lodz] Ghetto Poland. The Berwalds were deported from Prague on October 26, 1941. Hedwig Berwald, sixty-seven, died on March 27, 1942, five months after they were deported. Ludwig Berwald, fifty-nine, died on April 20, 1942.[9]

Americans knew that deportation might be delayed if the scholar produced a letter stating that a university position awaited him or her in the United States. "The principal thing for me is to have a Certificate to show our authorities that I probably have an opportunity of leaving this country [Czechoslovakia] as emigrant within the next few weeks," Walter Froehlich, who had taught mathematics at the German University of Prague, wrote Weyl of the Institute for Advanced Study in January 1940. "Such a certificate is necessary for me, as you will readily imagine." Weyl, a mathematician himself, suspected that "the last sentence may convey sinister implications about deportations," yet he still did not think he could provide that assurance. Froehlich "scientifically . . . was not particularly outstanding so that I foresee considerable difficulty in procuring an academic position for him," Weyl wrote, "but I will make his plight known as much as I can." Weyl later updated the case: "Dr. and Mrs.

Froehlich have been deported from Prague. New Address: Prager Transport B, Mr. 976 and 977, Warthegau, Hanseaten Strasse 3.7 Litzmannstradt [Lodz] Ghetto, Poland." Froehlich died on November 29, 1942, at the age of thirty-nine in the Lodz Ghetto.[10]

And Americans knew what deportation almost always meant. In February 1941, German historian and librarian Helene Wieruszowski, who was in Italy and trying to emigrate, reported receiving telegrams from friends throughout Germany that Jews were "being threatened with exportation to Poland." Having received Wieruszowski's cable, a friend wrote to an American Friends Service Committee staff member, Annelise Thieman, on Wieruszowski's behalf. The friend assumed that Thieman knew about the deportations and that "being sent to Poland [is] about as good as a death sentence." The friend was right about Thieman's understanding. "As you know," Thieman responded, "the deportation of Jewish people to Poland has started again, and there is no doubt if help is to be given to these refugees at all, it should be given immediately."[11]

This is not to say that every faculty member who decided not to offer a refugee scholar a position knew the decision could be a death sentence; but it does mean that most everyone regularly trying to place scholars had access to this information. The frequent references to "deportation to Poland" were not presented as shocking or out of the norm, but what was to be expected.

"A Great Many American Friends"

A refugee scholar's best hope was persuading an American university to hire him or her. Connections mattered. "University appointments are almost always the result of personal relationships," Esther Brunauer, the AAUW staffer who spearheaded its refugee efforts, advised Marianne Beth. Beth, a lawyer from Vienna, worried that her position as a criminologist at Reed College would not be extended in 1941. Hiring comes from "being known by men and women well established in the field who also know of openings and will make recommendations," Brunauer continued. Beth was able to extend her stay at Reed until 1945, but she never held a university position after that.[12]

American professors already knew some of the refugee scholars, particularly those who had made academic visits to the United States. "There is little doubt that of all the intellectuals in Europe who hoped to obtain a position here, those who had been in America on visits had the best chances," Laura Fermi wrote. She also pointed out that this often led to "cluster formations," in which a European was hired to lead a particular department and then hired other Europeans, resulting in the "Europeanization" of a few departments such as art historians and mathematicians at New York University and astronomers at Chicago. Established organizations, such as the Rockefeller Foundation, often had arranged these earlier visits and continued to take an interest in the foreign scholar. In his study of sixty-five political scientists, Alfons Sollner found that those who had "been Rockefeller fellows before 1933 were quite often the ones to be promoted further." In some disciplines, such as physics, the previously established connections were so strong that the scholars could get hired without requiring the assistance of the Emergency Committee. "Their successful search for positions was facilitated by the high degree of internationalization of the field and by personal contact that had been established so effectively during the 1920s and early 1930s," Marjorie Lamberti found.[13]

Other scholars had weaker but still important connections to American scholars whom they had met through participation in international conferences. As refugee advocates tried to place Edgar Rubin, a Danish psychologist, the American professors they contacted mentioned how they knew Rubin. "His reputation as a scholar is very high and we are indebted to him for organizing an International Congress of Psychology," Goodwin Watson, a professor at Columbia University's Teachers College, wrote of Rubin. Robert MacLeod of Swarthmore College also emphasized Rubin's connections. Rubin "visited this country in 1939 on the occasion of the International Congress of Psychology at Yale University, and at that time he made a great many American friends," MacLeod wrote. MacLeod also thought highly of Rubin's scholarly work, concluding that he would "be able to make a significant contribution to American psychology." Herbert Langfeld of Princeton University was less enthusiastic, finding him to be "quite above the average psychologist but not among the leaders." Langfeld noted a "piece of research on attention" but added that Rubin "has not done anything of much importance since." The Rockefeller Foundation earmarked $5,000 for Rubin, and he was invited to be an associate professor at the New School with a two-year appointment. But the invitation came too late. The school never heard from him from German-occupied Denmark. Rubin managed to escape to Sweden with most of the Danish Jews in the fall of 1943. He returned to Denmark after the war, but the difficult conditions of his escape may have hastened his death in 1951 at the age of sixty-six.[14]

"Really Valuable People"

Americans' already knowing a foreign scholar helped, but ultimately American universities were interested in hiring top scholars. Carl Sauer, a University of California geography professor, said that his university might consider adding some displaced scholars in 1936, "but they would have to be first class, particularly if they are Jews." Almost all the institutions assisting refugees—the Rockefeller Foundation, the Emergency Committee, the New School—agreed that the priority had to be on saving world-class men. New School philosophy professor Horace Kallen described Vladimir Jankélévitch as "among the most brilliant and lucid philosophical writers of the younger generation" and "very well worth saving." As Oskar Goldberg, a medically trained philosopher on Judaism and a German refugee himself, wrote in 1942 upon viewing a list of philosophers, "The last list contains persons who are respectable people and really worthy of being saved." In thanking Mildred Adams of the Emergency Rescue Committee for her help with author Hans Habe, Marie Ginsberg of the Comité International pour le Placement des Intellectuels Réfugiés wrote Adams that "the people in question are worthy of all our attention. Please be assured that your time and effort have been spent for really valuable people."[15]

The idea of rescuing scholars to enhance knowledge assumed that Americans were involved in an international academic community and therefore could assess the scholarship of individual European professors. Assistance organizations thus turned to American scholars in their respective disciplines to evaluate each refugee scholar's worth. Initially, the Rockefeller Foundation assigned grades to scholars. Grades of A and

A–s indicated a "man of distinct importance in his field," Flora Rhind, a Rockefeller Foundation secretary, explained in a 1933 memo. A grade of B– "in many cases merely means that the person concerned is younger and has a lesser reputation than those ranking in the 'A' category, but that they may be and probably are in many cases of equal promise." Finally, the "'B' mark merely implies that the men, while of more than average ability, cannot be considered in the very first rank." Rhind attached a list of one hundred scholars with their grades.[16]

The Emergency Committee also assigned grades early on. So did Phoebus Levene, the Rockefeller Institute's one-man placement agency for chemists and physicians. He assigned a letter grade to the four displaced chemists he knew on a list, ranging from C+ for Hans Kleinmann of Berlin, "who may be a good man in a hospital lab," to a B+ for Gerhard Schmidt of Frankfurt. Despite his C+, Kleinmann, who had been in the chemistry department of the University of Berlin's Biological Institute, joined the faculty of the Medical College of Virginia as an associate in pathology with grants from the Emergency Committee and the Rockefeller Foundation. Schmidt, whom a Rockefeller Foundation official had witnessed learning of his dismissal in 1933, joined Levene's lab at the Rockefeller Institute in 1937. He stayed only briefly, eventually joining the Tufts University School of Medicine faculty and having a distinguished forty-year research career that earned him membership in the National Academy of Sciences.[17]

Another evaluation strategy deployed in the early years of the crisis was to circulate lists of deposed scholars and ask scholars in their disciplines to comment on each of them. In September 1933, Prof. Walther Spielmeyer, a neuropathologist with the Forschungsanstalt für Psychiatrie in Munich, received a list of seventeen psychiatrists and neurologists in danger of losing their positions. Spielmeyer provided an assessment of each one to Robert Lambert of the Rockefeller Foundation in Paris. Lambert reported Spielmeyer's comments, which ranged from "one of the best; a real savant" for Gabriel Steiner and the "second best neurologist in the field of psychiatry in Germany" for Victor Kafka; to "a good young clinician" for Paul Jossmann; to "an egotist; talks too much but is not as bad as he seems" for Robert Wartenberg; to "has written nothing in past 10 years; just a routine man" for Franz Kramer. (Steiner, a neurologist at the University of Heidelberg who specialized in multiple sclerosis, immigrated to the United States in 1936 and became a professor at Wayne State University School of Medicine in Detroit. Kafka, a neuropathologist in Hamburg, fled to Norway and then to Sweden when Jews were deported. Jossmann joined the Boston University medical school. Wartenberg eventually became a clinical professor of neurology at the University of California. Kramer lost his position at the Psychiatric and Neurological Hospital in Berlin, fled to the Netherlands in 1938 and then to the Dutch Indies, where he practiced medicine and survived the war.)[18]

At the request of the Rockefeller Foundation, the celebrated economist Joseph Schumpeter, a recent Austrian immigrant who had joined the Harvard faculty, evaluated nine German economists in 1933, sometimes with a very critical eye. Emil Lederer of the University of Berlin, for example, "was a more than competent economist although he never published any well-rounded work." Adolf Löwe of the University of Frankfurt "has no single outstanding performance to his credit, but certainly [is] a very good man." Both Lederer and Löwe joined the New School faculty. Schumpeter was not all that critical of the Nazi regime, at least in May 1933. He assured a Rockefeller Foundation official that the foundation could assist two top economists who had been displaced without it being considered "an unfriendly act toward the German government . . . which indeed I should not approve of myself." Schumpeter continued: "I know something of the government which preceded Hitler's and I can only say that I am quite prepared to forgive him much by virtue of comparison."[19]

By the mid-1930s, direct correspondence about individual scholars took the place of circulating lists. Harlow Shapley's exchange with a fellow Harvard professor, Arthur Nock, a historian of religion, was typical of the efforts made to evaluate scholars. Shapley asked what Nock knew about Richard Kroner, a philosophy professor who had been dismissed from his position at the University of Kiel because of his Jewish ancestry. Kroner had converted to Christianity. "I know nothing further about him except that Dr. Erwin Freundlich, himself an exile and at St. Andrews, is sending Kroner to me for help," Shapley wrote Nock. "If your encyclopedic knowledge of scholars includes this name Kroner (R.) and you can pass on information concerning him, please let me hear from you at your convenience." Nock replied, "Kroner is just a name to me," and he suggested Shapley contact Harvard theology professor Seelye Bixler. Kroner came to the United States in 1940 and taught at Union Theological Seminary in New York.[20]

In rejecting foreign scholars, American academics often used language common in less fraught circumstances. "You will understand that we were able to select fewer than one in ten of the names submitted," the New School's Johnson wrote, "and that the person above [H. Levi], concerning whom we had correspondence with you, was omitted from our list only after careful consideration."[21]

Establishing a "Sequence of Importance"

Occasionally the comments were explicit about the need to save one scholar over others. Indeed, some reviewers seemed to feel obligated to pick the most accomplished among the candidates, almost as a test of their scholarly judgment. Robert Neuner of the Yale Law School weighed the advantages of Hugo Müller, an economics professor at the German Institute of Technology in Prague, against those of Franz Xaver Weiss, an economist at the German University, also in Prague: "If you are not able to help both Müller and Weiss, I think that Weiss has more merits, having a more powerful and original personality," Neuner wrote Johnson. Weiss managed to immigrate to Britain, although not with an academic appointment. It was not possible to discover what happened to Müller.[22]

Rudolf Carnap, a German émigré and UCLA faculty member, went into greater depth in his analysis of candidates. "Since you will be faced with the hard task of selecting a certain number out of a greater number of good scholars, I thought you might like to have an expression of my personal opinion on the people for whom I have written testimonials besides this official pronouncement," Carnap wrote Johnson. "If I had to establish a sequence of importance—a hard thing to do when one knows that they are all in danger—I should name Otto Neurath in the first place (not so much because of his scholarly contributions, but because of his vital organizing and activating ability for the whole Unity of Science

Movement), next [Friedrich] Waismann who really is an outstanding scholar." Waismann, an Austrian logical positivist, had already immigrated to England, where he became a lecturer at Oxford University. Neurath, another Austrian logical positivist, went to the Netherlands before the Anschluss. After the German invasion in 1940, he crossed the Channel in an open boat to England. When Neurath was interned in England as an enemy alien, U.S. scholars, including Carnap, promised to sign affidavits for him. Without a university appointment, however, he was not able to immigrate. He continued his research in England, dying there in 1945.[23]

The reviewers grasped what a negative evaluation could mean. Ernst Berl, a Carnegie Institute of Technology professor and émigré, wrote that Dr. A. Sander, who had been his assistant at the Technical University of Darmstadt, "has not done work which can be considered as outstanding," nor would he "develop here an activity which would be for the benefit of this country." Berl understood the consequences of this assessment, but "I know that many other very capable men staying in Central Europe or in the southern part of France whose work would really be important to this country want to come over and cannot come because they cannot get an American visa."[24]

Even being "world class" was not always enough. In October 1940, Walter Gropius, chairman of Harvard's Department of Architecture and world-renowned modernist, had been trying for more than a year and in "every way we knew how" to get architects Simon and Helena Syrkus out of Poland. L. Moholy-Nagy, director of Chicago's School of Design, echoed Gropius's assessment of the Syrkuses as Poland's "most outstanding architects" and "two of the most valuable members" of the young European architects' group led by Le Corbusier and Gropius. But efforts to get the Syrkuses (both of whom were Jewish) positions at Harvard and then the New School failed. When Gropius learned that Simon Syrkus had been sent to Auschwitz in 1942, he wrote a letter to Pope Pius XII— to no avail. Helena Syrkus was imprisoned in 1944. Both survived and went on to distinguished architecture careers in communist Poland.[25]

For those directly involved in rescue work, the emphasis on "world-class men" was as much a strategic posture, designed to minimize objections to the program, as a principled one. On his trip to the western

(10) CBS broadcaster Edward R. Murrow, former assistant
secretary of the Emergency Committee in Aid of
Displaced German Scholars, in 1939. By CBS Radio.

United States in late December 1934, the Emergency Committee's Edward R. Murrow detected universities' concerns over "possible resentment" of the foreign scholars but noted they "made an exception of the German scholars financed by this Committee on the basis that they are men of great distinction." Murrow added: "Even the educational nationalists when discussing our grantees seem to be willing to say—like Jonathan to his armor-bearer—'Thou art one man in a multitude.'"[26]

The New School also tried to avoid controversy by focusing on world-class men; the only difference was that director Johnson's judgment of a scholar's abilities was often enough to get him or her hired. "In asking men to come to this country we must bear in mind the American situation," Johnson wrote. "A powerful creative scholar helps to expand the field in which he works; the average scholar is merely a competitor of American scholars." Johnson put it more harshly in explaining why he agreed with the Rockefeller Institute's Alfred Cohn that Paul Biel, a physician from Vienna, lacked, as Cohn wrote, "any especial accomplishment that would entitle him to special consideration." Johnson added: "The run of the mine, although human and deserving of help, have to take their chances like the run of the mine anywhere in the world."[27]

Even some previous Rockefeller Foundation recipients were not considered worthy. When Johnson would not recommend Martin David, a law professor at the University of Leiden, for a Rockefeller fellowship that would enable him to come to the United States, David's brother-in-law wrote to point out that David had previously received such a fellowship. Johnson would not budge: "The people at the Rockefeller Foundation, like myself, respect the work of Dr. David. Unfortunately, however, we have but limited funds, and Dr. David has been considered along with other scholars of greater eminence." University of California–Berkeley law professor Max Radin, whom Johnson had asked for an evaluation, probably swayed Johnson. Radin noted that David's writings "are all competent, as one might expect." But Henri Levy-Bruhl, whom Johnson also was considering, was far better, Radin wrote, standing "well among the second class of men in his field." David, a legal historian who had fled to Holland from his native Germany after the Nazis assumed power, never received a visa for the United States. In March 1943, he and his family were sent to Barneveld, a transit camp for prominent Jews, and six months later to Westerbork, another transit camp in the Netherlands, where they remained for a year. In September 1944, they were shipped to Theresienstadt. David was liberated on March 8, 1945, and returned to Leiden and his position at the university.[28]

"First-Rate Men Unknown Outside of Germany"

One problem with having American scholars evaluate their European colleagues was that only those who did work known to Americans were able to find positions. In a few disciplines, the absence of American scholars toiling in that area helped. Mathematician Roland Richardson at Brown, for example, argued that refugees were essential to the teaching of applied mathematics in the United States. In discussions with the Emergency Committee, Richardson explained that this country had neglected the field and it was vital that the United States be able to hold its own against Germany, especially as the threat of war grew. "In the mathematics of aeronautics there was practically nothing being done in this country except by refugees," he stated. Brown's Division of Advanced Instruction and Research in Mechanics had four refugees teaching there in the spring and summer of 1941, out of six faculty members. American universities' curricular needs and national security seemed to outweigh Richardson's antisemitism, to which he frequently gave expression.[29]

Many scholars, however, were doomed by their disciplines. Murrow was already worried about that in 1934. He wrote Harvard government professor Carl Friedrich, "Every day brings to my desk added evidence of the number of really first-rate men who are comparatively unknown outside of Germany." That seemed to be the problem with two scholars who became philosophy luminaries. The New School did not submit an application to the Rockefeller Foundation to fund Jean-Paul Sartre because it was "not able to get enough recommendations from Americans." Asked to evaluate Sartre, an editor of the *Journal of Social Philosophy* confessed that the name "leaves an absolutely blank stare in my mental eye." A similar problem arose with another French philosopher, Maurice Merleau-Ponty: "We could not get anything on him and therefore was [sic] not able to do anything for him." Both Sartre and Merleau-Ponty, neither of whom was Jewish, remained in France during the war.[30]

American professors also expressed an inability to evaluate Jerzy Finkelkraut, a Polish jurisprudence scholar. Hugh Babb, head of Boston University's business school, was interested in hiring Finkelkraut, but he could not find anyone to assess his work. "I cannot read a word of his books and therefore cannot refer to them even by name," Babb wrote Johnson in January 1941. Babb indicated that University of Warsaw faculty and other scholars he met in the Polish city regarded Finkelkraut highly. "I am, indeed, sorry that there is no American scholar whose appraisal of his scholarship I can invoke. . . . Who among our legal scholars reads Russian or Polish?" Johnson then tried Radin at Berkeley, who also deferred because of his ignorance of both languages. Radin did venture that Finkelkraut "must have been unusually competent" because his name, "obviously of Jewish origin," would have put him at a "distinct disadvantage" even if he had been "otherwise completely Polonized." Radin suggested Babb try two other professors. Babb then began to worry about Finkelkraut's fate, noting that his last known address was in Warsaw: "I suppose that his home address would reach him *if he is still alive*" (emphasis in the original). Johnson then gave up, explaining that the Rockefeller Foundation was unlikely to make a grant to someone in occupied Poland. Finkelkraut is listed among Polish survivors of the Holocaust.[31]

American scholars also tended to discredit European scholars whose work differed from American research. Paul Hoch described the deep divide between experimental and theoretical physicists that made U.S. universities reluctant to hire the latter, who populated European universities. The American schools hired some of the top candidates but at least initially were not sure what to do with them, often cloistering them in math departments. Law schools were unlikely to hire more theoretically inclined criminologists. Sheldon Glueck of Harvard Law School declared that there was no point in trying to get an appointment for Max Grünhut, a criminologist. Grünhut engaged in "speculative, theoretical discussion of punishment and the like," while the American slant was "pragmatic and applied." Grünhut obtained a position at Oxford University in England.[32]

A similar problem existed for those who studied international law and Roman law. A 1940 Yale Law School study found that only eight of the seventy-nine U.S. law schools surveyed offered a course on Roman law and only seven a comparative law course—and so European law professors were told. "There are comparatively few law schools that make a real place for [international law], nor do the faculties of political science favor them," Johnson wrote a former law professor at the University of Berlin. Stephen Duggan at the Emergency Committee reached the same, despairing conclusion. "Frankly, I am at my wit's end to know what to suggest in these cases," he wrote. "We receive dozens of similar letters every week and of all possible fields international law is one of the worst from the standpoint of refugees."[33]

Kyle Graham identified a broader problem in American law schools. After a brief openness to comparative legal approaches in the 1920s, the U.S. legal academy rejected the continental model in the 1930s, Graham concluded, and "in doing so, American professors cultivated a resistance to pleas for aid predicated on respect for Continental scholarship or a spirit of global scientific kinship." Harvard's Thomas Reed Powell, for example, criticized Arthur Lenhoff, who had been a judge of the Austrian Constitutional Court and a prolific author, for "seeking universality" and urged him to "write some articles on contemporary problems." Lenhoff, who fled Austria in 1938 and started as a law librarian at the University of Buffalo, was able to reestablish his teaching and scholarly career at that law school, including a masterful 1951 study of law and literature, *Goethe as Lawyer and Statesman*.[34]

Realizing this, some law professors tried to reorient their scholarship. Even in exile and on the run, former University of Berlin law professor Erich Kaufmann continued to draft papers, one on "the relations between philosophy and law" and another on "the constitutional history of Germany between 1870 and 1932." In letters to American colleagues, Kaufmann emphasized the broad reach of his scholarship. "My only chance for survival appears to be some livelihood in the United States which will help me and my wife to get a non-quota-visa," Kaufmann wrote in June 1940 from the Hague, where he had fled. The Germans had invaded Holland a month earlier. His colleagues tried to find him a position. He received strong recommendations from Borchard at Yale and Karl Loewenstein at Amherst College. Kaufmann "is a desperate case and you would rescue from despair and possible destruction a scholar of the *very first* rank," Borchard wrote to Johnson. Johnson turned him down because at sixty years old "he is too much over age."[35]

In October 1940, Kaufmann was about to move again for "some more remote or sheltered place." He wanted his friend, Herbert von Beckerath, who was at Duke University teaching economics and political science, to inform American professors of his "rich experience in all fields of internal and international public life" and his desire for "a modest opening in an American academic institution." Kaufmann, who had right-wing sympathies, did not find an opening, though his field more than his politics seemed to be the reason. He remained in hiding in the Netherlands, survived the war, and returned to a prominent professorship in postwar Germany even though U.S. authorities doubted his commitment to democracy.[36]

Scholars' philosophical orientation also made them anathema to the American academy. Hans Joachim Schoeps, who had a Jewish mother but had been brought up in the Protestant faith, turned to Judaism both as a faith and as a scholarly endeavor, but in a way that led all the theological seminaries to reject him. "His brand of Jewish philosophy is extremely radical from the theological point of view and goes beyond the attitudes of even reformed institutions," Columbia University history professor Salo Baron acknowledged as he tried to find Schoeps a position. "Since his major contribution consists not in research but in independent thinking, such institutions might be inclined to invite him only if they felt spiritual kinship towards his philosophy, which is not the case." Julian Morgenstern, president of Hebrew Union College, said as much in rejecting Johnson's entreaty: "I have the distinct impression that he is not the type of man we would wish to engage even if there was a definite opening for a man in the field of theology here." Schoeps survived the war in Sweden and returned to Germany, even though his father had died in Theresienstadt and his mother in Auschwitz. Schoeps became a professor of religious history at the University of Erlangen and espoused conservative positions.[37]

The discipline of Jewish studies itself presented a problem. The Yiddish Scientific Institute, or YIVO, which had relocated from Vilna to New York after the German invasion of Lithuania, applied to the Rockefeller Foundation for a grant to hire Max Weinreich, one of its founders and head of its linguistic section. Having received high praise for both YIVO and Weinreich, including from Leo Spitzer at Johns Hopkins and Kurt Lewin at Iowa State University, the foundation initially agreed to a grant but then decided the Emergency Committee should provide it. It is not clear why. The Emergency Committee refused the YIVO grant. After "a rather detailed inquiry," the committee concluded that the institute's "own standing in this country were [*sic*] not very high." The committee would support Weinreich, but not YIVO. Weinreich still managed to serve as YIVO's research director from 1940 to 1950 while also teaching Yiddish at City College.[38]

One discipline that would seem to be a natural fit—German—proved problematic for primarily political reasons. Existing faculty in U.S. German departments often favored the Nazi regime, as did community members who supported the departments. "After 1933, scholars of German extraction, especially professors of German at small Midwestern universities, formed an important lobby active against the university professors expelled by the National Socialists, denouncing them as a 'fifth column' of socialists and as agitators against international understanding," Claus-Dieter Krohn concluded. During his 1936 tour of Midwestern universities, Walter Kotschnig encountered that attitude. George R. Throop, the chancellor of Washington University in St. Louis, was "very favorably disposed to displaced scholars," Kotschnig noted, hiring two of them, making an offer to a third, and asking for a list of scholars in various engineering fields. Still, when it came to hiring a professor in the German department, Throop told Kotschnig: "Owing to local circumstances, that professor should not be a Jew." In December 1939, Werner Richter was all set to obtain a position in the German department of an American college and then the head of the department received a decoration from the Nazi government and Richter's offer was withdrawn.[39]

American professors sensed what rejection would mean for the European scholars they pronounced "not particularly outstanding" or "talks too much." But choices had to be made. "The need for sifting is urgent," the Emergency Committee's Cohn explained. "We cannot aid everybody, only the most prominent and gifted—the more's the pity. About the rest and their fate, we have no plan, as yet."[40]

Age, Politics, Gender, and Money

The American academy wanted men who were old enough to have established a world-class reputation but not so old they were no longer productive. Halle law dean Max Fleischmann was considered world class, but he also was considered old. Yale law professor Edwin Borchard put Fleischmann "among the first rank of professors of international law," noting it was possible to tell just from his curriculum vitae "how important" Fleischmann was. But Fleischmann was sixty-two at the time he was fired in 1935 and only got older every year he sat in Halle unable to work or to leave.[1]

Alvin Johnson of the New School explained that the funding organizations insisted upon "scholars who have a long productive future ahead of them." Universities also worried about having to pay the pensions of scholars who had taught in their schools for only a few years. So what was too old? "The general rule was to appoint nobody over fifty-five," Johnson noted. That demarcation was not fixed, yet many scholars were turned away on the basis of their age. A handwritten note in Hugo Müller's New School folder is simple and to the point: "58 years old and not *too* important." The Emergency Committee's affiliated organization helping physicians advised Dr. Max Neuberger, who had lost his position at the University of Vienna, to remain in Vienna "because of his age (70) and the fact that he is receiving a pension." Neuberger, a professor of

(11) Max Fleischmann, dean of the University of Halle law
faculty. Courtesy of University Archive Halle-Wittenberg,
Rep. 40/VI, Nr. 2 Bild 41 (Max Fleischmann).

the history of medicine, apparently did not take the committee's advice,
fleeing to Great Britain where he worked in the Wellcome Historical Medical Museum. Neither the Emergency Committee nor the Rockefeller
Foundation would make a grant on "account of his age" to sixty-seven-

year-old Paul Langevin, a physicist who worked with the Curies and was considered "the most distinguished man in his field in all of France." Langevin was imprisoned in Paris after the occupation and survived to liberation.[2]

New School faculty member Arnold Brecht inquired about a position for sixty-five-year-old University of Heidelberg jurisprudence professor Leopold Perels, who had been deported on October 22, 1940, from Baden-Württemberg to the Gurs internment camp in France. "This unfortunately is one of the sad cases of which we have only too many," wrote Else Staudinger, who directed the New School's efforts to help those in France after the German invasion. "It seems to me that Professor Perels is too old to be taken care of by Dr. Johnson's present project." Perels, who was Protestant but had two Jewish grandparents and was one of the first Heidelberg professors to be fired, survived Gurs and returned to Germany.[3]

Nor would any university invite Rudolf Breitscheid, a leading Social Democrat, to join its faculty because of his "advanced age" of sixty-six. Johnson considered Breitscheid "a great parliamentarian and scholar and . . . a gallant and impressive personality" and made a last-ditch effort to save Breitscheid, who in 1941 had been sent back to Germany from France and imprisoned in Gestapo headquarters in Berlin at Prinz-Albrecht-Strasse 8. Johnson knew the danger Breitscheid faced, noting that "this morning's paper" reported that fellow Social Democrat and Marxist economist Rudolf Hilfreding, who had been handed over to the Gestapo by the Vichy government along with Breitscheid, had died in Gestapo custody. "But Breitscheid is still alive or was still alive until recently." Given that he could not get Breitscheid a faculty appointment, Johnson decided that "an invitation for a course of lectures" was "the only thing possible." Johnson persuaded Johns Hopkins University president Isaiah Bowman to invite Breitscheid to give ten lectures on "German economic and social developments since 1870" during the semester beginning February 1, 1942. Johnson promised Bowman that he "would find the money" to pay Breitscheid. The U.S. embassy in Berlin conveyed the university's invitation to Breitscheid on November 22, 1941. Soon thereafter, the United States and Germany went to war, ending any hope

of Breitscheid lecturing on "the development of agricultural coopera-
tives." Breitscheid died in Buchenwald in 1944.[4]

When a scholar was felt to be too old to get an academic appointment, the organizations sometimes tried to find someone to sign an affidavit so the scholar could possibly immigrate on a regular visa. That
could prove difficult too. At sixty, Richard Charmatz, a Viennese historian and newspaper editor, was one of those considered too old. Political
scientist Oscar Jaszi of Oberlin College, who said he could not provide
an affidavit for Charmatz and his wife, wrote to Alvin Johnson, to ask
"whether among your many influential acquaintances there is not someone who would be willing to save the life of this very worthy couple."
Johnson replied that he would try, "but the people I know are already
loaded up with as many affidavits as they are allowed." Johnson then
noted another problem: "Under the present conditions in Austria and
Germany every Jew is in peril of his life; many more want to come to this
country than the quota allows. Most people I talk to feel that the young
should have the first chance, because they can hope to fit into the life of
the country." A year later, in response to another appeal for an affidavit
for Charmatz, Johnson declined again, noting that his Jewish friends
were treating him as a "sort of combination of tax gatherer and troubled
conscience" because he so often asked for help with affidavits. Charmatz
survived the war, but it is not clear how.[5]

"Resentment Would Be Aroused" by Hiring Younger Men

At the other end of the spectrum, the emphasis on "first-rate men" disqualified most younger scholars. French philosopher Vladimir Jankélévitch was fired from a position in Lille for being Jewish after having been
severely wounded fighting for France. Horace Kallen, a philosopher
who was one of the founding members of the New School, considered
Jankélévitch "well worth saving," and Léon Brunschvicg of the Sorbonne
thought Jankélévitch would be a "very desirable acquisition for an American university." But at forty years old, Jankélévitch had a somewhat limited reputation. His supporters tried hard to find him an American position. Brunschvicg, who had lost his position at the Sorbonne for being

Jewish, wrote directly to Columbia's president Nicholas Murray Butler on Jankélévitch's behalf, praising his "charming turn of mind." As a "psychologist and a moralist," Jankélévitch has published "sparklingly brilliant pieces of work," Brunschvicg wrote. (Brunschvicg himself went into hiding in the free zone where he wrote studies of Descartes, Montaigne, and Pascal that were published in Switzerland. He died in 1944 at the age of seventy-four.) But another of Jankélévitch's recommenders, Henri Focillon, a French art historian then teaching at Yale, worried that many American professors might not be able to recognize Jankélévitch's talents.[6]

Focillon, who considered Jankélévitch "in the very first rank of French philosophers of his generation," was right to be worried. In February 1941, John Marshall, associate director of the Rockefeller Foundation's Division of the Humanities, would not recommend Jankélévitch because he was "little known in this country." Marshall based his assessment on the fact that "three American philosophers of standing have merely heard of him, but have no opinion of his work." Marshall then suggested referring the case back to Johnson at the New School so Johnson "could give us some further word as to how he would be utilized here." Johnson had in fact already assembled extremely positive assessments of Jankélévitch in late 1940 from several distinguished American philosophy professors, including Herbert Schneider of Columbia and Ralph Barton Perry of Harvard. Marshall either did not see these testimonials or did not trust them for some reason. He updated his assessment in March 1941. "My latest information indicates that he was generally regarded as the coming philosopher in France and a man of the most unusual attainments," Marshall wrote. "I'm more ready to act in his behalf than I was earlier." The New School ultimately made Jankélévitch an offer, funded by the Rockefeller Foundation, yet the delay cost him.[7]

The Emergency Committee and Rockefeller Foundation had another concern about scholars who were too young—they might compete directly with Americans for jobs, as Edward Murrow explained in rejecting Heinrich Liepmann's request for assistance from the Emergency Committee. Liepmann's "record looks good, but there is a superabundance of well-trained young economists, both native and foreign, looking for jobs in this country," Murrow explained to Walter Kotschnig, the former refugee high commissioner. "Whether we like it or not, and I personally do not like it, we must proceed with great care in making grants for younger scholars, particularly those in disciplines that are already crowded in this country."[8]

Although there was general agreement that older scholars should not receive assistance—with many exceptions—rescue advocates disagreed over the not-too-young policy. In 1934, Carl Friedrich of Harvard wanted to get additional funds to be able to hire as research assistants about "a dozen young men." Murrow agreed, asked the Carnegie Corporation for funds, and was turned down. That denial and committee conversations led Murrow to write a memo in September 1934 encouraging the committee to change its policy. Most of the committee's applications, Murrow noted, were in the "so-called younger group," men younger than forty-five. Yet at the committee's previous meeting two applications had been refused out of concern that "resentment would be aroused as a result of the appointment of younger men." Murrow insisted, however, that his conversations with college presidents and deans indicated they wanted to hire younger scholars and that they were the best judges of whether this would prompt criticism. "The fundamental problem involved appears to be whether or not the Committee now believes that it is in a better position than the various American colleges and universities to determine the age of the scholars to be invited to this country," Murrow wrote.[9]

Murrow's position was never completely adopted by the committee. It never quite abandoned its reluctance to fund younger scholars, and its correspondence is filled with missives about the "terrible time" younger scholars were having. Yet minutes of its executive committee suggested the committee's position was that it should not "lay down any hard and fast rule with regard to our treatment of younger scholars. If we had the case of a thoroughly good scholar, even under 40 years of age, we should consider it." Some Emergency Committee members eventually developed misgivings about both ends of the age policy. "Our policies have hardened in the course of time—as to the young, as to the old, as to the size of the stipends, in our attitude toward other organizations," Alfred Cohn wrote in 1940. He advocated the committee "soften its policy" on all these fronts. In responding to Cohn, Stephen Duggan seemed to agree that the committee's policies could be softened, although he did not offer any concrete changes.[10]

The Emergency Committee's overall approach can be seen in the ages of the scholars it funded through January 31, 1942: 168 of the 216 scholars whose ages it recorded were between thirty-five and fifty-four; only 16 were younger than thirty-five, and 32 were older than fifty-four. (At that point, the committee had funded 268 scholars, but some ages could not be determined.)[11]

Some Might Be "Classified as Communistic"

So the scholars could not be too old or too young. They also could not be too far to the left or too far to the right politically. In his study of sixty-five political scientists Alfons Sollner found that the Rockefeller Foundation preferred to make grants to those at institutions "that came closest to the American ideal of an integrated social science." In other words, the foundation favored scholars who identified with "political democracy, faith in science and human progress." It preferred mainstream scholars even when politics did not affect their academic work. The foundation provided only indirect support to two mathematicians, André Weil and Emil Gumbel, both of whom were German-Jewish exiles, because "they were prone to political views which differed markedly from the standard opinions of the American and European middle classes." Weil arrived in the United States in January 1941 and spent the war years teaching undergraduate math at Lehigh University; Gumbel arrived in 1940 and taught at the New School and at Columbia University. Community concerns and government pressure prevented socialists or, even worse, communists from being hired. Frani Touton, a University of Southern California vice president, worried that Friedrich Jaffe, a scholar the school was considering, would "soon be classified as communistic." She pointed out that the leaders of the Los Angeles German community would need to be persuaded "of the essential soundness of the economic thinking of any person whom we should invite from the exiled German group."[12]

Even when universities and funding organizations could overcome community concerns, they still had to worry that the U.S. government might refuse to issue scholars non-quota visas because of their political beliefs. Knowing the government's posture, the Emergency Committee and the Rockefeller Foundation tended not to support candidates who had socialist or communist leanings. Both organizations tended to accept the government's stance: "Communists can naturally be separated and refused admission," Cohn, who was involved with both groups, wrote in 1940. What concerned Cohn and the groups he represented was that the government used that concern to deny non-quota visas to refugee scholars in general because there might be communists among them. Cohn admitted he was "shocked by the notion," but only because of its blanket nature. Government objections became so prevalent that Columbia geneticist and Emergency Committee board member Leslie C. Dunn visited Washington at the end of 1939 to apply "political pressure." The State Department's political objections to non-quota visa candidates grew even worse after the fall of France.[13]

Such concerns affected the New School particularly. After relatively freewheeling hiring at its founding, the New School grew more circumspect by the end of the 1930s. In fact, it changed its charter in July 1940 to deny faculty appointments to any "communist or fellow traveler" and to affirm its appreciation of the United States as a "citadel of liberalism." That change may have kept the New School from helping Hans Mayer, who had a Ph.D. in philosophy and law and who had fled to France and then to Geneva. "For years now he has been sent from one of the so-called 'work camps' to another and has been forced to do work that he is unable to endure morally and physically for an indefinite time," Hans W. Schwerin, a writer and émigré from Breslau, wrote in trying to persuade the New School to hire Mayer. Johnson was unmoved. "I should be very doubtful that a man who had been active in the communist party would get any kind of visa for the United States," he explained to Edvard Hambro of Northwestern's history department, who also had written on Mayer's behalf. Mayer's colleagues continued to insist on his scholarly worth and his precarious situation. William E. Rappard, who ran the Graduate Institute of International Studies in Geneva, pleaded, "You would both be doing an act of mercy in favor of a German-Jewish refugee who has had his full load of suffering in the course of the last years and save for historical science a truly exceptional man." Johnson never offered a position to Mayer, who lived out the war in Geneva. Despite the wartime qualms about Mayer's politics, he worked for U.S. occupation forces during the postwar period.[14]

While the scholars could not be too left, they could not be too right either. The New School's files contain many small handwritten notes suggesting applicants might not have been sufficiently anti-Nazi or anti-Vichy. One note said: "Gershoy called. Can't imagine [French historian Louis] Madelin has any distaste for Vichy." Else Staudinger, who helped coordinate the rescue of scholars after the fall of France, spelled out the case against law professor Harald Mankiewicz, "known to be pro-fascist, who being a German Jew became a French citizen and later treated the German Jews very badly in the French concentration camp where he worked as a French interpreter. . . . He also wrote a book in favor of the Nazi legal system and was in constant relations with the German consulate at Lyon. . . . I think we can close his case here." Herbert Solow, who was assistant to the New School's president, then sent Mankiewicz a letter suggesting that he had been sent to Shanghai by the Vichy government and thus was "not likely to find" an American institution who would hire him "when so many anti-Nazi refugees are seeking posts here." Mankiewicz defended himself: "The last line of your letter does me, I believe, a great injustice in so far as it is open to the interpretation that I am not an anti-nazi. My own personal experiences and my views as expressed in numerous publications should serve to prevent such imputation." Mankiewicz survived the war in Shanghai.[15]

"Hopeless" Prospect of "Finding a University Appointment for a Woman"

The not-too-young, as well as the world-class requirement, had a disproportionate effect on female scholars, who also faced intense discrimination in both European and U.S. universities because of their gender. European universities had begun to convey advanced degrees to women in any numbers only in the twentieth century, so the women who held positions or aspired to academic careers tended to be relatively young and not well established. Alvin Johnson's evaluation of Katherina Wolf, a thirty-three-year-old Viennese psychologist, is typical. "Despite the excellent testimonials which we have received, she remains a young and promising person rather than one of eminence," Johnson explained to the Rockefeller Foundation as both organizations considered her candidacy. Wolf came to the United States a year later, although not on a non-quota visa, and worked on various research projects in New York. She eventually became a professor at Yale University's Child Study Center.[16]

Johnson recognized that a young female scholar might have more promise than a similarly situated man. "Generally speaking, a woman who has attained to the professorship is more likely to have real merit than a man with corresponding official career," he wrote to a Rockefeller Foundation official in 1940. Johnson even suggested adding "the names of a certain number of women scholars when first rate ones are found." Yet the New School's files, as well as those of the other organizations, are littered with examples of women who did not get appointments. For example, Johnson informed Countess Alexandra Tolstoy, the novelist's daughter, that he could not help a thirty-nine-year-old professor of Slavic history and culture. He acknowledged that she seemed "promising," but "the standing which she has attained is not . . . sufficiently compelling." Even when Johnson wanted to hire two Polish female philosophers, including one with recommendations from world-class philosophers Rudolf Carnap and Willard Van Orman Quine, he did not because the Rockefeller Foundation refused to fund them.[17]

In fact, the Rockefeller Foundation and the Emergency Committee had rules in place that hurt female scholars. Both organizations required grantees to have been professors or privatdozents in Europe, yet European universities often denied women those positions for discriminatory reasons. Jewish women faced a double penalty. The University of Vienna's refusal to award biologist Leonore Brecher habilitation in 1926 led to her life of wandering from one research laboratory to another. Käthe Spiegel, who had received her doctorate in medieval history from the German University in Prague, twice applied for habilitation that would have led to her being a privatdozent, and twice she was denied. Spiegel became a librarian and archivist instead. (Some Jewish men also faced discrimination in habilitation and became librarians, such as Leo Oppenheim, an Assyriologist and Oriental librarian at the University of Vienna.)[18]

(12) Marie Anna Schirmann in her laboratory at the University of Vienna Physical Institute. Manuscripts and Archives Division, the New York Public Library.

Marie Anna Schirmann may be the clearest case of prejudice. She earned her Ph.D. in physics with honors from the University of Vienna in 1918 at the age of twenty-five. For the next twelve years, Schirmann did research in the area of high-vacuum physics, including building a facility to study the physical appearance of the highest vacuums and obtaining patents on several devices she developed in order to conduct her experiments. In 1926, she became the first scientist to confirm static electricity between solid bodies and gases.

In 1930, she sought habilitation at Vienna's Physical Institute with a thesis on "new ways to create, maintain and measure the most extreme high vacuums and to study the physical properties of degassed matter in a vacuum, especially the static electricity between solid bodies and gases." Of the forty-one members of Schirmann's habilitation committee, thirty-four voted in favor of giving her habilitation; three were opposed

and four abstained. No objections materialized based on personal qual-
ities. But the final, much smaller committee rejected Schirmann's thesis,
concluding that her summarized collection of nine works and patents
did not meet the habilitation requirements and that she had not demonstrated "the level of general knowledge demanded by a lecturer." She
believed at the time, and subsequent scholars looking at her record con-
firmed, that her rejection was likely based on her being Jewish and a
woman. Only three female physicists received habilitation status before
World War II. (Breslau's Hedwig Kohn was one of them.) Denied habilitation and thus her chance of teaching, Schirmann returned to her
research.[19]

Americans could be just as prejudiced as Europeans. In December
1934, for example, Grete Bernstein, who had been a reporter at the *Frankfurter Zeitung* and taught at the University of Frankfurt, came to the
United States and met with the Emergency Committee's Murrow. Bernstein wanted to teach in a university. Murrow told her she could submit
a "research scheme" but indicated that she had "not a chance." He noted
that Bernstein was "intelligent and might teach German in secondary
school."[20]

Murrow's response probably reflected his own attitude as well as
his judgment of American universities, which were not particularly receptive to women scholars. Aid organizations understood that preference. Bennington College had an opening for a physics professor, as
AAUW's Esther Brunauer informed Charlotte Houtermans. Houtermans
had a Ph.D. in physics and had studied at the University of Göttingen
with luminaires such as Richard Courant, David Hilbert, and James
Franck. "The college wants a man for the position but it would surely do
no harm to try," Brunauer advised. "Your training at Göttingen might
compensate for your being a woman." Houtermans was not considered
for the Bennington position and eventually became a physics professor
at Sarah Lawrence College. In trying to place Eva Lehmann Fiesel, an
Etruscologist who had lost her position at the University of Munich and
had a temporary research position at Yale, a Yale professor acknowledged:
"There are not many places in the country where a woman scholar could
hope to get placed." Yale was not one of those few places, barring women
from teaching full time in its undergraduate college or its graduate school

of arts and sciences. Bryn Mawr College hired Fiesel for a temporary position when outside funding came through.[21]

Women's colleges were more welcoming, but tensions existed there too. Some sentiment surfaced that the addition of refugee scholars would hold back the appointment of American women. After attending a London meeting of the International Federation of University Women, whose purpose was at least partially to help university women in exile, Dean Virginia Gildersleeve of Barnard College told the *New York Times* that exile scholars were aggravating "our problem of placing women in teaching posts." The advanced research and teaching of European female professors also often did not fit the needs of women's colleges, which were, for the most part, colleges, not research universities. Although Bryn Mawr offered mathematician Hilda Geiringer a temporary position, the college never quite accepted her "highly specialized field of mathematical statistics." In asking the Emergency Committee to pay for Geiringer's position the following year, Bryn Mawr noted that it needed someone to teach statistics. In later communication with the committee, however, Bryn Mawr president Marion Park explained that the college offered only two statistics courses and Geiringer would be better off at a "university where she can do full time and permanent work." The Emergency Committee tried mightily to find her such a position. Universities hesitated to "do such an unconventional thing as invite a woman mathematician," acknowledged an Emergency Committee staffer in trying to interest the Illinois Institute of Technology in Geiringer. Another staffer wrote to the chairman of the University of Wyoming math department about Geiringer but admitted she did not "know of course whether you would hire a woman." Geiringer remained in a part-time position at Bryn Mawr, partially funded by the Emergency Committee.[22]

The State Department compounded female scholars' problems by interpreting the immigration law to deny non-quota visas to researchers, librarians, and archivists. Yet American universities' discriminatory practices meant women were much more likely to be hired as researchers, librarians, and archivists than as faculty. Female scholars thus faced a Catch 22: they needed American university jobs to qualify for non-quota visas, but the American university jobs they were most likely to get were not eligible for non-quota visas. W. Stull Holt of Johns Hopkins's history

department tried to dance around this dilemma in writing a recommendation for Helene Wieruszowski to obtain an Emergency Committee
grant. In 1918, Wieruszowski had obtained a Ph.D. from the University
of Bonn in early medieval history. Denied habilitation at the University
of Cologne, she retrained as a librarian and took a position at the Bonn
University Library. Fired in 1934 for being "of Jewish stock and protestant religion," as she put it, Wieruszowski fled to Spain and then Italy.
In exile, she energetically pursued her research. She was considered a
"scholar of the first rank," who had "devoted her life to research in the
field of Medieval History" and had a list of publications to prove it.[23]

Yet Holt did not stress those characteristics in his recommendation. Instead, he emphasized that Wieruszowski was a "trained librarian
with a knowledge of languages rarely to be found among librarians." Thus
she could be hired as a librarian. "In other words the prospect is not the
well-nigh hopeless one of finding a university appointment for a woman,"
Holt wrote. In fact, Holt contacted the Emergency Committee hoping it
would provide Wieruszowski with a grant to teach courses in Johns Hopkins's history and romance language departments even though there
was "no chance" the university would offer her a further appointment.
That way she could obtain a non-quota visa "from the very exacting consul at Naples." Wieruszowski was in fact denied a non-quota visa. She
immigrated to the United States in 1940 at age forty-seven, presumably
on a regular visa, and never gave up trying to become a professor, teaching short stints at several colleges, including Johns Hopkins. She eventually became a professor of history at City College of New York.[24]

Female scholars also faced a reality that confronted most female
exiles: it was easier for them to find employment as domestics, and thus
they often ended up doing that kind of work. Aside from professorial
and pastoral work, domestic employment was the one exception to the
immigration laws' contract labor provision, which denied immigration
visas to those who already had jobs in the United States. "If it should
take a very long time to find a position corresponding to my former profession," art historian Charlotte Giese wrote shortly after Kristallnacht,
"I beg to suggest that I should be glad to accept a position as companion
or housekeeper for a time, for I realise that it might become very urgent
for me to leave this country." Giese stressed her qualifications: "I am pro-

ficient in every domestic work, I have run my own household since I have been married even when I held a job."[25]

In January 1939, forty-nine-year-old Alice Mühsam, who had earned her Ph.D. in classical archeology and art history from the University of Berlin, wanted desperately to leave Germany. Mühsam, who had also been a successful music critic, would "do any kind of work in case I find nothing connected with my profession," she wrote an officer of the American Association of Museums. "I am not only an Art Historian and Archeologist, but a mother too, who is experienced in all household work." Mühsam, who came to the United States in 1940, spent the first five years earning her living babysitting and cleaning houses. "I hope ardently that there will be a possibility for me to return to scientific work," she wrote Esther Brunauer in 1941 as she tried to get a grant from the AAUW. New York University art historian and fellow refugee Karl Lehmann-Hartleben wrote on her behalf, concluding that Mühsam's research on Greek portraits of the Roman period will "make an extremely valuable contribution." Lehmann-Hartleben added that he admired Mühsam's courage in trying to make "a living by household work and hard physical labor," which was not easy for "a woman of her former background and of her intellectual training and abilities." Mühsam received two $250 grants from the AAUW and retrained to do art restoration work at the Brooklyn Museum. In 1944, she wrote to thank the AAUW for pointing her toward "an interesting craft" that had led to "contacts with interesting people" and was one that she could continue to do when she could no longer do "heavy work."[26]

Altogether, the Emergency Committee awarded grants to twenty-two women, or 6 percent of its total grants.

Friends Should "Bestir Themselves" to Fund a Salary

For all their insistence on hiring on merit within the parameters of age, politics, and gender, an additional factor swayed American universities—money. Many institutions hired scholars because an outside source—a wealthy business leader, concerned faculty, a committed philanthropist, family, or friends—agreed to pay their salaries. President Karl Compton of MIT acknowledged that the university hired physicist Arthur von

Hippel, who did not fill a particular faculty need, only because businessman Carl Boschwitz contributed $1,500 to von Hippel's salary of $3,500. (The Rockefeller Foundation contributed $2,000.) Compton wrote Boschwitz that the university "was very highly pleased with Dr. von Hippel's performance" and that Boschwitz should feel satisfied that he helped von Hippel settle "in what will probably be a permanent manner in this institution." It was. Von Hippel, who was a luminary in material physics, spent fifty years on the MIT faculty. He died in 2003 at the age of 105.[27]

Charles H. Colvin, an aeronautical engineer who cofounded the Pioneer Instrument Company, gave $2,400 for Arthur Korn's first-year salary at the Stevens Institute of Technology. (When the following year Colvin accepted a government job at "one-third of what I am accustomed to earning," he was no longer willing to cover Korn's salary. The Rockefeller Foundation and the Emergency Committee had to step in.) United States treasury secretary Henry Morgenthau personally pledged $600 a year for an indefinite number of years to support astronomer E. Finlay Freundlich, who was a personal friend. Freundlich, who had been raised Protestant, was fired from his position as director of the Einstein-Institut in 1933 because he had a Jewish grandmother and a Jewish wife. He fled first to the University of Istanbul and then in 1937 to German University in Prague. When the German occupation led to his being fired again, Morgenthau made the offer to pay part of Freundlich's salary at an American university. Morgenthau also "took up his case directly" with U.S. secretary of labor Frances Perkins during Freundlich's summer 1939 visit to the States, hoping Perkins could help change Freundlich's visitor visa to a permanent one. Freundlich received a position at St. Andrews in Scotland and never immigrated to the United States.[28]

A financial commitment without an affiliation with an institution of higher education did not work, as physicians learned in trying to get microbiologist Ludwig Hirszfeld out of Warsaw in 1940. Columbia Medical School professor Arthur Coca explained that American Cyanamid Company had agreed to transport Hirszfeld, his wife, and their daughter to the United States; Coca would let them live with him. Beth Israel Hospital in New York was considering offering him a research position. "The one obstacle to our plans is the lack of an institutional sponsorship," Coca conceded, meaning a university affiliation. A month earlier, Coca had written Felix Morley, president of Haverford College, "begging him to do what you can, at your next opportunity, to obtain the honorary appointment of Dr. Hirszfeld at Haverford." Coca advised Morley that to satisfy immigration rules Morley would need to offer Hirszfeld an assistant professorship for two years at a salary of $200 a month to be paid by a committee of U.S. physicians. The obstacles apparently were not overcome. Hirszfeld and his family were imprisoned in the Warsaw Ghetto in February 1941, where he organized vaccination campaigns against typhus as well as other antiepidemic measures. He also taught secret medical courses. The Hirszfeld family escaped the ghetto in 1943, using false names and changing hiding places to survive. His daughter died of tuberculosis during the war, but Hirszfeld survived and resumed his career as a microbiologist and medical school professor in Poland.[29]

Several U.S. university faculty members also pushed hiring by providing financial support. University of Chicago historian Louis Gottschalk and his wife, for example, created a "refugee aid fund" that provided salaries to a number of scholars, mostly younger men in research positions. The Gottschalks' fund also paid for three foreign lawyers to be retrained at American law schools.[30]

In theory, the Rockefeller Foundation and Emergency Committee decided whether to fund a scholar only once a university had already agreed to hire that scholar. In reality, the discussions about whether a university would hire a scholar and whether the committee and foundation would fund them often happened hand in hand. Bryn Mawr College's hiring of mathematician Hilda Geiringer, discussed above, illustrates the two-track system. Bryn Mawr initially hesitated to hire Geiringer, who had taught at the University of Berlin's Institute of Applied Mathematics. Dismissed in 1933 for being Jewish, Geiringer fled to Brussels and then Istanbul. She taught at the university there, along with her mentor and partner Richard von Mises, until 1938. Despite enthusiastic recommendations from von Mises, Albert Einstein, Richard Courant, and Oswald Veblen, Bryn Mawr balked at hiring Geiringer. Then Geiringer's brothers, who were in England, agreed to give the college $2,500 for a temporary, part-time position. She was hired in 1939.

When her brothers could not support Geiringer the following year,

Bryn Mawr decided it was not willing to take her on itself. For the next three years, the college agreed to extend Geiringer's appointment only because the Emergency Committee, the Oberlaender Trust, and a neighboring college kicked in some funds. Bryn Mawr did let Geiringer's teenage daughter, who had traveled with her from Berlin to Brussels to Istanbul and Lisbon, attend the college tuition-free. Not pleased with the temporary appointments, Geiringer kept looking for a permanent post. She finally got one at Wheaton College in Norton, Massachusetts, beginning in the fall of 1944. She and von Mises married that year.[31]

Geiringer was not the only scholar Bryn Mawr president Marion Park hired when the money materialized. She agreed to appoint on a temporary basis Emmy Noether, whom the University of Göttingen had expelled in 1933 and who was considered one of the leading mathematicians of her time. But once Noether was at Bryn Mawr, Park found her to be "too eccentric and unadaptable to be taken on permanently." When the question arose of hiring Noether for another year, Park hesitated. Eventually, she raised some private money and persuaded the Emergency Committee, the Rockefeller Foundation, and the Institute for Advanced Study to contribute enough for Noether's $3,000 annual salary. Park's willingness to continue to employ Noether was never tested, as Noether died following surgery in April 1935.[32]

By the fall of 1940, the Emergency Committee rethought its stated position of funding scholars strictly on the basis of merit, without considering their resources. The committee learned that fall that "several scholars" the committee helped had "money of their own or had wealthy relatives who were able to finance them." The committee voted to inquire in the future whether the scholars had their own resources or relatives who could help. Adolf Drucker, an Austrian émigré economist who taught at American University, seemed to be the beneficiary of the committee's new willingness to accept family contributions. His son, Peter Drucker, who became a well-known business professor and author, provided half of an Emergency Committee grant of $1,200 to pay his father's salary, on the condition that his father not be told. He then upped his contribution to the entire $1,800, again on the condition that neither his father nor anyone outside the committee was told.[33]

If the Emergency Committee reluctantly accepted the fact that out-

(13) Alvin Johnson, president of the New School for Social Research. Photograph by Ralph Crane. Reproduced with permission from the Crane heirs. Courtesy of New School Photograph Collection 1933–1984, 1944–1977, New School Archives and Special Collection, The New School, New York, NY.

side money might influence academic hiring, the New School did not hesitate to act on it. It offered positions to scholars who came with funding and encouraged others to make similar arrangements. Johnson's comments about the possible hiring of Ludwig Feuchtwanger suggest such arrangements were common. Feuchtwanger had run an academic publishing house in Germany and had been imprisoned in Dachau after Kristallnacht. "I should think that a place for Dr. Feuchtwanger could be found in one of the colleges of Southern California, if his friends would bestir themselves to fund a salary that would maintain him through a number of years," Johnson wrote in 1939. "As matters stand now, there is very little chance anywhere for an academic appointment unless the necessary salary fund can be raised." Feuchtwanger managed to get a visa to Great Britain, where he died in 1947.[34]

If the necessary salary could be raised, the New School would consider an offer. In 1940, financier Benjamin L. Sinzheimer visited Betty Drury of the Emergency Committee in her New York office on behalf of a relative, University of Frankfurt labor law and sociology of law professor Hugo Sinzheimer. He had lost his Frankfurt faculty position in 1933 and had been living in Holland, assuming professorships at the University of Amsterdam and the University of Leiden. At the time of his American relative's visit to the Emergency Committee, the sixty-five-year-old Hugo Sinzheimer, who had helped draft the Weimar Constitution, was imprisoned in a concentration camp (now known to be Theresienstadt). The Rockefeller Foundation already had indicated that Hugo Sinzheimer was too old for a grant, but Benjamin Sinzheimer thought the Emergency Committee might help. After Benjamin's visit, Drury informed the New School that he had promised to secure $1,000 for his relative's salary. The New School immediately agreed to hire Hugo Sinzheimer, who was released from Theresienstadt.[35]

The New School also accepted banker Erich Warburg's pledge of $4,000 to "any university which would take Dr. [Paul] Eppstein on their staff, thereby enabling him to come in quota-exempt." After losing his municipal appointment as director of Mannheim's adult education center, Eppstein, a prominent sociologist, ran the emigration department and did economic aid work for the Central Organization of German Jewry. In the fall of 1939, the Emergency Committee tried to interest Robert Clothier, president of Rutgers University, in hiring Eppstein, but Clothier declined. Warburg then did interest the New School in appointing Eppstein associate professor of social economics. Eppstein was to start January 1, 1940. In December 1939, however, Eppstein wrote Johnson to say he could not accept the appointment because he was unwilling to leave his position in the emigration department right away; he hoped to start at the New School by April 1, 1940. In September 1940 Eppstein was still in Berlin and wanted to delay accepting the offer for another two years. Johnson was obliging, but Eppstein's wife, Hedwig, also a sociologist, was not as sanguine, writing Johnson the following month from Berlin: "From the depth of my heart, I am wishing and hoping that your efforts may help us to reach our aim at the nearest future possible." Hedwig Eppstein's wishes did not materialize. The couple remained in Germany. In January 1943, they were deported to Theresienstadt, where Paul Eppstein served on the ghetto council. He was shot in September 1944; his wife was deported to Auschwitz, where she perished.[36]

The New School also made an offer to Leonard Polak, a professor of logic, epistemology, metaphysics, and ethics at the University of Gro-ningen in Holland, after Polak & Schwarz, a leading Dutch fragrance manufacturer, agreed to pay his yearly salary of $2,500 for two years. Polak, who was Jewish, was the son-in-law of the firm's founder and separately related to the family. Once the funds were guaranteed in May 1941 by the firm's New York office, Johnson invited Polak to join the New School faculty as an associate professor of philosophy and encouraged him to obtain a non-quota visa that would enable his wife, Henriette, and a minor daughter, seventeen-year-old Annie, to immigrate as well. The firm also was willing to pay for scholarships for his two older daugh-ters, Bettina and Antoinette, who were twenty-two and nineteen at the time, to attend the New School, enabling them to immigrate on non-quota visas for students. In July 1941, Bettina wrote to Johnson, express-ing thanks for her and her sister's acceptance, which enabled them to study art and psychology, respectively, and hoped that they would "get our visa for America soon."[37]

Johnson was somewhat uneasy with these arrangements because of what might happen if an individual did not come through with the promised funds for a salary. When columnist Dorothy Thompson wanted to pay the $4,000 salary (about $66,000 in contemporary dollars) of her friend Eugenia Schwarzwald, founder of a girls' school and proprietor of a literary salon in Vienna, Johnson warned Thompson of the substantial financial burden involved. "I am now in a good deal of difficulty over a case in which the person who pledged a salary could not come up with the funds," Johnson explained. "The beneficiary insists on the salary, and I have made a contract that is legally binding against the School. There-fore, I am impressed with the necessity of wariness, both for you and for me." Thompson wanted to go forward. Schwarzwald ended up staying in Zurich, where she had fled. Thompson sent her $100 every month. Schwarzwald died there of cancer in 1940.[38]

Too Jewish or Foreign

Universities were more likely to hire refugee scholars who were not too old or young, right or left, or female. Only one issue, however, menaced the entire endeavor—whether adding European scholars would make American faculties too Jewish.

Antisemitism marked the U.S. academy, perhaps more than other parts of American life. In the first decades of the twentieth century, many American universities refused to hire Jews to faculty positions. A Rockefeller Foundation official in 1930 considered not granting post-doctoral fellowships to Jewish applicants because they would not be able to obtain faculty positions anyway. A decade later, the situation had improved—but not much. Harvard law dean James Landis explained in 1939: "There are anti-Semitic tendencies with reference to the introduction of Jews into the teaching staffs of most universities. The quota along that direction is also regarded by many of the universities as filled and they refuse to listen to any increase." If they did not ban Jews outright, many departments had an informal "one-Jew rule." Hiring a refugee scholar would upset that balance. "Put plainly, German Jewish scholars threatened to destroy the anti-Jewish quota system then maintained by many American universities," Peter Rutkoff and William Scott concluded in their history of the New School.[1]

Those weighing whether to hire refugee applicants said as much. Johns Hopkins president Isaiah Bowman offered the one-Jew rule as his reason for not hiring Paul Friedlander, a philologist fired from his University of Halle professorship. Friedlander, who had arrived in the United States after being detained in a concentration camp, lectured at Johns Hopkins during the 1939–1940 academic year. "Dr. Friedlander is the kind of man whom we would like to have at this University and we cannot say enough in his praise," Bowman wrote. "But his specialty is Greek and we already have a Jew, Dr. Chermiss, in the Department of Greek. . . . We feel that it would be unwise to appoint a second person of the same faith." Bowman acknowledged that Friedlander is "a scholar of marked eminence whom, under other circumstances, we would greatly wish to keep." (Friedlander got a position at UCLA.) Hertha Kraus, a Bryn Mawr professor and German refugee herself, recommended that journalist and sociologist Julie Meyer not bother applying for a position at Connecticut College. "Since another and very important member of the department is Russian and Jewish, in addition to a German research assistant, it is certainly true that they can't afford another foreign scholar," Kraus advised.[2]

If hiring one refugee scholar could be a problem, hiring several was even more difficult. Alfred Richards, University of Pennsylvania vice president in charge of medical affairs, refused the request of Nobel Prize–winner Otto Meyerhof, a refugee with an appointment there in physiological chemistry, to hire another German-Jewish scholar as an assistant. "The concentration of too many German Jews in one department would increase anti-semitic feeling," Richards told Meyerhof. Meyerhof himself worried about adding too many more Jews at the University of Pennsylvania because "any further addition to the present number would seriously endanger the position of those who are there." (This prompted the Rockefeller Foundation's Alexander Makinsky, who was making his rounds of U.S. universities, to remark: "This reminds me of a Jewish friend, who, through much pressure to bear on the proprietor of 2, Sutton Place, was finally given an apartment, and who now violently opposes the candidacies of other prospective tenants who cannot produce clear records of purely Aryan grandmothers.") MIT president Karl Compton expressed a similar concern about adding a second Jewish member to that university's mathematics department. Compton claimed there was a "tactical danger of having too large a proportion of the mathematical staff from the Jewish race ... [since] the appointment of an additional member of the Jewish race would increase the proportion of such men in the Department far beyond the proportion of [Jews in the] population."[3]

A few American universities insisted on considering only the relatively small number of refugees, about 15 percent of the total, who were pure Aryans. "I've been playing with the idea that it might be possible for us to find an Aryan German or Austrian expatriate who would be desirable for our faculty," Hamilton College president William H. Cowley wrote Stephen Duggan of the Emergency Committee upon the impending retirement of the head of Hamilton's chemistry department. The Emergency Committee seemed nonplussed by the idea, matter-of-factly noting Hamilton's requirements for a chemistry professor: the person had to be an outstanding teacher, in this country so he could be interviewed, and Aryan. The committee cabled the London-based Notgemeinschaft for its suggestion for "outstanding chemist christian to succeed prominent scientist." As long as it was asking for Aryans, the committee included in the same cable a request from another college that sought an "Aryan Protestant mathematician" who could also teach German. The cable did not include the name of the university seeking the Aryan mathematician, but it was likely Eureka College in Illinois, best known as Ronald Reagan's alma mater.[4]

Hamilton and Eureka were not alone in their preference for Aryans. Tacoma College in Washington state would not hire a philosopher who was at the University of Chicago on a temporary Rockefeller Foundation grant because the college "decided they would prefer to have any Aryan." (Of course, some American universities had similar preferences in hiring Americans. T. M. Simpson, head of the University of Florida's math department, felt confident that Harvard mathematician George David Birkhoff would "know the type of man" Simpson wanted to fill a last-minute vacancy: "He should have the Ph.D. degree, should be a Protestant, a good teacher, and capable of at least a mild kind of research.")[5]

The Emergency Committee looked for Aryan chemists for Hamilton, contacting the American Committee for Christian German Refugees and the Committee for Catholic Refugees from Germany, as well as

the Notgemeinschaft. It tossed around several names but found it difficult. "There seem to be few Christians or aryan chemists who are recom-
mendable," Duggan explained. After a few weeks of searching, he wrote
Hamilton's president that the committee had "not yet been able to secure the papers of a desirable Aryan German or Austrian expatriate." He
reassured that "we will not give up the search" yet closed his letter by
noting: "There are of course many Jewish chemists who are available."
Cowley responded that he might reconsider: "If you know of any unusually able and personable Jewish chemist I'd be happy to hear of him." The
Emergency Committee then went on a hunt for an "unusually able personable professor Aryan or nonAryan." A month later, Cowley called off
the hunt, informing the committee that the college had "found our man,"
presumably not a refugee.[6]

Despite its brief, expressed willingness to consider a "personable
Jewish chemist," Hamilton had not actually changed its tune about non-
Aryan refugees. When the Emergency Committee learned in 1942 that
a Hamilton professor was being loaned to Princeton for war research, it
offered Cowley the services of a displaced physicist, Harry Dember, who
had led the physics department at the Technical University of Dresden
and then taught at the University of Istanbul. "I'd be grateful if you'd tell
me whether or not he's a Jew," Cowley responded. "I've hired three Jews
since I came to Hamilton—the first Jews ever on the Hamilton Faculty—
and thus I need to know this fact before proceeding." Dember's curriculum vitae indicated he was "of Jewish race and profession." Cowley then
"made a study of [Dember's] desirability for Hamilton" and concluded,
"he's not our man."[7]

Most American universities did not insist on a pure Aryan, but
they did prefer that the scholars not be too Jewish, meaning they did not
have too much Jewish blood or too many Jewish attributes. And, in fact,
many of the refugee scholars were only part Jewish. Because the German academy discriminated against Jews even before the rise of Nazism,
many aspiring academics converted to Protestantism or Catholicism or
were from families that had. Conversion was "the ticket to European
culture," as the poet Heinrich Heine, who had converted in 1825, put it.
Nazi-controlled universities, however, did not care whether the scholars
were practicing Jews or even self-identified as Jews; "of Jewish descent"

was the only relevant category. With a few exceptions, American universities were more receptive to those who fit in the non-Aryan category. Harvard's Landis "emphasized the extraordinary difficulties of placing one hundred per cent Jews." William D. Harkins, a chemistry professor at the University of Chicago, wanted to know whether any of the four scholars the chemistry department was interested in was "only remotely Jewish, which would make it very much easier for him to envisage possible invitations." Harkins told an Emergency Committee emissary that his department "was under fire because it contains a high percentage of Jewish members."[8]

Correspondence about which scholars to hire therefore often centered on how Jewish the candidate seemed. Dartmouth president Ernest Hopkins told the Rockefeller Foundation the college needed an economic historian but did not "want anyone who is obviously Jewish." The foundation suggested Paul Mantoux, whose "doctoral thesis on industrial revolution is still the outstanding work in the field of economic history." That, however, was not Mantoux's primary qualification. "Mantoux and his family do not have any obvious Jewish characteristics and have never considered themselves Jewish," the foundation's Tracy Kittredge wrote, noting that the family had been Catholic for two generations. "Most people who know him never suspect any Jewish origin. Hence he would not appear to fall under the category which President Hopkins has excluded from consideration."[9]

Another economic historian, Marc Bloch, who was "also a scholar of the first class rank," *was* excluded from consideration. Bloch was "more obviously Jewish" and "definitely labeled Jewish in France," according to the Emergency Committee's notes about placing him. Dartmouth offered neither Mantoux nor Bloch a position. (A former *New York Times* reporter hired by the Emergency Committee to assess antisemitism on U.S. campuses described Dartmouth in late 1939 as having "no refugee experience, and little interest in developing any.") Mantoux received offers from the New School and Bryn Mawr but decided in 1941 that he would not leave France until his son was demobilized from French military service. He never did leave. Mantoux survived the war, although it is not clear how, and became the director of the Graduate Institute of International Studies in Geneva until his death in 1956. Bloch remained in France where, with the German invasion, his future became more precarious.[10]

As Kittredge did in recommending Mantoux, many Americans emphasized that a particular scholar was not really Jewish. "Dr. [Friedrich] Jaffe is, I believe a Protestant," Columbia's Joseph Chamberlain wrote. "He is not of the Jewish faith, as only one of his grandparents was of that race and he is connected with some of the best and oldest established families of Baden and Wurttemberg." Chamberlain also noted that Jaffe's aunt was married to novelist D. H. Lawrence and that Jaffe's wife "is also a very attractive person." Other recommenders stressed that the scholars at the least did not seem Jewish. Roy C. Flickinger, an Iowa State classics professor, explained that Karl Lehmann-Hartleben of the University of Münster was of "non-Aryan stock, which I presume, means, Jewish, although he has never impressed me as being a Jew." Flickinger then recited Lehmann-Hartleben's gentile credentials—his family had been Protestant for two generations and his wife was "of pure German stock"— as well as his academic ones—"a wide reputation in the field of classical archeology." Lehmann-Hartleben spent two years in Italy before joining the New York University faculty in 1935, where he remained until his death in 1960.[11]

In urging the hiring of former University of Bonn law professor Eberhard Bruck, Alice Waldo of the American Committee for Christian German Refugees seemed to consider it relevant that "at no time have the Brucks considered themselves Jewish as they have been Protestants for all of Professor Bruck's life." Waldo also noted that "Mrs. Bruck is a so-called 'full Aryan.'" Earle Babcock, director of the Carnegie Foundation in Paris, wrote of Ernst Grunfeld, a professor at the University of Halle, "His wife, who is not Jewish, tells me that her husband, although he has Jewish blood was never looked upon as non-aryan before the accession of Hitler to power." Grunfeld, who received negative scholarly evaluations in trying to emigrate, committed suicide in 1938 while still in Germany. Appearance often played a large part in the assessment. "Dr. [Eva Lehmann] Fiesel looks entirely 'Aryan,' to use the unpleasant jargon of present-day German politics," Yale linguistics professor Eduard Prokosch wrote in 1935 in trying to get Fiesel a job at Bryn Mawr. "She is, however, on one side of her family 'non-Aryan' and this caused her dismissal from the faculty of the University of Munich." In fact, both Fiesel's parents came from Jewish families, and they converted to Protestantism after their wedding.[12]

"Never Knew He Was a Jew"

Even the most sympathetic Americans engaged in this type of appraisal. In recommending twenty-nine-year-old philologist Ruth Ehrmann to the president of Reed College for a position in the German department, Esther Brunauer of the AAUW noted that Ehrmann "is not what is usually considered 'Jewish' in appearance, but rather Slavic looking." (Reed did not offer Ehrmann, who was in Berlin, a position. Faced with a long wait for a regular quota, she immigrated to England on a domestic permit, taking a job as matron of a home for refugee girls. She then married a Berlin sculptor who had Chilean nationality, and they moved to Chile, where she spent the rest of her life.)[13]

The Bryn Mawr professor Hertha Kraus praised Friedrich Spiegelberg, who had studied with theologian Paul Tillich and assumed Tillich's position at the University of Dresden until Spiegelberg was himself fired in 1937: "This is a very nice family, 'Aryan,'" Kraus wrote, noting that Spiegelberg was "tall, good looking and an excellent speaker." Spiegelberg became a professor at Stanford University.[14]

In asking the AAUW to help her friend Margarete Merzbach-Kober, a historian of German literature, Katharine Keppler mentioned that Merzbach-Kober's daughter, Uta, was "a most charming, well-mannered and intelligent little girl, most 'nordic' and 'Aryan' in appearance." The AAUW could not help the Merzbach-Kober family. Merzbach-Kober was deported from Berlin to Theresienstadt on August 4, 1943, along with her husband and daughter. Once the camp was liberated, the family immigrated to the United States, where the parents became professors at what became Southwestern University in Georgetown, Texas. Their daughter became mathematics curator at the Smithsonian Institution in Washington, D.C., and taught at Johns Hopkins.[15]

To emphasize how "not Jewish" a particular candidate was, American recommenders sometimes stated they had not even known the person was Jewish. William A. Noyes, an emeritus chemistry professor at the University of Illinois, wrote of Else Hirschberg, a chemist from Hamburg who had sought help emigrating, "She is a Jewess but I knew her for some years before I knew this." Noyes and Hirschberg had met at a 1924 meeting in Germany and had exchanged letters and reprints over the years. Hirschberg had been trying to emigrate since she was first dismissed from her position at the University of Rostock in 1933. Beginning in 1937, she managed the laboratory of the Jewish hospital in Hamburg. In early 1939, she knew she would lose that position "because the Hospital cannot exist." Her teaching at the University of Rostock presumably qualified her for a non-quota visa, but she seemingly never received a university offer. On July 11, 1942, the fifty-year-old Hirschberg was among twenty-four Jews from Rostock on a Hamburg transport to what was most likely Auschwitz-Birkenau. Her name appears on a List of Murdered Jews from Germany.[16]

Frances G. Wick, a Vassar College physics professor, wrote to see whether the Emergency Committee could place Karl Przibram, with whom she had worked at Vienna's Radium Institute. (His brother Hans headed Vienna's biology institute.) "He is Jewish but not at all of the disagreeable type—in fact I worked with him for months and never knew he was a Jew until he told me himself," Wicks explained, noting that Przibram was "refined and delightful," with a non-Jewish wife. Wicks also advocated for other institute researchers, including Marietta Blau, who had escaped to Oslo and then to Mexico. Przibram never got an American university position. He spent the war hiding in Brussels and fighting with the Resistance. At the end of the war, he returned to Vienna and became a professor at the University of Vienna. Occasionally, a recommender felt obligated to acknowledge that a refugee scholar did seem too Jewish. Edwin Borchard of Yale Law School praised Arthur Nussbaum, who had been on the University of Berlin faculty, as "one of the finest legal hands now functioning in any part of the world." He then noted, "He is somewhat semitic in appearance, but a very delightful person." Nussbaum still managed to obtain a position on the Columbia law school faculty.[17]

Scholars themselves often listed their non-Jewish credentials on their curriculum vitae or in letters. Albert Ehrenzweig, who became a University of California law professor, highlighted in his curriculum

vitae that he was Catholic. Margherita Hirschberg, in trying to find a
teaching position that would allow her to emigrate from Italy after its
adoption of racial laws, noted, "I don't know if for teaching possibilities
it is of any interest that also being jewish by race I am catholic by faith."
In asking for help immigrating to the United States, Philipp August
Rappaport, an architect and town planner who lost his government job
in 1933, highlighted the fact that he was "educated as a good Christian
having a calm and conservative character." Hans Fried, a Viennese mathematician of the "Jewish confession," went so far as to suggest that he
would be willing to be baptized "since it is of utmost importance to me
to find a position." Fried immigrated to the United States in 1940 and
took a position at Swarthmore College. It is not clear whether he was
ever baptized.[18]

Sometimes "personality" problems seemed to be code for someone
who seemed too Jewish. "We simply must avoid sending people whose
personality and character are unattractive to American people and likely
to create anti-foreign feeling," Fritz Demuth of the Notgemeinschaft offered after a 1937 trip to the United States. That might have been Rockefeller Foundation official Daniel O'Brien's objection to David Nachmansohn, a chemist expelled from the University of Berlin and reestablished
at the Sorbonne. Nachmansohn was "rather on the pushing side and
somewhat tactless," O'Brien noted, even though he had "carried on active research of good quality in the field of study of chemical transmis-
sion in nervous tissue." O'Brien concluded: "He is worth keeping an eye
on—but preferably from someone else's glasses." Yale University had a
different perception, inviting Nachmansohn to join its faculty. He went
on to a distinguished career at Columbia's College of Physicians and
Surgeons, eventually being inducted into the National Academy of Sciences for his work on the molecular basis of bioelectricity.[19]

The reluctance to hire 100 percent Jews and the preference for those
who were merely non-Aryan presented a difficult challenge for the assistance organizations, one they never quite resolved. Should they acknowledge and cater to the prevailing antisemitism in the U.S. academy and
thus not place a significant number of scholars? Or should they challenge it and run the risk of inspiring a backlash that might prevent even
more scholars from being placed? Columbia anthropologist Franz Boas

expressed that concern early on in the refugee crisis. In seeking Columbia president Nicholas Murray Butler's help, Boas, who was himself Jewish, recommended against "the appointment of a large number of Jews to
permanent positions which might have the effect of increasing the anti-
semitic feeling which undoubtedly exists in our country." Julius Stieglitz,
a University of Chicago chemistry professor and younger brother of the
famous photographer Alfred Stieglitz, laid out his concerns to the Emergency Committee's Alfred Cohn. The seventy-year-old Stieglitz, who was
himself of German-Jewish ancestry and had studied in Germany, offered the names of people in the chemical industry he thought would be
sympathetic to refugees. He then offered a warning: "In our own experience, at least one-third and more likely one-half of all the calls we have
for chemists—and they are exceedingly numerous—bar the employment
of Jewish candidates. I am very much afraid that if your committee tries
to bring any large number of Jewish scholars in the varied branches of
science, art, letters, etc. this already great feeling, which is smouldering
throughout the country, will be fanned into an active flame." By 1939,
this challenge became a crisis.[20]

"Not at the Expense of Our American Graduates"

American universities had other concerns about refugee scholars that
also affected their employment decisions. In general, they preferred hiring Americans to foreigners, worried about Europeans' ability to teach
American undergraduates, and feared negative reactions from the public. Gregory Breit, then a University of Wisconsin physics professor,
expressed all three concerns in advising George Washington University
not to hire Edward Teller, a Hungarian-born, German-educated Jewish
physicist. Breit, who had been born in Russia, acknowledged that Teller
"was very good" yet added: "We have a very good crop of young theore-
ticians in this country too and I think they should be provided for first.
Also my observation has been that in universities Americans are usually
more effective in their work with students as well as contacts with the
administration. I believe G.W.U. will open itself to criticism for going in
for foreigners too heavily." George Washington hired Teller anyway, and
he became a legendary developer of the hydrogen bomb. He joined the

University of Chicago faculty after the war. Arthur Compton, chairman of the University of Chicago physics department, expressed similar concerns in 1935 but later hired Enrico Fermi and then Teller, who transformed the physics department.[21]

John Murlin of the University of Rochester's Department of Vital Economics gave expression to the pro-American sentiments: "We realize of course that the refugee problem is a terrific one, but we must not let our sentimentality blind our judgement in such matters. Where money can be provided by the Jewish people for an additional post in a university department, it does not displace a better qualified man, and the refugee worker then gets an opportunity to prove himself, which, of course, is what he should have, but not at the expense of our American graduates." Murlin then rejected the refugee whom Rockefeller Institute's Phoebus Levene had tried to place at the University of Rochester because of the refugee's supposed "ignorance of American progress" in the study of alimentation. Murlin's rationale reflects what Rutkoff and Scott found in their study of the New School—"the predictable defensiveness of American intellectuals toward European intellectuals, who often acted condescendingly toward American scholarship."[22]

The refugee scholars' ability to teach undergraduates in particular raised concerns. Academic administrators assumed that language problems, along with differences between American and European pedagogy, meant that the foreign scholars would have trouble in undergraduate classrooms. The case of Walter Sulzbach, who had been a University of Frankfurt sociology professor and taught at Claremont College, illustrates the problem. The Emergency Committee had to decide in 1939 whether it would again fund half of Sulzbach's $3,000 salary. A Claremont professor of social philosophy, Everett Dean Martin, had reported that Sulzbach was "a very able scholar and good teacher," who had been "very popular with students" when he taught during the previous summer session. Claremont president Russell Story disagreed, however, telling the committee that Sulzbach's "work with students is characterized by great 'remoteness,'" according to notes of the conversation among Story and committee members. "Personally a gentle and likeable man, Sulzbach . . . is not disinterested, but simply *oblivious* to any relationship between himself and the students." The discrepancy between the two versions might be explained in further correspondence, which suggested that the Claremont students were not "sufficiently advanced to follow his courses." Sulzbach's wife, a "blue-stocking" who was ill with diabetes, was also having trouble adjusting because she was "above the cultural level of the community" and held "herself somewhat aloof from her neighbors." The committee contemplated other placements, although Sulzbach remained at Claremont for another six years with the Emergency Committee's backing. He returned to Frankfurt and his position at the university in 1956.[23]

Comments about the community's reaction to Sulzbach's wife point to another issue about which universities fretted—a negative public response to foreign scholars. Not too long after he complained about Sulzbach, President Story informed the Emergency Committee: "The climate of opinion in which we now operate is much less hospitable to foreign scholars of German antecedents than it has been heretofore. Even those already with us are under some strain on account of rather irresponsible sentiments expressed in the outside community." The University of New Hampshire's president Fred Engelhardt explained his reluctance to hire refugee scholars: "Appointments are given wide publicity in the state, and even the best scholarly mind would be hard to defend if radical, foreign, or Jewish." The aid organizations had similar concerns. Demuth of the Notgemeinschaft insisted "the work must be done as noiselessly as possible, not attracting any attention from the public, the press or official quarters."[24]

It is hard to assess the degree to which these concerns were justified. At least on the national level, fears of public opposition seem to have been overblown. The National Refugee Service surveyed U.S. newspapers in 1940 and concluded that "the American press is sympathetic and understanding of its treatment of the refugee question, both in editorial comment and news coverage." Former *New York Times* reporter Percy Knauth, who visited seventy-five institutions for the Emergency Committee in 1939, found that "each Faculty appointment is given wide publicity" and therefore "the likely reaction of the general public must always be considered." But he advised the committee to be mindful of the public response, not to avoid publicity altogether.[25]

Language problems certainly arose in individual cases but seemed to be less of a factor than might have been assumed, presumably because it was not difficult to find refugees who spoke English. In a 1947 survey, Columbia sociologist Donald Kent concluded that "a distinguishing feature of this migration was the large number who arrived with some knowledge of English." The study acknowledged that the claim by more than 90 percent of those surveyed that they spoke English "well" was likely exaggerated. Still, the study found that many refugees were fluent on the basis of "the fact that at least one third of the study group were able to obtain professional posts in their own field within the first year in America," and that by the end of the war, 90 percent "were engaged in occupations requiring considerable facility in English." Scholars, in particular, knew English. Dismissed from their positions early in the Nazi era, many devoted themselves to learning the language. "I studied English thoroughly during the last years and shall be able to lecture in English," history professor Hedwig Hintze wrote from Berlin in January 1939.[26]

Whether the refugee scholars ultimately proved to be good teachers who adapted themselves to American universities is disputed. "Too many refugees have taken advantage of kindness, gained a foothold and have proven incompetent, or unworthy of their appointment," Ruth Pope found in her May 1940 study of fifty-six Southern colleges for the American Friends Service Committee. Laurens Seelye, the Emergency Committee's assistant director, reached a different conclusion after a visit to North Carolina, Tennessee, and Indiana "to call on displaced foreign scholars." He found them "almost universally well adjusted." Clemens Sommer had eighty students in his University of North Carolina course, which Seelye reported as "typical." He also found it "especially encouraging" that the scholars' children were "getting along well" and were almost always at the "head of their class in schools and colleges." In November 1940, the Rockefeller Foundation's Kittredge visited the Midwest and talked to representatives of universities there and came away with a favorable impression of opportunities for European scholars.[27]

Not all the appointments worked out of course. Julius Lips, who had been a professor of sociology and ethnology at the University of Cologne, resigned apparently before Howard University elected not to reappoint him. The Emergency Committee had warned Lips before he joined the Howard faculty that being a white professor at the historically black college required "the maximum degree of diplomacy" and "had begged him not to be too outspoken in his criticism." Lips went public with his criticisms in the *Washington Daily News* on June 12, 1939, being quoted as saying that he disliked "the ethical and scientific approach of some of the staff members" and painting a picture of "jealousy, toadying and general pettiness at the school." That prompted the dean of the College of Liberal Arts to make public his recommendation that Lips not be reappointed at least partly because of his "unfortunate temperament and personality." The dean described Lips's relationships with his social science colleagues as ranging from "polite indifference" to "suppressed hostility," making collaboration "highly improbable." Otto Nathan, an economist then at New York University, wrote to Betty Drury at the Emergency Committee to corroborate the Howard University dean's version of events and to encourage the committee not to fund Lips again. Lips "has abused the hospitality which Howard University has extended to him," Nathan wrote.[28]

Several scholars encountered anti-Jewish feeling and antipathy from the faculty where they were placed. Franz Mautner, a German literature scholar, for example, did not last at the University of Delaware because of "antagonism" on the part of the faculty. He eventually taught at Wesleyan, Kenyon, and then Swarthmore, where he spent most of his career. Despite these problems, the overall numbers, as well as the influential careers of individual scholars, point to a positive record. The 1947 survey found "62 percent of those who had been teachers abroad were able to continue teaching in the United States and had reached, at the time these data were collected, a position equal to that which they had held in Europe."[29]

Of course, many never recovered from the trauma and dislocation, as those gathered on June 1, 1945, for the funeral of refugee Werner F. Bruck expressed. Bruck had been a student of Martin Heidegger's and a promising philosopher. "In tracing his life, many of us are tracing our own lives, refugees from a country which no longer exists," the New School's Emil J. Gumbel said at the funeral. Gumbel acknowledged he knew Bruck "was profoundly unhappy" and "suffered not only through the usual material misfortunes, but especially through the separation

from his family." Eduard Heimann, a New School economist and sociologist, also eulogized Bruck:

> His lot was a comparatively easy one if we compare it with
> that of so many of our friends who went to the furnaces of
> Buchenwald and who all lie buried in the sands of Sahara. He
> was rescued by the University College of Cadiz and after sev-
> eral years joined the group of scholars whom Alvin Johnson
> had assembled at the New School. But there would be no
> sense at this moment in hiding the fact that he remained a
> helpless and restless man ever since. . . . His own work was
> almost unnoticed in this country and he was suffering from
> the uncertainty and humiliation of depending on the short
> term appointments which alone were available to men of his
> advanced age and state of health. . . . He lived in utter lone-
> liness until his heart broke under the stress, as the heart of a
> more robust man would have done.[30]

S • E • V • E • N

State Department Barriers

After seven years trying to help refugee scholars obtain non-quota visas, the New School's Alvin Johnson knew how obstructionist the U.S. State Department could be. He did not have much hope for two of the three Polish scholars to whom the New School had made offers once Germany invaded Poland in 1939. But Johnson thought Ludwik Ehrlich, a professor of international and constitutional law, might be different for a simple reason. Ehrlich's wife, Frances, was a U.S. citizen. Surely, the U.S. consul in Berlin would be willing to try to help her and their two children leave German-occupied Poland.

Johnson would be wrong. During the twelve years of the Nazi regime, the State Department made it as hard as possible for refugees to immigrate to the United States, and scholars and their spouses were no exception. The existence of the non-quota visa for professors and the prewar and postwar attention given refugee scholars has created the impression that the State Department did not throw as many roadblocks in their paths as it did for other possible immigrants. That was not the case. Even if professors were offered a university position, serious obstacles remained to their obtaining a non-quota visa. Without such a visa, the scholars would have to wait for a regular visa, often until it was too late. Knowing the importance of such visas, aid organizations and universities shaped their decisions around what they thought the State Department wanted.[1]

Section 4(d) of the Immigration Act of 1924 governed the granting of non-quota visas. It authorized provision of such a visa to immigrants who had been carrying on the vocation of professor continuously for two years before applying for admission to the United States and who were seeking admission to continue to carry on that vocation. Whether an individual applicant fit within that understanding depended on the determination of an individual official in a consulate abroad. An official in Berlin or Vienna or Rotterdam or Antwerp would assess an application and decide to issue a visa—or not. The official had complete discretion and almost never had to explain a decision. State Department officials in Washington sometimes issued guidelines on the preferred interpretation of a particular provision, including Section 4(d), but individual consular officials did not necessarily have to follow the guidelines, whose parameters changed all the time anyway. General consuls abroad sometimes created their own rules for the officials in their consulates, contributing to the inconsistency and confusion that permeated the process. It also meant that some consuls—in Rotterdam, Zurich, and Naples, for example—developed reputations as being particularly difficult. Amidst this maze of interpretations and random rules, there was one lodestar. To please their higher-ups, ambitious consulate officials simply followed the State Department's informal immigration policy during the Nazi era— deny visas to as many people as possible.[2]

As they issued shifting guidelines, State Department officials expressed concerns about the economic and security effect of admitting too many refugees. Yet the State Department's restrictive policy also reflected animus toward immigrants in general as well as refugee scholars in particular. George Messersmith, who was consul in Berlin, minister in Austria, and then assistant secretary of state in D.C., explained his views in a confidential 1933 report. Messersmith did not want to "open our doors without distinction" to the displaced professors. He argued that German scholars would take jobs from young American professors, were interested only in areas directly related to their fields, and were overall "of a very different type of man from the professor in the United States in a similar position." Most worrisome of all, according to Messersmith, was that "many of the Jewish professors were socialists of an advanced type."[3]

Although consuls did not have to explain why they were denying a visa, it often became apparent in their responses to inquiries about the status of individual refugees. Officials' interpretation of the non-quota visa provision hurt refugee scholars in several ways. For starters, non-quota visas were not available to intellectuals who were not affiliated with higher education institutions. Max Brod, a journalist, novelist, essayist, and Franz Kafka's editor and executor, could not obtain a non-quota visa despite his sustained efforts after the German invasion of his Prague home. Novelist Thomas Mann's assurances that Brod was a "very gifted man" and "scholar who would add to the distinction and honor of any institution" could not overcome the fact that Brod had not "held posts in recognized educational institutions," as the New School's Johnson explained to Mann in turning Brod down flat. Even Brod's promise that he would bring Kafka's manuscripts and books with him did not earn him an exemption. Brod fled to Palestine instead, Kafka's papers in tow.[4]

More controversially, consular officials determined what constituted a higher education institution. To qualify for a non-quota visa one had to have been professor of a "college, academy, seminary, or university." The author of a 1941 treatise on immigration law wrote confidently that the terms "academy and seminary" in Section 4(d) "are construed as applicable to any reputable institutions of learning which are equipped to prepare students for college." Yet in determining what types of European institutions fit the definition, government officials initially ruled out college preparatory schools that fell somewhere between high schools and universities. Logician Kurt Grelling was well known for discovering the heterological paradox, yet because he taught at a preparatory school, he found it difficult to immigrate.[5]

Seminaries also could be excluded. The Berlin consul accepted the German government's demotion of the Lehranstalt, that city's Jewish seminary, to an "institute" that therefore did not qualify as a "college, academy, seminary, or university." That determination made it difficult for any of its faculty to immigrate. After intense lobbying from officials of Hebrew Union College, which wanted to hire several of the seminary's scholars, the government eventually changed the designation in

March 1940—which was too late for Arthur Spanier. Hebrew Union College offered Spanier, a librarian who taught at the Lehranstalt, a position while he was imprisoned in Dachau following the November 1938 Kristallnacht pogrom. Denied a non-quota visa, Spanier took what he hoped would be temporary refuge in Amsterdam. The Rotterdam consul subsequently rejected his visa request. In 1942, Spanier was sent to Bergen-Belsen, where he died.[6]

American officials also decided an immigrant had to have been a classroom teacher; otherwise, they were "not a bona fide professor," as Betty Drury explained to Emergency Committee members. The statute itself did not mention teaching. "We have been restricted in our selections first of all by a legal factor," the New School's Johnson explained. "We could appoint only scholars eligible for a non-quota visa by virtue of having done sufficient teaching in a university." This was true even if aspiring professors were denied teaching positions because they were Jewish, as seemingly was the case for Czech lawyer Paul Hartmann. According to the Rockefeller Foundation, which had granted Hartmann a social science fellowship a decade earlier, he would have received a lectureship at German University in Prague except for "Nazi intrigue against him, as he is partly Jewish." (Hartmann escaped to England.) Even some teaching was not enough for some consuls. Johnson, who had overcome his initial objections to the "young and promising" psychology professor Katherina Wolf, discovered, when he tried to get her a visa, a problem with "the Consul at Zurich, who is difficult in general and who has been unpleasant to Dr. Wolf in particular." Johnson noted that the consul would not grant Wolf a non-quota visa "on the grounds that she has not done enough teaching." Wolf came to the United States a year later, although not on a non-quota visa.[7]

Requiring classroom teaching disqualified researchers. Albert Coyle, a New York lawyer, ran into that problem when he tried to get a non-quota visa for international lawyer Martin Domke, who in 1940 was imprisoned in a French internment camp. Johnson replied to both men that Domke could not get a teaching position, even though he did not need a salary. If research was recognized "as a teaching activity under the regulations this would not matter," Johnson later wrote to Coyle and Yale law professor Edwin Borchard, who also had taken up Domke's case.

"But they do not. We have tried to get in people as research assistants, but we have been consistently turned down." Domke managed to get to the United States in 1941, presumably on a quota visa, and became an adjunct professor at New York University Law School, and ultimately, an important figure in commercial arbitration.[8]

The interpretation also disqualified librarians. Helen Nathan had been director of a large Berlin public library until her ouster in 1933. She sought the AAUW's help. "May I hope that you will kindly lend me a helping hand?" she wrote Esther Brunauer in May 1940. Without her assistance, "I could not see the way how to enter your country. Believe me, dear Mrs. Brunauer." Brunauer could not help. The visa division judged Nathan unqualified for a non-quota visa because "her vocation heretofore has been primarily that of a librarian." Her "only claim" to a professorship was a connection to the Berlin School of Librarians and the socialist-oriented People's College. Acting visa chief Eliot Coulter concluded those institutions could not "be properly regarded as a college, academy, seminary or university."[9]

Julian Morgenstern, president of Hebrew Union College, was unusually accepting of this interpretation. He had sought a non-quota visa for Walter Gottschalk, whom he had offered a position. When Morgenstern discovered that Gottschalk was founder and director of the Arabic section of the Prussian State Library (not a Heidelberg professor, as he had assumed), he made no attempt to challenge the visa's denial. "The American consul in Antwerp of course had no alternative but to deny Dr. Gottschalk the non-quota visa," Morgenstern wrote in informing the Emergency Committee that Gottschalk would not need a grant. Morgenstern understood that Gottschalk, who in 1939 fled first to the Netherlands and then to Belgium, would not receive a regular visa for three or four years. Denied the Hebrew Union College position, Gottschalk sought a job as a librarian at the University of Istanbul. To maintain good relations with neutral Turkey, the Germans surprisingly let Gottschalk leave German-occupied Belgium in 1941 to take the job in Istanbul. Gottschalk spent the war years in Istanbul, where he helped develop Turkey's library system.[10]

The State Department decided that other scholars who had been "professors" in Europe were nonetheless ineligible for non-quota visas because they would not be able to carry on "the vocation of ... professor" in the United States; age or other reasons prevented them from becoming classroom teachers. In a private meeting, Harvard secretary Jerome Greene sought guidance on whether the State Department would grant non-quota visas to scholars whom the university assumed would do research and not teach. Avra Warren, chief of the State Department's visa division, responded with an unequivocal no. "Abuses of so liberal a definition by American institutions of doubtful standing made it impossible for that definition to be accepted," Warren told Greene, apparently without providing any examples of "abuse." Titles of "research fellows" or "research associates" were "often used as a pretext for getting aliens into this country," Warren said. Greene seemed to accept Warren's explanation without hesitation.[11]

A year and a half later, Yale's Borchard decided to take on the State Department's interpretation. He considered it "a very narrow construction to maintain that a man who has devoted his entire life to teaching in Europe cannot come here to do research because he is not then a teacher." Borchard, too, approached visa division chief Warren, who budged slightly. A research assistant engaged as a faculty member did not necessarily have to give "formal courses" but could "supervise student research or outside reading," Warren told Borchard, who was encouraged by the response. The New School's Johnson, however, doubted the State Department would in fact become more lenient: "We have little reason to believe that Mr. Warren makes liberal interpretations when he can find the possibility of the other kind." Julian Morgenstern had a similar reaction to the State Department and to Warren. "I have never been able to accomplish anything whatever with that State Department" without high-level pressure from the Roosevelt Administration, Morgenstern wrote in 1941 after two and a half years of trying to add refugees to the Hebrew Union College faculty.[12]

Still other consuls went even farther, considering themselves better judges of faculty needs than the institutions themselves. Hebrew Union College had offered Eugen Taubler, a historian of antiquity, a position on its faculty. The Berlin consul refused to issue a non-quota visa to Taubler and his wife, Selma Stern-Taubler, also a historian, because the consul determined that Hebrew Union College "having a staff of 19 teachers

(14) Law professor Edwin Borchard, Yale University, 1937.
Courtesy of Harris Ewing Collection at the Library of Congress.

and only 53 students, requires no further additions to its Faculty." Taubler eventually received his visa and joined the Hebrew Union College
faculty. Selma Stern-Taubler became an archivist at the American Jewish Archives.[13]

"The Absurdity of Demanding Two Years of Employment"

The State Department's interpretation of the teaching requirement presented another problem. Most of those trying to immigrate had been
expelled from their university positions beginning in 1933, which meant
that by the mid-to-late 1930s, they had not been professors "for at least
two years immediately preceding the [time of their] application for admission to the United States," as the law stated. The State Department's
Sumner Welles, an assistant secretary, acknowledged "the absurdity of
demanding two years of employment as a professor just previous to the

date of emigration." Welles, one of the few State officials sympathetic to refugees, believed "such a regulation was manifestly inapplicable to the majority of cases" and that research activity should be accepted in lieu of teaching.[14]

But many of the consuls, who ultimately made the determination, did not see it that way. A few considered the applicants to be "on furlough" and thus still qualified for a non-quota visa. Alice Waldo of the American Committee for Christian German Refugees used the "liberal" interpretation to help obtain a non-quota visa for law professor Eberhard Bruck, who had been dismissed from the University of Bonn in 1935. "Presumably he can ask for consideration on the ground of having been on furlough from 1936 until the present as he did not give up his teaching voluntarily," Waldo wrote. Bruck received a research fellowship in law at Harvard and was able to emigrate along with his wife. But many consuls did not consider applicants on furlough and routinely turned down applicants for not having taught immediately before immigration.[15]

After Kristallnacht led to a stampede of people trying to leave Germany, the State Department exhibited a slight and short-lived willingness to interpret the law to allow more refugees into the United States. Among other changes, it seemingly no longer required two years of continuous teaching before emigration for those who had been fired from their positions and broadened the types of institutions that qualified to include college preparatory schools and the Lehranstalt seminary. M. F. Baer of B'nai B'rith was told that the two-year teaching requirement "was not so strictly construed as to penalize those who were prevented from continuing in such a vocation by German authorities." The AAUW received the same information in January 1939 from the same source, acting visa division chief Coulter, who deemed the post-Kristallnacht flood of visa applicants an "emergency situation."[16]

The change probably saved Arthur Korn, who had been chair of physics at the Berlin Institute of Technology and had been offered a position at the Stevens Institute of Technology in New Jersey. In December 1938, Harvard's Harlow Shapley had warned Korn that he might not qualify for a non-quota visa. Korn wrote from Berlin the next month: "Please do your utmost with your colleagues to influence in Washington a liberal interpretation of the non-quota immigration law. As I had to resign my professorship here on the 7th of January 1936, I could not continue my teaching. . . . It may be taken into consideration that there was not any fault of mine. . . . You will agree that it is quite a desperate situation for us to wait for the quota immigration. Practically we cannot remain. Our only hope is U.S.A."[17]

In April 1939, Shapley reported that "a more liberal interpretation" of the teaching requirement meant that those, such as Korn, who had been dismissed for racial reasons "may be considered by your authorities as professor on furlow [sic]." Another problem had arisen, however. Korn's job offer at the Stevens Institute "is not recognized by the Consulate here [in Berlin] as a real university call," Korn wrote Shapley. "You know how much depends on this decision for me, my wife and my son, so please do, together with your colleagues, your utmost in order to help. Excuse my insisting letters." Korn's supporters argued that he would be teaching the laboratory staff and several students assigned to it. Korn finally obtained a non-quota visa and assumed the Stevens Institute position. His research is credited with leading to the invention of the fax machine. He died in 1945.[18]

But not all the consuls got the message, or at least followed it. Visa division head Coulter cabled the Naples consul in January 1939 that Auguste Jellinek, who had an offer from Washington University in St. Louis, should be issued a non-quota visa, even though she could not prove she had given lectures during the previous twenty-four months. The thirty-seven-year-old Jellinek, who did research on the physiology of hearing, had fled to Italy in 1933. Six years later a new law mandated that foreign Jews leave Italy, and she feared being sent back to Germany. Jellinek was so fearful that she also applied for visas to Palestine, Switzerland, Argentina, Paraguay, Bolivia, Guatemala, and the Netherlands. She had not received a reply from any of them. Still, the Naples consul, who had previously denied Jellinek's non-quota application, did not issue the non-quota visa immediately. Three months later, Jellinek received a regular visa "before the question of her possible clarification as a nonquota professor had been determined." She accepted the job at the Institute for the Deaf, which was affiliated with Washington University, and then established a private practice for speech disorders in New York.[19]

The uncertainty contributed to refugee scholars' anxiety that could verge on hysteria. The Rockefeller Foundation's Alexander Makinsky understood that Rafael Taubenschlag, formerly a University of Kraków law professor, would have to "present proof that he had been teaching for the past two years" to get a non-quota visa in September 1940. But Makinsky did not anticipate a problem because Taubenschlag, who fled Poland at the time of the German invasion, had been lecturing at the University of Aix-en-Provence. Still, Taubenschlag was not comforted, showing up at Makinsky's Lisbon apartment "in a terrible state of mind," Makinsky recorded in his diary, insisting that "the American consul had something against him personally" and threatening to commit suicide. Makinsky explained that Taubenschlag's was "a typical case of paranoia" and that he had "lost his family," including "a son in a concentration camp." Makinsky wrote he felt "deeply sorry for him." Taubenschlag's visa was granted the following month, and he assumed a position at the New School and later Columbia University.[20]

A final interpretive problem that afflicted scholars may have been the most perverse. The law specified that non-quota visas could be issued to a qualifying scholar's "wife, and his unmarried children under 18 years of age; if accompanying or following to join him." State Department officials concluded that because the provision specified "wife," it did not apply to the husbands of female scholars. They stuck to that position, even contributing to the defeat of a congressional bill that attempted to change the language to encompass husbands.[21]

"New Regulations Are Cast Iron"

Scholars also ran into the same bureaucracy and obstructionism that derailed so many refugees' immigration attempts. Determined to keep immigration below the numbers allowed by quota, the State Department instructed consuls that they had the right to deny visas to anyone "likely to become a public charge"—in other words, anyone who might not be able to support himself or herself in the United States. When in early 1933 U.S. consuls in Germany began using the clause to deny visas to almost everyone who applied, Jewish and liberal groups protested to the U.S. government. In the summer, new guidelines instructed consular officials to consider more than applicants' personal financial resources;

they also could consider statements from U.S. citizens vowing in sworn affidavits to support applicants once they arrived in the States. Because the German government stripped Jews of their resources upon leaving the country, affidavits of support became necessary for almost everyone hoping to immigrate to the United States. Yet many refugees could not get them. Affidavits were not sufficient, either. Consular officials often determined that the person providing the affidavit did not have a close enough relationship to the immigrant, or did not have enough financial resources, or had promised affidavits to too many people. Each consulate and indeed each consular official had their own understanding of not close enough, not enough resources, and too many people.

Librarian Helen Nathan, for example, had applied under the regular quota before she was turned down for a non-quota visa. The Berlin consul had deemed the affidavit she had provided to be insufficient because it was from a friend, not a relative. "In such cases the consulate requires an irrevocable credit amounting to 1000 dollars," Nathan explained to the AAUW's Brunauer (a requirement the Berlin consulate itself imposed). "Since 6 months my friends have been trying to collect this sum, but they have not yet succeeded and I am afraid they never will." The fifty-year-old Nathan considered the non-quota visa her "last chance." Within weeks of being notified she did not qualify, she committed suicide. The Berlin city library where she had once been director now bears her name.[22]

The outbreak of war in September 1939 provided another rationale for denying visas, including non-quota ones. Four weeks into the war, Assistant Secretary of State Messersmith instructed all consuls to "examine with unusual care" all applicants for non-quota visas, as well as those under the immigrant quotas to ensure no one admitted would threaten public safety. In the early 1940s, the State Department moved to issue even fewer visas because of the perceived threat of a "fifth column" of Nazi spies among the refugees. The State Department instructed its consuls to deny visas "if there is any doubt whatsoever concerning the alien." It then told the consuls they should bar anyone who had close relatives remaining in German territory. "The American Consulate has received instructions not to grant new visas to foreigners who are leaving any member of their family behind in Europe," Makinsky recorded in his diary entry of June 13, 1941. "The reason for this is that it is feared that Germany may later bring pressure to bear on those foreigners, and that the latter, because of the fact that their families are in German hands, may be 'accessible' to German pressure." At the same time, the State Department invalidated the affidavits of all immigrants and required them to obtain new ones. It also insisted on two affidavits, not one, along with a biographical statement and proof of transportation possibilities. These new regulations proved to be extremely burdensome.[23]

"This makes immigration very difficult at the present time, especially since almost every refugee who wants to come here has relatives in occupied territories," Ellen Hilb, a World Jewish Congress staffer, explained. The new regulations "are supposed to be flexible, but in reality are cast iron," Johnson wrote in August 1941 to Paul Haensel of Northwestern University, who had tried repeatedly to get his friend and fellow public finance professor Alexander Michelson out of France. "They won't admit anyone who leaves behind his parents, wife's parents, sisters or brothers of either, or children, in German or German occupied territory," Johnson explained. "If Professor Michelson has no relatives in this position there is a fair chance of bringing him over. If he has, the chance is very slight." Michelson was a well-to-do Russian émigré who had fled Paris to Pau in southwestern France. He had been offered a position at the New School yet may have delayed his departure because his son did not have a visa. With many relatives in German territory (he cabled the Rockefeller Foundation a list of their names and locations in July 1941), it was too late. "His case is not the only one of a scholar waiting around for members of his family until the difficulties have become almost insurmountable," Johnson noted. A law office informed the New School that Michelson had left Europe on the Portuguese ship *Serpa Pinto* on November 15, 1942. A passenger list, however, did not include Michelson's name, and no further record was found of him after that date.[24]

After the German invasion of France, a similar fate befell historian Marc Bloch, who, as we have seen, had been considered "too Jewish" for Dartmouth to hire. Having lost his job at the Sorbonne, which then was closed, Bloch moved south, to near Lyons. The New School had offered him a position, but he initially was reluctant to leave his mother, who was in her eighties, and two of his six children, who were older than seventeen and thus unable to obtain non-quota visas. "MB does not want to leave half of his family behind," John Marshall of the Rockefeller Foundation's humanities division recorded in his officer's diary. "Hence the difficulty." When his mother died in the spring of 1941, Bloch accepted the New School's offer and made plans to leave with his wife, Simonne, and his three remaining underage children (in the intervening months, a third child had turned eighteen and thus had become ineligible for a non-quota visa), with the promise that additional visas would be forthcoming in June. By June, however, the State Department instituted the close relatives policy. Bloch, like many other Rockefeller Foundation grantees, anxiously telegraphed the names of their close relatives, who in most cases were in occupied territory. Unable to leave France, Bloch joined the French Resistance in Lyons. In March 1944, French militia captured Bloch and turned him over to the Gestapo. A few weeks after the Normandy invasion, the Gestapo shot Bloch and seven hundred other prisoners.[25]

The close relatives policy also blocked the immigration of psychiatrist Alfred Storch, who received an offer from the New School after the Emergency Committee in Aid of Displaced Foreign Medical Scientists agreed to pay his $2,200 salary for a year. Johnson wrote Storch in December 1941 with detailed instructions on how to approach the U.S. consul after the New School had negotiated with the State Department in Washington, D.C. But Storch's mother-in-law, sister, brother-in-law, and niece were still in Germany. Because his brother-in-law had been imprisoned in Hamburg since 1939, Storch had hoped the policy would not interfere with his emigration. "Considering the causes which have prevented my relatives from emigrating until now I hope that there will be no objection from this side to the immigration of myself, of my wife and of our child," the fifty-three-year-old Storch wrote in January 1942 from Münsingen, Switzerland, where he had been living since 1933. Later reports indicated that his sister and her seventeen-year-old daughter had been deported. His seventy-five-year-old mother-in-law was apparently still in Berlin. Storch's visa application, which was filed March 23, 1942, seemingly made little headway in the State Department. In July 1942, the committee reviewing applications was hearing cases filed the previous November, December, and January, meaning the soonest Storch's case would be heard was October 1942. Storch never received a visa, surviving the war in Switzerland, where he lived the rest of his life.[26]

The close relative requirement also derailed the immigration plans of the Polak family, whose father, Leonard, a Groningen philosophy professor, had an offer from the New School and whose eldest daughters were to be students there. Polak and his daughters received their offers at the end of May 1941. The State Department changed its rules the following month, invalidating the family's original visas and making it unlikely that they would receive new ones. The executives of the family-owned fragrance firm that had been willing to pay the senior Polak's New School salary and the girls' tuition decided in July to try to get visas that would allow the family to go to Cuba. By that time, the sixty-one-year-old Leonard Polak had been sent to the Sachsenhausen concentration camp. At the end of 1941, he injured a testicle and underwent surgery. A day later, he was forced to carry stones as his work assignment and died shortly thereafter. The family firm, Polak & Schwarz, learned the news, informing the New School by telephone on March 24, 1942. The New School then gently inquired about what to do with the guarantee. Leonard's wife, Henriette Polak, was discovered in hiding and deported to Westerbork. Polak & Schwarz managed to save her at the last moment. After the war, she became a philanthropist and art preservationist. Two daughters, Betinna and the youngest daughter, Annie, also survived the war; records indicate Betinna, who had studied art at the University of Utrecht, was in the Barneveld and Westerbork transit camps. Antoinette, who had studied medicine for two years at the University of Groningen and had hoped to study psychiatry and psychology at the New School, entered the Ravensbrück camp on February 21, 1942. She was sent to Auschwitz nine months later, where she was gassed at the age of twenty-one.[27]

Even hesitation over the close relatives policy cost some scholars their lives. German logician Kurt Grelling, for whom the Rockefeller Foundation had arranged a professorship in January 1941, apparently hesitated when he assumed that his wife, who was in Brussels, would not be able to get a visa. On September 16, 1942, Grelling was sent from Drancy with Convoy #33 to Poland, arriving two days later at Auschwitz, where he probably died that day. His wife also perished.[28]

"Drowned in a Flood of Bureaucratic Difficulties"

The New School's Johnson knew all that history in 1941, yet he still expected the State Department to extend basic cordialities to a U.S. citizen, the wife of a distinguished legal scholar. For eighteen months, he tried to get various State Department officials to help him obtain a visa for Ludwik Ehrlich, a professor at the Jan Kazimierz University in Lwów, as well as a passport for Ehrlich's American-born wife, Frances. Born a Jew in Tarnopol, Poland, in 1889, Ehrlich had spent considerable time in the United States, lecturing at the University of California from 1916 to 1919 and directing the Polish Information Bureau in New York from 1919 to 1921. In 1923, Ehrlich married Frances Thornton Lawton in New York City. (In 1914, Lawton won the Daughters of the American Revolution Prize for best historical essay at Rogers High School in Newport, Rhode Island.) The Ehrlichs moved together to Poland where Ludwik became a Lwów professor and served as a judge on the World Court in the Hague from 1930 to 1936. (Raphael Lemkin, who developed the concept of genocide, took his first international law course from Ehrlich in Lwów.)

Under the Hitler-Stalin Pact in 1939, Lwów became part of the Soviet Union. In January 1940, the university fired Ehrlich from his professorship; eleven months later, the New School offered him a position as an associate professor. Ehrlich left Soviet-occupied Lwów to join his wife and two children, sixteen-year-old Krystyna and twelve-year-old Andrzej, at their country home in Falejowka, just across the demarcation line in German-occupied Poland. The Germans had established a forced labor camp in the nearby village of Zasław for the Jews in the surrounding area, mostly the approximately fifty-four hundred Jews who lived in the small city of Sanok. The New School appealed to the U.S. embassy, which was still in Berlin, to forward its offer letter to Ehrlich via diplomatic pouch. The embassy refused, the first sign that the State Department was going to be less than cooperative. Surprisingly, Ehrlich received the offer letter through ordinary air mail, which the New School learned indirectly. Ehrlich did not reply, however. Johnson interpreted that to mean he faced "obstacles which may prove insuperable."[29]

Johnson still hoped that the family might be able to get out on the basis of Frances Ehrlich's U.S. citizenship. If she could get to Berlin, the

U.S. embassy there would be able to issue her a passport. Without a passport, however, the Germans were not convinced she was a U.S. citizen and would not let her travel to Berlin. The U.S. consul refused to do anything to help her persuade the Germans of her U.S. citizenship. In March 1941, her father, Charles Lawton of New York City, forwarded his daughter's birth certificate and marriage license to Assistant Secretary of State Breckinridge Long in Washington, D.C., hoping he would pressure the Berlin consul. It did not work. H. F. Cunningham Jr., the U.S. vice consul in Berlin, wrote a chilly letter, offering no assistance to Frances Ehrlich and declining to indicate whether the consulate would issue her a passport. The problem of Frances getting to Berlin was between "alien visa applicants and the local authorities, and the Embassy can be of no assistance in this connection," Cunningham wrote. He did not address whether proof of Frances's citizenship might make any difference. He did point out that even if Frances obtained a U.S. passport and was able to go to the United States, "there is, however, no reason to believe that her doing so would enable her husband and children to join her." They were "aliens," whom the Germans would not grant permission to travel to Berlin to apply for visas.[30]

In the meantime, Johnson received a letter from Ludwik Ehrlich in German-occupied Falejowka, laying out additional hurdles the U.S. consul imposed on granting his non-quota visa application. The consul required proof that Ehrlich had been teaching the previous two years and a shipping company letter indicating the family had a passage booked. "We are doing everything we can from this remote spot," Ehrlich wrote Johnson, "but I should be most grateful if the Embassy could be induced not only to promise the visas but also perhaps to take up the matter of supporting our case."[31]

The Rockefeller Foundation, which provided the grant for Ehrlich's New School professorship, also got into the act in June 1941, hoping a new first secretary in the Berlin embassy might be more favorably disposed. Johnson finally gave up in June 1942, and the Rockefeller Foundation canceled its grant. Correspondence at the time implied that Frances Ehrlich and the children made their way to friends in Germany in January 1943. Polish sources, however, tell a much grimmer story. German authorities held Frances in Kraków's notorious Gestapo-run Montelupich prison for a year, presumably housed in the nearby convent that held female prisoners. The Germans detained their daughter, Krystyna, in Warsaw and then sent her and a friend to Majdanek, the concentration and extermination camp near Lublin. The friend's father paid to have them released three months later. Ludwik Ehrlich went into hiding. He moved north from his country home to the Zamość area, where he documented German atrocities. The Germans captured him in mid-September 1943. The Polish Home Army freed him the same month, and the fifty-four-year-old joined its ranks, adopting the alias "Farley" for John Murphy Farley, who had been the Catholic archbishop of New York when Ehrlich lived in the city. The Ehrlichs' sixteen-year-old son, Andrzej, participated in the Warsaw Uprising in October 1944, while their twenty-year-old daughter served as a medic.[32]

On August 27, 1945, Ehrlich wrote to Johnson to inform him that "I (and my family) have survived our very varied experiences" and to lament that he had not been able to accept the New School's "very kind offer" three years earlier. Ehrlich added, "The Embassy at Berlin seemed, indeed, to have drowned it all in a flood of bureaucratic difficulties." He still wanted to teach at the New School, but Johnson informed him the offer was no longer open. Ehrlich continued his academic career at Jagiellonian University in Kraków and served as an expert witness at the trials of Nazi war criminals.[33]

An International Crisis

L ike many German Jews, musicologist Mieczyslaw Kolinski fled
to Czechoslovakia after the Nazis took power and found some
refuge in the new state. Living in Prague, Kolinski had just
enough money to survive and had been able to continue and
even deepen his scholarship. Throughout 1935 and 1936, he had transcribed and analyzed Dahomean songs of West Africa for Northwestern
anthropologist Melville Herskovits. Herskovits found Kolinski's analysis "interesting in the extreme." His junior colleague was identifying
complex rhythmic traditions to challenge the conventional wisdom that
American Negro music had primarily European origins. Herskovits kept
shipping Kolinski his Dahomean recordings: twenty-nine songs on fifteen records in April 1935; sixty-six songs on forty records in June 1935;
a batch of cards with the accompanying words almost every week. From
his previous work for Herskovits, Kolinski contributed a chapter on Su-
rinamese music to Herskovits's book *Suriname Folk-Lore*. He also continued to work as a pianist and composer, having his ballet performed
in Salzburg in 1935 and in Czech cities, including Prague.[1]

By 1937, Kolinski had finished the West African songs and moved
on to songs Melville and Frances Herskovits had recorded in Haiti
during the summer of 1934. The Carnegie Corporation provided $1,800
to Northwestern to pay Kolinski to transcribe and analyze the Haitian

songs. As the evidence of the African roots of American Negro music grew, Herskovits began to think about bringing his collaborator to the United States. "I hope that on the basis of your transcriptions of these three collections," he wrote in January 1937, "it will eventually be possible for us to get you to this country actually to work with American Negro music in the field and to analyse it from the point of view of its aboriginal origins." In the meantime, Herskovits worried that Kolinski could not find American Negro music in Prague. "Do you, for example, know the collections of secular songs recently published by the Lomaxes, father and son?" Herskovits asked, referring to the fruits of John and Alan Lomax's first trips collecting folksongs in the Deep South for the Library of Congress. Herskovits then sent Kolinski his own copy of *Slave Songs of the United States* and his book *Life in a Haitian Village* and requested publishers send Kolinski collections of both religious and secular Negro music.[2]

As the books and recordings arrived in Prague, Kolinski's world turned upside down. The German crisis was quickly becoming an international one. In March 1938, Germany annexed Austria. In October, it added the Sudetenland region of Czechoslovakia where Kolinski had done fieldwork years before. In November, Kristallnacht made conditions even more dire for the Jews in Germany. In March 1939, the Germans marched into the Czech provinces of Bohemia and Moravia that included Prague. Czechoslovakia was no more, and its territory was no longer a refuge for thousands of German Jews who had escaped there or the four hundred thousand Jews who lived there. Almost two hundred thousand Jews in Austria also needed to escape, and the three hundred thousand Jews still in Germany knew that staying was no longer an option.

As nearly a million Jews in the Reich sought to leave, scholars faced unique pressures. Austrian and Czechoslovakian universities, which had had a significant Nazi presence throughout the 1930s, immediately dismissed their non-Aryan professors. In October 1938, Italy ousted non-Aryans from its universities, including many German Jews who had found positions there and who were threatened with a forced return to Germany. Abraham Flexner of the Institute for Advanced Study described "an awful autumn and early winter" in which he "had been driven as never before by an uninterrupted cry for help from German and Italian Jews."[3]

Historian and librarian Helene Wieruszowski was among those crying for help. She had fled to Spain and then Italy after losing her position at the Bonn University Library in 1934. In Italy, she worked at the Biblioteca Nazionale Centrale and Archivio di State until Italy's 1938 racial laws forced her from those jobs. "Since the loss of my position in Germany due to the new laws against the hebrews I have tried twice to build up my life both in Spain and Italy," she wrote in September 1938. "Twice I had to submit to stronger powers in the moment of final and great success." But Wieruszowski was a dedicated scholar. "In her months of extreme adversity" in Italy, she had "kept on with fortitude and a rare faith in her work," according to Charles Singleton, a Johns Hopkins romance language professor who encountered Wieruszowski in the summer of 1939 while he was in Florence. She was "literally forced to live from week to week." Unable to work for pay in Italy, she relied on the visits of friends from Germany to "bring some money." Wieruszowski still made considerable progress on the last item of her bibliography, prepared a critical edition of a commentary on Dante's *Divine Comedy,* and would soon publish an edition of a thirteenth-century letter form book. "Her fine character only reveals itself the more through [human cruelty and political] persecution," Singleton wrote.[4]

Public outrage after the Anschluss and Kristallnacht pushed the Roosevelt Administration to combine and fill the existing Austrian and German quotas, 1939 being the only year the German quota reached the maximum allowable during the Nazi era. But that still meant only 27,370 Germans or Austrians a year could immigrate to the United States when hundreds of thousands wanted to. For those living in the Reich but born in countries with quotas a fraction of the German one, such as Poland, Rumania, or Hungary, the wait stretched for a decade. After receiving many letters in early 1939 from strangers seeking affidavits and knowing that, even with affidavits, it would take five or six years to immigrate, Alfred Cohn of the Rockefeller Institute wrote the National Coordinating Committee's Cecilia Razovsky in despair: "I hesitate very much to trouble you but would find it comforting if I could share my sense of helplessness with you. Will you, if a method of salvation occurs, let me know what I am to do?"[5]

Razovsky replied: "Your letter of March 3rd really made me feel very sad. It is true that all we can do is write comforting and consoling letters to the people who turn to us for advice and assistance in these dark days." Razovsky did offer a ray of hope—"South American countries will be opening their doors soon." But as she was dictating the letter, she received a cable indicating that Venezuela would return 165 people to Hamburg unless the National Coordinating Committee deposited $20,000 ($341,000 in contemporary dollars) for them as a bond. "When you hear of such things," she continued, "you really know how desperate the whole situation has become and how absolutely *impossible* it is for any *private* organization to try to cope with it." She again reiterated that providing affidavits did not help because "the quotas are so oversubscribed now that it is almost futile to prepare affidavits as they will be outdated by the time the immigrant is called for his examination." Then Razovsky shared her own feelings: "I, myself, am getting to the point where it seems to me more than we can bear; each day brings so many tragedies to our knowledge. I think the only thing we can hope to do is to keep our sanity and our health and try to be of as much help as we can to the best of our ability."[6]

As immigrating under the regular quota grew next to impossible, anyone who could argue plausibly that he or she deserved a non-quota visa did. So a month after Kristallnacht, Philipp August Rappaport, an architect and town planner from Essen, Germany, sought a U.S. teaching position. He realized it would take at least two years to get a quota visa, and he had "neither relations nor acquaintances" in the United States "to give me the affidavit." An American professorship seemed his best prospect. But Rappaport had not been teaching for two years before emigration, as the law required, explained Alvin Johnson of the New School, who fielded his appeal. Besides, an American university was not likely to hire an architect. Unable to get a visa of any kind, Rappaport eventually was imprisoned in Lenne, a camp for those of mixed race.[7]

Erna Barschak had a better claim but not a better chance. Apologizing for her delay in responding, Betty Drury of the Emergency Committee wrote Barschak in October 1938, "We have been swamped with correspondence concerning displaced scholars from Germany, Austria, Czechoslovakia and Italy and have gotten far behind in our correspondence." The fifty-year-old Barschak had taught psychology and education at a teacher training college in Berlin until her dismissal in 1933. Advised that "it is becoming increasingly difficult to place people in colleges," Barschak did what many scholars did when faced with bleak prospects for a regular visa and for a non-quota visa—she sought both. Stuck in Berlin in January 1939, she had quota number 40,635 and little likelihood of a university job. Fortunately, Barschak, who had studied in England and then returned to Germany to teach in Jewish educational institutions, managed to get to Wales to work as a domestic.[8]

"It Looks Hopeless in Austria Now"

On March 12, 1938, Wehrmacht troops moved into Austria and were met by delirious crowds. The next day, Germany officially annexed Austria to its Reich. Immediately, swastika banners and Hitler photographs adorned buildings and buses. Parading soldiers filled the streets. The word *Jude* defaced Jewish shop fronts. Mobs forced Jews to scrub sidewalks with toothbrushes and slashed sidelocks off observant men. The Nuremberg Laws went into effect in May. The education ministry in Berlin took control of Austrian universities, subjecting them immediately to German educational legislation. What had happened to German universities now happened to Austrian universities, just in double time. Universities immediately barred non-Aryans, losing almost 40 percent of their students and faculty in a matter of hours.

As they had in Germany five years earlier, Rockefeller Foundation officials took account. Two months after Germany's annexation, Tracy Kittredge wrote to the Paris office attaching a list of thirty-one professors and lecturers who had been displaced in his area, law and the social sciences. Kittredge also noted how precious a non-quota visa had become as demand for regular visas skyrocketed. The U.S. consul in Vienna informed Kittredge that the office had received about forty-six thousand applications for 1,413 annual quota spots, meaning it would take more than thirty years to allow in everyone who wanted to go to the United

States. Even combining the German and Austrian annual quota would add just five thousand to ten thousand visas for Austrians—at the expense of German Jews.[9]

Affidavits from U.S. citizens supporting the applications were in particularly short supply. When Ellen Menzies of Hickory, North Carolina, wrote Johnson to ask him to assist Austrian journalist Viktor Becker, Johnson replied: "I am sorry the Austrian Aid organization informs me that they already have so many applications for affidavits that they are not able to take on any more. I suppose it remains for each one of us who is interested in any particular Austrian to go through the circle of his friends until he finds someone who has the humanity to give this sort of aid." For all her interest in Becker, Menzies was not willing to tap her circle: "Most of my friends are very sympathetic, but, like myself, are financially unable to take on all the responsibility involved in the signing of affidavits." Menzies insisted she would not "give up yet."[10]

Austrian displaced scholars began the desperate hunt for an American university job, and U.S. and British organizations began the laborious process of evaluating those scholars. Renowned Austrian economist Friedrich Hayek, who was then on the London School of Economics faculty, traveled to Vienna at the request of the Society for the Protection of Science and Learning, the British agency charged with aiding refugee scholars. Hayek evaluated twenty or so scholars, mostly privatdozents. His report was forwarded to the Rockefeller Foundation. The American Council of Learned Societies, a federation of scholarly organizations, sought the opinion of 150 people about Austrian scholars who might be displaced. Of the sixty names offered, the council's Mortimer Graves judged "not more than half a dozen would be sufficiently outstanding cases to secure wholehearted recommendation on the part of the Council."[11]

LEONORE BRECHER

Leonore Brecher, who had resumed her research position at Vienna's Institute for Experimental Biology after her University of Kiel lab had been shut down in 1933, found herself once again out of a job. In March, she was fired, along with the institute's fifteen other Jewish employees.

They made up half its staff, including its founder and director Hans Przibram and all its department heads. Przibram and two other scientists had started the private institute with their own funds and then donated it to the Austrian Academy of Sciences. When the Nazis took over, Przibram could no longer enter the institute, reclaim privately owned equipment and a research library, or have access to the endowment fund he and a colleague had started.[12]

"Through the changed circumstances here, I have no more the possibility to continue my research . . . and have no more the possibility for subsistence," Brecher wrote on April 9, 1938, to the AAUW, whose international association had awarded her a fellowship in 1923–1924. "I beg you to help me to continue the research, because I am without any means." Brecher had written a similar letter two days before to Leslie Dunn, the Columbia professor and Emergency Committee board member whom she knew. Dunn responded on April 22: "I am sorry to learn of the change in your circumstances and shall do what I can to help. . . . I am unable to make specific suggestions at the present time. I thank you for your paper of December 1936." Not to be dissuaded, Brecher wrote Dunn again on June 6, updating him on her research on "the histogenesis of the pigmentation in the pupa" and the results from her last experiments in 1936 and 1937. "I was preparing this material for the histological examination, when my work had to be interrupted at once. I have taken the preserved material with me and will try to bring it safely to the new research place, when I will be accepted somewhere to work," Brecher wrote Dunn. "Apart from my research work, I could be research assistant and help in other research work. Here too I was many years research assistant to Professor Przibram and helped Professor Przibram in his work. . . . I would be happy in the most modest conditions of living, the principal thing is, if I could have again the possibility for work, and if [I] could be of use." Over the summer Dunn made one attempt to find a position for Brecher, contacting Samuel Pond, a scientist at the Marine Biological Laboratory at Woods Hole, Massachusetts. Pond replied: "Things do not look too hopeful for her and for many others in Austria." Dunn took no more actions on Brecher's behalf.[13]

Brecher's case came to the Emergency Committee through a different route. Barnard professor Margaret Maltby, who had received Brecher's letter from the AAUW, wrote Betty Drury two weeks later. "I wish I could do something to help members of the Austrian Federation of University Women who are friends of mine," wrote Maltby, who had earned her Ph.D. in physics at the University of Göttingen. "It looks pretty hopeless in Austria now. I never thought I'd live to see the European world go back so far toward the Middle Ages." Drury replied: "The situation is a ghastly one, and according to the papers is spreading rapidly. What guarantee have we that it will not reach here."[14]

Over the next few months, Austrian Jews' property was appropriated, their homes were pillaged, and their lives were threatened by arrests and attacks. Brecher resorted to teaching at Kleine Sperlgasse 2A, a newly designated Jewish school. In September 1938, she registered with the U.S. consulate in Vienna supported by an affidavit from Lena Madesin Phillips, president of the International Federation of Professional and Business Women. Phillips, a fifty-seven-year-old American lawyer and champion of liberal causes, founded the federation to push for women's equality in the business world. Brecher was not optimistic about immigrating under the quota. Having been born in Rumania, she came under its U.S. quota of just 603 immigrants a year. In November 1938, Brecher found a temporary, unpaid research position at Cardiff University in Wales. But her request for financial assistance from the Society for the Protection of Science and Learning was rejected. Its records indicate that at age forty-seven, she was considered too old and her field was too specialized.[15]

Brecher still considered an American university position and a non-quota visa her best hope. She had worked with several of Europe's most renowned biologists, including Przibram, Rudolf Hober, and Hans Winterstein. She spoke and wrote French, English, Rumanian, and German well. In February 1939, she wrote to "the Dean, Vassar College," listing Przibram as a reference as well as John Gerould of Dartmouth College's biology department and F. B. Sumner of Scripps Institution of Oceanography. The Vassar dean and Maltby at Barnard both got in touch with the AAUW, but neither Vassar nor Barnard helped Brecher directly.[16]

During the summer of 1939, the Reich government shut down hundreds of Jewish factories and stores. In October, more than one thousand young and old Jews were sent to Buchenwald. Two other transports were sent to Nikso, Poland, as part of Germany's plan to establish a reservation for Jews near Lublin. The next month, Robert Sims, a New York friend of Brecher's, tried to convey to the AAUW the situation in Vienna that "is much worse than ever." Sims pleaded: "Miss Brecher is condemned to perish if some outside help is not given very soon. I am taking the liberty of bringing this to your attention and begging you to help her in some way that she could emigrate to this Country and fulfill her life work for humanity. Hope you will try and help Miss Brecher as she hasn't any one in the World to help her and the situation is precarious." Sims wrote a similar letter on the same day to the Emergency Committee, which prompted Drury to write back that the organization had known about Brecher "for many years." But "there seems to be nothing at the present time that we can do to help Dr. Brecher."[17]

In February 1940, Brecher expressed dismay that her research had languished for so long. "I wish very much to continue my research work," she wrote to Esther Brunauer at the AAUW, noting that the research had been interrupted in April 1938 and because she was barred from libraries, preparing papers based on previous research was impossible. "The analysis of colour adaption in chrysalids, on which I have been devoted so many years was very near conclusion and I should have liked very much to finish it, so that I may be able to give a description of the whole process of the colour adaption in those light-variable butterfly chrysalids," Brecher wrote. She was not optimistic about immigrating under the Rumania quota. "I do not even know how long I will have to wait, because the Consulate has so much work that it cannot give information," she wrote. "But as I am not in a position to go forward with my research work so long as I am here and as I am not in a position to support myself where I am and cannot wait my quota number here, I was applying to you to help me to come as soon as possible to the United States. I should wish very much to come at once to the United States." If that was not possible, Brecher sought help in getting temporary admission to another country "where I could await my quota number, continue my research, have admission to the libraries."[18]

She contacted the Emergency Committee again, including a six-page handwritten letter explaining her research and following that with a plea for help immigrating to any country. She concluded: "I beg you very much to help me to come very soon to the United States, because it is very urgent for me." Drury turned to Emergency Committee board member Dunn, but he responded that he had already done whatever he could for Brecher: "I corresponded with her some years ago and was unable to offer her any encouragement concerning a post in this country although I suggested her name to several medical institutions." Dunn attributed Brecher's difficulty in finding an American position to her "personality," though she was "an indefatigable worker." Drury then wrote Brecher: "I am exceedingly sorry that there is practically nothing we can do to assist you." Drury assured her that the committee "would keep you in mind even though there is little chance of our learning of a suitable opportunity."[19]

MARIE ANNA SCHIRMANN

Physicist Marie Anna Schirmann was in a similar position, having been fired from her University of Vienna laboratory. "Now I am displaced and have lost my existence and possibility to continue my scientific work," she wrote. Like Brecher, Schirmann had been denied habilitation because of her gender and religion and found herself without a full faculty position. She had been born in 1893 into what she described as an "old scholarly and artistic family" in Vienna. Her father was a music professor at the Vienna Conservatory, and her mother attended medical school and worked at St. Anna Children's Hospital but could not practice medicine because women then were not allowed to be medical doctors. Schirmann became a physicist with a specialty in high vacuum physics. Denied habilitation in 1930, she continued to work at the University of Vienna's Institute of Physics, performing experiments, supervising doctoral theses, publishing papers, and obtaining patents for devices to use in research.[20]

After the Anschluss, the forty-five-year-old Schirmann started a frantic effort to emigrate, contacting both the National Coordinating Committee for help in obtaining affidavits to immigrate under the U.S. quota and the Emergency Committee to obtain a university position that would enable her to immigrate with a non-quota visa. Schirmann registered for a quota number with the Vienna consulate on November

30, 1938, and received a quota number of 4,958, yet she still needed affidavits of support. She turned to Cecilia Razovsky of the National Coordinating Committee, who replied with what Schirmann described as a
"promising letter." She expressed her gratitude: "For in this place, every
day, every hour bring us such affliction and grief as any hope gives us
consolation." With no relatives in neutral countries, Schirmann asked
Razovsky to contact several "interested and wealthy friends" in the
United States who might provide an affidavit: the wife and son of a de-
ceased colleague; two former Institute of Physics colleagues, one at Vassar, the other whose address she did not know; her former University of
Vienna professor then at Notre Dame University; and a former University of Berlin professor at the seismological laboratory in Pasadena.
Schirmann closed her letter with a plea: "I hope you will succeed in
helping an University Woman, who without own guilt has to leave home,
property, position and all her relatives and friends."[21]

Schirmann had started her emigration quest with the Emergency
Committee hoping to receive a university appointment. She apparently
had run into difficulty because her laboratory position might not have
qualified her as a professor. She explained that she was not "a simple laboratory assistant" but had the qualifications to be a privatdozent; however, the state had denied her the official title to avoid paying her a pension, even though the University of Vienna had approved it. This would
not have been an issue had she received habilitation, which automatically conferred privatdozent status. Schirmann also volunteered that she
could work in an industrial lab, having practical experience in "incan-
descent lamps, Luminious and X-ray tubes, Photoelectric cells for Television, Radio, Valves" and other practical applications. She concluded
this letter, written a day after the one to Razovsky, with a similar plea: "I
hope you will succeed in helping a woman scholar who without guilt has
soon to leave home, property, position and all her relatives and friends."[22]

The Emergency Committee did not have any luck finding Schir-
mann a position in the United States, so it tried another avenue: an
appointment in the College of Engineering at the University of the
Philippines in the field of electrical communication. Drury instructed
Schirmann to make a formal application if she was interested. She was.
In the meantime, Schirmann had received a temporary position in En-

gland, working in Gordon Miller Bourne Dobson's meteorology lab
at the University of Oxford. The International Federation of University
Women, of which Schirmann had been a fellow, had arranged for the
Oxford job, but it was conditioned on her having a position waiting for
her in the United States in one or two years. Schirmann hoped Drury
might be able to come up with documents indicating she would have
an American position so she could take the Oxford job and leave Vienna
immediately.[23]

As she was trying to get a university appointment, Schirmann also
wrote repeatedly to Razovsky for help in obtaining affidavits from Schirmann's American acquaintances. She received no reply. At the end of
1939, Schirmann grew increasingly concerned that her many registered
letters had not been answered and that she had lost the possibility of
going to England because of the outbreak of war three months earlier.
She was still willing to go to the Philippines, or even temporarily to Sweden. "I beg you not to forget my condition in this place, I am not able to
describe," Schirmann wrote. "But you are sure to know that I am *obliged*
to leave this country and it is impossible for me to continue my scientific
work in this place." At the end of 1939, Schirmann had no prospects for
leaving "this place."[24]

"It's Extremely Difficult to Get Anyone Out of Germany"

As the Reich expanded into Austria and Czechoslovakia, it also intensified its persecution of Jews in Germany proper. During the pogrom
known as Kristallnacht, on November 8 and 9, 1938, rampaging mobs
across the country damaged synagogues, Jewish cemeteries, and Jewish-
owned shops and department stores. They ransacked Jewish homes and
assaulted Jewish men and women. All the while German police stood
by, instructed to interfere only if the attacks were on non-Jewish property. More than thirty thousand German-Jewish men were arrested and
sent to the concentration camps of Buchenwald, Dachau, and Sachsenhausen. Similar outbreaks in Austria led to the burning of forty-two
synagogues and the looting of four thousand shops in Vienna alone and
the arrest of eight thousand men.

Germany's remaining Jews took Kristallnacht as a sign they had to try to get out—immediately. Before the outbreak, University of Berlin law professor Fritz Schulz had gone to the United States, but finding no "openings for me whatever in America," he had returned to his homeland in the hope he might be able to "live on in Germany" and continue his work. "The events of the last weeks have smashed this hope," Schulz wrote to UC Berkeley law professor Max Radin three weeks after Kristallnacht. "I am very far from being in a panic, but it seems to me quite clear now: the game is up."[25]

But emigration from Germany had never been more difficult. Although U.S. State Department officials finally were letting as many Germans immigrate as the law allowed, they tended to favor those who were already in other countries, particularly Great Britain. In addition, the number of openings was still tiny compared with the demand, and the combination of the Austrian and German quotas took spots from Germans. Displaced scholars at least had an option besides waiting for their quota number to be called. Charlotte S. Salmon of the American Friends Service Committee summarized the situation in Germany in April 1939:

> There are in Germany hundreds of college and university professors who are not allowed to teach because one or more of their grandparents were Jewish. Others have lost their jobs because of their political beliefs or because their wives were labeled "non-aryan." Many of them were thrown into concentration camps and released only on condition that they leave Germany within a few months; yet the quota of immigrants to be admitted from Germany is already filled for several years ahead. Their one chance lies in the provision of the United States immigration law which admits outside the quota professors who have been offered positions in American colleges.

To Alvin Johnson as well, a non-quota visa was one of the only lifelines for German Jews. "It's extremely difficult to get anyone out of Germany," he wrote in January 1941, "and the only way that is at all open is the non-quota visa which presupposes that the applicant has been regularly employed as a professor."[26]

HEDWIG KOHN

Hedwig Kohn had been working in laboratories and trying to emigrate since she lost her position as a Breslau physics professor in December 1933. Even this tenuous existence ended with Kristallnacht, during which all Breslau's synagogues and Jewish schools were destroyed. Stores now bore signs banning Jews. Jews who ventured out were beaten in the streets as epithets were hurled at them. A few months after Kristallnacht, Rudolf Ladenburg, Kohn's Breslau thesis advisor, now a Princeton physics professor, renewed his interest in her case and wrote again to the Emergency Committee. The committee declined to help, however, referring Ladenburg to "our regulations," which "you of course know"—that is, a university had to make an offer before the committee could act. Ladenburg traveled to Washington to talk in person with the AAUW's Brunauer. He told her that Kohn had no way to earn a living and no relatives to help her financially; she was depending on colleagues to support her. Ladenburg did not believe Kohn could get an American university post because she was not well known in international circles. He did think her research on illumination and radar technology could be useful to industry. Ladenburg volunteered to provide Kohn an affidavit and cover living expenses.[27]

In March 1939, Kohn wrote to Brunauer explaining her emigration strategy so far and seeking help going forward. She initially had decided to seek a non-quota visa to the United States. Knowing she needed proof that she had been teaching two years before immigration, she had continued to supervise graduate students, "hoping this fact would enable me to come to the United States with a non-quota visa." But Kohn made a mistake based on incorrect information. She did not apply under the quota, "as I have been informed that it is not allowed to take the two ways simultaneously." She also feared that without relatives or friends in the United States to provide an affidavit, "I should have to recourse to some protectors' kindness."[28]

By March 1939, Kohn was regretting that decision, having learned it "has become exceedingly difficult to find an academical post." She sought Brunauer's advice on whether to pursue a quota visa, knowing it would take at least three years to obtain one. She also wanted to know whether the AAUW might help in obtaining affidavits for her should she register under the quota. Immigrating to a South American country did not seem likely because Kohn knew neither Spanish nor Portuguese. Besides, to enter those countries "a rather high landing money is to be shown which I cannot procure."[29]

Kohn had another idea. Perhaps she could work in an observatory in neutral Sweden or Switzerland, as she had in 1935, while she waited for a permanent post in the United States. To receive a permit to enter those countries, however, she required proof she would soon leave and that she had the means to support herself while there. "My savings will probably be sufficient for my subsistence in the present year and for the costs of emigration (passage, luggage)," she wrote Brunauer, but she would not be able to support herself past that in a neutral country. "As long as I could, I tried to fight it out by myself," Kohn wrote, "but it is no more possible to do so."[30]

Her emigration prospects did not look good. Erna Hollitscher, who headed emergency relief for the International Federation of University Women, of which the AAUW was a part, sent Brunauer a discouraging reply from A. Vibert Douglas, who was in the physics department at McGill University. Douglas wrote that his university had no funds available for hiring Kohn and that industrial labs in Canada were not an option. "A woman of middle age even with a grand record stands no chance," Douglas wrote. "I am sadly forced to tell you I can do nothing to suggest a place for Miss Kohn here. . . . It sounds heartless and terrible and it *is* terrible but not heartless." Based on Douglas's assessment of Canada and another professor's assessment of the chances in England, Hollitscher determined "the only thing to be done is to approach Australia."[31]

Australia was not approached, as in the meantime, Kohn had gotten good news—J. A. Carroll of the University of Aberdeen in Scotland offered her a position in his lab. In August 1939, Kohn received a permit to travel to England. Before she could get her German emigration papers, however, war broke out and her permit for England was canceled. Kohn was stuck in Breslau.[32]

MAX FLEISCHMANN

Things were not much better in Halle for Max Fleischmann, who had been dean of the university's law faculty until 1935. The following year his former university appointed a notorious antisemite to a lectureship on the history of the Jews who started delivering what would prove to be close to ninety seminars and lectures on the need to combat Jews and Jewish influence. The city of Halle had never had a large Jewish population, only thirteen hundred Jews lived there in 1933, one-half of 1 percent of the total population. The minuteness of its numbers, however, did not spare that population from the ravages of Kristallnacht. On November 10, Nazis destroyed the city's synagogue and communal center. Two hundred men were arrested and sent to Buchenwald; three of them died.[33]

As a Protestant convert with a Catholic wife, Fleischmann enjoyed some protection from the worst persecution. He still knew he had to leave, and a non-quota visa was a possibility, even though he had been told when he lost his job three years before that he was too old to be hired by an American university. Fleischmann and his supporters had not given up, and Kristallnacht added urgency to the efforts. Yale law professor Edwin Borchard had tried to get State Department officials to interpret the non-quota visa provision to allow older scholars such as Fleischmann to immigrate as researchers without the expectation of classroom teaching. The State Department had not been persuaded. "I have not been able to discover any way of arranging for a non-quota visa for professor Fleischmann, or for any of the other [international law] teachers whose cases have become so particularly urgent," Stephen Duggan of the Emergency Committee wrote Borchard in March 1939. Bryn Mawr's Hertha Kraus, herself a refugee, asked rhetorically, "Don't you think it is entirely hopeless to present his case to any American Institution since after all professors are forced to retire at 65?" Erich Hula, an Austrian political scientist then at the New School, also concluded that Fleischmann "was out of the picture."[34]

As his supporters tried to find him a university position, Fleischmann registered for a quota visa. On January 25, 1939, he received the number of 59,576. He obtained affidavits for himself and his wife, Josephine, from his cousin, Max Pflaum, a U.S. citizen living in Minneapolis, and Harold Field, whose wife, Gladys, was also Fleischmann's cousin. Fleischmann turned to the American Friends Service Committee. The American Jewish Joint Distribution Committee seemingly would not help Fleischmann because of his and his wife's religious affiliation. The quota number did not comfort Fleischmann much, and the U.S. consul informed him it would be three years before he would be able to immigrate. And he had received official notification that he had to leave Germany as soon as possible. Only a letter Fleischmann had received from Borchard dated February 10, 1939, had "brought hope into a house otherwise burdened by many worries."[35]

More than a year later, Fleischmann's number still had not been called, and no university had offered him a job. His brother, George, who had immigrated to New York, grew increasingly worried. At the end of 1939 and into 1940, the *New York Times* carried many small stories about the deportations to the Lublin reservation. In February 1940, the *Times* reported in stunning detail about the deportation in freight cars of eleven hundred Jews from Stettin, a German port city, to the reservation. In March, the *Times* followed up with the news that two hundred of the Stettin Jews had already died because of inadequate shelter and food. On March 14, 1940, George Fleischmann and his wife went to the Emergency Committee's New York office to meet personally with Betty Drury. "Gestapo now after poor Professor Fleischmann," Drury noted in a memorandum following their conversation. "If he doesn't leave they will send him to Poland. Awfully distressing situation, and awfully distressed people up against an insoluble problem." Deprived of any consolation from the Emergency Committee, George Fleischmann continued to worry about his brother being deported to Poland.[36]

In May 1940, a possible position arose. The International Institute for Social Research, which was affiliated with Columbia University, had agreed to hire an international law specialist, but he had died in Paris just before his planned departure for the United States. Borchard thought Fleischmann might be suitable for the newly available position. "In this case, as in others the sorrow of one family may prove a blessing to another," wrote Tatiana Schaufuss, who assisted refugees through the Tolstoy Foundation. Borchard and Philip Jessup of Columbia approached the institute about hiring Fleischmann. Max Horkheimer, who had

founded the institute in Frankfurt and established its affiliation with
Columbia, praised Fleischmann as "one of the few outstanding German
lawyers," though Horkheimer too had some reservations because of
Fleischmann's age. The institute did not offer Fleischmann a job. "What
he is threatened with now is deportation to some wretched hole in Poland where his chances even of physical survival are extremely slight,"
wrote Berkeley law professor Max Radin in June 1940.[37]

HEDWIG HINTZE

In Berlin, historian Hedwig Hintze's problems had only grown. After returning in 1935 to that city from Paris, Hintze spent the next three years
caring for her husband, Otto, and managing to "continue my research
work to a certain degree." She became interested "in the problem of
modern Jewish colonisation in Palestine and occasionally taught young
Jews who prepared for their migration to Palestine." Continuing her
work became impossible in 1938. That year, Otto, who was considered
the foremost historian of Germany's late empire, had himself been subjected to Nazi humiliation. The Royal Prussian Academy of Sciences had
conducted an inquiry into Otto Hintze, who had been an academy member since 1914. (In 1915, Albert Einstein presented his field equations of
general relativity to the academy.) Asked by the academy whether he
was in a mixed marriage, the derogatory *Judische versippt*, Otto answered "yes" and resigned. Not long after, the couple's quiet home life in
a handsome five-story apartment building in the Charlottenburg neigh-
borhood had been shattered. With its large Jewish population, Charlottenburg suffered some of the worst devastation during Kristallnacht.
Windows of Jewish shops along the posh Kurfürstendamm boulevard
were smashed. The Fasanenstrasse Synagogue, which had been shuttered
in 1936, burned to the ground. Three weeks later, on December 3, the
Judenbann law prevented Jews from entering government offices, including universities and libraries. That month, German authorities also began
evicting Jews from their homes in prestigious parts of Berlin, including
Charlottenburg.[38]

  "I beg you to help me in my very great plight," Hintze began her
March 1939 letter to the Emergency Committee. Unlike many other

(15) Historian Hedwig Hintze, University of Berlin
lecturer, 1930. ullstein bild Dtl./Getty Images.

scholars, she had not contacted the committee before; in fact, her letter
was addressed to no one in particular at the "Institute for Displaced
German Scholars." She explained that she had not emigrated "definitely"
in 1933 because of her husband, who was "aryan" and "aged." "My situation is quite unbearable now," she wrote. "I am not allowed to enter any
public library or university building. I cannot continue my research work
and I do not know how long I shall be allowed to share my husband's

flat." Hedwig feared that rather than continue to live in Charlottenburg with Otto, she would be forced to live in one of the *Judenhäuser* (Jewish houses) being established in the city.[39]

Hintze had registered under the regular quota but had not been able to obtain an affidavit to support her application. She hoped to obtain a non-quota visa but worried that she would not qualify. "Unfortunately I had not opportunity to lecture regularly during the last two years," she wrote. "Would it be possible to get a non-quota visa for research work?" She explained that she could teach "French and German as well as History and Sociology." Hintze noted that she was "on the waiting list of the American Consulate General of Berlin but I cannot possibly wait in Germany until my number will be called up." She meant it. Before 1939 was done, Hintze had fled again, this time to Holland.[40]

"Fighting for Free German Science" at Prague's German University

Even before the Germans marched into Bohemia and Moravia in March 1939, Nazi influence was felt in Czech universities. Prague's six-century-old Charles-Ferdinand University had split in two at the end of the nineteenth century. Its German-language half, German University, enjoyed a strong reputation before World War I, boasting a faculty that included Albert Einstein and students who included Franz Kafka. By the late 1930s, its Nazification was well under way. As England and France were ceding the Sudetenland to Germany in October 1938, Stephen Duggan received a plaintive letter from geneticist and biologist Hans Kalmus. Kalmus wrote on behalf of "the about 30–35 democratic and non-aryan professors, dozents and assistents [*sic*] fighting for free German Science on the theoretical field." Kalmus, who was from a Jewish family but had been brought up Protestant, explained that the future of the German University faculty "was in great danger and so we are obliged to call for assistance." No assistance was forthcoming. Kalmus fled to London with his wife and two children two days before the Germans took over Prague. He joined the zoology department at University College London, where he spent the rest of his career.[41]

In November 1938, the Czech government barred Jewish refugees from commerce and the liberal professions. In January 1939, the government began sending Jewish families questionnaires to establish their race, religion, nationality, and associations. The actual German takeover of Bohemia and Moravia in March made things worse. At first, the German government and the authorities of the Czech Protectorate—the name of the region once Slovakia split to form a separate fascist state allied with Germany—exercised overlapping and haphazard jurisdiction over Jewish affairs. In June, the Germans took control of the process of the appropriation of Jewish property. In July 1939 Germans took control of "emigration," forcing anyone considered Jewish under the Nuremberg Laws to register and imposing a compulsory "Jewish emigration tax." Jewish books and periodicals were banned. The Reich Ministry of Education officially took control of German University on September 1, 1939. Student demonstrations broke out in October, and during one, a medical student was killed. That led to more and bigger demonstrations. All Czech universities were then closed for the rest of the war, more than twelve hundred students were sent to concentration camps, and nine student leaders and professors were executed.

KÄTHE SPIEGEL

In January 1940, Käthe Spiegel, the historian who had become a librarian and archivist after having been denied habilitation at the German University, lost her positions at both the National and University Library and the Archives of Bohemia. "Now I have to find a new start," the forty-two-year-old Spiegel wrote to the AAUW in February 1940, invoking her time as a Rockefeller Foundation fellow in Washington, D.C., in 1927 and 1928. She had become acquainted with many AAUW officials, including Brunauer. Spiegel added that she was of "Non-Aryan blood" though she had converted to Catholicism. Spiegel later explained that she had waited to register under the regular quota. An only child, whose father, a prominent German University law professor, had died in 1926, Spiegel had been unwilling to emigrate and leave her mother behind. "I couldn't think of leaving her, because she was very dependent," Spiegel wrote. When her mother's doctors told Spiegel following a July 1939 operation that her mother was not likely to live long, "I felt I have to register." She did, on August 2, 1939, but the delay meant she got a high quota number. "That makes, that my number is supposed not to be called up for many years!" Spiegel wrote to Brunauer. "Therefore I have to come on a Non-Quota Visa or, I supposed, I shall not be able to come at all." Brunauer understood, however, that as a librarian Spiegel had little chance of obtaining a non-quota visa. "I knew Dr. Spiegel when she was here and liked her very much," Brunauer wrote a colleague. "I am very much distressed about her case but there is little that I can do."[42]

Brunauer decided to concentrate on Spiegel's immigration under the regular quota. Spiegel suggested obtaining an affidavit from her friend, Mrs. Frank C. Wilkins of Warner, New Hampshire. "I heard that it is very useful for the authorities here to be able to show them, that someone in USA is willing to give the affidavit," Spiegel explained. Brunauer then wrote Wilkins. "I suspect that if she has [an affidavit] to show the secret police she hopes to be allowed to stay in Prague and not be shipped into Poland," Brunauer wrote. A group of Moravian Jews had been sent to the Lublin reservation in October 1939 along with Jews from other parts of the Reich. Brunauer confessed that she did not think providing an affidavit would do much good. "The actual time to use it would probably not arrive for a long time," Brunauer wrote, and when it did, a new affidavit would be needed anyway. Still, Wilkins provided an affidavit, as did two other women associated with the AAUW.[43]

Brunauer then explored other immigration possibilities, including whether Spiegel could get into Switzerland. Spiegel herself persisted in trying to get a non-quota visa, writing to the Emergency Committee in May 1940 and rounding up testimonials from academics who had commented on years-old manuscripts. By November 1940, her immigration efforts had not progressed, and despair and loneliness began to creep into her letters. "I am just working privately at my table and have enough to work to arrange my daily affairs," she wrote Brunauer. "Of course, you may be sure, I should love much better to be in full swing again—but nobody can make out what future days will demand." Spiegel wrote that she had found old papers and letters that referred to parties their group of women had attended during the years she was in Washington. She had lived for a while in the AAUW's house and then in a Brookings Institution house. "I found again all your names in your own handwriting,"

Spiegel wrote, then pleaded: "Ask my friends please, to write me—I suppose that their letters must have been lost."[44]

MIECZYSLAW KOLINSKI

By early 1938, Mieczyslaw Kolinski was taking seriously Hitler's rumblings about moving into Austria and the Sudetenland. Even before the Anschluss, he instructed Melville Herskovits to stop sending checks to his Prague address. Kolinski borrowed money from a friend to support himself during what would turn out to be his last six months in Prague. He promised to repay the loan with the money Herskovits was holding for him abroad. After first trying for a visa to France, Kolinski in August got a three-week visitor visa to Belgium. Knowing Herskovits would be in France during the summer, Kolinski also obtained a short-term travel visa to France. He met Herskovits in Paris in mid-August to talk over his alternatives. After their meeting, Kolinski went to Brussels on his visitor visa, which expired in three weeks. Herskovits wrote professors he knew in Belgium, England, and France to see whether anything could be done for Kolinski in those countries. "He is one of the best men in his field in the world, and has had more experience with primitive Negro music than anyone else," Herskovits wrote Belgian professor Georges Smets in August 1938, noting Kolinski had transcribed more than one thousand songs Herskovits had recorded. To another professor, Herskovits wrote that Kolinski's analysis of Dahomean songs "is a beautiful job" and "throws more light on the problem of the origins of spirituals than anything that has ever been done."[45]

His visa expired, Kolinski stayed in Brussels, unwilling to make too many inquiries to legalize his status. Everything connected to the police seemed to be in "hibernation," he wrote, and he did not feel inclined to disturb that sleep. Kolinski met with Smets and another Belgian anthropologist, Frans Olbrechts, and both told him he would not be able to have a career in Belgium. When the Czech government ceded the Sudetenland to Germany in the fall, Herskovits and Kolinski expressed relief he was not in Prague. "Of my friends in Prague, I hear the worst," Kolinski wrote Herskovits, even though "the Nazi [influence] has only recently and gradually ripened." Kolinski was glad to have escaped the Czecho-

slovakian "hell" just in time, and hoped to soon leave Belgian "purga-
tory" and enter "paradise."[46]

By December 1938, Herskovits began plotting to get Kolinski a position in the United States. Northwestern had formed a committee to
bring refugee students and professors to campus, and Herskovits submitted Kolinski's name. "I see by this morning's paper that Prague is
moving to eject its refugees, which means that Kolinski if he is still in
Brussels has no place to go," Herskovits wrote to Waldo Leland of the
American Council of Learned Societies, which funded some of Kolinski's work. "I don't know what the answer is; I don't see how the poor
fellow works in the midst of the uncertainties of life, but he seems to
go on anyway and I admire him for it." In the meantime, Herskovits got
another grant for Kolinski to finish work on the Haitian music, which
would take several more months. In February 1939, Kolinski had $605
he could draw upon in Belgium. He tried to maintain his equilibrium,
especially after learning that he could stay in Belgium just until August.
"I don't take this warning too tragically," Kolinski wrote. "It was a stroke
of good luck that I left Prague just in time; in any case it remains to be
seen whether I've jumped from the frying pan into the fire."[47]

That spring Northwestern agreed to make Kolinski a lecturer in the
Department of Anthropology for the 1939–1940 academic year, as long
as outside money funded the position. Herskovits sent dozens of letters
seeking the funding. There were two reasons "beyond the usual humanitarian ones" to fund Kolinski, Herskovits wrote to Betty Drury in March
1939. "His particular field, the study of primitive music, is one in which
only a very few persons are competent." Plus, Herskovits continued, "the
music on which Dr. Kolinski has worked holds particular interest for
this country" because of correspondences between African music and
Negro spirituals. Herskovits added he had met Kolinski in Paris. "I was
impressed with his modesty and charm . . . I am certain he will have no
trouble fitting into the American academic environment." Two Columbia University anthropologists, Franz Boas and George Herzog, shared
Herskovits's assessment of Kolinski. Boas wrote that Kolinski "is one of
our best authorities on primitive music, and might be particularly valuable here on account of his extensive knowledge of African and American Negro music." Herzog wrote, "I know his scholarly work intimately

(16) Anthropologist Melville Herskovits, Northwestern University.
Courtesy of Northwestern University Archives.

and consider it among the very best there is anywhere," noting that
scientific work on Negro music is "in its beginnings in spite of the great
popular interest."[48]

The Emergency Committee agreed to provide $1,200 for Kolinski's
Northwestern salary for the 1939–1940 academic year, and the Jewish

Welfare Fund of Chicago provided another $1,800. The American Council of Learned Societies contributed $500 for transportation. Kolinski still needed a non-quota visa to enter the United States, but Herskovits assumed that was a formality. Northwestern's president wrote directly to the U.S. consul in Belgium in May 1939, and the dean of the College of Liberal Arts wrote to the head of the visa division in June. Neither received a reply. Drury also wrote the visa division head in June without a response. Herskovits was so confident that Kolinski would be teaching at Northwestern in the fall that he had Kolinski's courses listed in the school bulletin: comparative musicology in the fall and methods of studying primitive music in the spring. Twenty students signed up for Kolinski's fall course. Because he planned to be in Trinidad doing fieldwork during the summer, Herskovits arranged for others to greet Kolinski when he arrived in New York City.[49]

But then in early June Kolinski informed Herskovits he had been turned down for a non-quota visa. The U.S. consul in Antwerp had a reputation for putting obstacles in the way of those applying for visas, Kolinski wrote in July. "I can't imagine that all these efforts will be without result, and it would be truly absurd if the whole business came to nothing because of the Antwerp consul's mood!"[50]

Lacking an official explanation, the Americans helping Kolinski surmised the Antwerp consul thought Kolinski's University of Berlin assistantship did not make him a professor. Kolinski, who earned his Ph.D. in 1930, had been a month or two from coming up for habilitation and a privatdozent position when the Nazis assumed power. "It seems to us here at the university that his status as a scholar, the fact that he has actually been on the payroll of this institution for five years, and the contribution he can make to American scholarship, all tend to give force to the argument that the law might reasonably be interpreted in his case so as to afford him a non-quota visa," Herskovits wrote to the immigration and naturalization commissioner in September, one of the many appeals to government officials made on Kolinski's behalf in the months after his visa application was rejected.[51]

Bombarded by polite but aghast letters from university leaders, distinguished professors, the American Musicological Society, and the American Council of Learned Societies, the State Department finally felt obligated to respond. In October, four months after the consul's decision, visa division chief Avra Warren explained to Northwestern's dean of the college that Kolinski's "possible classification" as a professor "rests almost entirely on his former connection" to the Phonogramm-Archiv, where he was "engaged primarily in arranging and cataloguing the national collection of gramophone records and in maintaining records and transcriptions." Louis Sussdorf Jr., the Antwerp consul-general, wrote to the head of the American Musicological Society that it would not have been necessary for Kolinski "to show that he has been engaged in instructing students" had he been "a person of high scholastic or scientific attainments" with "the title of 'professor,' or an equivalent title, continuously during the last two years." (Sussdorf's statement demonstrates again that the consuls' interpretation of the law varied greatly; many consuls required non-quota visa applicants to have been instructing students, and others did not assess an applicant's "scholastic or scientific attainments.") Sussdorf stated that Kolinski could apply under the Polish quota, which allowed 6,524 immigrants a year to enter the United States. "It would now appear that there will be a very protracted period, doubtless some years," before Kolinski would qualify, Sussdorf wrote.[52]

As had been the case in Berlin and Prague, Kolinski knew better than to hang around Brussels. He had another destination in mind: Haiti. He could work on Herskovits's latest recordings while studying Negro music and trying again for a non-quota visa. The U.S. consul in Haiti might not be "such a monster as the Antwerp Consul General," Kolinski wrote in November 1939. Herskovits had misgivings: "I am a little afraid of it, but think that, lacking anything better, it might be worthwhile trying." Herskovits did. On January 15, 1940, he wrote to Jacques Antoine of the Haitian legation in Washington, D.C., whom Herskovits knew from his time on the island. Four days later, Antoine replied favorably. Within three weeks, Haiti had authorized a visa be issued to Kolinski.[53]

Herskovits also kept up the pressure on the Antwerp consul, asking the Department of Labor and Senator Scott Lucas of Illinois to file complaints. The Labor Department would not. Lucas did, provoking a long and somewhat nasty response from the Antwerp consul. Boas too challenged the consul's decision, noting that Kolinski "was actually one of the active men" in the Phonogramm-Archiv, carrying on "scientific work" and working with individual students "who learned from him as is usually done in university laboratories." Nothing worked. The Antwerp consul's denial of Kolinski's visa "made it practically impossible to obtain a review of the case by the State Department," Herskovits explained in February 1940.[54]

Haiti again looked like the best and probably only option. But there was a problem. Kolinski needed to pick up his Haitian visa from the Haitian legation in Washington, D.C., which meant that he needed to persuade the U.S. consul in Antwerp to give him a transit visa to the United States. Even if that was accomplished, Herskovits needed to raise money to pay Kolinski's fare to Washington and then to Port-au-Prince, as well as his living expenses in both cities. Kolinski could not leave Brussels without the funds in hand. He doubted that the Antwerp consul would give him even a transit visa and suggested instead that he go to Genoa and then to Havana. Herskovits started the process of getting the money and making alternative travel arrangements, but by then it was May 6, 1940. The Germans were about to make their move on Belgium.[55]

NINE

More Need, Less Help

Just as the plight of refugee scholars became more precarious at the end of the 1930s, American universities became less welcoming. A number of factors coalesced to make hiring foreign scholars particularly difficult. As we have seen, universities received many more requests for positions from newly displaced or increasingly desperate European scholars. Pleading letters often landed directly on administrators' desks, adding to the sense that this was an insurmountable crisis. Ruth Pope of the American Friends Service Committee wrote after her May 1940 tour of Southern colleges: "One dear old gentlemen [*sic*] recently interviewed said that he put all such letters in his 'conscience pile' but did nothing further. Many frankly admitted that they put these inquiries and pleas into a wastebasket." Universities had a sense that having hired some refugee scholars, they had done enough; any more would constitute a tipping point of too many foreigners, or perhaps too many Jews, on U.S. campuses.[1]

At the same time, the organizations aiding refugee scholars faced their own crises as scholars' temporary appointments expired. Universities were unwilling to pay the salaries of professors whom they had previously gotten for free, despite the fact that the slowly improving U.S. gross national product was close to pre-1929 levels. (Unemployment was down from a high of 25 percent but still was at 15 percent by the end of the 1930s.) The refugee groups had to decide whether to continue to fund the positions. The Emergency Committee in particular seemed to devote more of its energies at the end of the decade to figuring out what to do with the scholars already in the country than to helping the growing number of scholars—such as Leonore Brecher, Marie Anna Schirmann, Hedwig Kohn, Max Fleischmann, Hedwig Hintze, Käthe Spiegel, and Mieczyslaw Kolinski—trying to get out of Austria, Germany, Czechoslovakia, and Belgium.

Persuading universities to provide and pay for permanent positions had long been difficult. The decision to offer temporary positions, which seemed a smart strategic move initially, proved problematic. "We were too optimistic in assuming that if people could be maintained on temporary maintenance grants of one or two years, most of them would be automatically absorbed," Walter Kotschnig of the high commissioner's office wrote to Alan Gregg of the Rockefeller Foundation in 1935. "A longer period of absorption is necessary and, above all, there has to be real economic pick-up before the process of permanent absorption will actually get going." There was a personal cost as well. "I am really worried about some of the professors that are hear [sic], and who are apparently not going to be continued," Joseph Chamberlain of the National Coordinating Committee wrote Stephen Duggan after a refugee scholar attempted suicide, apparently upon learning his contract would not be renewed.[2]

Even universities that continued temporary appointments after the initial two-year period did not do so out of their regular budgets, as the New York University president explained. "On the whole our experience has been satisfactory," President Harry Woodburn Chase wrote of the hiring of foreign scholars over the previous six years, yet "we have not found it possible to provide salaries for any of these temporary appointees out of our regular budget." Instead, NYU turned to individuals to provide the refugees' salaries or returned to the original funding sources. (Less than a year later, Chase was more enthusiastic. "Our experience with these scholars whom you have helped and others whose salaries have been paid from other sources, has been in general, excellent," Chase wrote Duggan, noting in particular that refugee Richard Courant had become head of NYU's math department.)[3]

Public universities often found it particularly hard to extend scholars' appointments because they relied on legislatures to budget the amounts. (Some faced even more difficulties. For instance, a 1917 state law required the University of Tennessee to hire only U.S.-born faculty, and Illinois and Kentucky tried to enact such legislation during this period, with the support of their university presidents.) Ohio State, for example, wanted to fund the salary of sociologist and economist Arthur Salz, who as a Jew had been dismissed from the University of Heidelberg in 1933. The Emergency Committee and Fred Lazarus Jr., the founder of a department store chain that became Federated Department Stores, provided the initial funds. The chair of the economics department wanted to retain Salz, whom the chair considered a "valuable member of the department." But the university needed the legislature to increase its budget before it could commit to paying Salz's $4,000 annual salary. Somehow Salz remained at Ohio State until his death in 1963.[4]

Both the Rockefeller Foundation and the Emergency Committee ended up doing what they had vowed not to do—extend grants to many of those with temporary appointments. Johns Hopkins University's Institute of the History of Medicine considered Ludwig Edelstein, who had been at the University of Berlin, "a man that we just can not afford to lose," according to the institute's director Henry Sigerist. And yet the university would not fund his position. In 1935, the Rockefeller Foundation and the Emergency Committee provided $3,000 to support Edelstein for a third year, as they had for the previous two. Edelstein remained at Johns Hopkins until 1947 and then joined the faculty at the University of Washington and the University of California, ultimately returning to Johns Hopkins. He died in 1965.[5]

The temporary appointments also proved an impediment to further hiring because universities feared taking on someone they could not support in the long term. University of Michigan Law School dean Harry Bates fretted about adding a scholar: "An able scholar is brought to an American university in this way. He takes root; to some extent, his colleagues become attached to him and interested to have him stay; then the Foundation support is withdrawn and the University may be in no position to pay the salary from its own resources. The resulting situation is very trying and embarrassing to all concerned." Bates's counterpart at

Michigan's medical school refused to hire psychiatrist Alfred Storch for that reason. "Past experience has taught that even though these individuals are subsidized by some philanthropic organization for a year or two, we, invariably, find them on our doorstep in the end. Consequently, the Executive Committee is very unwilling to consider any of these individuals on the basis of a temporary grant." (Storch was ultimately offered a position at the New School but was unable to obtain a visa.)[6]

"A Rather Tragic Situation"

One scholar's case was so vexing that his name, Victor Jollos, became synonymous with the problem. In 1934, the University of Wisconsin's zoology department had hired Jollos, a geneticist, to a temporary position funded by the Emergency Committee and the Rockefeller Foundation. The year before, the University of Berlin had fired Jollos from his position as an associate professor in its zoology department. When Jollos's year-and-a-half Wisconsin appointment ended in July 1935, the Emergency Committee informed the university that it did not intend to renew his grant. The committee asked Franz Scharder, a Columbia zoology professor, to help Jollos. According to Betty Drury's notes, Scharder responded, "There were plenty of biological geneticists without work anyway, and lots of them were smarter than Jollos." Scharder "is washing his hands of the matter," Drury wrote. The university then informed the Executive Committee it did not intend to reappoint Jollos for budgetary reasons.[7]

The Executive Committee offered to renew the grant for a year if the university would hire Jollos permanently at the end of the year. The university again said no, with faculty members objecting to what they perceived as pressure from the committee. To make matters worse, a position in the zoology department had opened up, yet the faculty apparently did not want Jollos for it. Despite his expertise in genetics, parasitology, and tropical diseases, which was probably greater than that of anyone on the Wisconsin faculty, Jollos had had trouble adjusting to American methods of teaching undergraduates. Leon Cole, the head of Wisconsin's genetics department, tried to place him at other state universities without success. The Emergency Committee decided not to renew

(17) Victor Jollos, former University of Berlin zoology
professor. Courtesy of Embryo Project Encyclopedia
(1934), Marine Biological Laboratory Archives.

Jollos's grant in 1936, making him "the only one of our scholars for whom
no provision has been made," the Emergency Committee noted.[8]

The committee's decision turned Jollos's case into something of a
cause célèbre. John Whyte, the Emergency Committee's assistant secretary, described Jollos's predicament as "a rather tragic situation." Some
committee members second-guessed the decision to refuse to fund Jollos because he did not necessarily have "a worse scientific record than
others who had been renewed." Columbia zoologist and committee
board member Leslie Dunn, in particular, came to his defense, noting
that Jollos's work in genetics "had fallen short of a very ambitious objec-

tive" but that his previous work in protozoology "was generally judged to be first class." Dunn tried to get Jollos a position at the University of Puerto Rico where his expertise in protozoology would "prove helpful." In January 1937, the committee agreed to provide Jollos with a $2,000 grant to teach at the University of Puerto Rico, but the university did not consider the amount sufficient and applied for a Rockefeller grant. The foundation would provide the grant only if the university agreed to give Jollos a permanent position once his grant expired, which it would not do. The Emergency Committee then canceled its grant as well, and Jollos was left unemployed in Wisconsin.[9]

The financial circumstances of the Jollos family grew dire, and they had little support in the community. Even though both Jollos and his wife, a pianist, were of Jewish origin, they considered themselves "non-Aryans" and thus did not associate with the Jewish community. While on the Wisconsin faculty, Jollos had antagonized his colleagues by assuming he already had a permanent position. His wife had irritated them by expressing her horror at the fact that faculty wives did their own housework. She refused, leading the family's landlady to try to get them to move because of the house's filthy condition. In February 1937, the Jollos family faced eviction from its home in Madison. Dunn agreed to sell off the last of Jollos's Persian and Turkish rugs. "With these gone he is completely destitute and if and when this is discovered he will be subject to deportation," Dunn wrote Whyte. "I think we have properly avoided the relief part of the refugee problem, but I think we now have to face it in this one case." Dunn proposed that the committee appropriate $500 to send Jollos on a lecture tour; Dunn had already secured engagements for him at the Rockefeller Institute for Medical Research, Princeton, Yale, and Johns Hopkins. The National Coordinating Committee might then be willing to give the family $100 a month for six months.[10]

Jollos, who had suffered two heart attacks in 1937, delivered lectures at several universities on the East Coast in the fall. In the meantime, the University of Wisconsin barred him from access to its labs that year, and an aid organization stepped in to help the family survive. The Chicago arm of the Joint Committee for the Readjustment of German Jews loaned Jollos $60 to cover his rent and $20 for coal for a month and living expenses for two weeks. But its officers were none too happy, blaming the Emergency Committee for withdrawing its support and leaving the family to run up bills with local merchants that it could not pay. They also thought the case could have greater ramifications. "The shift of responsibility for the family's support to the family themselves and the faculty members seems to have created an unfavorable ground, at least at the University of Wisconsin, for further placement not only of German refugees but indirectly of American Jewish instructors," wrote the joint committee's Mildred Lasker Kahn. Within three months, the Chicago group had stopped giving the family money and had proposed moving them to New York. Dunn objected and tried to find Jollos work in Chicago.[11]

The Jolloses muddled along for the next few years in Madison, living on Mrs. Jollos's meager income from giving music lessons. Even though the family had not approached the Madison Jewish community, one of its members still intervened. "This man needs help," William Nathenson implored the Emergency Committee in March 1940. Two weeks later, board member and Rockefeller Institute physician Alfred Cohn wrote to Drury: "It is obvious that our arrangements for taking care of people are not complete. Poor Dr. Jollos falls between stools. I wonder if there is any organization that does sufficient case work to take him on and to find him a teaching position." The committee made one last attempt in February 1941, exploring the possibility of Jollos working at the School of Tropical Medicine in San Juan, Puerto Rico. Jollos died on July 5, 1941, at the age of fifty-four without obtaining another academic post.[12]

"Criminal to Turn a Scholar of His Caliber Adrift"

Jollos was just the worst of many cases in which the Emergency Committee struggled to find permanent positions. By 1937, the committee became preoccupied with this issue—most of the minutes of most meetings were devoted to it. On December 8, 1937, for example, the minutes tick off the situations of twenty-seven scholars whose positions either had not been renewed or were in danger. The situation of Eugen Altschul, an economist who taught halftime at the University of Minnesota, was typical. Having been fired from the University of Frankfurt in 1933 for being Jewish, Altschul made his way first to London and then sought the committee's assistance to find a position in the United States. Ross Gortner, a biochemist who headed the University of Minnesota's committee on German scholars, helped bring him to that university with what Gortner thought was the understanding that Altschul would not join the permanent faculty. But as the years went on and Altschul did not obtain another position, the expectation grew that he would stay with the Emergency Committee's support. Minnesota dean R. A. Stevens wrote that he "was entirely satisfied with the work that [Altschul] is doing" and "pleased to have him on the campus," yet his "particular aptitudes" could not justify more than a half-time appointment "under present budget limits." Unlike Jollos's situation, Minnesota managed to work something out, with both the university and the Emergency Committee contributing to Altschul's half-time position. Altschul remained at Minnesota until 1943, eventually becoming a professor at the University of Kansas, from where he retired in 1952.[13]

Individual professors also made valiant efforts on behalf of scholars in this country. For example, Conyers Read, graduate head of the University of Pennsylvania's history department, fought to get Richard Salomon, a medievalist, reappointed as a lecturer at Penn, as well as at neighboring Swarthmore and Bryn Mawr. When the Penn administration rejected the history department's recommendation that Salomon be reappointed, considering his courses "a luxury," Read took up his case. "I think it would be little short of criminal to turn a scholar of his caliber adrift for the sake of the small amount of money which needs to be secured," Read wrote to Duggan. Read also advised Salomon not to be discouraged and "don't allow your wife and children to be discouraged," adding, "You have done a fine job this year and those of us who have associated with you will leave no stone unturned to find further provision for you and yours." Salomon was reappointed for another year. In 1939, he received a permanent position at Kenyon College, where he remained until his retirement in 1962.[14]

The Emergency Committee's concerns over finding appointments for scholars in the United States almost overtook its central mission of helping scholars find teaching jobs so they could obtain non-quota visas and leave Europe. In 1938, only 55 of 125 scholars placed had received permanent appointments. The Emergency Committee that year changed its policy to make grants only to those who had a chance of their positions becoming permanent, limiting the number of foreign scholars it could help emigrate. At the same time, universities continued to refuse to hire anyone without outside support. Knowing that its exchange programs would not be operating in the midst of a war, the Institute of International Education in September 1940 asked colleges and universities that usually participated whether they would redirect funds allocated to exchange students to accept on their staffs "eminent refugee scholars either on their own budget or with financial assistance." Only Russell Sage College indicated a willingness to hire a refugee on its own budget; the rest agreed to hire a foreign scholar if outside sources provided part of the salary. Some institutions even offered refugees positions without pay, whether to help the refugees or to take advantage of the situation, or some combination. Drury cited examples of unpaid positions in a 1939 memo: West Virginia State College, "a negro institution," sought someone to teach German, French, Spanish, and possibly Italian; Kansas Wesleyan University offered a position without salary and sought a grant from the Christian Committee to cover room and board; and Yale took on Friedrich Lenz, a classical philologist, to allow him to stay in this country.[15]

"The Callousness of Official Harvard"

The problem of permanent positions for those already in the United States grew so severe that university presidents met in 1939 to try to find a solution. Harvard's president James Conant put forward a plan, also endorsed by Columbia's president Nicholas Murray Butler, to provide an endowment to fund one hundred permanent positions at $2,000 each. Universities would hire the foreigners and provide them with offices, laboratories, and library privileges so they could continue their research; but they would teach no classes and would have no possibility of advancing to a faculty position. In this way, they would not compete with American scholars. Harvard astronomer Harlow Shapley, who developed the plan, assumed he would need an endowment of at least $6 million (or about $110 million in contemporary dollars) to get his "asylum fellowships" off the ground. Butler apparently thought that amount "could be raised from rich Jews."[16]

But the same "rich Jews" seemed to be the target of many refugee groups, leading to acrimony over the plan. When the national effort fizzled, mostly because of Conant's inattention, Shapley moved to do it just at Harvard. The Harvard Corporation (the name of the university's board of trustees) agreed to allow sixteen people to whom Harvard had already committed to remain to conduct research if Shapley got more outside money. Shapley wanted to raise $150,000 for the sixteen fellowships. He started with one of the Emergency Committee's major donors, Henry Ittleson Jr., chair of the Commercial Credit and Investment Company, which Ittleson's father had founded. In February 1940, Shapley wrote Ittleson that he was trying to arrange emergency funds for temporary Harvard appointments for sixteen men so "they could get into the country and escape the concentration camps of Europe." Shapley acknowledged that other academics took the position that "we must give the native-born the first break." But Shapley wrote: "I . . . refuse to sacrifice any more scientists and scholars than necessary in the interests of a narrow 'Americanism.' If the best intellects can be salvaged, the current attack on civilization is softened."[17]

Along with his overall efforts, Shapley took on five refugees at the Harvard Observatory as of September 1940. But he too made hard choices. After a colleague was not much impressed by the work of German physicist and pacifist Herbert Jehle, concluding that if Jehle is "rescued, it must be on primarily humanitarian grounds," Shapley wrote Jehle a discouraging letter. Shapley also did not help Felix DeRoy, an internationally recognized Belgian amateur astronomer and journalist who made significant contributions to variable star research. Shapley offered to help discover what had happened to DeRoy's sons, who were in the Belgium Army when the country was overrun in May 1940, but did not offer assistance on the academic front.[18]

Ittleson agreed to donate $15,000 and possibly another $15,000. Shapley scaled back the proposal to eight or ten research fellowships with stipends of $1,200 to $2,000 annually. The grants would be made to men already at Harvard receiving tiny emergency grants including luminaries

(18) Harlow Shapley, director of the Harvard
College Observatory. Bettman/Getty Images.

such as physicist-turned-philosopher Philipp Frank, Polish mathematician Alfred Tarski, and Austrian seismologist Victor Conrad.[19]

When the Emergency Committee board member Charles Liebman
got wind of Shapley's overture to Ittleson and to another major donor,
the New York Foundation, he wrote an aggrieved letter to Ittleson. Liebman explained that Shapley's plan "would immeasurably hurt the pains-
taking work" the Emergency Committee had done in placing 230 scholars and also in "maintaining public relations with the whole academic

world in such a way that in no case that I know of has it engendered any anti-semitism." Liebman warned: "If there is one spot where anti-semitism in its ugliest aspect might arise, it is in our universities and colleges." He urged Ittleson not to ignite "the smouldering but unextin-guished fires of anti-semitism" by giving to the fund and further dissi-pating limited monies for refugees. Instead, Liebman argued that the eight people Shapley wanted to support ("all deserving men," though one, paleontologist Tilly Edinger, was a woman) should seek the usual two-year grants from the Emergency Committee.[20]

On April 10, 1940, after "a long and full discussion," the Emergency Committee voted to disapprove Shapley's plan. It would help "a limited number of foreign scholars . . . for the remainders of their lives," engen-dering resentment that might "prejudice the chances of success" of the committee's ongoing project. Both Duggan and Cohn wrote statements explaining the committee's decision: the proposal threatened the com-mittee's fund-raising by tapping the same sources; it gave Harvard pre-eminence in the field by funding just its researchers; and it depended on relations with Shapley, a difficult personality. Duggan stated the fund-raising concerns directly. "The Emergency Committee has to look pri-marily to the foundations for grants to enable it to carry on its work," he wrote. "Professor Shapley's plan could hardly fail to divert funds from the Emergency Committee which despite the generosity of support hitherto accorded it has always been circumscribed in its work for lack of neces-sary monies." Cohn objected so strongly to the plan that he was happy to circulate his objections to "whomever is concerned with this problem." He wrote a somewhat more conciliatory note to Shapley, insisting that they shared the objective of helping as many scholars as possible but dis-agreed about how to achieve it.[21]

Shapley was not buying it. He wrote that he was "beginning to lose heart" because of the "unjustified and petty attitudes of well-meaning men." He singled out Cohn, whom Felix Frankfurter had told him had "the biggest heart and wisest head on earth." Shapley argued that Cohn did not understand that there could be different approaches to hiring scholars and that his plan was aimed particularly at those older than sixty. Shapley and Cohn met in New York on May 17, 1940, but did not reach an accommodation, Shapley writing that he just could not understand Cohn's point of view. Shapley ended the letter: "Perhaps both the planet and I am too weary and worried to be unconfused easily." Cohn was no more pleased with the meeting, describing Shapley as "very skillful" yet "not always fair." He continued to object to any plan that would address the problems of older scholars: "In the end I fear a method of approach like this [of dividing the scholars into old and young] will serve to perpetuate and accentuate the differences between Harvard University and ourselves." Cohn decided that inviting Shapley to join the Emergency Committee board might help to paper over their differences, so Shapley joined the board's executive committee. He then "rearranged" his plan. Ten scholars, including some on Shapley's original list of sixteen, received appointments paid out of the money Shapley had already raised (including from Ittleson) and some through regular Emergency Committee grants, such as the funds supporting Polish mathematician Tarski.[22]

President Conant of Harvard may have proposed and then abandoned a national plan to help refugee scholars, but his stance on hiring to the Harvard faculty had remained the same since the start of the refugee crisis. Adding fewer than a dozen researchers, most of whom were already there, was one thing, but adding more refugees to the permanent faculty was another. Shapley's limited plan was as far as Conant was willing to go at his university. He doubled down in 1940 as refugees' need to escape Europe became acute. The Harvard Corporation, at Conant's request, pledged to hire to the faculty only eminent men it would support financially for their entire lives. It would not hire scholars who needed academic appointments to get non-quota visas but did not need Harvard to pay their salaries. The Harvard administration, with Conant as the driving force, refused to make such offers even when the faculty requested them.[23]

Harvard would not even provide university affiliations to physicians with permanent hospital jobs who needed an academic appointment to qualify for non-quota visas—an idea Cohn had floated in the dark days after Kristallnacht. In 1939 and into the 1940s, many doctors were in that position. For example, psychiatrist Henry D. von Witzleben needed "a small position" in Harvard's Department of Psychiatry to qualify for a non-quota visa. Von Witzleben had an offer of a permanent job at McLean Hospital, freeing Harvard of any "financial responsibility." Harvard neurologist Stanley Cobb "strongly" recommended that von Witzleben "be one of the acute cases for salvage." But Harvard Medical School dean Sidney Burwell decided von Witzleben did not have a "sufficiently strong" case to "ask the President to take it to the Corporation as an exception." In another example, Harvard would not provide a university affiliation for Peter Ladewig, a German-Jewish pathologist who was teaching at the University of Istanbul and whose situation in Turkey had become dangerous. Ladewig had a position at a U.S. hospital and financial support but sought Harvard's affiliation to qualify for a nonquota visa. Ladewig remained in Istanbul and immigrated to the United States in 1946.[24]

Shapley could not even get a position at his observatory for David Belorizky, an assistant astronomer at the Marseille Observatory and a widower with a three-year-old son. Belorizky "is not one of the topnotch astronomers of France, but a very versatile person in mathematics, photometry, and astrometry," Shapley wrote to the Rockefeller Foundation in October 1942. (Belorizky may have been more of a pathbreaking astronomer than Americans understood: in 1938 he proposed two ways to observe planets around other stars, the Doppler and transit methods. Publishing his results in French he did not get credit for the results—American Otto Struve did for his 1952 publication that allowed thousands of exoplanets to be discovered using the same methods.) Shapley added: "The racial laws that Hitler forced on France have thrown him out of his position and during the past year he has been in pretty desperate straits. The laws may get worse and he may perish."[25]

Shapley was willing to sponsor him and provide employment and salary for at least a year, probably more. But Shapley was not able to proceed. "At this point the red tape and callousness of official Harvard stopped me," he scrawled in a one-sentence note in the file. In a letter to C. D. Shane, a Berkeley astronomy professor, he explained the situation a bit more: "Unfortunately Harvard University has filled itself up so much with refugees that there is official ruling against any more being incorporated in the staff of any department. But I hope we shall be able to do something, and the trying to do something has its merits."[26]

So Harvard, which at the beginning of 1939 proposed a nationwide asylum plan, ended up with a Harvard-only scheme to keep ten researchers supported by outside funds. The national problem festered. The Emergency Committee took its own limited steps. In December 1941, the committee voted unanimously to set aside $10,000 for the renewal of grants in support of scholars previously aided. Ultimately, most of the scholars received full-time positions as the economy picked up during and immediately after the war. By 1947, 77 percent of the refugee scholars had faculty positions. Yet the damage had been done. The need to take care of refugee scholars in the United States had deflected the aid organizations' energy and resources from the task of saving scholars still in Europe.[27]

"We Have Reached a Point of Saturation"

In refusing to fund refugee scholars, American universities merely may have been balking at paying for something they had grown accustomed to receiving for free. Yet something more may have been afoot. Refugee advocates received reports about growing discontent on American campuses. Harvard dean George David Birkhoff in a well-publicized September 1938 address on the fiftieth anniversary of the American Mathematical Society warned that "we have reached a point of saturation" for refugee scholars and "we must definitely avoid this danger." Birkhoff's compatriot at Brown, Roland Richardson, picked up the theme six months later. "In the American Mathematical Society we are resisting as much as we can the entrance of more foreigners at this time," wrote Richardson, who earlier had considered it essential to hire foreign applied mathematicians. "Even those who have been helped feel that we have done so much as is wise at the moment. It would not be wise to build up strong anti-foreign feeling if we can help it."[28]

The American Association of University Professors (AAUP) had similar concerns. Around the time of Birkhoff's speech, Ralph E. Himstead Jr., AAUP's general secretary, told Duggan he believed the saturation point for foreign scholars had almost been reached. Complaints about refugee scholars arose at an AAUP conference that year, according to Betty Drury, who had attended. In April 1939, Himstead wrote directly to Duggan: "From many sources I have received reports that

American teachers, particularly our younger teachers in colleges and universities, are disturbed and apprehensive about the influx of refugee teachers. We have so many qualified, well trained men and women seeking in vain for college and university teaching positions that the reaction indicated above is to be expected. . . . My own view is that the situation created by refugee teachers seeking positions in our schools and colleges is rather a serious one." Himstead seemingly tried to head off the hiring of foreign scholars by recommending that his members insist that the Emergency Committee verify the credentials of any possible foreign hires at their universities. "During recent years many émigré teachers have sought positions in our colleges and universities," Himstead wrote in a letter to AAUP chapters. "Some of these teachers are well trained while others are not. Information received at this office indicates that in some cases the émigré teacher's academic training and experience have not been carefully investigated."[29]

If the ground was so saturated it could not absorb any more refugees, then such a backlash might have been understandable. Other than the anxiety of American scholars, however, there was not much evidence of too many foreign hires. In fact, faculty employment had recovered relatively quickly from the Depression's depths. By 1935–1936 the number of teaching staff at American universities exceeded the number in 1931–1932. So when Birkhoff publicly declared in 1938 that the saturation point had been reached, refugee advocates were prepared to push back. Abraham Flexner of the Institute for Advanced Study insisted that hiring top professors only increased demand. "If we could place fifty Einsteins in America, we could probably within the next few years create a demand from other institutions for several hundred," he wrote Birkhoff in response to his speech. Flexner had experienced such demand firsthand—and not just with Einstein, who was indeed at his institute. In thanking the Emergency Committee for making it possible to "bring this great scholar," Ernst Herzfeld, to the United States, Flexner noted that the archeologist specializing in Iran had been "fairly overwhelmed with applications from promising young men, many of them having established reputations, who desire to work with him." Flexner's Institute colleague Oswald Veblen argued that the "more prominent universities" might be reaching their limit but that "there are still a great many less well known academic institutions in which refugees could be placed with substantial advantage to the individual and to the institution."[30]

The concern about too many foreign scholars may really have been a concern about too many Jews, as an exchange between Rockefeller Foundation officials suggests. In July 1940, foundation trustee Douglas S. Freeman, who was editor of the *Richmond News Leader,* warned that the saturation point for scholars had likely been reached two years before. The foundation's president, Raymond Fosdick, however, took talk of a saturation point as code for antisemitism: "The 'saturation' point . . . was in part, at least, due to certain inevitable anti-Semitic prejudices that sometimes arise even in the best of academic institutions," he wrote Freeman. Fosdick indicated he would not necessarily fight those prejudices, assuring Freeman that in the current emergency situation a number of "outstanding non-Jewish scholars in France, England, Spain and Portugal are in real personal danger." Other foundation officials assessed the situation similarly at a staff conference held later that month, with one official pointing out that "this is not a Jewish problem," and another noting that "the types of scholars now coming over . . . do not raise old racial questions." Freeman may have proved the point himself, noting that there was indeed room for non-Jews.[31]

In pointing to antisemitic prejudices that "arise even in the best of academic institutions," Fosdick may have had Birkhoff in particular in mind. Birkhoff had a history of antisemitism. In 1932, he turned down Flexner's offer to head the Institute's School of Mathematics apparently because he did not want to be part of an enterprise that Jews directed and funded. He opposed Solomon Lefschetz's election as president of the American Mathematical Society because, as Birkhoff wrote to Richardson, "he will work strongly and positively for his own race. . . . The racial interests will get deeper as Einstein's and all of them do." In February 1938, Birkhoff wrote G. C. Evans of the University of California, Berkeley, about the "racial origin" of John B. Green, who was seeking membership in Harvard's Society of Fellows. Birkhoff noted that the name "Green" usually suggested "English blood," but "I know that names are changed in a rather surprising manner." Asking Evans what he knew about "the situation," Birkhoff wrote: "There are already four or five other

Junior Fellows who are 'Non-Aryan' or at least partly so; otherwise I wouldn't take the trouble to write. Please keep this inquiry of mine in confidence." Evans assured Birkhoff that Green was not Jewish, following "some Protestant denomination." Birkhoff wrote Evans a month later saying he had offered Green the position. Birkhoff did hire "non-Aryans" in Harvard's math department but not for tenured positions. He justified that posture on the basis of his belief that Jews matured early in their mathematics work but then lacked staying power. Birkhoff also took the position that Jews should be represented in the Harvard student body in the same proportion, less than 3 percent, that they were represented in the overall population.[32]

Long before he spoke publicly about a "saturation point" in 1938, Birkhoff had been working to keep refugee scholars from being hired at both Harvard and other institutions. Three years earlier, his negative assessment of Otto Szasz, who had been a professor at the University of Frankfurt, probably kept Szasz from getting a job at one of the top Eastern universities—MIT, Harvard, and Brown—where he held temporary positions. Although Szasz was "an active, highly competent and stimulating mathematician, he did not teach undergraduates very well," Birkhoff wrote in 1935. More important, Birkhoff told his friend Richardson, "America had already absorbed a considerable number of German refugees," which had prevented "very promising young Americans" from obtaining mathematical positions within "the last year or two." Birkhoff cited one instance of a young man "who was forced to enter secondary work." Birkhoff concluded: "It would seem to me to be a serious matter if Professor Szasz should take a position which would normally go to one of our American mathematicians." Szasz ended up at the University of Cincinnati.[33]

Birkhoff raised the same concern a little more than a year later in explaining to Hungarian physicist and astronomer Bela Lengyel, who had spent a year at Harvard, that neither the department of physics nor the department of astronomy there had a position for him. Birkhoff explained that "several doctors" in his department had yet to obtain jobs. One of them had come to see him that morning, so discouraged he was considering "something other than teaching." Lengyel immigrated two years later in 1939, assuming a position at Rensselaer Polytechnic Institute.[34]

In late 1937, the University of Rochester considered hiring Karl Menger, an Austrian mathematician who came highly recommended by Oswald Veblen. Birkhoff and Richardson both pushed for the hiring of "a native American at this time." Birkhoff elaborated in a subsequent letter to the University of Rochester's dean, noting that Rochester's mathematics department already had Wladimir Seidel, "who was born in Russia and only came to the United States in his teens." Interestingly, Birkhoff had urged the university to hire Seidel because Rochester was not a good enough institution to deny Seidel a position because he was Jewish. But now that Rochester had one foreign Jew, it could not risk adding another. "Hence, if you obtain Professor Menger (who, incidentally, has some Jewish blood) you will be in my opinion overweighing with foreigners your small Department," Birkhoff explained in 1937. Instead, Birkhoff advised Rochester to hire an American. He then suggested several possibilities, all of whom were not only Americans but also were not Jewish. Menger remained at the University of Notre Dame until 1946, completing his career at the Illinois Institute of Technology.[35]

"Sympathetic but Not Sacrificial"

Whether academic leaders such as Birkhoff actually believed in a "saturation point" or used it as an excuse to curb hiring, refugee advocates wrestled with what to do in response. They worried that the idea that universities had already hired too many scholars would not just curtail future hiring; they feared it could provoke a backlash that would inflame hatred against American Jews generally. This was a common fear stoked by some scholars' popular writing. Refugee advocates were both extremely sensitive to those concerns and skeptical of them at the same time, engaging in heated debate among themselves. The Emergency Committee split, though not perfectly, along religious lines, with Jewish members tending to be the most concerned about arousing antisemitism and non-Jewish members trying to tamp down concerns.[36]

The debate grew particularly intense in fall 1938. Bernard Flexner (Abraham's brother) and Duggan argued that taking more scholars, particularly youngers ones, would stir up resentment and ultimately hurt their efforts. Flexner claimed "the country had been flooded with young

Viennese psychologists since the Austrian Anschluss." Cornell's president Livingston Farrand, who chaired the board, and Liebman did not think there were so many cases as to be a problem. At a subsequent meeting, Columbia's Dunn maintained that if anything, there was now a "more sympathetic attitude toward the plight of the refugees than heretofore," and that universities were more willing to take scholars than Flexner and some others thought, particularly exiles who could teach art history, fine arts, music, and astronomy. Dunn said they were "in a better position now as far as their chance of finding employment" than any time since 1933. Fred Stein interjected that "his observation and experience" differed. (Since its inception, Stein had wanted the Emergency Committee to be cautious, helping only the most distinguished scholars and doing everything it could not to stir up antisemitism.) When other committee members raised the specter of public opposition to greater immigration, from people picketing Macy's because of the (false) claim it hired refugees to replace native-born workers to their writing protest letters after a congressman suggested liberalizing immigration laws, Dunn replied, "The world situation has reached the point where Americans must face some of this sort of thing." In the wake of Kristallnacht, criticism of refugee scholars was at least muffled. Drury reported to Duggan that "sympathy for refugee scholars was very strong" and "no feeling of resentment" had been publicly expressed among American professors who taught German though there had been "private comments."[37]

A British refugee advocate's plan to visit American colleges in spring 1939 provoked another intense round of infighting. Committee members tried to persuade the Society for the Protection of Science and Learning not to send its new general secretary, David Cleghorn Thomson, a Scottish journalist and former member of Parliament for the Labor Party, to visit the United States. Duggan provided several reasons, but chief among them was the increase in antisemitism that "has invaded some of our institutions of higher learning." Duggan argued that an "unusual knowledge of the situation in particular parts of the country" was required to confront antisemitism, knowledge a foreigner was unlikely to possess.[38]

Yet concern among American Jews about arousing widespread popular antisemitism may have been more of a problem than actual anti-semitism. The Rockefeller Foundation's Alan Gregg seemed to put his finger on the problem: "It would be easy to exaggerate the dangers of the under-current of anti-Semitism now running in this country and its universities, but it would be hard to exaggerate the intensity of the anxiety of American Jews lest English efforts here . . . expose . . . all Jews to the very resentment they are powerless to control." Unable to be at some of the committee meetings that the society's Thomson attended, Dunn wrote to his fellow committee members to keep them focused on what he saw as the committee's essential task. The committee should not allow concerns about provoking domestic antisemitism or taking jobs from Americans deter "Jews or non-Jews from keeping our doors open or from welcoming all those who wish to come as we or our ancestors came," he wrote. Although Dunn did not state it directly, he implied that other committee members were too concerned about the impact on American Jews. He also did not accept that further immigration would affect the economy because "the numbers now admitted to the United States are very small and the country is large."[39]

Dunn's letter seemed to lead Cohn to walk back some of his concerns and endorse Dunn's position that fear should not lead to the rejection of refugees. He obliquely acknowledged the position of American Jews: "I am not certain that I would be willing to do injury to another man to save my own skin although that would be the natural thing to do." And Cohn admitted that the substantive issues—stirring up xenophobia and antisemitism—were probably less important in the committee members' reaction to Thomson's visit than the personal ones. Despite occasional concerns about turf, the Emergency Committee had worked well with the society's previous general secretary, Walter Adams. But Thomson did not seem to be as respectful. The committee learned about his proposed trip, not from the society, but from a *New York Times* science reporter seeking help for Thomson. This was obviously a breach of protocol from which the committee never recovered. "Our English friends after years of co-operation obviously attempted to shunt the Emergency Committee," Cohn wrote to Duggan. "That Thomson was not an endearing character became an element having essentially nothing to do with the problem, but in practice, a great deal." Thomson went ahead with his trip, which, for all the anxiety its announcement provoked, proved relatively uneventful.[40]

To its credit, the Emergency Committee was not willing to let board members' impressions dictate its approach. The committee commissioned a Gallup poll of university presidents to gauge the sentiment on American campuses. Of those surveyed 79 percent showed "sympathy for displaced scholars," a Gallup official concluded and anticipated that that percentage had grown because of "the effects of recent events" (presumably Kristallnacht and its aftermath). But the Gallup official also fretted that "the largest institutions"—Chicago, Columbia, Princeton, Harvard, and Yale—did not participate in the survey, and "they have the facilities to make the greatest contribution toward the solution of the problem." As a result, the official speculated, the percentage expressing a willingness to take refugees was not as high as those expressing sympathy. The survey found 46 percent welcomed refugee scholars; 25 percent said they did not; and 29 percent gave no answer. The Gallup official attributed the quarter who did not welcome scholars at least partly to the high response rate from smaller universities without the necessary resources.[41]

He also noted that the survey could not resolve the issue of whether a saturation point had been reached because 83 percent of those responding did not answer that question. Of the university presidents surveyed who had hired a refugee scholar, a "high average" rated the experience as "excellent" or near excellent in "his contribution to intellectual life of college," "his relations with colleagues," and "his relations with the student body." Interestingly, the presidents responded overwhelmingly that "language and literature" was the discipline in which refugee scholars could make a unique contribution "not to be matched by Americans." Only twenty-one presidents offered up the next discipline, "physical sciences," a third fewer than had chosen language and literature. Gallup also sorted through the comments the presidents wrote on the survey. The most common "remark" (after "we don't have any experience with refugees") was, "We could take on a refugee if we could get the right one!" (thirty comments). Some comments reflected concerns about taking on too many refugees and a possible backlash. Having read through the comments, Betty Drury concluded, "The general sentiment seems to be (as one college president put it) 'sympathetic but not sacrificial'!"[42]

All Faculties Have "a Fear of Numbers"

In addition to commissioning the Gallup poll, the Emergency Committee also hired Percy Knauth, a former *New York Times* reporter who had been stationed in Berlin, to visit U.S. colleges and universities. Knauth was to assess how refugee scholars were doing and how receptive each school was to taking Jews. On October 9, 1939, Knauth attended an executive committee meeting held at Duggan's office on 45th Street, during which he was given his instructions. Discovering whether institutions would be willing to take refugee scholars would be "delicate but not complicated," as board member and acting City College of New York president Nelson Mead put it. Knauth set out a week later and spent the next three months touring seventy-five American universities. He traveled 7,584 miles by car until he reached Omaha and then rode another 5,470 miles by train and 549 by bus. He produced a forty-five-page report that discussed separately each of the institutions he visited.[43]

Knauth listed institutions by "Liberal, and able to accept Jews" (twenty-five names), "likely to find racial prejudice" (six names: the University of Vermont, Mather-Western Reserve [what is now Case Western Reserve University in Cleveland], Syracuse University, Bates College, Dartmouth College, and the University of New Hampshire), and "trustees unfriendly to Jewish appointments" (one name: Williams College; apparently Williams's trustees would not even let him visit). Knauth explained some of his assessments, noting that Bates College in Maine had no Jews on its faculty and "there was some hesitancy in expressing the welcome a Jew would receive." Interestingly, Knauth found no "racial prejudice" at two other small Maine colleges, Bowdoin and Colby. The University of Vermont also had no Jewish faculty, and the appointment of Jews "would be likely to find community opposition." At Colgate University, Knauth found "two unobtrusively Jewish men" and five Jewish students out of one thousand. Knauth concluded that St. Lawrence University would welcome "a fine Jew."[44]

"While it is true that there is very little evident antagonism and prejudice towards Jews, it must be recognized that there is present in all faculties a fear of numbers," Knauth concluded. "No comment, in the group of institutions which had accepted men, was as common as 'So many, no more.'" Knauth cited a few examples of this attitude: The president of the University of the Pacific complained that a Jewish member of the faculty had been sending friends and acquaintances to see him, and he resented the pressure. Upon the announcement that Kurt Lewin, a prominent refugee sociologist, would join Iowa State's faculty, six Jews apparently arrived on campus in a car with New York license plates to register at the school. "This sudden incursion did not go unnoticed," Knauth recorded. Both the administration and local Jewish students at Emory University, which had received the support of "the finer Jews in Atlanta," "resist the infiltration of what they call the 'Brooklyn Jews,'" who could not get into northeastern colleges. Knauth was not immune to these prejudices, punctuating his report with references to "fine Jews" and "not too obtrusive Jews," as well as insisting that the "real or incipient defence against numbers" did not reflect any "prejudice as to race or creed."[45]

The reason for this sentiment, however, did not seem to be that European scholars were actually taking jobs from Americans. "There were not many colleges in which the competition of American scholars was mentioned," Knauth noted. In addition to Knauth's report, there were other indications that concerns about competition were exaggerated. Charles Oldfather, dean of the Liberal Arts College at the University of Nebraska, acknowledged in the winter of 1936, "while there were many American scholars without jobs it was found extremely difficult to find adequate candidates for existing openings." Despite the anxiety of the Emergency Committee and other groups throughout this period, few reports surfaced of actual jobs being taken from American scholars. A State of Connecticut education official reported in 1940 that the department had received "a complaint" that "preference was being given to refugee scholars in their appointments to colleges and universities." The official backed off very quickly, however, when Duggan wrote him and enclosed an Emergency Committee report.[46]

In 1938, the Emergency Committee received a complaint from Paul Flory, a philosophy and psychology professor (not the Nobel Prize-winning chemist of the same name), who claimed he had been "forced out" of his position at Olivet College in Michigan because the school hired a "Jewish refugee from Germany," Friedrich Solmsen. Flory offered no proof, but the committee took the charge very seriously. Since the committee had formed in 1933, it had feared such a case, as the minutes of the meeting during which the charge was discussed reflect. The members decided that Columbia law professor Joseph Chamberlain should investigate the charge. Ultimately, nothing came of it. Solmsen stayed at Olivet until 1940 when he moved to Cornell University, eventually becoming head of its classics department. He ended his career at the University of Wisconsin.[47]

"Resources Are Completely Exhausted"

After years of struggling with a problem that grew only worse, at the end of the 1930s exhaustion more than anything else may have settled in among American academics. Even inviting art historians Hans and Charlotte Giese to deliver a series of lectures in early 1939 proved too much for some of the nation's most prestigious institutions. Hans was a University of Berlin professor of the history of art and architecture; Charlotte wrote essays for scientific journals and newspapers and did research for the German Federation of Art-Science. The couple had married in 1919. In 1933, Charlotte, who was of "non-aryan descent," offered to divorce Hans. He refused, and in 1937, the University of Berlin dismissed him without a pension. The following year Charlotte wrote to the AAUW explaining that she and her husband "do not find any possibility to earn our livelihood." She attached her curriculum vitae, four references, and a bibliography as well as "my husband's papers." A week after Kristallnacht, she wrote the AAUW again, offering to "do any kind of work" and touting her proficiency "in every domestic work."[48]

Advised that their best bet for university appointments would be to come to the United States first on visitor visas, the couple tried to set up a lecture tour during a possible visit. Charlotte explained that lecture dates would make it easier to get visitor visas; State Department officials were increasingly withholding such visas on the theory that European visitors would not be able (or willing) to return home. Walter W. S. Cook of New York University's Institute of Fine Arts, who had received several letters from both Charlotte and Hans "begging me to try and find a position for them," refused to even try to set up a lecture for Hans. "It is very late in the season" and "most museums and universities plan their lectures program several months in advance," Cook wrote, while acknowledging that "the only hope that Dr. Giese or his wife would have would be to come to this country on a visitor's visa" to make personal contacts. Cook then suggested that Kathryn McHale, the AAUW's head, write to the heads of other art history departments.[49]

McHale did. They all declined to invite the Gieses to lecture. Charles Morey of Princeton University's Department of Art and Archeology explained: "We have had Dr. and Mrs. Giese on our list of candidates for some time, and I am well aware of the merits of both and the trying character of their position." But Princeton had already "taxed its resources providing for cases of this sort" and "our funds are already overdrawn for lectures." As for openings at other universities, Morey admonished that "we always have to keep in mind the necessity of taking care of our own graduates and Americans of merit who are unemployed." Erwin Panofsky of the Institute for Advanced Study also begged off, citing that "the resources of this Institute are completely exhausted . . . it seems impossible to put new names on a list already filled beyond capacity." Paul Sachs at Harvard's Fogg Art Museum wrote, "I am handling so many cases already that I am at a loss to know what to suggest."[50]

The Gieses never came to the United States on a lecture tour. No record could be found of Hans Giese. All that is known of Charlotte Giese's fate is that a 1943/1944 Gestapo book from Lissa in Poland included her name.[51]

T • E • N

A Last Chance in France

In the spring of 1940, the Germans ended what had been known as the quiet war, the seven months following the invasion of Poland, by blitzing through Norway, Denmark, the Netherlands, Belgium, Luxembourg, and France. Faced with a catastrophe that seemed to spell the end of Western Civilization, refugee advocates rallied once more to try to save scholars and scholarship.

As the financial engine behind much of the intellectual migration and the organization with the most clout, the Rockefeller Foundation knew it had to take the lead in deciding how to respond and to do so quickly. Soon after France's fall, the foundation moved its Paris office to Lisbon and took stock of what it had left behind. Daniel O'Brien, who had been in the Paris office's medical division for more than a decade, checked on the status of laboratories in France. Frédéric Joliot-Curie, for example, was managing to sustain his research after striking a deal with the Germans. Alexander Makinsky, who headed the foundation's Health Commission headquarters in Paris, tracked individual scholars in distress. The forty-year-old Makinsky, who graduated from law school in St. Petersburg in 1918 and earned subsequent degrees in political science from French universities, wrote in his copious officer's diary what he knew and what he was told about the scholars caught up in the invasion. Linguist André Mazon was not far from Chateauroux in the free zone and wanted to come to the United States. Ernst Honigmann, a historian who specialized in the Byzantine Empire, was imprisoned in the Saint-Cyprien concentration camp in the south of France. Paul Wittek, an Austrian whose field was Ottoman Studies, had been in Belgium but "seems to have disappeared," having last been seen in Ghent on May 13, 1940.[1]

As German soldiers were marching into France, the Rockefeller Foundation understood that it faced a situation it had never faced before. Many foundation officials believed they were witnessing the likely end of the European Enlightenment, with the United States as the only bulwark against the onslaught. For all their despair at the prospect, they continued to perceive an opportunity for the best men and for the American academy. Bombs fell on Paris, and the last British troops escaped Dunkirk, as Joseph Willets, the Rockefeller Foundation's director of the Division of the Social Sciences, prepared an "If Hitler Wins" memo. The June 3, 1940, memo assumed the Nazis would control all of Europe, including Great Britain. Willets, who had just left the deanship of the University of Pennsylvania's Wharton School, advocated that the foundation "shop for the best" and bring to the Americas "100 of the best minds from Great Britain, 75 from France, and smaller numbers from other countries." He suggested "as quietly as possible" assembling "a list of the men and women in the various social science fields whom we would most like to see here" so the foundation would be ready "if the final tragedy occurs." The emphasis, he insisted, "should be on the highest quality."[2]

While Willets was expecting the worst, he was plotting to get out the best. Four days after German troops took Paris, he noted the Germans' impending control of all of France. "Night appears to be settling down on the people who have given the finest meaning to the word 'culture,'" he wrote. The foundation's obligation was clear—"to preserve the best of the scientists and scholars of France for civilization." This could be difficult. "The task of reaching and discovering the ones we want without being deluged with ones we do not want is complicated," he noted. Foundation officials began discreetly assembling lists. As it had in less harried circumstances, the foundation sought advice from American scholars about whom to rescue. With the foundation's assistance, *Foreign Affairs* editor Hamilton Fish Armstrong cabled State Department assis-

(19) Joseph Willets, director of the Rockefeller
Foundation Division of the Social Sciences.
Courtesy of Rockefeller Archive Center.

tant secretary Breckinridge Long on June 21 with a list of twenty-seven
"French intellectuals now likely to be in particular danger" and suggested that the Lisbon consul be told to grant visitor visas immediately
"to any person on this list." Armstrong numbered the names so numbers could replace names in future correspondence. Foundation official
Tracy Kittredge added a list of twenty younger French scholars whom he
implied might be better suited for permanent positions and presumably
non-quota visas. Solomon Lefschetz of the University of Michigan consulted with colleagues and came up with a list of five French mathemati-

cians who should be helped. Harvard government professor Carl Fried-rich contributed his own list of outstanding French scholars in the social sciences, including comments on each.[3]

Not everyone agreed on helping only the best. In fact, not every-one agreed on helping anyone. On July 9, two weeks after France's offi-cial surrender, Rockefeller Foundation vice president Thomas Appleget wrote to fellow foundation officials that perhaps the foundation should stay out entirely: "There would be inevitable confusion between the hard-boiled desire to save intellect and the humanitarian desire to save lives. And this would be complicated by the fact that, because of aid to institu-tions and our fellowship programs, we have thousands of friends among the scholars of Europe. To select a few of these for aid and refuse the rest would cause widespread disappointment and bitterness in an area where we want goodwill." But Appleget, who had been a Brown University ad-ministrator before working for John D. Rockefeller and then joining the Rockefeller Foundation, seemed to change his mind quickly. Two days later he wrote, "The collapse of European civilization" offered an oppor-tunity to enhance American culture; therefore, the foundation "is will-ing to bring to America a limited number of really first-class men."[4]

Appleget's concerns about favoritism seemed to be well founded. The State Department had forwarded the list Armstrong assembled and Kittridge supplemented to its consuls in Lisbon, Marseille, and Bor-deaux, calling it the "Foundation list." The Rockefeller Foundation then received two or three cables seeking to add names to it. Within a week, foundation president Raymond Fosdick instructed Makinsky to go to the U.S. consul in Lisbon and clarify the situation. "I would hate to have our friends in Europe get the impression that a list with which we had only a casual connection represented our considered judgment as to who should or should not come to the United States," an obviously per-turbed Fosdick wrote. Makinsky did as he was told, visiting both the U.S. ambassador and the consul-general in Lisbon the morning of July 25. Both officials told Makinsky that the consul would make his own decisions about granting visas without regard to a "Foundation list." The consul also wanted it known that "the consulate here is the worst place in Europe from which to apply for a visa," Makinsky told Fosdick. In fact, the Lisbon consul wanted Fosdick to encourage anyone he corresponded with in France, Switzerland, or Spain to apply to emigrate from those countries rather than Portugal. Makinsky, however, reassured Fosdick that he did not think the consul would "create any particular trouble" for their grantees despite his warning.[5]

As Europe crumbled around them, top Rockefeller officials signed off on a plan to save the continent's scholars and to bend their rules to do it. They knew there was no time for the usual procedure of waiting for universities to make offers and then deciding separately whether to fund them. Instead, both the Rockefeller Foundation and the Emergency Committee decided to work through Alvin Johnson and the New School, who "are relatively free, aggressive and ingenious," as Appleget put it in a July 11 memo. Appleget assumed that "Johnson, if we select carefully will take any scholar we assign to him," at least in the social sciences or humanities, the New School's bailiwick. Johnson would recommend to other institutions scholars in the natural and medical sciences. The plan was to find positions for one hundred scholars of the first rank. Most were in France, but some were in Poland, the Netherlands, Austria, Belgium, or the territories that once made up Czechoslovakia. The Rockefeller Foundation agreed to provide $400,000 for salaries, $100,000 for transportation, and $65,000 to the New School for administrative costs. Makinsky would be in Lisbon to help individual refugees. The Emergency Committee would provide contacts and funds. The New School assumed responsibility for all other details, which included negotiating with foreign governments and the State Department.[6]

To coordinate this effort, the New School created the American Council for Émigrés in the Professions under the direction of Else Staudinger, a German refugee who had a doctorate in economics. Her husband, Hans Staudinger, had been a top official in the Weimar Republic and was a New School faculty member. The Emergency Committee began to worry that the foundation's reliance on the New School might eclipse its work. In August 1940, the Emergency Committee's executive committee board members had a relatively tense meeting with Johnson and a representative of the Rockefeller Foundation. The solution seemed to be to have Johnson join the Emergency Committee executive board and to develop jointly several rescue plans. Consumed with caring for its grantees already in the States, the committee did end up with a backseat role.[7]

No One Who Is "Merely Run-of-the Mill"

Once the procedure was established, the question remained: Which scholars should be saved? During an October 1940 staff conference, Alan Gregg, director of the medical sciences division, asked whether the foundation's emphasis should be primarily on humanitarian or scholarly objectives. John Marshall, associate director of the Division of the Humanities, replied by identifying four criteria: "1. eminence 2. age (with some weighting towards younger men); 3. need of the man—danger or no prospect of continued productivity 4. need in this country—utilization in undeveloped fields or where other personnel is lacking." To social sciences division head Willets, the first two criteria, age and eminence, mattered most. The foundation agreed to fund the additional one hundred scholars "if they are of real quality." As before, quality was to be determined by American scholars. Willets explained the foundation's criteria to Johns Hopkins president Isaiah Bowman in November 1940: "Are the men of real distinction so that their extinction would be a genuine loss to the scholarly world? We do not see much point to bringing over people who are merely run-of the-mill." They should also be in "some potential danger" and "young enough" to make important future contributions. Willets admitted these may not be the "right tests but they are the ones we have been roughly trying to apply."[8]

The foundation apparently applied that test to Rudolf Keller, a Prague biochemist. "Dr. Keller himself is not of sufficient scientific distinction to compete on anything like an equal basis with most of the European scientific refugees who constitute an already too large number for aid from any single organization," H. M. Miller, the Rockefeller Foundation's assistant director for natural sciences, wrote in September 1940. "It is therefore, with regret that we feel such aid as we are able to give must be extended to persons of greater scientific distinction and with promise of useful production in science over a longer period of years." Keller, who along with being a researcher had married into the family that co-owned the *Prager Tagblatt*, the city's top newspaper, left Prague for Sweden, then Great Britain, and finally the United States.[9]

Ignace Meyerson, a Warsaw-born physician and psychologist, was described as "not a first rate scientist—but a very nice man." The initial references for Meyerson, who had translated Freud's *Interpretation of Dreams* into French, were negative. Smith College psychology professor Kurt Koffka panned Meyerson, referring to his lack of productivity, even though he had done "some excellent work on the intelligence of chimpanzees." Wolfgang Kohler of Swarthmore found Meyerson to be "handicapped by a slightly neurotic attitude toward the world in general and scientific work in particular." And Herbert Langfeld of Princeton described him as "an assistant rather than a leader." References gathered a year later were much better, including one from Cornell University's dean of arts and sciences, but by then it was too late. The forty-two-year-old Meyerson fled Paris for Toulouse, where he joined the Resistance forces led by historian Jean-Pierre Vernant. Meyerson survived the war. French linguist George Gougenheim, a former professor of phonetics and grammar at the University of Strasbourg, was "regarded as a mediocre professor" and sent a "letter of regret July 31, 1941."[10]

Although its main effort was in France, the New School also assessed scholars in other German-occupied countries. Erwin Goodenough, a Yale history professor, tried to be careful in evaluating Edmund Stein, a professor at the Warsaw Institute of Jewish Studies. "I do not want in any way to appear to damn Dr. Stein for he may be a person of great promise," Goodenough wrote in October 1940. Still, his assessment was quite damning. "I know of Stein only as the author" of two studies of Philo of Alexandria that "are competent and thorough but not brilliant, the sort of thing which good young men in Germany turnout almost automatically." Columbia history professor Salo Baron and Rabbi Abraham Heschel had a more favorable impression. Heschel described Stein as "one of the foremost experts on Jewish Hellenistic literature and history," who was "successful in his academic position both at Cracow University and the Institute for Jewish Studies." Stein never received a position in the United States. He was imprisoned in the Warsaw Ghetto, where he trained students in Judaic studies and wrote for the ghetto newspaper. His work for a textile workshop gave him immunity from deportation, but after his wife and son were transported to the Treblinka extermination center, he refused an offer of refuge outside the ghetto on the Aryan side. In January 1943 he was transported to Trawniki and from there to Majdanek, where he was murdered.[11]

"Too Frail to Stand the Strain"

Some American professors did more than evaluate refugee scholars; they worked passionately and persistently to try to save them. Michel Gorlin, the Russian-born literature scholar who had settled in Paris when the Nazis assumed power in Germany, had those kinds of backers. Gorlin had made something of a life for himself in France. He took a job as a librarian at the University of Paris's Institute of Slavic Studies and assisted the institute's president, André Mazon. His partner, Raissa Bloch, wrote poetry and worked for a journal on the history of pharmacology, contributing articles on Tibetan medicine and remedies for canine rabies. The couple continued to host literary evenings, such as one on Russian poetry of the nineteenth century. They were not as integrated into the Russian exile community as they had been in Berlin. Like many German refugees in France, they had trouble making ends meet; a friend described the couple as destitute. They married in 1935 and had a daughter, Dora, the following year. Gorlin wrote that Dora was born "like almost everything in my life—at the last minute: at five minutes to midnight. Notwithstanding this, she's a marvelous lass." Once the war began in 1939, Gorlin, who was not a French citizen, considered immigrating to Brussels or even the United States.[12]

At first, the Rockefeller Foundation was not the least interested in Gorlin, a young scholar without a world-class reputation. On May 14, 1941, the Paris police grabbed the thirty-two-year-old Gorlin along with five thousand other Jewish men between the ages of eighteen and forty in the first wave of mass arrests in France. Gorlin was sent to the Pithiviers internment camp, about fifty miles from Paris. Mazon and other colleagues tried to secure his release but to no avail. Gorlin was assigned to forced labor on a farm near the camp.

At that point, Mazon activated the Slavic scholarly community both in France and abroad. On July 14, 1941, Wacław Lednicki, a Polish professor of Russian literature who was then a Harvard lecturer, went in person to the Rockefeller Foundation offices to explain Gorlin's situation and spoke with John Marshall. That same day, Marshall, who had both a bachelor's and a master's degree in English from Harvard, wrote to Harvard Slavic scholar Samuel Cross. "Quite apart from his difficult situation in France—to put it mildly—is he someone who we ought to have over here?" Marshall asked Cross. "Can he be regarded as 'eminent' enough to rank with the men whom we have helped to bring over?" If Cross thought Gorlin "especially deserving," Marshall promised "to see what might be done" despite the difficulties of getting people out of France.[13]

Cross responded in the affirmative, citing two prominent linguists who vouched for "the high quality of Gorlin's talents." Marshall tried to dampen Cross's expectations about the foundation's ability to extract someone from France, particularly in light of Makinsky's imminent departure. "I hope that you are right that the withdrawal of our Lisbon representative would not hinder the chances of [Gorlin's] getting over," Marshall wrote, "but if you knew all that [Makinsky] had done in Lisbon to help these refugees, even in times less difficult than the present, I think you would be less optimistic than you are about Gorlin's getting out. Of course, the Hicem, the international Jewish organization, is pretty efficient, but sometimes more than efficiency is necessary."[14]

Marshall still had not committed to finding and funding a position for Gorlin. He next contacted Francis Whitfield, a specialist in Slavic languages and literature at the Library of Congress. Marshall asked Whitfield to put something together for Gorlin that would approximate a curriculum vitae. He also asked whether Whitfield agreed with Cross and Lednicki that Gorlin held a place "of unquestioned eminence in his field, or of prospective eminence if he was young, as I understand Gorlin is." Whitfield replied that he was "overjoyed to hear that you have at least a little news of [Gorlin] and perhaps some prospects of helping him." Gorlin "is certainly worthy of any assistance you can give him," he wrote.[15]

Whitfield, who had known both Gorlin and Raissa Bloch-Gorlin in Paris, then assembled as much information about the two as he could, including two articles and an edited volume, as well as Gorlin's "long study" of what eighteenth-century Russians knew of Russia during the Middle Ages. Whitfield also noted that Bloch-Gorlin's Ph.D. was on the relationship between emperors and popes during the Middle Ages and that she had published two volumes of poetry. (It may be reflective of biases of the academic organizations that Gorlin, not Bloch-Gorlin, was considered for a university post.) Lednicki, who also knew Gorlin from Paris, pitched in, sending Marshall more of Gorlin's books and articles and elaborating upon his work and reputation. "I believe that he fully merits being saved from the concentration camp in which, if he remains, he probably will die, as his health is too frail to stand the strain," Lednicki wrote.[16]

Gorlin, whose health was indeed poor, survived that summer of 1941 on the camp's meager rations. In September, he received a bit of a reprieve, working as a librarian in the city of Pithiviers during the day and then returning to the camp at night. His wife managed to see him occasionally, and he even resumed his research. Gorlin also seemingly had a future in the United States. The New School agreed in August to appoint him professor of comparative Slavonic literature with a $6,000 grant from the Rockefeller Foundation. The two-year grant covered $2,500 a year in salary and $1,000 in transportation costs. Gorlin's academic community seemed to have saved his life.[17]

Don't "Refuse Any Kind of Passage"

While the Rockefeller Foundation, the Emergency Committee, and the New School tried to rescue scholars by securing university posts that offered at least a shot at a non-quota visa, other U.S. organizations helped procure regular visas, visitor visas, and new emergency visas. Established Jewish aid organizations, such as the Hebrew Immigrant Aid Society (HIAS or HICEM, its French branch) and the American Jewish Joint Distribution Committee, operated in France and Portugal, as did Christian groups such as the American Friends Service Committee and the Unitarian Service Committee. The most overlap in mission occurred with the Emergency Rescue Committee, a private organization supported by well-known American artists and writers that was founded after the fall of France specifically to assist about two thousand artists, intellectuals, and political dissidents.

Under pressure from liberal and academic circles, the Roosevelt

Administration decided to grant emergency visitor visas to select refugees allowing them to come to the United States and stay past the usual
six-month limit. (At the same time, the State Department was increasingly denying regular visitor visas to those in Europe.) The President's
Advisory Committee on Political Refugees was to generate a list of special refugees in France entitled to the temporary emergency visas. The
Emergency Rescue Committee sent journalist Varian Fry to Marseille to
assist those on the list to escape. The list, however, turned into a fiasco.
Groups in the United States fought over who should appear on it, and
the State Department objected both to who appeared on the list and to
the very existence of the list. (It opposed any exceptions to existing rules,
including extending the length of stay for a visitor visa.) Fry and his
team in Marseille targeted those on the list, but they also went beyond
their mandate to help whomever they could. Fry assisted about two thousand refugees, including many prominent artists and intellectuals, before
the State Department pulled his visa. Explanations for taking Fry's visa
vary from a Marseille consul official's personal animus to the department's concern that Fry was endangering U.S. relations with the Vichy
government. Either way, Fry had to leave France in September 1941.[18]

   Everyone trying to help refugee scholars (as well as other refugees)
faced a daunting task. France had been divided into two zones as part of
its peace deal with the Germans. The Germans occupied the northern
part of the country, including Paris, while the French controlled the
south, with its government in Vichy. Refugee advocates first had to lo-
cate the scholars, many of whom had fled to the unoccupied zone and
might be in hiding. Scholars also could be in one of almost forty internment camps established for foreign Jews and political dissidents in both
the occupied and unoccupied zones. Rescuers knew conditions in the
camps were horrific and time was of the essence. In an April 1941 fund-
raising appeal, the Emergency Rescue Committee noted that twenty-five
people a day were dying in the Gurs camp in the unoccupied zone and
that "a gift of $350 will evacuate one of them." An eleven-page commit-
tee report contained thirty-one first-person, named accounts of people
interned in several French camps, along with heart-wrenching letters
from those in the camps. "My future is dark and my chances of escape
are not very great," economist and sociologist Heinz Langerhaus, who

was imprisoned in Gurs in July 1940, wrote a friend in the United States. "My personal conditions are, of course, for the moment full of difficulties. Little to eat, no shoes, etc. etc." The thirty-six-year-old Langerhaus, who had studied at Frankfurt's International Institute of Social Research, had already survived three years of imprisonment in Germany for publishing an antifascist newspaper and two years in the German concentration camp of Sachsenhausen. He had escaped to Belgium where he was arrested during the German invasion and sent to Gurs. Langerhaus concluded his letter: "He who survives will have much work to do. I am not despondent."[19]

As they searched for a particular scholar amidst the chaos, the aid organizations also sought a faculty position at an American university, either the New School or another institution. Recommendations had to be gathered in order to make the scholar's case. Should a university post be secured, the aid group then had to ensure that the scholar received a non-quota visa. If a faculty position and a non-quota visa were not forthcoming, aid organizations tried to facilitate immigration under a regular quota, though that too had become more difficult. Emergency visas were another possibility, though they also involved an arduous bureaucratic process with little likelihood of success. Finally, passage had to be booked on one of the private ocean liners sailing from Marseille or Lisbon. (Emergency Committee board member and Columbia zoologist Leslie Dunn proposed that the U.S. Congress "authorize and finance American vessels' transportation of refugees with visas for American countries." But Dunn could not get any newspaper to publicize his proposal, beyond a letter to the editor in the *New York Times*. U.S. government or government-paid-for ships did not carry refugees, even when troop transports returned to the United States empty, having dropped their cargo in England or North Africa.) For those hoping to leave from Marseille, the Vichy government required an exit visa, which it often denied. To leave from Lisbon, refugees had to cross Spain, which required entry and exit visas, as did Portugal. Obtaining any of these visas, from the United States, France, Spain, or Portugal, required proof of a reservation on a ship with a specific sailing date. Refugees who were not able to line up all the necessary paperwork in time for the ship's departure had to start all over again. If they could not get a ship reservation, all the other paperwork became worthless.[20]

Alexander Makinsky juggled all these demands as he assisted scores of scholars. Rather than orderly notes of visits to grantees, his official Rockefeller Foundation diary entries during this period are as frantic and desperate as the times: lists of underlined names of those he was trying to help and the status of their visas, ship debarkations, hotel rooms, and consulate visits; the arrival of visitors from the States; meetings and other communication with aid workers from the Unitarian Service Committee, American Friends Service Committee, and HIAS. In his February 1941 officer's diary, Makinsky records the comings and goings of various scholars: International lawyer Leo Gross postpones his arrival from Madrid by one day. Anthropologist Claude Lévi-Strauss's contract with the New School arrives by cable. Walter Meyerhof, a Nobel Prize winner's son, writes that the Spanish consulate at Marseille will issue his visa and wants to reserve a place on a boat sailing in mid-February. The wife of medical professor Maurice Wolf delivers two copies of her husband's curriculum vitae and scientific publications. Political geographer Jacques Ancel is in Paris, having been dismissed from all his posts. Political economy professor Robert Mosse, who is Jewish, as is his wife, is no longer on the Grenoble law and economics faculty. H. Mankiewicz is in Lisbon on his way to Shanghai. French sociologist Albert Bayet is "in danger," though "there is probably very little that we can do."[21]

The February diary also reflects Makinsky's interactions with other aid organizations, consuls, and shipping lines. On February 27, for example, he meets with Marjorie Bennet Fellows Schauffler of the American Friends Service Committee. Schauffler is on her way to a camp in Spain to check on the status of fifteen hundred people being held for trying to cross the border without a Spanish entrance visa or a Spanish exit visa. Eighty percent of them are Jews. Makinsky describes a "long talk" on the refugee situation in Spain and Portugal with Schauffler, "a woman of considerable energy and ability."[22]

On that same day, Makinsky plans to call on the U.S. consular officer who has told "Mrs. Emil Gumbel" her visa would not be extended "without seeing 'whole dossier.'" The problem: Marieluise Gumbel, whose mathematician husband had been invited to join the New School faculty, had a non-quota visa through her husband, while her mother and her nineteen-year-old son had visitor visas. Waiting for the dossier to arrive from Lyons would delay the family's departure several weeks at least and would mean Gumbel would have to cancel her reservation on the ship *Excalibur*. She would not be able to get another reservation for at least two months. Makinsky plans to visit the consul, "explain the situation, and will see what can be done," even though he doubts he will be able to change the consul's mind.[23]

At the end of the day, Makinsky meets with a "Mr. Hart of Export Lines," a shipping company, and receives very specific instructions on how to reserve five places on a boat sailing April 18. Makinsky also gets disturbing news. The State Department had told Hart not to allow any more foreigners on his ships from now (February) to June; all available space is to be reserved for Americans. "H. says that all they can do is follow instructions which the State Department gives them," Makinsky writes, mulling whether it would be better for Rockefeller official Appleget or the New School's Johnson to take up the matter with the State Department "and see whether New School professors can be placed on the priority list of the Export Lines. Otherwise we shall have considerable trouble."[24]

In the midst of great distress and calamity, people still had their foibles, and Makinsky had to deal with those who were forgetful, demanding, stubborn, or otherwise difficult. For instance, as Makinsky tried to get Byzantine scholar Henri Gregoire out of France, he noted that Gregoire had left his contract to teach at the New School "somewhere in Marseilles." Gregoire later retrieved notes of introduction he had left on Makinsky's desk only to lose them again, leaving them in a taxi. At another time, a clearly exasperated Makinsky indicated that Boris Mirkine-Guetzévitch, former director of the Paris Institute of Comparative Law, instructed him to insist that the Export Lines accept a personal check for $700. He also asked Makinsky to see about his luggage because Mirkine-Guetzévitch was "having some cardiac trouble." "I am afraid MG is a bit demanding," Makinsky recorded on March 1, 1941. "I do not see why his wife and daughter cannot take care of his luggage; they do not seem to be involved in MG's heart trouble." Mirkine-

Guetzévitch arrived in the United States to take a position at the New School. Perhaps most aggravating of all, film producer Jean Benoit-Levy, who had a position waiting for him at the New School, refused to sail with his family on the *Navemar* in June 1941 because of the ship's lack of comforts. "If I were in Prof. Benoit Levy's position, I think I would hesitate to refuse any kind of passage," Makinsky notes. Benoit-Levy, his wife, and two daughters arrived in the United States in September 1941 on another ship.[25]

As 1941 turned into 1942, the situation for refugees, particularly Jews, deteriorated still further. Refugee aid organizations that were still operating in France relayed the information to the home front. In September 1942, Katherine Lessy sought the American Friends Service Committee's help for her cousin, Ernst Emil Schweitzer, a jurisprudence scholar who was in Gurs. As previously noted, Schweitzer's imprisonment had already led to his losing so much weight that another aid organization had noted that his life was in danger. Schweitzer "is a very sick man, starving and asked me to help with food and money," Lessy wrote the committee. She begged the aid organization to send "food, (milk chocolate, sweetened canned milk, sweetened cocoa)" or, if that was not possible, money. Two weeks later, a committee official sent a letter to Lessy in Dorchester, Massachusetts, returning the $10 she had asked to be transferred to Schweitzer. "Drastic changes in the refugee population make it difficult for our Marseille office to locate beneficiaries," the form letter stated. Beginning in August 1942, convoys sent thousands of Gurs internees to Auschwitz-Birkenau, which is presumably what the committee message meant. Schweitzer likely was on the transport that left the Drancy transit camp on August 19, 1942, for Auschwitz.[26]

A committee official sent a more direct message in December 1942 to the Muenzes living on the Grand Concourse in the Bronx who had inquired about Walter Froehlich:

> A letter received from our Marseille Office dated November 5 includes a long list of transfers which they were unable to make because the beneficiaries had left Unoccupied France for destinations unknown. We regret to tell you that we find on the list the name of Walter Froehlich. . . . Our Marseille

staff has asked us to convey their sympathy to friends and
relatives in this country because of these deportations—and
we need not tell you how much we regret the necessity of
sending this sad message to you. Of course, recent events
have completely cut off our communications with our workers in France and there is nothing we can do at this time to
help the refugees.

The "recent events" were the Allied landing in North Africa, the Germans' move into the southern half of France, and the subsequent sev-
ering of the U.S. relationship with the Vichy government. Froehlich
was likely a twenty-four-year-old Vienna native who was deported to
Auschwitz on September 9, 1942, not the Prague mathematician with the
same name.[27]

"The Most Incredible Hardships"

For those remaining in wartime France, conditions were brutal. Astronomer David Belorizky, the forty-one-year-old widower with a three-year-
old son, almost escaped in fall 1942 when Harvard Observatory head
Harlow Shapley offered him a position. Belorizky had left Russia in 1920
at age nineteen and studied science in Paris. After a short stay in Palestine, he returned to France, earning a doctorate in mathematics and becoming a citizen in 1933. Belorizky took a job as an assistant astronomer
at the Marseille Observatory. His son, Elie, was born on August 4, 1939,
a month before the war began. Not long after, Belorizky's wife, Judith,
died at the age of thirty-six. An elderly nurse cared for Elie while Belorizky served in the French Army.[28]

    With the French surrender in 1940, Belorizky returned to his po-
sition at the Marseille Observatory, but the Vichy government's racial
laws soon endangered his job. Only the intervention of Jean Bosler, the
observatory's director, allowed Belorizky to hold on until 1942. He was
then fired and began working in a radio repair shop. The nurse, who was
not Jewish, hid Elie in the cellar of their home, allowing the toddler to
emerge only in the evenings. Shapley had his eye on Belorizky for a
while and, given the dire circumstances, even managed to persuade the

Rockefeller Foundation to fund a Harvard position. But in October 1942, the Harvard administration refused Shapley's request to hire Belorizky. Shapley continued to look for options. A few weeks later, he thought he had found one, a two-year position at the Swarthmore Observatory in Pennsylvania. Shapley told Bosler to inform the U.S. consul in Marseille and Belorizky himself. Four days later, the United States and the Vichy government severed diplomatic relations, ending the Belorizkys' hope of escape.[29]

By 1943, Marseille had become extremely dangerous for Jews, with German officials and French militia grabbing them off the streets. The most notorious roundup occurred in January 1943 when French and German authorities demanded the identity papers of forty thousand people over three days, finding two thousand Jews and sending them to three internment camps and then to extermination centers. Belorizky was caught in one such roundup. Noticing the police had cordoned off an area, he jumped on a tram. Two militia men were onboard. One demanded his identity card, which was clearly marked *Juif* and included his home address. It would lead to his son. For some reason, the man decided not to arrest him, and his colleague had not noticed the Jewish identity card. Shaken, Belorizky returned home but knew he could not stay long. With Bosler's help, he and Elie and Elie's nurse moved in the dead of night into the Haute-Provence Observatory north of Marseille. Four other Jewish families were hiding there, including astrophysicist Evry Schatzman. Surviving the war, Belorizky returned to the Marseille Observatory and died in 1982. Elie Belorizky became a physics professor at the Joseph Fourier University of Grenoble.[30]

Hellmuth Simons, a bacteriologist who had been on the University of Düsseldorf faculty, also found himself in Marseille during the war. He had been trying to immigrate to the United States since 1934. After some time in England, and then in Russia, he went to France, working at the Pasteur Institute and writing summaries of articles in European journals for the University of Pennsylvania's *Biological Abstracts*. Three months after the German invasion of France, at "the first sign of life," Simons wrote to the editor, John R. Flynn, recounting his "appalling war adventures." Simons had been interned by the French and freed as the Germans approached, marching south with twelve hundred men, twenty-nine of whom were killed in machine gun fire. After working on a farm to stave off starvation, he walked an additional fifty-five miles in thirty days to Marseille. He resumed his research even though he could no longer consult "many precious Dictionaries and English or American textbooks" in his personal collection. The libraries in Marseille "are *much* worse," he wrote.[31]

After catching Flynn up on the status of his work, Simons asked the editor to write to the U.S. consul in Marseille to help him obtain a non-quota visa. He included two postscripts with more detailed directions following further conversations with the consul. Flynn reached out to Alvin Johnson on the basis of Simons's "excellent work for us" that assured the availability in English of a large body of European research. Johnson responded that Simons did not fit into his plan for the New School. He suggested instead that Flynn write to the consul and agree to provide Simons with an affidavit pledging financial support. Flynn likely supplied the affidavit because in June 1941 Simons received a visa dependent on his leaving Marseille via Martinique. When that was not possible, his visa was canceled.[32]

In January 1942, a month after Pearl Harbor, the *Abstracts'* assistant editor, Jean MacCreight, penned a letter to Secretary of State Cordell Hull. MacCreight touted Simons's work, "done with the utmost devotion, working under conditions unbelievably tragic," and his family connection (brother of a renowned neurophysiologist and descendant of Heinrich Heine). MacCreight concluded with a plea: "Every day that Dr. Simons remains in Marseille brings him closer to death by starvation and yet he continues to send his abstracts—working with rare courage, refusing defeat. To let such a man down is to condemn to failure the very ideals that give us the strength to meet the tragedy of the war and win." A handwritten note dated February 19, 1942, indicates that MacCreight never received a reply to her letter to Hull.[33]

Three months later Simons's friend Walter Bornstein, a physician in New York City, wrote to Johnson, quoting from a recent letter from Simons and describing the ongoing fight with the State Department. Simons was still in Marseille. On April 24, 1942, he had written, "We are living under the most incredible hardships of starvation." His weight had dropped to about eighty-six pounds. Simons continued to try to work.

"I constructed an oil-lamp by means of old sardine-tin (in order to work longer during the night) . . . I feed this 'devil's lamp' with . . . [the] oil [that is] my fat ration. . . . So, I have been able to write today's manuscript. . . . I am getting so weak in my fingers that writing begins to become a physical pain." Simons was still trying to work with the Marseille consulate, but an American vice consul was discouraging, telling him "America is no Jewish hotel." Simons included a plea: "Please, do everything in your power to push, push and push against the incredibly slow (people in Washington). The only really reliable hope seems to me to get the USA visa." Simons never got a U.S. visa during the war, though he did manage to escape to Switzerland and to immigrate to the United States after the war.[34]

E·L·E·V·E·N

Security Fears

ellmuth Simons, the bacteriologist trapped in Marseille, was not the only scholar urging his American supporters to push back against the State Department. Many did, and some refugee advocates listened. As more visas were rejected with increasingly grave consequences, refugee aid organizations decided they had to take on the State Department and its policies directly. Since 1933, State Department officials had been interpreting the language of the Section 4(d) non-quota visa provision to limit the type of institutions and the type of scholars covered. Different consuls used different rationales, yet they still relied on the provision's wording. At the onset of the European war, State Department officials took it upon themselves to reject non-quota visa applicants on grounds that were nowhere in the statutory language. They began examining the political backgrounds of those applying for non-quota visas and rejecting whoever did not meet their standards.

After the fall of France, the Emergency Committee ran into so many problems getting its grantees visas that Columbia professor Leslie Dunn contacted State Department assistant secretary Adolf Berle, an important advisor to President Roosevelt with whom Dunn thought he had an in. But Dunn found Berle "frigid about political prisoners in France" because, according to Berle, "some of them might be commu-

nists and . . . we already had enough aliens to shadow." (In meeting with
Berle, Dunn had his sights on an even bigger objective—to pressure
President Roosevelt and Secretary of State Cordell Hull to agree to support the creation of a category of political refugee under immigration
law who could come to the United States on an emergency basis. Dunn
did not succeed and, as was true of so many trying to help the refugees,
was on the verge of despair, writing in August 1940: "I know that many
groups see the point and many efforts go on for individual refugees, but
we have yet to learn of one person among those responsible for U.S.
policy who has spoken out. If this should happen soon it would give us
courage to go on with our letters and delegations and press campaigns.
If it does not we shall have to retire.")[1]

Dunn described his meeting with Berle to his fellow Emergency
Committee member Alfred Cohn, who also knew the assistant secretary.
Cohn then wrote Berle to express his "great distress" that "scholars, scientists, patriots, of greatest human value in themselves and in all prob-
ability capable of great contributions to our country . . . should be excluded on no very good grounds or on no grounds deemed reasonable
by good Americans." Cohn obviously struggled with whether he should
write Berle at all, finally concluding: "It is a desperate situation. All the
more ought profound and sympathetic human feeling be applied to it."[2]

Berle responded: "We have arranged to salvage a good many of the
kind of people you speak of in France," presumably referring to the special refugees who qualified for emergency visas. He acknowledged, however, "we do like to know about the people who come in." He put forward
the argument that would be used repeatedly during the war years to re-
strict immigration—a "considerable amount of espionage work has been
done under the guise of 'refugees,'" including by those with relatives in
Germany who could be coerced into spying. But fears of refugee espionage proved to be a red herring—of the twenty-three thousand "enemy
aliens" who arrived in 1940 from German and Soviet territory (the Soviet Union being Germany's ally at that point), fewer than one-half of 1
percent were taken into custody for questioning, and only a fraction of
those were indicted, and then for violating immigration regulations, not
for espionage. Refugee espionage was an effective fear tactic nonetheless.[3]

As it did with the "likely to become a public charge" clause, the

State Department initially used its administrative discretion to limit immigration on the basis of security. Breckinridge Long, the new assistant
secretary in charge of the visa division, laid out the department's strategy in a June 26, 1940, memo: "We can delay and effectively stop for a
temporary period of indefinite length the number of immigrants into
the United States. We could do this by simply advising our consuls to
put every obstacle in the way and to require additional evidence and to
resort to various administrative devices which would postpone and postpone and postpone the granting of the visas." The strategy worked well.
Consuls granted visas to fewer than 20 percent of those who applied in
1940 and 1941. The country-by-country quotas were not filled in 1940 or
any subsequent wartime year.[4]

"Speed Is of the Essence"

Musicologist Mieczyslaw Kolinski had already run into the State Department's obstructionism in Brussels in 1939 and 1940, when the Antwerp
consul denied him a non-quota visa and then delayed deciding whether
to issue him a transit visa to enable him to get his visa to Haiti. As Kolinski waited in his Brussels apartment on May 10, 1940, to hear whether
the U.S. consul would issue the transit visa, German soldiers crossed
into Belgium. "Since this morning, the long-feared Hitler-invasion of
Belgium has unfortunately become a fact, and it remains to be seen what
will be the immediate consequences of it for me," Kolinski wrote Melville Herskovits at Northwestern. Kolinski asked Herskovits to redouble
his efforts to secure Kolinski a visa. Across the ocean, Herskovits also
heard the news of Germany's invasion of Belgium. Four days later, he
wrote Kolinski, informing him he would not send the regular check for
Kolinski's work analyzing musical recordings until Herskovits was sure
it would reach him. "I do not know if this letter will ever get to you,"
Herskovits wrote mournfully on May 14, 1940, "but I am writing to you
at your Brussels address in the hope that it will eventually reach you."
Belgium surrendered to Germany on May 28.[5]

For the next six months, Herskovits heard nothing. Then a refugee
who had managed to reach New York cabled him news from Kolinski.
The thirty-nine-year-old was in the same Brussels apartment at 108 rue

Goffart, working on Herskovits's recordings. "Kolinski, who I thought must be either in a concentration camp or a Polish ghetto at best, is apparently being permitted to work undisturbed for the moment in Brussels," Herskovits wrote to a friend in November 1940. Kolinski may have been able to live and work in his apartment, but he knew he was not safe in Brussels. The German occupation of Belgium was proceeding along a familiar and devastating path. A month earlier, the military government had passed anti-Jewish laws similar to the Nuremberg Laws and to ones being adopted in France and Holland at the same time. Jewish shops bore the marks of their owners' religion, and Jewish-owned economic assets were registered. Before 1941 ended, sixty-three hundred Jewish-owned businesses were liquidated and six hundred Aryanized.[6]

Kolinski faced the same problem as he had had before the invasion—convincing the U.S. consul to issue him a transit visa so he could travel to Washington, D.C., to retrieve his Haitian visa from the legation there. In the cable he sent to Herskovits through friends, Kolinski asked him to get in touch with the Haitian consulate and to raise travel money. Kolinski promised to repay the travel expenses as soon as he started receiving his Northwestern salary, a promise he repeated a few months later.[7]

As soon as he received Kolinski's cable, Herskovits began pestering the State Department. The department did not reply for more than two months. On February 11, 1941, visa division chief Avra Warren wrote to Herskovits: "You understand, of course, that in order for Dr. Kolinski to qualify for an American transit visa, he must demonstrate to the satisfaction of the American consulate in Brussels both his intention and his ability to proceed directly to Haiti." Warren explained that the State Department needed to obtain verification of Kolinski's Haitian visa through the U.S. legation in Port-au-Prince. An exasperated Herskovits replied that he understood the need for verification, even though it should be obvious Kolinski planned to go to Haiti because he would be working for Herskovits there. "I should like to stress, however, that speed is of the essence in this case," Herskovits wrote, so perhaps State should accept the Haitian legation's certification "since this will obviate the time-consuming necessity for communication with our legation" in Haiti.[8]

Warren ignored Herskovits's suggestion, writing three weeks later that "in accordance with the usual practice" the department had cabled the U.S. legation in Port-au-Prince to contact the Haitian government and was awaiting a response. Herskovits was billed for the cable. On March 19, Warren wrote: "The Foreign Office of Haiti has refused a visa. . . . no further action is being taken." Herskovits, who could not believe the Haitian government changed its mind about Kolinski's visa, frantically tried to find out what had happened. Seemingly nothing. Sometime over the next three weeks, the Haitian legation telephoned the State Department to find out where it should cable its authorization for Kolinski's visa. The State Department then said it would issue Kolinski a transit visa. It had been five months since Herskovits first tried to get the department to agree to issue a transit visa. It was taking its time, even though Kolinski too kept emphasizing the need for speed. "It is necessary to act quickly and not lose time regarding this," he urged Herskovits, suggesting that Herskovits "handle everything via telegram."[9]

As Kolinski learned the U.S. consul would issue a transit visa, he received even better news. His number under the Polish quota to immigrate to the United States had been called. What he thought would take multiple years took fewer than two, presumably because so few Poles were able to leave the country since the German invasion. Although welcome news, the issuance of a quota visa required an entirely different bureaucratic procedure. Kolinski needed an affidavit of financial support and another attesting to his "loyalty and morality," both from U.S. citizens. He required proof of transportation from Europe paid in U.S. dollars. Just in case, Herskovits continued working on the Haitian visa. The U.S. consul threw up another obstacle, insisting that Haitian officials provide detailed information about Kolinski that the Haitians did not have and that U.S. officials presumably did. Herskovits noted that the U.S. consulate has "a full file, NO. VD 811.111 on [Kolinski], where all this information is at hand." Still, Herskovits fed a Haitian official all the necessary information on Kolinski "since nothing is certain in this world."[10]

Before he could fulfill the quota visa requirements, Herskovits had to make sure Northwestern would let Kolinski teach during the 1941–1942 academic year, that both the Emergency Committee and the Jewish Welfare Fund would renew their financial commitments, and that transportation expenses were secured. He enlisted his mentor Franz Boas in the effort; but before Kolinski's future employment was nailed down and his documents collected, Kolinski's visa application ran into the State Department's new regulations.[11]

"Several Months to Take Action"

In June 1941, the U.S. Congress enacted a law that explicitly gave State the authority to deny visas to any alien who might endanger public safety, including those who had close relatives remaining in German territory. On its own, the State Department then erected new bureaucratic procedures for both quota and non-quota visa applicants that assured the immigration process would be dauntingly complex and exceedingly slow. Consulates in German territory were closed, meaning refugees in Berlin or Vienna or Prague or Brussels would need to travel to neutral countries to apply to immigrate to the United States. The department voided all current applications and required them to be reinitiated with new forms, provided by the department in Washington, D.C., that were to be filled out by U.S. citizens or legal residents willing to take responsibility for the "aliens." The Americans had to attest to detailed biographical information about applicants, vouch for the applicants' willingness to uphold American values, and promise to financially support them.

Form B, the biographical part, required a preposterous amount of information from refugees who were barely surviving in war-torn countries. The form contained twenty-three categories of questions about the applicant including names; schools and universities attended and during what years; degree earned and field of study; employers since 1930, including positions and dates; all children's dates of birth, present residences, and marital status; names and locations of close relatives in Europe, Asia, or North Africa; membership affiliation in parties, groups, and societies, with detailed information on each provided on a separate sheet. Another question asked whether the applicant had been a communist or an anarchist. The U.S. citizen then needed to swear his or her own allegiance to the U.S. government and disavow membership in any radical groups.[12]

Form C established a U.S. citizen's or a resident alien's willingness to sponsor an alien and his or her financial ability to do so. The form asked for that person's income supported by the latest federal income tax return and an affidavit from a bank officer showing the date the account was opened, the balance, deposits made, and whether in small or large amounts. Similar affidavits had to be provided from responsible people with knowledge of other assets. The potential sponsor then needed to list his or her dependents, any other immigrants he or she had sponsored, whether those sponsored were self-supporting, and pledge his or her fidelity to the United States and acknowledge membership in any politically radical organizations. The sponsor further had to swear not to have paid for the alien's transportation to the United States or to have promised the alien employment here, which would constitute inducements to immigrate. Finally, the sponsor had to promise that he or she would ensure the alien never became a public charge.

Form D, the shortest of the three, required a more general pledge from a U.S. citizen or resident alien that a "visa applicant is friendly toward the United States and disposed to the good order and happiness of its people." Each of the three forms necessitated two additional U.S. citizens to serve as references for the sponsors, attesting to their "good standing and character." All the documents had to be notarized and certified.[13]

The new forms and procedure roiled the refugee aid community, including those in Europe trying to save scholars. The Rockefeller Foundation's Alexander Makinsky explained all the steps a university would need to take in 1942 to extract someone from unoccupied France. Foreign Jews could not get exit visas and were being deported to Poland so their situation was hopeless. For French Jews, the university needed to send an application for a visa to the State Department's chief of the visa division and request six copies of Form B. The university then needed to answer all the questions on Form B in detail. If it could not and needed the scholar to provide answers (which was highly likely), the university should cable the scholar, including a note to the censor to ensure the cable went through. Of course, many of the applicants were in hiding or in internment camps and not easily reachable. A university did not need to provide information about its own financial status, as required of an individual sponsor on Form C. Instead, to satisfy the non-quota visa requirements, the university needed to indicate the faculty position to be filled, the salary to be paid, and a guarantee of two-year employment.

Consuls could turn down applications if the university's offer was not for enough money or for a long enough time period or if the consul decided the university did not seem to have a need for the applicant. None of this was specified in any statute.[14]

Absurdly detailed forms were not the only State Department procedure introduced in June 1941 to stop, or at least slow, immigration. State also created a D.C.-based apparatus to handle the applications and a new process for assessing visa applicants. An Interdepartmental Advisory Committee that included State's visa division, the Immigration and Naturalization Service, the Department of Justice, the Federal Bureau of Investigation, the Military Intelligence Service, and the Office of Naval Intelligence would conduct a three-to-six-week investigation and then send a recommendation to the relevant consulate abroad, with the consulate retaining the right to reject a positive recommendation. In conducting its review, the D.C. committee was supposed to take into account whether the applicant had close relatives in German territory, information the new forms elicited. Most of the applicants did, and that in itself proved to be almost completely disqualifying. Of the 985 applications received by September 1941, more than 800 were rejected.[15]

If the application was approved, the State Department would send the forms to the appropriate consul. "It usually takes several weeks—and frequently several months—for the Department of State to take action on applications," Makinsky wrote. In July 1942, for example, the reviewing committee was considering applications filed the previous November. During those eight months, the persecution of Jews in occupied countries intensified—curfews, restricted rations, curtailed living quarters, branding with a Jewish Star of David, deportations east to disease-and-starvation-ridden ghettos. The extermination camps also began operation during these eight months, with "kill rates of extreme magnitude," among the highest of the Holocaust. A quarter of all the Jews who were killed died between March 1942 and November 1943.[16]

Even if the visa was approved, it was good only for the remainder of the fiscal year. If the applicant was not able to arrange transportation to the United States during that time, which meant a $500 deposit and travel plans to the debarkation location, he or she would have to start the application process again. An appeals process, which was seemingly intended to help refugees, did so only slightly. Refugees who had been denied a visa by the six-agency review committee could appeal to another committee made up of representatives of the same agencies. The second committee could hear testimony from sponsors or other representatives of the refugee. If the second committee sided with the refugee and the State Department did not object, the recommendation to grant a visa was forwarded to the appropriate consulate abroad. The consulate could still object to issuing a visa, but it had to provide an explanation. If the second committee agreed with the initial reviewing committee that a visa should not be offered, the applicant could then appeal to a two-person board appointed by the president. If that board split or the State Department objected to the board's decision, State's position prevailed. The review committee sustained the primary committee 85 to 90 percent of the time. The two-person review board was somewhat more sympathetic to refugees; 20 to 25 percent of the cases changed from being disapproved to accepted. All of this took a great deal of time that the refugees did not have.[17]

Events "Throw Us Back" Two Steps

By the time Mieczyslaw Kolinski was ready to apply for a regular quota visa in June 1941, the new, more onerous requirements were in place. John Marshall, who approved the Rockefeller Foundation's expenditure of $500 for Kolinski's travel expenses, signaled the first problem: Did Kolinski have any close relatives remaining in German-occupied territory? Kolinski was single. He had not heard from his father and brother, who presumably were in Poland, for two years. But before that potential problem could be dealt with, an even more pressing deadline loomed. On July 15, 1941, the U.S. consulates in Belgium and throughout occupied Europe were to be closed, making "all speed imperative if anything is to be done," Herskovits wrote to Northwestern's president Franklyn Snyder. Herskovits hoped, probably foolishly, that he could get Kolinski a visa from a Belgium consulate before it closed. "I hope I am not too late with all this, but you know how things have to be fitted together like a mosaic," Herskovits wrote to Boas on July 5. In a less restrained mood, Herskovits expressed his frustration to a Columbia administrator who

(20) John Marshall, associate director of the
Rockefeller Foundation Division of Humanities.
Courtesy of Rockefeller Archive Center.

had been helping him with the paperwork: "I've been writing and writing and writing these things . . . and millions of others like 'em now."[18]

The consulates closed. Kolinski did not have his visa. His only hope
was to travel to a neutral country and obtain one from a U.S. consulate
there. Makinsky, who had left Lisbon a month earlier, tried to be helpful.
In a memo, he explained the many, probably futile, steps Kolinski would
need to take to get out of Europe. It was as if, after years trudging along
a tortuous path, Kolinski had been blown back to his starting point.
Should he set out again, he would face hurricane-force winds.

The starting point was a non-quota visa, which the Antwerp consul had rejected in 1940. Northwestern needed to persuade the State De-

partment to have a consulate in a neutral country, preferably Portugal, issue Kolinski a non-quota visa, Makinsky stated. The consul in Lisbon might prove more sympathetic than the one in Antwerp. Northwestern would have to fill out all the questions on Forms B and D, cabling Kolinski for answers the university might not have (which, presumably, would be many). Because it would not be possible for Kolinski to get a visa to enter Portugal without having the U.S. visa in hand (which he would not, because he had not been to Lisbon yet), he would need a visa from another country that issued visas in Belgium. Cuba was the best option. This would require a $500 deposit that U.S. officials would need to authorize. The authorization would take as long as a month. After the $500 was deposited, Kolinski would need to notify the Cuban consul in Brussels to issue him a visa. He would then need an exit visa from the German authorities in Belgium and a reservation on a boat sailing from Lisbon to Cuba, with half the cost paid up front. The Portuguese consul and the Madrid consul both would need to issue transit visas. If all that was accomplished, Kolinski should travel to Lisbon. "*Then* he will have to forget all about Cuba, and start working on his American visa," Makinsky explained. The only good news was that Kolinski could probably book a ship reservation on Export Lines in Lisbon, using the place of someone else who could not get there.[19]

The New School and the Rockefeller Foundation tried the same Cuban gambit with biologist Hans Przibram and law professor Hugo Sinzheimer. Przibram, who had been fired from the Viennese biology institute he founded and where Leonore Brecher worked, fled Austria along with his wife, Elisabeth, to Amsterdam. They waited there for a regular visa to the United States to become available under the Austrian quota. When the Germans invaded Holland, waiting became impossible. The New School tried to extract Przibram in July 1941 by getting him a visa through the Cuban consul in Amsterdam. Sinzheimer, a University of Frankfurt labor law professor whose U.S. relative originally agreed to fund his New School position, had spent four months in Theresienstadt. Upon his release, he cabled the New School in November 1941 for help leaving Holland. Without a U.S. consulate in the German-occupied country, the New School decided to "buy Cuban visas" for Sinzheimer and his family.[20]

Despite the odds, both Kolinski and Herskovits seemed ready in August 1941 to try for a Cuban visa. "The Kolinski case seems to get more and more fantastic; every time we take one step forward, events seem to throw us back two," Herskovits wrote to Northwestern president Snyder on August 7. Complicating already ridiculously complex matters, Herskovits planned to leave at the end of August for a one-year trip to Brazil to do fieldwork. Someone else would have to handle all the letter writing and paperwork. Sailing from New York City, Herskovits was set to meet with Marshall and Makinsky at their Rockefeller Foundation offices on August 25. Then Marshall wrote: "Just had word that the Cuban Consulates in France, Belgium, Holland and Germany have just been closed. I am afraid that takes much of the hope out of Kolinski's prospect of coming to this country."[21]

Przibram's hope of leaving Holland also evaporated. In April 1943, Hans and Elisabeth Przibram were deported to Theresienstadt. He was imprisoned there for a year, dying on May 20, 1944, apparently of starvation. Elisabeth committed suicide the next day. The Sinzheimers also were trapped in Europe. The Jewish Council in Holland selected Hugo Sinzheimer and his wife Paula as two of ten Jews to be exempted from deportation to Poland. Hugo then spent the rest of the war hiding in attics of friends in Amsterdam, Haarlem, and Bloemendaal. Paula hid in a different location in Holland. They both survived the war. The years of hiding and hunger, however, took their toll on the law professor. Sinzheimer died in September 1945 of a brain hemorrhage at age seventy, a day before his planned valedictory speech at the reopening of the University of Amsterdam and before he received word that all four of his grown children had survived the camps.[22]

Herskovits sailed for Brazil, having heard nothing from Kolinski. Once there he continued to try to get Kolinski out of Europe, securing a staff position for him at the National Museum in Rio de Janeiro. Then Brazil broke off diplomatic relations with the Axis powers. "The unfortunate thing was that, through no fault of my own we were always just one step behind the developing political scene," Herskovits wrote Betty Drury in December 1942. Drury had just informed him that "under present circumstances in Europe, there seems little point in keeping our grant [the Emergency Committee grant to Kolinski] open." Herskovits reluctantly agreed. "I have no word of Dr. Kolinski for more than a year and a half," Herskovits wrote, "and I fear greatly that he has been shipped to Poland."[23]

"Nothing to Add to the War Effort"

Refugees in France had a somewhat easier time immigrating to the United States than did those in Belgium or Holland; consulates in France remained open until the United States broke diplomatic relations with the Vichy government in November 1942. But they had no easier time with the State Department in Washington, D.C. In October 1941, twenty-five scholars had American positions waiting for them funded by the Rockefeller Foundation, but only "about 6 had a fair chance of getting in" because of State Department roadblocks. The attack on Pearl Harbor seven weeks later made the State Department even more determined to keep people out. "The State Department is not anxious, apparently, to bring over many new aliens," Makinsky recorded a month and a half after the attack, and was primarily admitting scholars who were considered useful to the national defense effort.[24]

The State Department made its own determinations of what was useful to the national defense. The Rockefeller Foundation decided that Paul Wittek, "one of the leading, if not the leading, scholars in the field of Turkish language and culture" was "urgently needed in this country." State did not agree. Wittek, an Austrian by birth, had lost his position at the German Archeological Institute in 1933. He fled to Belgium, where he took a position at the University of Brussels. During the invasion of Belgium, Wittek tried to reach Great Britain with his wife and three children, aged twelve to sixteen. The family was separated, Wittek making it to London and his wife and children returning to Brussels. The Rockefeller Foundation then arranged for Wittek to work at the Library of Congress, developing an Arabic and Islamic section. He was considered the only person available of "high scholarship who commands all three of the requisite languages, Turkish, Arabic and Persian." He also would be a New School faculty member with a $6,000 Rockefeller Foundation grant of $2,500 a year, plus $1,000 for travel expenses for Wittek and his family.[25]

After the State Department's Sumner Welles intervened, Wittek initially received a visa, but he was not able to use it immediately. With his wife and three children in Brussels, his mother in Baden, and his brother in Berlin, Wittek ran afoul of the newly adopted close relatives policy. This policy was "the monkeywrench" in Wittek's immigration, wrote Marshall, noting that "prior to the ruling the State Department had seen to it that he had a Clipper reservation, but the ruling washed all that out." Officials of the Library of Congress "have undertaken to assure the State Department that Wittek will not overthrow the government of the United States," Marshall wrote with more than a hint of sarcasm. It apparently did not work. The Interdepartmental Advisory Committee reviewed Wittek's case and denied it because of his close relatives' presence in German territory and his own internment as an enemy alien in Great Britain. (Great Britain interned almost all adult male German nationals during the war's first two years.) During a telephone conversation, State's Adolf Berle told Archibald MacLeish, the Librarian of Congress, that not a single member of the committee reviewing Wittek's case voted to grant him a visa.[26]

Marshall did not give up. He tried again in February 1942 but then had trouble booking passage for Wittek on a liner to the United States; waiting lists dated back to July 1940. "Presumably to get passage, nothing short of high governmental priority would be effective," Marshall wrote MacLeish. Marshall sought MacLeish's judgment on whether Wittek "is so urgently needed here that extreme measures are justified." MacLeish responded, "We might as well close the Wittek case." Wittek never got a U.S. visa. He took a position at the University of London's School of Oriental and African Studies. The foundation and the Society for the Protection of Science and Learning then began quibbling over which organization should help Wittek with living expenses.[27]

On Saturday, January 24, 1942, the State Department's Avra Warren summoned Makinsky to explain the disposition of the foundation's visa requests for ten potential grantees. Warren told Makinsky that four of the scholars had been denied visas because they would "not contribute to the war effort." Oddly, one of them, Arabist Guilbert Boris, might in fact have proved useful to the Allies; the Vichy government seems to have denied him an exit visa on the basis of his knowledge of North

Africa, where Allied troops would land within the year. Boris was then in Tunis. The other three denied U.S. visas were André Philip, an economics and finance professor at the University of Lyon who had been a Rockefeller Foundation fellow at the University of Wisconsin and Columbia University and active in French politics; Vladimir Jankélévitch, the forty-year-old philosopher whom Horace Kallen considered "well worth saving"; and Michel Gorlin, the Russian literature scholar. Six other scholars' visas were being held up by the State Department but had not yet been denied. Warren also explained that State did not look favorably at the New School's offers to so many French antifascists because "maintaining good relations with Vichy and France was deemed essential for the time being, hence their hesitancy to admit too many people who may prove to be too actively on the other side." (The United States would not sever ties to Vichy for another ten months.)[28]

Makinsky returned to the State Department on Thursday, February 5, and spent the afternoon being questioned by ten people from the FBI, Naval Intelligence, the Immigration and Naturalization Service, and State's visa department about each of the foundation scholars supposedly on their way to the United States and a few who were here. Makinsky described the proceedings as "very formal," with "three shorthand typists" taking down "everyone [sic] of my statements." Some applications were "examined with particular care": historian Elias Bickerman, because he had a German name; French economist Raymond Warnier, because he had been writing for Le Temps, a Paris newspaper; another French economist, Robert Mosse, because he had a passeport de service, a passport for those performing state-sponsored missions abroad without diplomatic status; and philosopher Jean André Wahl, because he had been released from a concentration camp. "The questions asked showed a lack of familiarity with European conditions," Makinsky wrote.[29]

For some, State Department scrutiny caused only a temporary delay. Bickerman received a visa in April 1942, came to the United States, and became a professor of ancient history, first at the New School and then at Columbia University. Mosse and Wahl eventually joined the New School faculty, along with international law professor Alfredo Mendizabal, whose visa application had also been held up at the time. But for others, the visa denial left them trapped in Europe. The Rockefeller Foundation never learned what happened to Boris; it simply recorded him as failing to arrive in the United States. All that is known is that he was listed in Tunisia on June 15, 1944. What happened to Warnier also could not be determined. The State Department informed the consul in France in June 1942 that Philip and his wife should be given U.S. visas, but at that point the Gestapo was hunting him. He managed to escape to London the following month, and his wife and five children went to the United States.[30]

Jankélévitch's visa was apparently authorized in April 1942, but he still had not received it by July 9, when he was supposed to sail on the *Nyassa* via Casablanca to the United States. He was set to leave again in October, out of Marseille, supposedly with his U.S. visa in hand. At the last minute, he did not board because Vichy authorities had arrested his brother-in-law and he did not want to leave his sister alone. Jankélévitch joined the Resistance, writing and teaching clandestinely in Toulouse. He survived the war, assuming a chair in moral philosophy at the Sorbonne and writing books on philosophy and music, including ones that dealt with the topics of evil and forgiveness.[31]

Michel Gorlin's non-quota visa was denied in early 1942 because he had "little or nothing to add to the war effort." As his potential appeals languished in the State Department in the spring of 1942, Gorlin's younger sister Lalla, who had immigrated to the United States, kept after the New School and the Rockefeller Foundation, assuming the latter would be more effective. "Things in France being as they are I am terribly afraid that if help will not come soon it might be too late," Lalla Gorlin, who lived in New York, wrote Marshall in April 1942. "I should appreciate it very much if you could see your way to grant me an interview." Marshall did not see much point. "I should be glad to talk his situation over with you if I thought there were anything further that I could do. But I have talked it over with Mr. Makinsky and am convinced that everything has been done that is possible at present," Marshall responded. "I am afraid for the present there is nothing to do but to wait and hope."[32]

Ultimately, the Rockefeller Foundation brought over only fifty-two of the one hundred or so scholars they had identified as worthy of a U.S. university position, twenty-three of them teaching at the New School.

About half the scholars offered New School posts received non-quota visas, a better than average rate most likely because of the Rockefeller Foundation's influence. Between Pearl Harbor and the war's end, the quotas from Axis-controlled countries were only 10 percent filled, with just twenty-one thousand refugees, or about five hundred a month, entering the United States from Nazi Europe.[33]

T · W · E · L · V · E

Final Appeals

Since the first deportations to the Lublin reservation in 1939, mass murder stalked Jews trapped in German-occupied Europe. The trains from Western Europe deposited Jews to live in enclosed ghettos in Riga, Minsk, Lodz, and many of the three hundred other Eastern European cities and towns already overcrowded with local Jewish residents. In the larger ghettos, thousands died every day from disease, starvation, and sporadic violence. In June 1941, German and local death squads began liquidating the ghettos and machine-gunning Jews in the towns where they lived in Eastern Europe. At the end of 1941, camps for mass gassings had been set up in Chelmno, north of Lodz, and Birkenau, part of the Auschwitz facility in Silesia. By June 1942, the major extermination centers, Chelmno, Belzec, Sobibor, Birkenau, Majdanek, and Treblinka, were in operation. The first trains rolling directly into the killing centers came from Slovakia and France, followed by those from almost every part of Western and Eastern Europe.

In 1941 and 1942, many American professors and professionals advocating for refugee scholars had contact with those in Europe who were still begging for help. Faced with reality and their own exhaustion and despair, some gave up. Others could not.

Michel Gorlin

Lalla Gorlin feared that unless help came soon, it would be too late for her brother, the Slavic scholar Michel Gorlin, who was in a French internment camp in the spring of 1942. Denied a non-quota visa in early January, and with no appeal proceeding in sight, Gorlin struggled in the Pithiviers camp. But Gorlin and his friends in France decided to do more than wait and hope, as the Rockefeller Foundation's John Marshall had advised Lalla. They plotted an escape from Pithiviers to Spain. It failed. Gorlin lost his privileges as a librarian that had allowed him to work in town during the day. He was now confined to the internment camp at all times.[1]

On March 27, 1942, the first convoy of French Jews left Drancy outside Paris for Auschwitz with 1,112 people on board. Four more convoys of 4,037 people left for the same destination over the next four months. On the evening of July 16, 1942, Gorlin and almost 1,000 other prisoners were shoved into cattle cars, 70 to 80 people to a car. There was no water or food. It was very hot. The following morning, at 6:15, Convoy #6 left Pithiviers for the three-day trip to Auschwitz with 809 men and 119 women on board. The novelist Irène Némirovsky, author of *Suite Française,* was one of the women. Upon arrival at Auschwitz, all the deportees were selected for slave labor. Gorlin was assigned to transport heavy material, load coal, and dig on construction sites. He did not last long. He died on September 5, 1942, at 9:10 p.m. at the age of thirty-three. His death was recorded on September 16, 1942; the reason stated was pneumonia, and his occupation was listed as librarian.[2]

That same month, the New School succeeded in getting the State Department to grant Gorlin a non-quota visa, and the consul in Lyon was advised to issue it. At that point, however, the New School was not able to reach him.[3]

After her husband's deportation, Raissa Bloch-Gorlin tried to stay one step ahead of the Germans. She left her six-year-old daughter, Dora, with André Mazon, head of the linguistics institute where her husband had worked. Bloch-Gorlin took on a new identity as Michelle Miraille and fled Paris. She went to Vic-sur-Cère in central France, where under her assumed identity she worked as a teacher in a facility for Jewish chil-

(21) Raissa Bloch-Gorlin, poet and medieval
historian. Courtesy of Yad Vashem Photo
Archive, Jerusalem, CAS-195147.

dren run by the Oeuvres de Secours aux Enfants, or Children's Aid Society. She also became part of the Resistance. In October 1942, she arranged for Dora to join her. Two days after Dora arrived, the little girl
became ill and died on October 27, 1942, from a viral infection. Bloch-
Gorlin stayed at the facility for a while but then headed to the town of
Clermont-Ferrand.[4]

As conditions worsened in 1943, she decided to try to cross the
border into Switzerland; Swiss officials arrested her on October 18, 1943.
Despite her friends' efforts to free her, Bloch-Gorlin was sent to Drancy
and then on to Auschwitz-Birkenau on Convoy #62. The train started
with twelve hundred Jews on board; nineteen men escaped by jumping
off the train, and many more died along the way. As she headed to Silesia,

Bloch-Gorlin managed to toss a note from the train, thanking her friends and teachers for their support. The note found its way to the Institute of Slavic Studies. By then, she was dead. Convoy #62 arrived at Auschwitz around 4 a.m. on November 23; 241 men and 47 women were selected to work. Bloch-Gorlin was sent immediately to the gas chambers at Birkenau. She was forty-five.[5]

Almost a year later, the Rockefeller Foundation's Marshall was about to head to liberated Paris. "We never heard anything further from either Dr. Gorlin or Professor Mazon," the New School's Else Staudinger wrote Marshall on October 5, 1944, asking him to see whether he could learn anything of their fates. "I am sure that Dr. Johnson as well as Miss Gorlin would deeply appreciate any news and any assistance that could be given Dr. Gorlin."[6]

Gorlin had been dead for two years; Gorlin-Bloch for a year. Mazon survived. As a tribute to its young colleagues, the Institute of Slavic Studies published in 1956 a volume of articles by Michel Gorlin and Raissa Bloch-Gorlin.

Mieczyslaw Kolinski

Melville Herskovitz last heard from his colleague Mieczyslaw Kolinski in Brussels in the summer of 1941. When the Emergency Committee finally withdrew Kolinski's grant to teach at Northwestern in December 1942, Herskovits assumed Kolinski had been sent to Poland. Earlier that year, Kolinski had indeed been on the verge of being deported.

In November 1941, the German occupiers created the Association of Jews in Belgium that was to help administer the Germans' extermination program. The association began registering Jews and used those lists to call up people for deportation. On May 27, 1942, all Jews in Belgium were required to wear a black badge with a yellow Star of David inscribed with a *J* for *Juif* in French and *Jood* in Dutch. On August 4, 1942, the first convoy left the Mechelen transit camp with stateless Jews on board on the way to Auschwitz. Before October 1942, seventeen convoys with 16,600 people had left Belgium for extermination camps.

During that time, Kolinski had been called to report, supposedly to be transported to a labor camp, a common pretext for being sent to

Auschwitz. He had been ready to report until a friend persuaded him to go into hiding. Kolinski had an idea who could help him. As soon as he arrived in Belgium, Herskovits had put Kolinski in touch with linguist and anthropologist Frans M. Olbrechts, another disciple of Franz Boas who was a professor at the University of Ghent. Kolinski met Olbrechts's assistant, Edith van den Berghe, the daughter of a well-known Belgian expressionist and surrealist painter. From 1931 until his death in 1939, Frits van den Berghe had been a cartoonist for a leftist newspaper, often caricaturing Hitler and fascism. Edith van den Berghe agreed to let Kolinski live with her and her mother in their house in Ghent.

Kolinski spent the next two years hiding in the port city in the Flemish region of Belgium. (As many as 40 percent of Jews in Belgium were in hiding during the war.) In the van den Berghe house, Kolinski continued to work on Herskovits's recordings, developing analytical methods for the cross-cultural study of tempo, melody, and harmony. The music and the work also helped to keep him going. On September 6, 1944, the British 7th Armoured Division liberated Ghent, and in November, Herskovits heard his first news of Kolinski in more than two years. A British lieutenant who had participated in the city's liberation wrote Herskovits that Kolinski was healthy and had married Edith van den Berghe. A month later, Herskovits heard from Kolinski directly. "I hasten to give you sign of life," Kolinski wrote. "I have got safely through the terrible cataclysm." He mentioned his marriage and his work. "During all that time, I worked at the establishment of new methods to analyse the structure of primitive music, which I apply to your collection of West African songs."[7]

Hedwig Hintze

Unable to tolerate living in Germany any longer, historian Hedwig Hintze left Berlin for Holland in 1939. Otto, her non-Jewish husband, had stayed behind. The couple exchanged cards and cables almost daily until Otto Hintze died in April 1940. The following month, Germany invaded Holland, which soon barred Jews from the civil service and required them to register their business assets. At first, Hintze seemed somewhat fortunate. The New School and the Rockefeller Foundation tapped her as one of the one hundred scholars they considered worthy of rescue. The New School offered her a faculty position, and the foundation agreed to fund it.[8]

As German authorities required all Jews in Holland to register in January 1941, including the twenty-five thousand refugees who had migrated there from the Reich, Hintze sought a non-quota visa from the U.S. consul in Rotterdam. The consul first rejected her request apparently because she had not been teaching during the two years before she applied to immigrate. The consul also may have "raised objections on account of the lady's age"; Hintze was fifty-seven. The American Friends Service Committee in Amsterdam, which had been helping the baptized Hintze, encouraged her to try to get the Rotterdam consul to apply the more lenient standard some other consuls were using. In cases where scholars had been dismissed for racial reasons, the two-years-teaching-before-immigration requirement was overlooked. Indeed, the consul did seem to drop that objection. The New School's Alvin Johnson noted that the consul had "stopped badgering Hintze about her academic record."[9]

That did not signal the end of the badgering, however. "We seem to be dealing with a Consul who is the ultimate in obstructionism," Herbert Solow, Johnson's assistant, wrote. In February 1941, the Rotterdam consul imposed new requirements for Hintze's immigration application. She had to provide two good-conduct certificates from the police in the place she had lived for the past five years. She also needed three character affidavits and three letters of recommendation in "affidavit form from well known and disinterested persons" who had known her for more than five years and could include "detailed information" about her "business, social and political activities." Finally, she needed evidence of her ability to obtain exit and transit visas. These were the Rotterdam consulate's rules; the new State Department requirements, which were different, would not go into effect for four months.[10]

Johnson doubted that Hintze, who had been living in Berlin four of the previous five years, would be able to "get testimonials from the Gestapo" in order to fulfill the first criterion. Johnson did think it possible for her to get character affidavits and recommendation letters, including from "people on this side of the water." The Rockefeller Foundation's Tracy Kittredge obtained six signed and notarized affidavits and recommendation letters and in April 1941 supplied the four copies of each the consul requested. Kittredge, who had known Hintze since the foundation funded her salary at the University of Paris in 1933, wrote one of them himself. He described her as a "scholar of excellent reputation" who had "published a number of books and articles in France." He added that in terms of her "personal position," she was "regarded with dignity and respect."[11]

Even with the affidavits and recommendations in hand, the Rotterdam consulate still did not issue Hintze a visa. It would not even return her papers to her. And then the consulate closed in July, along with all the other U.S. consulates in German territory. "Can you do anything for me in my desperate situation?" Hintze wrote Johnson in August 1941. "I entreat you once more to do for me whatever you can." By then, German and Dutch authorities had begun segregating Jews from the general Dutch population and sending foreign and stateless Jews to the Westerbork transit camp. In September 1941, with no sign Hintze would get a U.S. visa, her American supporters considered obtaining a visa to Cuba (like they had for Kolinski, Przibram, and Sinzheimer). This offered the only possible escape. After debating whether the additional expense of securing a Cuban visa was justified, foundation officials agreed to pay $150 more for the visa to avoid posting a $2,000 bond. The Cuban consul in Berlin authorized the visa and an agent in the Netherlands secured a German exit visa, transit visas, and railroad tickets to Lisbon.[12]

As Hintze made her way to Lisbon, she learned her Cuban visa had been revoked. She was forced to return to Holland and live with friends near Utrecht. The New School then received a refund of $1,139.70 for the trip Hintze never made to Cuba and the United States. The cost of the Cuban visa, $403.31, was not refundable.[13]

In November 1941, a German decree made the property of all Jews living abroad the property of the Reich. Hintze lost access to her husband's pension, which was her only means of support and which she had fought to keep. She tried again to immigrate, this time to Switzerland, but was rejected. On April 29, 1942, government authorities ordered Jews in the Netherlands to wear a yellow Star of David on their clothing. In June, Hintze received a demand to turn over to a German agency her remaining silver, a tea caddy, and six spoons. That summer, deportations from

Holland to Auschwitz began. Hintze chose suicide, dying in a hospital in
Utrecht on July 19, 1942.[14]

Marie Anna Schirmann

In July 1940, Viennese physicist Marie Anna Schirmann learned that the
Emergency Committee's efforts to get her an appointment at the University of the Philippines had failed. Two months later, she wrote to the
International Federation of University Women, the organization that had
arranged for the temporary position in England that had fallen through
at the outbreak of war. "As a passionate defender of the feminist movement I am thoroughly convinced only a femal [sic] academic organization (Committee) will be in a position to help me in finding a new scientific activity in U.S.A.," Schirmann wrote in September 1940. "If I am
able to obtain any University (College) position in U.S.A. I can come to
U.S.A. immediately, without any waiting till my turn on the immigration quota has come." At the end of her letter, she wrote: "By reason of
various circumstances I am not able to describe my condition here and
all the mental suffering to be separated from my scientific work. Remain
only the hope to find good colleagues in U.S.A., who are ready to help
me for the sake of culture and science." Schirmann never heard from the
federation.[15]

And the Emergency Committee never heard from Schirmann directly again. On March 5, 1941, Schirmann, forty-six, reported to a
school building at 35 Castellezgasse in Vienna and was then taken to the
Aspangbahnhof station. She was prisoner 107. Because there were not
enough boxcars, the prisoners were ordered to leave their luggage behind. Along with 981 other Viennese Jews on Transport #4, Schirmann
undertook the 425-mile journey to a small Polish town, Modliborzyce,
near Lublin. A ghetto had been established there for the town's Jews, as
well as deportees from other parts of Poland and the Reich. The deportees crammed into the homes of local Jews or huddled in the town's synagogue. German authorities allowed Jewish community leaders in Vienna to forward the left-behind bags to the now ghetto residents with a
stern warning not to sneak in any additional luggage.[16]

The Emergency Committee learned of Schirmann's deportation a month later from Helmut Landsberg of Pennsylvania State University's Geophysical Laboratory. Schirmann had written Landsberg asking for help finding employment in the United States. "In the last few days I have received also an airmail letter from Dr. Linke of the University of Frankfurt, for whom Dr. Schirmann has been working for the last few months, indicating that she had been deported from Vienna to some place in Poland," Landsberg wrote Betty Drury on April 5, 1941. Landsberg, who had been at the University of Frankfurt until 1934, explained that Penn State did not have a position for Schirmann. "I thought I had better get in touch with you and find out exactly what her status is and whether your Committee sees any possibility of helping her." Drury responded: "I am afraid we are helpless here to do anything for her." Drury noted that in the three and half years that the committee "had her papers on file we have had only one opportunity to suggest her as a candidate," referring to the position in the Philippines.[17]

Drury received further news in December 1941. A friend of Schirmann's, a former librarian at the University of Vienna who was in Sweden, wrote Drury that she had heard from Schirmann in Modliborzyce. She "is living there in a very hard situation," K. A. Kolischer wrote. "Having no means she was forced to sell her dress and—as I am informed by her—also her winter-dress is pawned." (Ghetto residents survived by selling their meager last possessions, as Schirmann apparently had done.) Kolischer wanted Drury to send Schirmann money and food; "otherwise I could not hope this most learned and unhappy lady could life [sic] any longer—I think rather she is to perish there." Kolischer added that she herself sometimes finds "good hearted people to send her any crowns but this is absolutely insufficient." Kolischer then provided Schirmann's address: "Modliborzyce Kr. Janew Lubelski, Kr. Krassnik, German Gen. Gouv. Polen."[18]

Drury had an assistant telephone the American Red Cross. Whomever the assistant spoke with at the Red Cross told the assistant that the organization "had no facilities for aiding such people," yet promised to try to get in touch with Schirmann through the International Red Cross's contact with the German Red Cross. The "Red Cross held out little hope, however, that anything could be done to relieve her tragic situation," the assistant reported.[19]

It is not known whether Schirmann succumbed to malnutrition, disease, or the regular attacks on ghetto residents by the German police and SS. Or she may have survived to the ghetto's liquidation on October 8, 1942. On that date, the old and the sick were slaughtered in the ghetto. The others were taken to the Zaklikow station and sent to one of three extermination centers, Belzec, Sobibor, or Treblinka. Of the one thousand Austrian Jews transported to Poland on March 5, 1941, only thirteen survived. Marie Anna Schirmann was not among them.[20]

Max Fleischmann

By 1940, the New School and the Emergency Committee had given up on law professor Max Fleischmann. When he was fired as the University of Halle's law dean in 1935, the sixty-two-year-old Fleischmann was considered too old to teach in the United States. Five years later, he was five years older. But Fleischmann's family, friends, and the American Friends Service Committee were not done yet.

In the fall of 1940, Fleischmann's brother, George, who was in New York and had already made a personal appeal to the Emergency Committee, tried a new approach. As founder and director of Halle's newspaper institute, Max Fleischmann in 1928 had helped pioneer the academic study of journalism. He directed scholars who researched the role of media in society, primarily through analysis of daily newspapers. "It would surely be possible to found something of the same kind at the New School or another university," George Fleischmann wrote to Alvin Johnson, "and to employ my brother for this purpose, since he already has the relevant experience." If Johnson did not think a university would be interested, George Fleischmann had another idea—"the owners of the large newspaper concerns" might be interested. Johnson shut down the idea immediately. "I do not know of any newspaper that would undertake the maintenance of such an institution, nor would I know of any other possibility for raising the necessary funds," he responded.[21]

Yale law professor Edwin Borchard, who did not know Fleischmann personally yet had been promoting his cause for years, made one last attempt in 1941 to get Fleischmann a university position as a researcher. The ever-optimistic Borchard detected a softening in the State Department's interpretation of the non-quota visa provision's language that might allow researchers to obtain non-quota visas. The State Department seemed to suggest it would be willing to provide non-quota visas to those who supervised students, even if they did not give formal courses. Borchard seized upon the opening. "I infer from the letter that if we can present the case of a man over sixty who will be useful in the research work of an established educational institution, they might find a way of granting him a visa under a more liberal construction of the word 'teacher,'" Borchard wrote Johnson. Borchard then suggested raising Fleischmann's case in particular with the State Department. Johnson was not convinced the State Department would take a different approach and thought Fleischmann's case presented additional problems. In July 1941, Johnson pointed out that Fleischmann would need to be supported for years and that "new visa regulations have made matters more difficult than ever."[22]

In the meantime, Fleischmann was trying to immigrate under the quota with the help of the relief arm of the American Friends Service Committee. "Dr. Fleischmann is an outstanding scholar—no danger of becoming public charge," a Service Committee note in his file stated. "Very wealthy relatives here." The wealthy relatives, the Fields and the Pflaums, had provided affidavits of support to Fleischmann and his wife, Josephine, and had sought help from the Service Committee in arranging transportation for them. The family dynamics, however, were complicated. While the cousins in the Midwest were using the Service Committee to book passage on one shipping line, Fleischmann's brother and nephew on the East Coast booked passage on another.[23]

The Fields, owners of a theater chain, disparaged George Fleischmann's efforts. "There's no possibility of George Fleischmann receiving transportation and offering any other aid," Gladys Field wrote the Service Committee's Annelise Thieman in May 1941. "I understand he is very old and very poor." Field seemed to have only slightly more use for the Pflaums, "who are very old—in their 70's." Field, who had contributed $387 for part of the transportation costs, suggested that the Service Committee ask the Pflaums for "the rest of the transportation money as soon as there is the slightest chance of getting passage" in case they changed their minds. "I know their families are very unsympathetic to the whole project," Field wrote. Her husband, Harold, was just as dismissive of Karl Steinauer, Fleischmann's nephew, who was also trying to help his uncle immigrate. "Mr. Steinauer is a refugee himself and so far has made absolutely no progress along the lines of self-support," Field wrote Thieman, encouraging her to make her own arrangements for the Fleischmanns and ignore his nephew and brother.[24]

The State Department's new regulations and closure of its consulates in German territory quickly overshadowed the family spat; immigration to the United States was unlikely, no matter who arranged it. "The general immigration situation at this time looks quite black and we are afraid that the closing of the American Consulate in Berlin as far as visas go already has become a fact," Thieman wrote Harold Field on June 27, 1941. Fleischmann and his wife had left Halle for Berlin earlier that year. "In other words, if the Fleischmanns were not able to get their American visas just during the last few days (which we have no reason to believe they did), their chances to come to the United States are now postponed indefinitely."[25]

Fleischmann never obtained a teaching position, a research position, a non-quota visa, or a regular visa. When he arrived in Berlin from Halle in early 1941, he joined about 70,000 other Jews in the capital, reduced from the 160,000 who once had lived there. The first deportations from Berlin to Poland began in October 1941. By January 1942, 10,000 Jews had been shipped to the Lodz, Minsk, Riga, and Kovno ghettos; elderly Jews were sent to Theresienstadt. That year, Jews began to be sent directly from Berlin to extermination centers, primarily Auschwitz-Birkenau.

Fleischmann was not on the earliest transports. He became involved in the German Resistance, one of the few Jews known to have taken part. The former law professor also prepared drafts of a new German constitution that would be ready when Hitler was finally deposed. On January 14, 1943, the Gestapo summoned Fleischmann to the home of former justice minister Eugen Schiffer and informed him he was to be arrested for refusing to wear the Jewish star. Granted his request to gather some things at his home, Fleischmann returned to his apartment and took a large dose of the barbiturate Veronal. Not yet seventy years old, Fleischmann died that day in Berlin. Within three months, the

University of Tubingen's library for public law learned it could acquire Fleischmann's valuable private library for a few thousand Reichsmark. In June 1943 the university sent his widow, Josephine Fleischmann, a check and seized the books.[26]

Käthe Spiegel

Since the Nazis assumed power in Germany and the first Jews and non-Aryans were dismissed from the German Federation of University Women, Esther Caukin Brunauer had used her staff position at the AAUW to help university women in Nazi-controlled Europe. Aware that she was all that stood between them and death in Poland, Brunauer kept trying.

When the Czech medieval historian and archivist Käthe Spiegel wrote a joint letter in November 1940 to Brunauer and other friends, she had waxed nostalgic about their time together in Washington, D.C., in 1927 and 1928. When Spiegel next wrote, in March 1941, she seemed to be coming undone. In a three-page typed letter to "my dear, dear friends," Spiegel, forty-two, recalled how happy she had been in the United States, researching her book, sharing her thoughts with her friends, and traveling to California ("nearly a trip through paradise itself"). The letter quickly took a dark turn: "I confess I am very miserable now and it is really an SOB letter I am sending you and ask you to help me as much as you can. Things are drifting a way which seems to become unbearable in a fearly [sic] near future and I have the feeling to have to ask my friends for help and not to perish without saying a word."[27]

Spiegel made her fear clear: "There are beginning now *deportations to Poland!*" Since the fall of 1939, Jews from Austria, Moravia, and Germany proper had been sent to the Lublin region. "Nobody knows when there will be started to deport people from Prague too," Spiegel wrote. "Deportation to Poland doesn't mean anything else for me than to perish there." She included a list of people to whom the AAUW could turn for help. She also believed, mistakenly, that an affidavit from a U.S. citizen could save her. "People who can prove that they have the permission to enter *later* a foreign country are exempted from deportation," she wrote. (Although affidavits promising financial support were essential to immigration under the quota, they did not in any way guarantee ad-

(22) Käthe Spiegel, Prague historian,
librarian, and archivist, 1941. Courtesy
of AAUW Archives, Washington, DC.

mission to the United States.) Spiegel also contemplated going to a South
American country, "Chile or Ecuador or Mexico or Brazil or somewhere
else. . . . But I have no connections there." She suggested several American professors she thought might be of assistance.[28]

Spiegel concluded the long, rambling letter:

> May be you clever American women know something better
> than all these things . . . of which I am speaking here—arrange

all things for me as you think it best. . . . It is now the question to be or not be and I am asking now life and death. . . . Now my dear, please do excuse my disturbing you, but I think may be it wouldn't be fair to you to perish without saying a word having friends across the great water who are so full of cordiality and friendship as all of you are![29]

Realizing that Spiegel as a librarian was unlikely to qualify for a non-quota visa, Brunauer had been working on enabling her to immigrate under the regular quota. But Spiegel was panicked. She decided that a non-quota visa was a possibility and that she could appeal directly to the U.S. consul in Vienna. She typed up praise she had received in 1931 and 1933 for manuscripts she had sent various Americans, including J. F. Jameson, chief of the Library of Congress's division of manuscripts. She recalled "how wonderful the Tidal Basin must be" now that it was spring in D.C. and longed "to start new with you in your country." She also sent more subdued letters to the Emergency Committee, and even a last-minute plea to the Brookings Institution.[30]

In the meantime, Spiegel's prospects for immigrating under the Czech quota had improved. Three AAUW associates had signed affidavits for her. Spiegel wrote to thank "dear, dear, true and golden friends" for "a beautiful song of friendship." She then continued "prosaically," explaining that to apply for a visa she had to prove she was booked on a ship to the United States. Spiegel believed the Rockefeller Foundation, which had supported her U.S. fellowship, would grant her another one and pay her transportation expenses. For a full page, she threw out possibilities.[31]

At a May 10, 1941, board meeting, the AAUW agreed to pay $500 each for the transportation of Spiegel and two other women out of German-occupied Europe. It was a last-ditch attempt to save the women, all three of whom had been involved in its international operation. In addition to her AAUW acquaintances from D.C., Spiegel had been president of the German section of the Czechoslovak association. In early June, Brunauer contacted U.S. consular officials in Vienna and was told not to send Spiegel's documents right away; the U.S. government was about to change its immigration requirements. Regardless, Brunauer made reservations and deposited money for Spiegel to travel on the Hamburg-America Line. Spiegel waited for the final word from the AAUW.[32]

But then, as it did for so many refugees, a more restrictive U.S. immigration policy and the closing of U.S. consulates in German-occupied countries made it impossible for Spiegel to leave. In September, Spiegel sent Brunauer a card with her picture. No more was heard. On December 8, the Hamburg-America Line wrote Brunauer to return the deposit on Spiegel's booking with "deep regret." Six months later, a visitor from Germany provided an update on the possibilities of emigration from Prague. The AAUW "determined, we thought, beyond all doubt that it was impossible for Dr. Spiegel to emigrate," but "if there is still a chance that she may be able to get out of Germany and come to the United States . . . we want to do all in our power to help her."[33]

There was nothing in the AAUW's power to do. Eight months earlier, the deportations from Prague that Spiegel had so feared began. In October and November 1941, six thousand Jews from Prague and Brno were deported directly to the Lodz and Minsk ghettos in Poland. Spiegel received a notice on October 18 to report to the Prague fairground with belongings weighing no more than fifty-five pounds. She and thousands of other Jews waited there for three days with little food or water. On October 21, they were transferred to the train station and boarded a third-class passenger car. Spiegel was on the second transport from Prague, Transport B, known cynically as the "VIP" transport because it consisted of academics, lawyers, physicians, artists, and businesspeople. About one thousand Jews were on Transport B, including 116 children. They arrived the next day in the late afternoon in poor weather at the outskirts of the Lodz ghetto. The Prague Jews were quickly unloaded and registered. Spiegel either died in Lodz or was among the Prague deportees sent within the next ten months to the Chelmno extermination camp and murdered upon arrival.[34]

Leonore Brecher

Like Schirmann and Spiegel, the Viennese biologist Leonore Brecher had turned to both the Emergency Committee and the AAUW to help her survive. In April 1940, the Emergency Committee had squelched any possibility of her obtaining an American university position. She thus fixed all her remaining hope on Brunauer and the AAUW. In the year since she had received the devastating news from the Emergency Committee, Brecher had been forced to move to Leopoldstadt, where all the city's Jews were to live, crammed into collective apartments with other families. Her chances of immigrating under the regular Rumanian quota had not improved. Her number of 3,749 meant she would not be called for another six years.[35]

Lena Madesin Phillips, the president of the International Federation of Professional and Business Women, who had provided Brecher's affidavit, thought she and Brunauer might be able to stave off Brecher's deportation by at least guaranteeing her transportation expenses of $400. Brunauer agreed to contribute but did not think it would do any good. "Just about everything has been done on this side now that can be done for Dr. Brecher," Brunauer told Phillips in June 1941. The main problem was that Brecher could not get any quota preference. She was not eligible for a non-quota visa, having "not been in a teaching position" and "not coming to a teaching position in this country." (The latter seemed to be more of a problem than the former; the Emergency Committee's Drury said that Brecher might qualify, but no teaching offers were forthcoming.) Brunauer concluded: "We have had to send disappointing information to many university women abroad who thought that just because they were scientists and scholars they would have preference under the quota."[36]

Brunauer's letter to Brecher four days later was a bit less grim, notifying her that the university women would pay for her transportation and the money had been deposited with the American Jewish Joint Distribution Committee. She would be able to come to the United States as soon as her quota number came up, which Brunauer considered her only chance. Brunauer concluded: "Hoping that it will not be very long before your number is called up."[37]

Brecher, however, realized it would be a long time. Three months later in September 1941, she reinvigorated her efforts to obtain a non-quota visa, providing a testimonial to the AAUW from Hans Przibram, with whom she had worked. The testimonial indicated that she had con-

ducted "the practical university courses for experimental zoology," seemingly establishing her teaching credentials. "Professor Przibram writes
that he hopes it will serve me to obtain a non quota visa," Brecher wrote.
"I hope too that it may help me obtain a non quota visa." A clearly agitated Brecher could not remember whether she had sent the testimonial
previously. "I beg you very much to help me if possible to emigrate very
soon, in which way this may be possible," she concluded her letter.[38]

On October 15, 1941, the first systematic deportation of Jews from
Vienna began. (Schirmann had been caught up in an earlier, more limited action.) Ten days later, Brunauer wired Phillips, explaining that she
had received a cable from the AAUW's contact in Switzerland. It read:
"brecher in greatest danger deportation stop contact phillips about cuba
visa." Brunauer's cable to Phillips asked plaintively: "what do you suggest
be done. please wire." Aware of the danger, Brecher tried to take matters
into her own hands as much as she could. She knew she needed to go to
a U.S. consulate (the State Department had closed the one in Vienna in
the summer) and arrange for a transit visa to Spain. But to get the Spanish visa, she needed a U.S. visa allowing her to travel to the United States
from Spain. She asked Brunauer to contact the State Department or, if
State did not come through, to help her obtain a tourist visa to Cuba that
would enable her to leave at once. "It is now very urgent for me to emigrate," Brecher wrote. She followed up by providing Phillips with the
names and addresses of three immigration lawyers in New York City.
Phillips advised Brunauer that they should try to obtain a tourist visa
to Cuba for Brecher, which will involve "an additional several hundred
dollars if necessary."[39]

The last hope seemed to trickle away the following month with
the suspension of American Export Lines from Lisbon. Phillips cabled
Brunauer on December 10, 1941, indicating that Brecher had not replied
to her cable. The same day Brunauer received a cable reading: "fear there
is little hope now and brecher's silence may indicate expectation of nazi
authorities that migration even to cuba will soon be impossible." Two
weeks later Phillips seemed resigned to Brecher's fate: "There seems nothing to be done for poor Dr. Brecher at the moment." Phillips received
a letter from Brecher on January 6, 1942, asking for help obtaining a
Cuban visa, but the letter was almost two months old. "So far as I can see

nothing can be done about this," Phillips wrote. "The post office here advises us that even letters may no longer be sent to German occupied territories."[40]

Six months later, the American Jewish Joint Distribution Committee "collected conclusive proof that Dr. Leonore Brecher has no possibility to migrate and is still in Germany or German-occupied territory." In September 1942, Brecher was ordered to report to Sperlschule, the school where she had worked briefly after being fired from her institute position. The school had been converted to a deportation center in February 1941. Deportees could wait there for days, sleeping on the floor without proper sanitation. On September 14, Brecher boarded a train at the Aspangbahnhof station at 7:08 p.m. along with about a thousand other Jews. She was prisoner 703 on Transport #41. Two days later, the deportees were transferred to freight cars at the main train station in Wolkowysk. They arrived at 4:30 a.m. at Maly Trostinec, the largest extermination camp in Belarus, located on the outskirts of Minsk. Only seventeen Viennese Jews are known to have survived Maly Trostinec. The fifty-five-year-old Brecher was almost certainly among the Jews herded immediately to the open pits in the nearby forest and shot to death.[41]

Hedwig Kohn

When the start of the European war derailed her plans to go to Scotland to work in a lab, physicist Hedwig Kohn, like Spiegel and Brecher, turned to Esther Brunauer. The AAUW had been one of several organizations that had been helping Kohn since she lost her professorship at the University of Breslau in December 1933. In early 1940, Kohn decided to pursue the option she had described to Brunauer a year earlier. She tried to get permits to enter either Sweden or Switzerland. She would use the small grants awarded her by Princeton, the university women, and a Dutch committee to support her while she waited for her U.S. visa. In April, Erna Hollitscher of the International Federation of University Women informed Brunauer that the money Kohn had would not be enough. The Jewish Community of Stockholm, Kohn's guarantor, would be responsible for her only if 150 kronor were available every month for as long as she had to stay in Sweden, which, as Hollitscher wrote with emphasis, "may be several years!" Hollitscher asked: "Do you think that Dr. Kohn's American friends will undertake to give the Jewish Community of Stockholm such a far-reaching guarantee?"[42]

Before Brunauer could respond, Princeton professor Rudolf Ladenburg, who assisted German physicists' emigration efforts, learned Kohn could not wait any longer. He wrote Brunauer on May 7, 1940, that he had received a letter from Kohn the previous day, indicating that she had "to know definitively by the middle of June where to go, otherwise it is too late." Ladenburg added that he had learned "indirectly that the Gestapo presses her; if she has no country to go to, she will be transported by force, probably to Poland, and that means practically death." As he was writing the letter to Brunauer, Ladenburg received a cable from Sweden saying Kohn would be deported within weeks.[43]

Ladenburg followed up with a concrete suggestion. Kohn was having trouble getting a Swedish permit because her American quota number was too high, meaning it looked like she would have a long stay in Sweden. It might help, Ladenburg suggested, if Kohn had official letters showing that she had been invited to join an American university in a year or so. Brunauer got on it, though she warned Ladenburg she was not optimistic. She had already tried to place Kohn "with no success at all." Most women's colleges did not have the money to hire anyone permanently, and those that did preferred refugees who were already in the States and could be interviewed. Yet Brunauer said she would write again to "some of the college presidents whom I think would be most sympathetic" on the chance they might "reconsider the problem in light of Dr. Kohn's pending deportation to Poland."[44]

That same day, Brunauer sent a letter to the presidents of seven women's colleges, asking whether he or she could provide a letter inviting Kohn for the 1941–1942 academic year. Brunauer got the response she had anticipated from President Constance Warren of Sarah Lawrence ("We feel that it would be utterly impossible for us to offer a position, sight-unseen") and President David Robertson of Goucher (the college cannot add staff).[45]

But President Meta Glass of Sweet Briar College stepped up. She acknowledged that hiring Kohn would be difficult for both the college and for Kohn. As a small undergraduate institution, Sweet Briar had a tiny physics department with just one professor; it could not possibly make use of Kohn's abilities as an advanced physicist with a specialized research agenda. Still, Glass was willing to invite Kohn for 1941–1942, cover her living expenses, and have her lecture occasionally and pursue her research "if we have any apparatus that will be useful in what she is trying to do." Glass understood Kohn's predicament. "What we have to offer is plainly a makeshift," Glass wrote. "She may, however, rather have this than deportation to Poland."[46]

Glass sent the invitation to Kohn on June 3. Brunauer informed Ladenburg. She then received another, more hesitant response from President Mildred McAfee at Wellesley. McAfee had difficulty persuading "some of our men lest Dr. Kohn be a 'front' for propaganda purposes." As long as Brunauer could assure her Kohn was "a bona fide refugee" and that she would be the only one the college was asked to hire, McAfee was ready to invite her as a "visiting research worker."[47]

Brunauer initially assumed the Sweet Briar offer would be enough to make Kohn a good candidate for a U.S. non-quota visa, but then Ladenburg indicated Kohn would probably need two years of employment, not just one. So Brunauer cabled McAfee: "Dr. Kohn seems in immediate danger of deportation to Poland which in present circumstances amounts to slavery, starvation or both. It would be tremendously helpful if Wellesley would offer second year under conditions suggested." It worked: Kohn had an offer from Sweet Briar for 1941–1942 and from Wellesley for 1942–1943. At the same time Duke University professor Hertha Sponer, a German refugee physicist, separately had arranged for a position for Kohn with the Women's College in Greensboro, which was affiliated with the University of North Carolina. The offer was for the academic year beginning in a few months. "The plan is get her immediately to Sweden or Switzerland and have her apply for a non-quota visa there," Brunauer wrote.[48]

At the end of June 1940, Kohn wrote Brunauer that as a result of the American universities' offers, she had obtained a permit to enter Sweden. She arrived in Stockholm on July 9. Her American sponsors still needed to shepherd her through the non-quota visa process and figure out how the $500 available for her would be apportioned. Sponer informed Brunauer she had told UNC's president that Kohn's salary would be paid using those funds. It also was apparent that Kohn would not arrive in the States in time for the fall 1940 term.[49]

Kohn boarded a Trans-Siberian Railway train on October 12, 1940, for Vladivostok, where she waited for three weeks for a boat to Yokohama. By the time she reached Japan, her scheduled steamship had already left for Seattle. She waited some more, finally taking a South American boat to San Francisco. After a long cross-country trip, she arrived in Greensboro. Among her first tasks was to write Brunauer to thank her for her help. "I have heard from Professor Sponer and Professor Ladenburg how much you have done for me till the last moment," Kohn wrote on January 12, 1941, from the safety of North Carolina. "I know it is especially to your help that I owe the positions at the Women's Colleges and only those positions enabled me to get out of Europe, to come to this country and to live here—in other words to find a new life in this difficult time."[50]

Epilogue

In May 1942, a trickle of refugees was still leaving Europe; eight hundred to nine hundred were expected to arrive in the United States within the next month or two. But it was becoming more difficult by the day as more ports refused to let ships depart and more governments refused to let refugees in. The Rockefeller Foundation thus concentrated on finding positions for scholars already in this country, particularly as researchers rather than as professors. It also explored possible positions in Latin America.[1]

By 1942, universities were actively looking for foreign scholars even though the U.S. involvement in the war meant that many of the candidates were enemy aliens. "We are all confronted by the general question of how far we as a public institution can go in employing individuals who are technically from enemy alien countries," wrote University of Minnesota's Malcolm Wiley, dean and assistant to the president. "How can we draw a line between enemy aliens and friendly aliens? I am certain there is a distinction between these two groups and yet I do not know that we could convince some of our constituents of it."[2]

The need for professors seemed to overcome these hesitations in many instances. The Emergency Committee's executive committee reported in March 1942 that "despite growing discrimination against aliens, the Committee has heard of five opportunities in the past week alone in the following fields: physics, languages, dramatics and philosophy." Four months later, the Emergency Committee counted forty-one institutions in the hunt, many listing several positions, including Princeton, Boston College, and the University of Connecticut. (Some on the list noted that they would not hire women or enemy aliens.) In the meantime, refugee scholars became caught up in the U.S. fight against Nazi Germany. The Emergency Committee tallied the war work done by its 304 grantees as of June 30, 1942: of the 263 who replied (scholars at Hebrew University in Jerusalem had not been heard from "doubtless because of distance"), 31 were employed by the government and another 87 were engaged in the war effort in some way, from being involved in military training programs to being civilian defense volunteers and blood donors. Several of their children were in the military.[3]

With little possibility of getting anyone out of Europe in 1943, the Emergency Committee was no longer placing scholars from overseas, but instead was taking care of people who were already here. In addition to funneling them to universities newly in need of personnel, the committee began awarding small grants to refugee scholars to pursue academic projects in the United States. From the forms these scholars filled out seeking grants, it was evident that their lives were not, and would never be, like those of other academics. Asked to describe their "social status," many responded along the lines of "wife and children last heard were in Poland, presumed dead." Ernst Honigmann's application listed his discipline (geography), his age (fifty-two), his academic status (librarian), his previous affiliation (Berlin Prussian State Library), his specialty (ancient and medieval geography), and his social status (widower, two children in Belgium whose fate was unknown). When sociologist Joseph Bunzel sought a grant to write a book on the social history of theater, a committee official noted on his application: "Dr. Bunzel's wife is ill and depressed. His own father was killed by the Nazis; his mother and another relative and his wife's parents were 'deported' by Nazis."[4]

As the war neared its end and the Emergency Committee prepared to close up shop, some key players from the committee and from the New School formed a new organization. In 1945, Stephen Duggan, Nelson Mead (a history professor at the City College of New York and Emergency Committee member), Alfred Cohn, and Alvin Johnson created the American Committee for Émigré Scholars, Writers and Artists. The American Committee would help refugee scholars and artists in the United States through a "modest" grant program for research, writing, and other creative projects. When hiring picked up after the war, the new committee turned to job placement, calling "the attention of over 1500 college presidents to the great pool of potential teaching talents." Informed of more than 250 college openings, the committee was optimistic that "eventually all refugee intellectuals who have real contributions to make in the field of teaching can be absorbed into our educational system."[5]

The American Committee also realized that a new influx of "professors, research specialists, writers and artists" would be arriving in the United States who had undergone the horrors of the extermination campaign. This group could not move right into faculty positions; they required "short-term sympathetic and highly specialized assistance." In addition, the American Committee provided "modest financial assistance" to these new refugees "to tide them over" so they could "reestablish their equilibrium, resume their studies and become familiar with American customs and institutions." The committee received funding from the National Refugee Service and the American Christian Committee for Refugees, as well as small contributions from foundations and private sources. By December 1946, the American Committee had placed thirty-one scholars at small and lesser-known colleges where the "scholars are regarded as great prizes."[6]

For the scholars whose lives and deaths are chronicled in this book, the only remaining question is whether and how they were, and are, remembered. Traces appear, some physical, some in the cyber world. A commemorative stepping stone rests outside Max Fleischmann's house at 14 Rathenauplatz (then Kaiserplatz) in Halle, explaining that "here lived Prof. Dr. med. Max Fleischmann." A plaque honoring Otto and Hedwig Hintze adorns their apartment building in Charlottenburg, Berlin. Free University awards a Hedwig Hintze Prize for the Advancement of Women to a female scholar who has written an outstanding dissertation in history. The Austrian Academy of Sciences includes Leonore Brecher as one of its victims of National Socialism. Marie Anna Schirmann is listed among the most important Austrian scientists. The University of Vienna recounts her difficult experiences at that institution. Käthe Spiegel is the subject of articles in German journals. Even occasional citations to their work float to the surface, such as a footnote in a recent article on Catholic identity that described Spiegel's "pioneering" 1929 paper on Polish universities. In death, Michel Gorlin seems to have been eclipsed by his wife, Raissa Bloch-Gorlin, whose poems have been reprinted, whose time in the French Resistance has been recounted, and whose life is the subject of a 2017 book.[7]

Those who survived, Hedwig Kohn and Mieczyslaw Kolinski, pursued academic careers in the United States. In 1941, Kohn began teaching at the University of North Carolina's Women's College. She decided to forgo the Sweet Briar offer and stay at the Women's College for another year, replacing a professor who went to the Naval Academy. President Meta Glass, who had agreed quickly to offer Kohn a position in 1940, was understanding. Kohn did go to Wellesley for the prearranged academic year. She remained there as a professor, setting up a modest lab for flame spectroscopy that introduced students to research. In 1952, the West German government awarded Kohn a pension and the title of professor emeritus. That year, she retired from Wellesley, but not from research. Duke professor Hertha Sponer, who had found the Women's College position for Kohn a decade earlier, arranged for her to become a research associate in a Duke laboratory. Kohn finally returned to the research she was forced to abandon in the 1930s—measuring the absorption and concentration of atomic species in flames. She published several works based on this research, including a section on radiometry for a textbook. Kohn worked in the Duke lab until shortly before her death in 1964 at the age of seventy-seven.[8]

In the immediate postwar years, Mieczyslaw Kolinski and his wife, Edith, continued to live in Belgium. They both were active in the musical scene—Mieczyslaw composing another ballet based on a scenario his wife developed, and Edith performing her own piano sonatas at the Amsterdam Concertgebouw and other compositions at the Palais des Beaux Arts in Brussels. In 1951, the couple moved to New York, where Mieczyslaw was a music therapist, an editor for a music press, and a cofounder of the Society for Ethnomusicology. His scholarly work at that time relied on the Herskovits's recordings to challenge the perception that European and African musical elements were too different to meld into a musical whole. He sought to identify and emphasize the links between musical languages from populations spread across the globe. In 1966—twenty-seven years after he received the offer at Northwestern University—Kolinski finally had his chance to teach as well as write and compose, joining the University of Toronto music faculty. He continued to develop methods to analyze melodies and rhythms across cultures, adding Iroquois, French Canadian, and British Isles music to his studies. And he continued to compose, from simple bagatelles to larger pieces in a modernist style. When he retired from the University of Toronto a decade after he began, Kolinski received the title emeritus, the first time the university had bestowed that honor. He died in Toronto on May 7, 1981, at the age of seventy-nine.[9]

The Emergency Committee ended operations in 1946. The New School's graduate program became just another graduate school. The AAUW focused once again on the advancement of American scholars. And the Rockefeller Foundation returned to making career-building, not life-saving grants. Some of the American professors and professionals who had dedicated a decade of their lives to trying to save refugee scholars turned to helping them survive in the United States, as Duggan and Cohn did at the American Committee. In 1946, Stephen Duggan retired from the Institute of International Education that he founded and that gave birth to the Emergency Committee. He died in 1950 at the age of eighty. Alfred Cohn continued to work as a cardiologist at the Rockefeller Institute until he died in 1957 at the age of seventy-eight. Rudolf Ladenburg retired from Princeton in 1950 and died two years later at the age of sixty-nine.[10]

Other refugee advocates continued the humanitarian work and liberal advocacy that had brought them to the refugee issue. One did not. The Rockefeller Foundation's Alexander Makinsky, who had helped dozens of refugee scholars in Lisbon in 1940 and 1941, initially followed the path of several other advocates, including his foundation colleague, Alan Gregg, in helping to launch the United Nations. Three years later, however, Makinsky went in a different direction. In 1946, he became a European executive with the Coca-Cola company, helping to launch the all-American drink in France.[11]

Alvin Johnson retired from the New School in 1945 after twenty-four years leading the university. He was seventy-one. He had left academia in 1917 to spend four years as an editor at the relaunched *New Republic,* an important organ of liberal opinion, and then joined the New School for the next two decades. Upon retirement from the New School, Johnson returned to his writing roots. He penned his autobiography, *Pioneer's Progress* (1952), and published dozens of articles in both academic and popular journals, extolling liberal values in education and in society. He wrote several that touched on his refugee work ("The Jewish Problem in America," 1947) and the new state of Israel ("The Scientific Future of Israel," 1948). He died in 1971 at the age of ninety-six.

Yale law professor Edwin Borchard, a fervent isolationist on the basis of his belief in neutrality as a legal principle, continued to oppose U.S. foreign policy, though he muted his criticism of the Second World War. He represented the American Civil Liberties Union in the infamous 1944 U.S. Supreme Court case of *Korematsu v. United States* that upheld the internment of U.S. citizens of Japanese ancestry. Borchard and the ACLU were on the losing side. Borchard's most lasting legacy, however, was not in the international arena. He was among the first legal scholars to highlight cases of defendants who had been wrongly convicted and to argue for their right to compensation. In 2007, *Justice Denied,* a magazine for the wrongly convicted, recognized Borchard "as the first consistent voice in the country for innocent people enmeshed in the legal system." The honor came fifty-six years after this death in 1951 at the age of sixty-six.[12]

Northwestern's Melville Herskovits also became a pioneer, in the new discipline of African American studies. In his scholarly work, including *The Myth of the Negro Past* (1941), Herskovits argued that being black in the United States did not so much reflect a racial category as a cultural inheritance. Music and his work with Mieczyslaw Kolinski helped lead him to the understanding that African Americans had not lost all connection to their cultural origins. In 1948, Herskovits founded the first major interdisciplinary program in African studies at Northwestern, followed six years later by the establishment of a library to hold the world's largest collection of Africana. In 1957, he founded the African Studies Association and became its first president. Herskovits also argued during the postwar period for the independence of African colonies from their European rulers. After Herskovits's death in 1963 at the age of sixty-seven, the Black Panthers and other black nationalists used his work in making their case for the importance of their African heritage.

Several of the refugee advocates' dedicated liberalism and internationalism led to run-ins with the government during the McCarthy era. Columbia's Leslie C. Dunn became one of the nation's leading geneticists, known for contesting the idea of fixed and absolute biological differences due to race. His research led to his election to the National Academy of Sciences and the American Philosophical Society. Along with his scientific work, Dunn continued to champion liberal causes. He urged the abolition of the House Committee on Un-American Activities in 1948, defended a physicist attacked for his membership in the Communist Party, and called for a cessation of the U.S. manufacture of atomic weaponry. He died in 1974 at the age of eighty.

Harlow Shapley continued to direct the Harvard College Observatory, though during the immediate postwar years he increasingly took on a national and international role. He presided over the American Astronomical Society, the American Association for the Advancement of Science, and the National Society of Sigma Xi. He remained a committed internationalist, helping to found UNESCO and championing cooperation with Soviet intellectuals even in the depths of the Cold War. His political activities got him hauled before the House Committee on Un-American Activities. "I have never seen a witness treat a committee with more contempt," its chair, John Rankin, said after emerging from a closed-door meeting with Shapley. Rankin apparently objected to Shapley bringing with him a lawyer and a secretary to take notes of the proceeding, both of whom were kicked out of the hearing. They also wrangled over Shapley's efforts to bring foreign scientists to the United States and his leadership of a left-leaning group that donated to the campaign of a liberal Massachusetts congressional candidate. Rankin eventually dropped contempt charges against Shapley. Senator Joseph McCarthy later called Shapley one of five communists connected to the State Department. The Senate Foreign Relations Committee exonerated him the same year. It was eventually discovered that during this period, from 1946 to 1953, the FBI had been spying on Shapley. He retired as observatory director in 1952, though he continued to teach and lecture. Shapley died in 1972 at the age of eighty-seven.[13]

Esther Caukin Brunauer did not get off as easily from her encounter with McCarthyism and McCarthy. Long a critic of isolationism and appeasement and supporter of international organizations, Brunauer left the AAUW in 1944 to join the State Department. She worked on laying the postwar groundwork for international cooperation, helping draft the plans for UNESCO (along with Harlow Shapley) and serving as an advisor to the delegation at the San Francisco conference establishing the United Nations. She was promoted to the rank of minister, the third woman to obtain that standing in the State Department. After rumblings from right-wing newspapers and congressmen that Brunauer was a communist fellow traveler, Senator McCarthy in 1950 turned his fire directly upon her. He identified Brunauer as one of the State employees whose disloyalty he could prove, supplying her name along with nine others to a Senate committee for investigation. With the strong backing of several AAUW officials and politicians and her own unequivocal testimony before the committee ("I am not a Communist. I have never engaged in Communist activities"), the committee exonerated her.[14]

Brunauer's ordeal, however, was not over. Her Hungarian-born husband, Stephen, had been a member of a communist-front group in his youth. Trained as a chemist, Stephen Brunauer joined the U.S. Naval Reserve during World War II and headed its high explosives research group. After the war, he continued to work for the navy as a civilian scientist, passing four security clearance investigations. In 1951, the navy suspended his clearance to do another review. The State Department then suspended Esther Brunauer and subjected her to another security review. Stephen resigned from the navy. Esther persisted but was forced from the State Department as "a security risk" in 1952. The attacks on Brunauer and the AAUW (another AAUW member, a judge and activist, also made McCarthy's list) continued into the mid-1950s in the pro-McCarthy press. The Brunauers relocated to Evanston, Illinois, where Esther worked for the Film Council of America and in publishing. She never recovered from the political assault, dying in 1959 at the age of fifty-seven.[15]

Another veteran of scholar rescue advocacy played a key role in the McCarthy trauma. Edward R. Murrow, the Emergency Committee's first secretary, left in 1935 to join CBS News. During the subsequent decade, he maintained a connection to the committee, remaining on its board, attending meetings when he was in the States, and corresponding frequently with Alfred Cohn, who had become a close friend. Murrow also was building his legendary radio career. He covered the Anschluss from Vienna, the Blitz from London, and the air war from the skies over Europe, flying on twenty-five combat missions. At war's end, Murrow stepped into the hell of Buchenwald. Murrow is probably best known for his attack on McCarthy in March 1954 on his television show *See It Now*, which is credited with helping to topple the Wisconsin senator. Murrow died in 1965 at the age of fifty-seven.

At the State Department, visa division chief Avra Warren served another decade in the department, including four ambassadorships. He died in 1957 at the age of sixty-three. His boss, Assistant Secretary of State Breckinridge Long, eventually overstepped in pushing his anti-immigrant agenda. In 1943, Long testified before a U.S. congressional committee considering establishing a rescue agency and falsely implied that the majority of the 580,000 refugees admitted from Europe during the previous decade were Jewish. In fact, only 545,000 visas had been issued, and far fewer than half of those were to Jewish refugees. The public disclosure of his false testimony became a scandal in early 1944. Long was demoted and not long afterward resigned. He died in 1958 at the age of seventy-five. The names of the consular officials who piled on paperwork and denied visas to helpless refugees have mostly been lost to history, along with an accounting of their individual culpability. What should not be lost is an understanding of how they used the law as an excuse for the cold-blooded execution of a government policy to limit immigration.

Columbia president Nicholas Murray Butler and Harvard president James Conant both served long tenures as heads of their respective universities. Butler was Columbia's president for forty-three years, retiring in 1945 and dying two years later at the age of eighty-five. Conant was Harvard's president for twenty years until President Eisenhower tapped him to be U.S. ambassador to Germany in 1953. He died in 1978 at the age of eighty-four. Both Butler and Conant are remembered, mostly, with reverence.

And what of the overall legacy of universities? German universities have yet to recover from the blow of losing more than a third of their faculty members in a half dozen years, and other European institutions suffered from similar losses. Across the ocean, U.S. universities clearly benefited from adding top European intellectuals to their ranks before and after the World War II years. Because of that lopsided success, American universities have not had to grapple with the more troubling aspects of their responses during the Nazi era. In the 1930s and early 1940s, American universities had the opportunity to hire far more refugee scholars and help them escape Europe than they did. In deciding whether to help, the academic community possessed critical information about the European scholars' cruel circumstances. From the first dismissals to the last deportations, professors and administrators received personal letters, association newsletters, and foundation appeals. They read newspapers and academic articles on the refugee scholars' plight. They attended conferences and meetings where the situation was discussed. What was at stake in hiring a refugee was not a secret. Yet many American professors expressed more concern about the dicey career paths of American graduate students and young professors than they did about the certain expulsion, persecution, and annihilation foreign scholars faced. If they did not know, it was only because they did not bother to learn. A lack of compassion led to a lack of understanding, not the other way around.

Of course, American universities were not engaged simply in rescuing European scholars; they were engaged in deciding whom to rescue. They had to make choices, and the choices were not easy. Genuine economic constraints limited hiring as the economy remained in the grip of the Depression. Even though most positions were funded from outside, universities did have to worry about what would happen when the money ran out. Almost everyone they considered was imperiled, and only so many could be employed. It made a certain sense to hire those "well worth saving." Still, it is chilling to read the casual dismissals—"not particularly outstanding," "just a routine man," "never published any well-rounded work," "competent and thorough but not brilliant," "an assistant not a leader," "not a first rate scientist—but a very nice man"—knowing what rejection meant. The American academy maintained a rigid approach to hiring, and, more particularly, to hiring Jews, when the times demanded sympathy and flexibility.

The American academy was far from alone in its indifference to the suffering of European Jews. From the military to the media, from the government to the church, U.S. institutions all failed to respond adequately, and often with greater consequences. American universities bear a particular burden, however. They did not confront undifferentiated mass misery in numbers too large to imagine. They encountered Leonore Brecher and Marie Anna Schirmann and Max Fleischmann and hundreds of other people with names and faces and histories. In faculty conference rooms throughout the country, academics scoured refugees' curriculum vitae and probed personal predicaments and decided the fates of individual human beings.

American professors also were not powerless in the face of persecution, as many other Americans were. They had a concrete, immediate way to help. Some tried in heroic ways, but many more did not. And the academy as a whole never took concerted action. Professors did not organize, as they did in Great Britain, to raise funds to support foreign scholars so that private organizations would not have to rely on the same "rich Jews." They did not present a united front to challenge U.S. consuls' contradictory interpretations of the non-quota visa provisions, leaving it to Edwin Borchard and a few others to go back and back again to the State Department. They did not support the efforts of some scholars, such as Columbia's Leslie Dunn, to pressure the government to create a "refugee" category under immigration law, or to provide government ships to transport refugees with U.S. visas. No major leader in the American academy took up the mantle of trying to save scholars and scholarship in the face of a threat not just to them, but to the entire idea of a global community dedicated to pursuing knowledge.

In 1936, just three years into the refugee scholar project, the Rockefeller Institute's Alfred Cohn grappled with what drove him and those like him. "The difference between people has been and is: have they compassion—the bowels of compassion some call it," Cohn wrote. Others would ask him, "'Why are you borrowing trouble?' I don't know, except there's nothing else to borrow and having a heart, and a mind too, you can't help it. As long as I can I mean to help."[16]

Appendix 1: U.S. Organizations and Personnel

The following organizations played a central role in determining whether refugee scholars could come to the United States.

American Association of University Professors
Ralph E. Himstead Jr., general secretary

American Association of University Women
Esther Caukin Brunauer, associate, international relations program
Kathryn McHale, general director

American Committee for Christian German Refugees
Alice Waldo, personnel secretary

American Friends Service Committee
Ruth Pope, educational counselor
Annelise Thieman, staff

Brown University
Roland Richardson, mathematics professor and dean of the graduate school

Bryn Mawr College
Hertha Kraus, professor, social work and social research
Marion Park, president

Columbia University
Franz Boas, anthropology professor
Nicholas Murray Butler, president
Joseph Chamberlain, law professor
Leslie C. Dunn, geneticist and zoology professor
Frank Fackenthal, secretary

Duke University
　　Hertha Sponer, physics professor

Emergency Committee in Aid of Displaced Foreign Scholars
　　Alfred E. Cohn, founder and executive committee board member
　　Betty Drury, assistant secretary
　　Stephen Duggan, secretary and chair
　　Leslie C. Dunn, executive committee board member
　　Livingston Farrand, chair
　　Bernard Flexner, founder and executive committee board member
　　Charles Liebman, executive committee board member
　　Edward R. Murrow, assistant director
　　Laurens Seelye, assistant director
　　Fred M. Stein, founder, treasurer, executive committee board member
　　John Whyte, assistant secretary

Emergency Committee in Aid of Displaced Foreign Medical Scientists
　　Alfred Cohn, founder
　　Bernard Sachs, founder and chair

Emergency Rescue Committee
　　Varian Fry, emissary

Harvard University
　　George H. Chase, dean, graduate school of arts and sciences
　　George David Birkhoff, mathematics professor and dean, arts and sciences
　　C. Sidney Burwell, dean, medical school
　　James Conant, president
　　David Edsall, dean, medical school
　　Felix Frankfurter, law professor
　　Carl Friedrich, government professor
　　Jerome Greene, secretary
　　A. Lawrence Lowell, president
　　Harlow Shapley, director, Harvard College Observatory

Hebrew Union College
　　Julian Morgenstern, president

Institute for Advanced Study
　　Frank Aydelotte, director
　　Albert Einstein, physicist
　　Abraham Flexner, director
　　Oswald Veblen, mathematician
　　Hermann Weyl, mathematician

International Federation of Professional and Business Women
　　Lena Madesin Phillips, president

International Federation of University Women
    Erna Hollitscher, head of emergency relief
    Karin Kock, vice president

Johns Hopkins University
    Isaiah Bowman, president

National Refugee Service (National Coordinating Committee)
    Joseph Chamberlain, chair
    Cecilia Razovsky, director, migration department

New School for Social Research
    Alvin Johnson, president
    Herbert Solow, assistant to the president
    Else Staudinger, coordinator of affiliate, American Council for Émigrés in the Professions

Northwestern University
    Melville Herskovits, anthropology professor

Princeton University
    Rudolf Ladenburg, physics professor

Rockefeller Foundation
    Thomas Appleget, vice president
    August Wilhelm Fehling, German representative, social sciences, Berlin
    Raymond Fosdick, president
    Alan Gregg, director, medical services division
    Tracy Kittredge, assistant director, social sciences division, Paris
    Robert Lambert, program director, Paris
    Alexander Makinsky, director, health commission, Paris
    John Marshall, associate director, humanities division
    Max Mason, president
    Daniel O'Brien, assistant director, medical services division, Paris
    John Van Sickle, assistant director, social sciences division, Paris
    Joseph Willets, director, social sciences division

Rockefeller Institute for Medical Research
    Alfred E. Cohn, cardiologist and clinical researcher
    Phoebus Levene, head, biochemical laboratory

Sweet Briar College
    Meta Glass, president

U.S. State Department
    Adolf Berle, assistant secretary
    Eliot Coulter, acting visa division chief
    H. F. Cunningham Jr., vice consul, Berlin
    Breckinridge Long, assistant secretary

George Messersmith, consul, Berlin; minister, Austria; assistant secretary
of state
Louis Sussdorf Jr., consul-general, Antwerp
Avra Warren, visa division chief
Sumner Welles, assistant secretary of state

University of Buffalo
David Riesman, law professor

University of California, Berkeley
Max Radin, law professor

Wellesley College
Mildred McAfee, president

Yale University
Edwin Borchard, law professor

Appendix 2: Displaced Scholars and How They Fared

This list includes all the displaced scholars mentioned in this book with the exception of the eight scholars followed most closely. When appropriate, it includes the name of the U.S. university that hired the scholar, enabling him or her to immigrate. It does not include other U.S. universities at which the scholar may have worked.

Eugen Altschul	Economics, University of Frankfurt; dismissed 1933	Fled to Great Britain; University of Minnesota
Jacques Ancel	Political geography, University of Paris; dismissed 1940	Survived in France
Erna Barschak	Psychology, education, public institute for teaching vocational education, Berlin; dismissed 1933	Fled to Great Britain, returned to Germany, returned to Great Britain; Wilson College, 1940
Albert Bayet	Sociology, École pratique des hautes études, Paris	Survived in France
David Belorizky	Astronomy, Marseille Observatory; dismissed 1942	Survived, hiding in France
Jean Benoit-Levy	Film, Paris	New School for Social Research, 1941

Max Bergmann	Chemistry, Kaiser Wilhelm Institute for Leather Research; dismissed 1934	Rockefeller Institute for Medical Research, 1934
Felix Bernstein	Mathematics, University of Göttingen; dismissed 1933	Columbia University, 1934
Grete Bernstein	Journalism, University of Frankfurt; dismissed 1933	Fate unknown
Marta Navarra Bernstein	French, English literature, Jewish High School, Milan; dismissed 1938	Survived in Italy
Ludwig Berwald	Mathematics, German University, Prague	Died in Lodz Ghetto, 1942
Marianne Beth	Law, sociology, Vienna	Reed College, 1939
Elias Bickerman	History, University of Berlin; dismissed 1933	Fled to France; New School for Social Research, 1941
Franz Bielschowsky	Medicine, biochemistry, University of Freiberg; dismissed 1933	Fled to the Netherlands, Spain, Great Britain
Marc Bloch	History, Sorbonne until 1940, University of Montpellier; dismissed 1942	Joined Resistance; executed by German firing squad, 1944
Harald Bohr	Mathematics, University of Copenhagen	Fled to Sweden, 1943, Great Britain, United States
Niels Bohr	Physics, University of Copenhagen	Fled to Sweden, Great Britain, United States
Moritz Bonn	Economics, Berlin Business School; dismissed 1933	Fled to Great Britain, United States
Guilbert Boris	Arab studies	Fate unknown
Rudolf Breitscheid	Economics, Social Democratic Party delegate to Reichstag	Died in Buchenwald, 1944
Max Brod	Journalism, literature, Prague	Fled to Tel Aviv
Eberhard Bruck	Law, University of Bonn; dismissed 1936	Harvard University

Martin Buber	Jewish Studies, University of Frankfurt; resigned upon Hitler becoming chancellor, then barred from teaching 1933	Hebrew University
Richard Charmatz	Journalism, history, Vienna	Survived the war
Victor Conrad	Seismology, University of Vienna; put on leave 1934, retired 1936	Harvard University, 1938
Martin David	Law, University of Leiden, the Netherlands	Sent to Barneveld, Westerbork transit camps, Theresienstadt; survived
Harry Dember	Physics, Technical University, Dresden; dismissed 1933	University of Istanbul, Rutgers College
Felix DeRoy	Astronomy, journalism, Brussels	Fled to France, returned to Brussels, died there, 1942
Adolf Drucker	Economics, Vienna	American University
Ludwig Edelstein	History of medicine, University of Berlin; dismissed 1933	Johns Hopkins University, 1934
Tilly Edinger	Paleontology, Naturmuseum Senckenber, Frankfurt; dismissed 1933, worked in secret until 1938	Fled to Great Britain, 1939; Harvard University, 1940
Albert Ehrenzweig	Law, University of Vienna	Fled to Great Britain, United States
Ludwik Ehrlich	Law, Jan Kazimierz University, Lwów; fired 1940	Survived in hiding in Poland, joined Resistance
Ruth Ehrmann	Philology, Kalinski School, Berlin	Fled to Great Britain, 1939; Chile, 1940
Gustav Embden	Physiology, University of Frankfurt; dismissed 1933	Died 1933
Paul Eppstein	Sociology, University of Mannheim	Died in Theresienstadt, 1944
Oscar Fehr	Medicine, Virchow Hospital, Berlin	Fled to Great Britain

Ludwig Feuchtwanger	Publishing, academic house	Fled to Great Britain
Eva Lehmann Fiesel	Etruscology, University of Munich; dismissed 1933	Yale University
Jerzy Finkelkraut	Jurisprudence, University of Warsaw	Fate unclear
Victor Egon Fleischmann	Medicine; lost position at German annexation of Austria	Died in Dachau, 1940
Philipp Frank	Physics, mathematics, philosophy, German University, Prague; left 1938	Harvard University, 1939
E. Finlay Freundlich	Astronomy, director of Einstein-Institut, Potsdam; dismissed 1933	University of Istanbul; German University, Prague; St. Andrews, Scotland
Herbert Freundlich	Chemistry, Kaiser Wilhelm Institut für Elektrochemie, Berlin; dismissed 1933	Fled to the Netherlands, Great Britain; University of Minnesota
Hans Fried	Mathematics, Vienna	Swarthmore College
Paul Friedlander	Philology, University of Halle; dismissed 1935	Johns Hopkins University, 1939
Walter Froehlich	Mathematics, German University, Prague	Died in Lodz Ghetto, 1942
Hilda Geiringer	Mathematics, University of Berlin; dismissed 1933	Fled to Brussels, University of Istanbul; Bryn Mawr College
Charlotte Giese	Art, Berlin	Fate unknown
Hans Giese	Art history, architecture, University of Berlin; dismissed 1937	Fate unknown
Walter Gottschalk	Library science, Prussian State Library	Fled to the Netherlands, Brussels; University of Istanbul, 1942
George Gougenheim	Linguistics, University of Strasbourg, France	Survived in France
Henri Gregoire	History, Free University of Brussels	New School for Social Research, 1941

Kurt Grelling	Logic, secondary schools, Germany; left 1937	Fled to Brussels, sent to France, 1940; deported to Auschwitz, 1942, and died there
Leo Gross	Law, University of Cologne; dismissed 1933	Fled to Switzerland, Great Britain, France; Tufts University
Ernst Grunfeld	University of Halle	Committed suicide in Germany, 1938
Max Grünhut	Law, University of Jena; dismissed, 1933	University of Oxford
Hans Guggenheimer	Medicine, University of Berlin; dismissed	Fled to Sweden, 1939
Emil Gumbel	Mathematics, University of Heidelberg; forced out 1932	Fled to France; New School for Social Research, 1941
Hans Habe	Journalism, literature, Vienna	Fled to France, United States
Else Hirschberg	Chemistry, University of Rostock; dismissed 1933	Died in Auschwitz, 1942
Ludwig Hirszfeld	Bacteriology, University of Warsaw; dismissed 1940	Imprisoned in Warsaw Ghetto, survived in hiding
Rudolf Hober	Physiology, University of Kiel; dismissed 1933	University of Pennsylvania
Herman Hoepke	Anatomy, University of Heidelberg; dismissed 1939; wife "first-class mixed race"	Survived in Heidelberg
Ernst Honigmann	History, librarian, France	Imprisoned in Saint-Cyprien concentration camp, 1940; United States
Max Horkheimer	Philosophy, Institute of Social Research, Frankfurt; institute closed 1933	Fled to Geneva; Columbia University, 1934
Charlotte Houtermans	Physics, University of Göttingen; left 1933	Fled to Great Britain, Soviet Union, Denmark, Great Britain, United States
Helene Jacobi	Biology, Institute for Experimental Biology, Vienna	Died at Maly Trostinec extermination center, 1942

Vladimir Jankélévitch	Philosophy, University of Lille; dismissed 1940	Joined the Resistance, survived in France
Herbert Jehle	Physics, research assistant, British and Belgian universities and institutes	Imprisoned in Gurs concentration camp, 1940; Harvard University, 1942
Auguste Jellinek	Physiology, neurology, University of Rome; dismissed 1939	Fled Germany to Italy; Washington University, 1939
Victor Jollos	Zoology, University of Berlin; dismissed 1935	University of Wisconsin
Paul Jossmann	Medicine, Charité Hospital, University of Berlin; dismissed 1935	Boston University
Victor Kafka	Neuropathology, University of Hamburg	Fled to Norway, Sweden
Hans Kalmus	Genetics, biology, German University, Prague	University College London, 1939
Fritz Kant	Psychiatry, University of Munich	Harvard University
Regine Kapeller-Alder	Medicine, Vienna	University of Edinburgh
Erich Kaufmann	Law, University of Berlin	Survived in hiding in the Netherlands
Rudolf Keller	Biochemistry, private laboratory, Prague	Fled to Sweden, 1939; Great Britain; United States
Paul Kimmelsteil	Medicine, Hamburg-Eppendorf; dismissed 1933	Harvard University
Hans Kleinmann	Chemistry, Berlin University; dismissed 1933	Medical College of Virginia
Gustav Kollmann	Biochemistry, Austria	Fate unknown
Arthur Korn	Physics, Berlin Institute of Technology; dismissed 1935	Stevens Institute of Technology, 1940
Franz Kramer	Neuropsychiatry, Charité Hospital, University of Berlin; dismissed 1935	Fled to the Netherlands, Dutch East Indies
Hans Krebs	Medicine, biochemistry, University of Freiberg; dismissed 1933	Cambridge University

Richard Kroner	Philosophy, University of Kiel; dismissed 1933	Fled to Great Britain; Union Theological Seminary
Peter Ladewig	Pathology, Berlin; left 1935	University of Istanbul, 1935
Heinz Langerhaus	Economics, sociology	Imprisoned in Germany, 1933; transferred to Sachsenhausen concentration camp, 1936; Brussels, 1939; Gurs concentration camp, 1940; Gettysburg College, 1942
Paul Langevin	Physics, director École de Physique et Chimie, Paris	Held under house arrest throughout the war
Emil Lederer	Economics, University of Berlin; dismissed 1933	New School for Social Research, 1933
Karl Lehmann-Hartleben	Archeology, University of Münster; dismissed 1933	Fled to Italy; New York University
Bela Lengyel	Physics, astronomy, Pázmány University, Hungary; left 1935	Harvard University, 1936
Arthur Lenhoff	Law, University of Vienna; dismissed 1938	University of Buffalo
Claude Lévi-Strauss	Anthropology, lycée, Montpellier; dismissed 1940	New School for Social Research, 1941
Heinrich Liepmann	Economics, University of Heidelberg	Fled to Great Britain
Julius Lips	Ethnology, sociology, University of Cologne; dismissed 1933	Sorbonne; Columbia University, 1934
Otto Loewi	Medicine, pharmacology, University of Graz; dismissed 1938	Fled to Great Britain; New York University
Adolf Löwe	Economics, University of Frankfurt; dismissed 1933	University of Manchester; New School for Social Research
Otto Lowenstein	Neuropsychiatry, Bonn; dismissed 1933	University of Geneva; New York University
Louis Madelin	History, France	Remained in France
Harald Mankiewicz	Law, University of Lyon	Fled to Shanghai

Paul Mantoux	History, France	Remained in France
Franz Mautner	German literature, Vienna	University of Delaware, 1938
Hans Mayer	Philosophy, law	Fled to France, Switzerland
André Mazon	Linguistics, Institute of Slavic Studies, Paris	Survived in France
Alfredo Mendizabal	Law, University of Oviedo, Spain	Fled to France during Spanish Civil War; New School for Social Research, 1942
Karl Menger	Mathematics, University of Vienna; left 1931	Harvard University, 1931
Maurice Merleau-Ponty	Philosophy, France	Remained in France
Margarete Merzbach-Kober	German literature, Berlin	Deported to Theresienstadt, 1943; survived
Julie Meyer	Sociology, journalism	New School for Social Research
Otto Meyerhof	Medicine, Kaiser Wilhelm Institute for Medical Research, Heidelberg; left 1938	Fled to France; University of Pennsylvania
Ignace Meyerson	Medicine, psychology, Paris, Toulouse	Joined the French Resistance, survived
Alexander Michelson	Public finance, Pau, France	Fate unknown
Boris Mirkine-Guetzévitch	Law, Paris Institute of Comparative Law	New School for Social Research, 1941
Robert Mosse	Law, economics, University of Grenoble; dismissed 1940	New School for Social Research, 1941
Alice Mühsam	Art history, classical archeology	Fled to United States, 1939
Hugo Müller	Economics, German Institute of Technology, Prague	Fate unknown
David Nachmansohn	Biochemistry, University of Berlin	Sorbonne, 1933; Yale University, 1939
Helen Nathan	Library science, Berlin School of Librarians	Committed suicide in Berlin, 1940

Max Neuberger	History of medicine, University of Vienna; lost position 1933	Fled to Great Britain
Otto Neurath	Philosophy	Great Britain
Emmy Noether	Mathematics, University of Göttingen; dismissed 1933	Bryn Mawr College, 1934
Arthur Nussbaum	Law, University of Berlin; dismissed 1933	Columbia University, 1934
Leopold Perels	Jurisprudence, University of Heidelberg; dismissed 1933	Survived Gurs internment camp
André Philip	Economics, finance, University of Lyon	Fled to Great Britain
Alfred Philippson	Geography, University of Bonn; dismissed	Deported to Theresienstadt, 1942, survived
Ludwig Pick	Pathology, Friedrichshain-Berlin Hospital	Died in Theresienstadt, 1944
Felix Plaut	Psychiatry, Deutsche Forschungsanstalt für Psychiatrie, Munich; dismissed 1935	Died, Great Britain, 1935
Leonard Polak	Philosophy, University of Groningen; dismissed 1940	Died in Sachsenhausen concentration camp, 1941
Hans Pollnow	Neuropsychiatry, Charité Hospital, University of Berlin; dismissed 1935	Fled to France; died in Mauthausen concentration camp, 1943
Hans Przibram	Biology, Institute for Experimental Biology, Vienna; dismissed 1938	Fled to the Netherlands; died in Theresienstadt, 1944
Karl Przibram	Physics, Radium Institute, Vienna; dismissed 1938	Fled to Belgium, survived in hiding
Philipp August Rappaport	Architecture, Essen, Germany	Imprisoned in Lenne, mixed-race camp; escaped 1945
Bruno Rossi	Physics, University of Padua; dismissed 1938	Denmark, Great Britain; University of Chicago, 1939
Edgar Rubin	Psychology, University of Copenhagen	Fled to Sweden, 1943

Gottfried Salomon	Sociology, University of Frankfurt; dismissed 1933	Fled to France; New School for Social Research
Richard Salomon	History, University of Hamburg; dismissed 1934	Rotating positions at Bryn Mawr, Swarthmore, University of Pennsylvania, 1937
Arthur Salz	Sociology, economics, University of Heidelberg; dismissed 1933	Fled to Great Britain; Ohio State University, 1934
Jean-Paul Sartre	Philosophy, France	Remained in France
Richard Schatzki	Medicine, University Hospital, Leipzig; dismissed 1933	Harvard University
Gerhard Schmidt	Physiology, University of Frankfurt; dismissed 1933	Fled to Italy, Sweden, Canada; Tufts University
Hans Joachim Schoeps	Religion, University of Erlangen	Fled to Sweden
Elly Elisabeth Schuck	Austrian Federation of University Women	Deported to Theresienstadt, 1942; Auschwitz, 1944, died there
Fritz Schulz	Law, University of Berlin; transferred to University of Frankfurt, 1934; dismissed 1935	Fled to the Netherlands, 1939; Great Britain
Eugenia Schwarzwald	Education, head of girls' school, Austria	Fled to Switzerland
Ernst Emil Schweitzer	Jurisprudence, Berlin	Imprisoned at Gurs concentration camp; deported to Auschwitz, 1942, likely died there
Hellmuth Simons	Bacteriology, University of Dusseldorf	Fled to Great Britain, Soviet Union, France, Switzerland
Hugo Sinzheimer	Law, University of Frankfurt; dismissed 1933	Fled to the Netherlands; deported to Theresienstadt, 1940; released and survived in hiding
Friedrich Solmsen	Classics, University of Berlin; left Germany mid-1930s	Olivet College

Clemens Sommer	Art history, Greifswald University; left 1937	Sweden, University of North Carolina
Arthur Spanier	Librarian, Lehranstalt Seminary, Berlin	Fled to the Netherlands; died at Bergen-Belsen, 1942
Friedrich Spiegelberg	Theology, University of Dresden; dismissed 1937	Columbia University, 1937
Walther Spielmeyer	Neuropathology, Anatomisches Laboratorium der Psychiatrischen und Nervenklinik, Munich	Died of tuberculosis, 1935
Edmund Stein	Jewish Studies, Warsaw Institute of Jewish Studies	Died at Majdanek extermination center, 1943
Gabriel Steiner	Neurology, University of Heidelberg	Wayne State University
Selma Stern-Taubler	History, Akademie für die Wissenschaft des Judentums, Berlin	Hebrew Union College, 1941
Alfred Storch	Psychiatry, Psychiatric University Hospital Giessen; dismissed 1933	Fled to Switzerland, 1934
Walter Sulzbach	Sociology, University of Frankfurt; dismissed 1933	Claremont College, 1937
Helena Syrkus	Architecture, Warsaw	Imprisoned in Poland, 1944; survived
Simon Syrkus	Architecture, Warsaw	Sent to Auschwitz, 1942; survived
Otto Szasz	Mathematics, University of Frankfurt; dismissed 1933	Massachusetts Institute of Technology, 1934
Alfred Tarski	Mathematics, University of Warsaw; left 1939	Harvard University, 1939
Rafael Taubenschlag	Law, University of Kraków; left 1939	Fled to France; New School for Social Research, 1941
Eugen Taubler	History, University of Heidelberg; dismissed 1933	Hebrew Union College, 1941

Edward Teller	Physics, University of Göttingen; left 1933	Fled to Great Britain, Denmark, Great Britain; George Washington University, 1933
Siegfried Thannhauser	Medicine, University of Freiberg	Tufts University
Paul Tillich	Theology, University of Frankfurt; dismissed 1933	Columbia University, 1933
Arthur von Hippel	Physics, University of Göttingen	University of Istanbul; Denmark; Massachusetts Institute of Technology, 1936
Eric von Hornbostel	Musicology, ethnography, University of Berlin	Fled to Great Britain; died there, 1935
Henry D. von Witzleben	Psychiatry, superintendent, State Institute for Nervous and Mental Diseases, Kreischa, Germany	United States, 1939
Jean André Wahl	Philosophy, Sorbonne	Imprisoned in Drancy camp, escaped; New School for Social Research, 1942
Friedrich Waismann	Philosophy, Vienna	University of Oxford
Raymond Warnier	Economics, French Institute, Lisbon	Fate unknown
Robert Wartenberg	Neurology, University of Freiberg; left Germany 1935	University of California, Berkeley
André Weil	Mathematics, University of Strasbourg; dismissed 1940	Lehigh University
Max Weinreich	Linguistics, Yiddish Scientific Institute, Vilna	City College of New York
Franz Xaver Weiss	Economics, German University, Prague	Fled to Great Britain
Helene Wieruszowski	Library science, Bonn University Library; dismissed 1934	Fled to Spain, Italy, United States
Hans Winterstein	Physiology, University of Breslau	University of Istanbul

Paul Wittek	Ottoman Studies, German Archaeological Institute; dismissed 1933	Fled to Brussels; Great Britain, 1940
Katherina Wolf	Psychology, Vienna	Yale University
Georg Wunderlich	International law; forced to leave Germany 1936	United States

Notes

Archives and abbreviations are as follows.

AAUWA	American Association of University Women Archives, Washington, DC
AFSC	American Friends Service Committee
AFSC Case Files	American Friends Service Committee Refugee Assistance Case Files 2002.296, U.S. Holocaust Memorial Museum, Washington, DC
Alfred Cohn Papers	Alfred E. Cohn Papers, Record Group 450 C661, Rockefeller University Archives, Rockefeller Archive Center, Sleepy Hollow, NY
APS	American Philosophical Society, Philadelphia
CJH	Center for Jewish History, New York
Emergency Committee	Emergency Committee in Aid of Displaced Foreign Scholars
Emergency Committee Papers	Emergency Committee in Aid of Displaced Foreign Scholars Papers, MSSCOL 922, Manuscripts and Archives Division, New York Public Library
FCLM	Francis A. Countway Library of Medicine, Boston
HUA	Harvard University Archives, Cambridge, MA
Melville Herskovits Papers	Melville Herskovits Papers, General Files 1906–1942, Northwestern University Archives, Evanston, IL
NYPL	New York Public Library, New York
RAC	Rockefeller Archive Center, Sleepy Hollow, NY
RF	Rockefeller Foundation

RG   Record Group

UACL   University Archives and Columbiana Library, New York

UASUNY   American Council for Émigrés in the Professions Papers, German and
            Jewish Intellectual Émigré Collection, University at Albany, State
            University of New York

USHMM   U.S. Holocaust Memorial Museum, Washington, DC

YUA   Yale University Archives, New Haven, CT

Introduction

1. Ladenburg to Brunauer, May 7, 1940; Ladenburg to Brunauer, May 24, 1940; Brunauer to Ladenburg, May 25, 1940, all Box 839, Folder Hedwig Kohn, Committee Records 8111, AAUWA. Helping Kohn in Sweden were Karin Kock, a lecturer at the University of Stockholm involved with the International Federation of University Women, and Lise Meitner, a former Kaiser Wilhelm Institute professor who had fled to Sweden in 1938. Meitner is considered to have been unfairly denied the Nobel Prize awarded to her long-time collaborator Otto Hahn in 1944.

2. Ladenburg to Brunauer, May 7, 1940, ibid.

3. Brunauer to Glass, May 25, 1940, ibid. On the same date the same letter was sent to the presidents of Goucher, Connecticut College, New Jersey College for Women, Wellesley, Vassar, and Sarah Lawrence.

4. U.S. Department of State, Press Releases, January 21, 1939, Box 814, Folder International Relations Committee Records, Committee Records 8111, AAUWA; Bat-Ami Zucker, *In Search of Refuge: Jews and the American Consuls in Nazi German 1933–1941* (London: Vallentine Mitchell, 2001), 159.

5. This is the final tally of the Emergency Committee. Stephen Duggan and Betty Drury, *The Rescue of Science and Learning: The Story of the Emergency Committee in Aid of Displaced Foreign Scholars* (New York: Macmillan, 1948); Johnson to Gannett, December 5, 1938, Box 4, Folder 58; Johnson to Florence, August 1, 1941, Box 4, Folder 154, both UASUNY; a later accounting of fifty-eight scholars the foundation had tried to help included six who "failed to reach America."

6. Appleget, "The Foundation's Experience with Refugee Scholars," March 5, 1946, Box 1, Folder 11, Record of the Emergency Committee, RG-19.061, USHMM.

7. Turkey took in 190 refugee scholars. Arin Namal and Arnold Reisman, "Friedrich Dessauer Transferred Leading Edge Western Radiology Knowhow to the Young Turkish Republic While a Refugee from Nazism," European Association for the Study of Science and Technology, *EASST Review* 26, nos. 3/4 (2007), http://docplayer.net/41520932-Easst-review-volume-26-3-4-european-association-for-the-study-of-science-and-technology-september-easst-review-volume-26-2007-number-3-4.html. Two studies of Canadian institutions found that Canada had a worse record than either the United States or Great Britain. "In total, only five scholars were permanently placed in Canadian universities, and one additional person held a temporary appointment. This left Canada behind Egypt, India, Brazil, and Australia. . . . The situation becomes even worse when one

considers that all of those scholars who found permanent academic positions in Canadian universities were funded by a special program of the American-based Carnegie Foundation. Before the Second World War, not a single academic refugee was fully funded from Canadian sources." David Zimmerman, "'Narrow-Minded People': Canadian Universities and the Academic Refugee Crises, 1933–1941," *Canadian Historical Review* 88 (June 2007): 294, 315. See also Paul Stortz, "'Rescue of Our Family from a Living Death': Refugee Professors and the Canadian Society for the Protection of Science and Learning at the University of Toronto, 1935–1946," *Journal of the CHA 2003 Revue de la S.H.C.* 14 (2003): 231–61.

8. There is a voluminous scholarly literature on the intellectual migration and its impact on the American academy. See, for instance, Mitchell G. Ash and Alfons Sollner, eds., *Forced Migration and Scientific Change: Émigré German-Speaking Scientists and Scholars After 1933* (Washington, DC: German Historical Institute, Cambridge University Press, 1996); Norman Bentwich, *The Rescue and Achievement of Refugee Scholars: The Story of Displaced Scholars and Scientists 1933–1952* (The Hague: Martinus Nijhoff, 1953); Lord Beveridge, *A Defence of Free Learning* (London: Oxford University Press, 1959); Richard Bodek and Simon Lewis, eds., *The Fruits of Exile: Central European Intellectual Immigration to America in the Age of Fascism* (Columbia: University of South Carolina Press, 2010); Lewis A. Coser, *Refugee Scholars in America* (New Haven: Yale University Press, 1984); Duggan and Drury, *The Rescue of Science and Learning;* Gabrielle Simon Edgcomb, *From Swastika to Jim Crow: Refugee Scholars at Black Colleges* (Malabar, FL: Krieger, 1993); Axel Fair-Schulz and Mario Kessler, *German Scholars in Exile* (Lanham, MD: Lexington Books, 2011); Laura Fermi, *Illustrious Immigrants: The Intellectual Migration from Europe 1930–41,* 2nd ed. (Chicago: University of Chicago Press, 1971); Donald Fleming and Bernard Bailyn, *The Intellectual Migration: Europe and America, 1930–1960* (Cambridge: Harvard University Press, 1969); Anthony Heilbut, *Exiled in Paradise: German Refugee Artists and Intellectuals in America, from the 1930s to the Present* (New York: Viking, 1983); H. Stuart Hughes, *The Sea Change: The Migration of Social Thought, 1930–1965* (New York: McGraw-Hill, 1977); Jarrell C. Jackman and Carla M. Borden, eds., *The Muses Flee Hitler: Cultural Transfer and Adaptation 1930–1945* (Washington, DC: Smithsonian Institution, 1983); Claus-Dieter Krohn, *Intellectuals in Exile: Refugee Scholars and the New School for Social Research* (Amherst: University of Massachusetts Press, 1993); Jean-Michel Palmier, *Weimar in Exile: The Antifascist Emigration in Europe and America* (London: Verso, 2006); Helmut F. Pfanner, *Exile in New York: German and Austrian Writers After 1933* (Detroit: Wayne State University Press, 1983); and Peter I. Rose, ed., *The Dispossessed: An Anatomy of Exile* (Amherst: University of Massachusetts Press, 2005). There are also many biographies of individual scholars and journal articles too numerous to list. Stephen H. Norwood's important book, *The Third Reich in the Ivory Tower: Complicity and Conflict on American Campuses* (New York: Cambridge University Press, 2009), 29–33, touches on American universities' reception of refugee scholars, but his focus is primarily on the academy's stance on Nazi Germany more generally.

9. Christian Fleck, "Emigration of Social Scientists' Schools from Austria," in Ash and Sollner, eds., *Forced Migration and Scientific Change,* 219. See also Lewis J. Edinger,

German Exile Politics (Berkeley: University of California Press, 1956), ix; Catherine Epstein, "Schicksalsgeschichte: Refugee Historians in the United States," in Harmutt Lehmann and James J. Sheehan, eds., *An Interrupted Past: German-Speaking Refugee Historians in the United States After 1933* (Cambridge: Cambridge University Press, 1991), 116–17; Karen J. Greenberg, "The Mentor Within: The German Refugee Scholars of the Nazi Period and Their American Context," PhD diss., Yale University, 1987.

10. John M. Spalek and Robert F. Bell, eds., *Exile: The Writer's Experience* (Chapel Hill: University of North Carolina Press, 1982), xiii. That estimate of the number of autobiographies was made in 1982, so undoubtedly more autobiographies have been published although the pace has slowed in more recent years; Wilfred M. McClay, "Weimar in America," *American Scholar* 55, no. 120 (Winter 1985/1986): 71.

11. Erika and Klaus Mann, *Escape to Life* (Boston: Houghton Mifflin, 1939), 194–98, 299–301; see Richard Breitman and Alan Kraut, *American Refugee Policy and European Jewry, 1933–1945* (Bloomington: Indiana University Press, 1987); Richard Breitman and Allan J. Lichtman, *FDR and the Jews* (Cambridge: Harvard University Press, 2013); Henry Feingold, *The Politics of Rescue: The Roosevelt Administration and the Holocaust 1938–1945* (New York: Walden, 1980); Saul S. Friedman, *No Haven for the Oppressed: United States Policy Toward Jewish Refugees, 1938–1945* (Detroit: Wayne State University Press, 1973); David Wyman, *The Abandonment of the Jews: America and the Jews, 1941–1945* (New York: Pantheon, 1984); and David Wyman, *Paper Walls: America and the Refugee Crisis 1938–1941* (New York: Pantheon, 1985). Only Zucker, *In Search of Refuge*, 159–60, discusses the separate immigration issues of professors, but only briefly. Michael A. Meyer provided one of the first accounts of the immigration process in examining refugee scholars, but he focused on a small group hired by Hebrew Union College. "The Refugee Scholars Project of the Hebrew Union," in Bertram Wallace Korn, ed., *A Bicentennial Festschrift for Jacob Radar Marcus* (New York: Ktav, 1976), 359–75.

12. Reinhard Siegmund-Schultze, *Mathematicians Fleeing from Nazi Germany: Individual Fates and Global Impact* (Princeton, NJ: Princeton University Press, 2009), explicitly takes up this mission, yet the book's focus remains on the refugees, not the American universities. Nathan Reingold, "Refugee Mathematicians in the United States, 1933–1941: Reception and Reaction," in Jackman and Borden, eds., *The Muses Flee Hitler*, 205–32, also examines mathematicians. There has been excellent work in other individual disciplines. See Paul K. Hoch, "The Reception of Central European Refugee Physicists of the 1930s: U.S.S.R., U.K., U.S.A.," *Annals of Science* 40 (1983): 217–46; Kyle Graham, "The Refuge Jurist and American Law Schools, 1933–1941," *American Journal of Comparative Law* 50, no. 4 (Fall 2002): 777–818; Michael Groth, "The Road to New York: The Emigration of Berlin Journalists 1933–1945," PhD diss., University of Iowa, 1983 (focuses more on the adjustment to the United States and less on the actual immigration process); and Karen J. Greenberg, "'Uphill Work': The German Refugee Historian and American Institutions of Higher Learning," in Lehmann and Sheehan, eds., *An Interrupted Past*, 94–101. Epstein, "Schicksalsgeschichte," 116–17, studied all ninety "'first-generation' individuals who eventually taught history or published extensively on historical topics in the United States." She found a mixed record of success. Fleck, "Emigration of Social Scien-

tists' Schools from Austria," 209, 219, found that most Austrian émigrés in the social sciences "were able to establish themselves permanently in the countries to which they fled." Still, he noted many "had considerable difficulties in exile," including Edgar Zilsel, a social theorist and philosopher of science who committed suicide in the United States. Alfons Sollner found a similar phenomenon with the sixty-four political scientists he studied; 85 percent obtained a permanent position in political science in the United States. "From Public Law to Political Science? The Emigration of German Scholars After 1933 and Their Influence on the Transformation of a Discipline," in Ash and Sollner, eds., *Forced Migration and Scientific Change,* 254. Bernard Grossfeld and Peter Winship, "The Law Professor Refugee," *Syracuse Journal of International Law and Commerce* 18, no. 3 (1992): 1–18, contrasted the lives of law professors Arthur Lenhoff and Ernst Rabel, both of whom found relative success in the United States but who experienced tribulations and frustrations. Yael Epstein, "When the Nobel Prize Was Not Enough: Jewish Chemists from the Nazi Regime as Refugees in the United States," in Bodek and Lewis, eds., *The Fruits of Exile,* 127–55, attempts to explain chemists' unique difficulties both in immigrating to the United States and in adjusting to the industry and academy here. Epstein's acknowledgment of the refugee chemists' difficulties and her willingness to tackle American antisemitism are admirable, yet her lack of understanding of the immigration process and the operations of assistance organizations makes many of her conclusions questionable. Guy Stern, "Writers in Extremis," *Simon Wiesenthal Center Annual* 3 (1985), Museum of Tolerance Online, Multimedia Learning Center, http://motlc.wiesenthal.com /site/pp.asp?c=gvKVLcMVIuG&b=395031, looked at the lives of several artists and writers who were not able to emigrate, or what he terms "thwarted exile," among the "hundreds" who "perished in the concentration camps." He does not examine their attempts at emigrating. That the story is still not well known is evident from the reaction of Rutgers University law professor Richard Hyland in his review of *Roman Lawyers and the Holocaust: Max Radin, Cartas Romanisticas (1923–50)* in *The American Journal of Comparative Law* 51 (April 2003): 457–70. Although the book focuses primarily on Radin's posture on Roman law, Hyland is most interested in and most shocked by the correspondence over hiring refugee scholars. "In this book, real life erupts in our midst. We witness the best—or at least the most prestigious—members of our profession as they make fateful decisions. Today these decisions seem horrifying—or even worse, inexplicable. Each time I try to imagine whether I would have reacted differently I feel a shortness of breath. This is not a book for the faint of heart" (460). What led Hyland to be heartsick was the unwillingness of distinguished legal scholars, such as Roscoe Pound, dean of the Harvard Law School, and Charles Clark, dean of the Yale Law School, to help Hermann Kantorowicz, "one of the most distinguished legal scholars in Germany, a teacher who had taught in this country—a teacher who in fact had taught them" (464). Hyland recounts the repeated rejections of dozens of distinguished legal scholars and then concludes: "The humiliation, and worse, of dozens of the world's leading legal scholars could have been prevented by a couple of phone calls from the dean to sympathetic alumni. Yet at the defining moment of the twentieth century, our nation's great law schools refused. Whatever we think of it, this is our heritage" (470).

13. Brunauer to Ladenburg, June 5, 1940, Box 839, Folder Hedwig Kohn, Committee Records 8111, AAUWA.

Chapter 1. The Nazi University

1. Peter M. Rutkoff and William B. Scott, *New School: A History of the New School for Social Research* (New York: Free Press, 1986), 88. See also Claus-Dieter Krohn, *Intellectuals in Exile: Refugee Scholars and the New School for Social Research* (Amherst: University of Massachusetts Press, 1993), 41.

2. Officer's Diary, O'Brien, Box 115, Folder 1933–1934, RF RG12.1, RAC.

3. Ibid.; O'Brien to Gregg, April 11, 1933, Box 91, Folder 725, RF RG2, RAC. Embden died that year; the circumstances of his death are not clear. Schmidt fled Germany and after some wandering found his way to the United States and a successful research career at Tufts University. Herman Kalckar, "Gerhard Schmidt, 1901–1981," *Biographical Memoir* (Washington, DC: National Academy of Sciences, 1987), http://www.nasonline.org/publications/biographical-memoirs/memoir-pdfs/schmidt-gerhard.pdf.

4. Thannhauser to Lambert, O'Brien, April 10, 1933, Box 1, Folder 27, Alfred Cohn Papers. Thannhauser asked the Rockefeller Foundation to grant fellowships outside of Germany to the two assistants, Franz Bielschowsky and Hans Krebs. Krebs, whom the Rockefeller Foundation helped go to Cambridge University, became a professor of biochemistry at the University of Oxford and won a Nobel Prize. Bielschowsky escaped to the Netherlands and eventually settled in New Zealand. Thannhauser himself immigrated to the United States in 1934 and joined the Tufts medical school faculty; Officer's Diary, O'Brien, Box 115, Folder 1933–1934, RF RG12.1, RAC; O'Brien to Gregg, April 11, 1933, Box 91, Folder 725, RF RG2, RAC.

5. Doron Niederland, "The Emigration of Jewish Academics and Professionals from Germany in the First Years of Nazi Rule," *Year Book* 33 (1988): 291.

6. "University Disturbances Dismissal of Professors by the Minister of Education," Box 91, Folder 726, RF 2 (1933), RAC.

7. Memo, May 15, 1933, Box 91, Folder 724, RF RG2, RAC; Sachs to Boas, August 10, 1933, Box 164, Folder 6, Emergency Committee Papers.

8. Officer's Diary, Lambert, May 8, 1933, Box 91, Folder 725, RF RG1.1, RAC.

9. Officer's Diary, O'Brien, April 2–3, 1933, Box 115, Folder 1933–1934; O'Brien to Gregg, April 11, 1933, Box 91, Folder 725, RF RG2, RAC. See Eric D. Kohler, "Relicensing Central European Physicians in the United States, 1933–1945," *Simon Wiesenthal Center Annual* 6 (1987): Chapter 1, Museum of Tolerance Online, Multimedia Learning Center, http://motlc.wiesenthal.com/site/pp.asp?c=gvKVLcMVIuG&b=395145; Harriet Pass Freidenreich, *Female, Jewish and Educated* (Bloomington: Indiana University Press, 2002), 81; and Herbert A. Strauss, ed., *Jewish Immigrants of the Nazi Period in the USA* (New York: K. G. Sauer, 1987), 160. O'Brien to Gregg, April 11, 1933; Van Sickle to Day, May 1, 1933; Van Sickle to Day, April 29, 1933, all Box 91, Folder 725, RF RG2, RAC.

10. Van Sickle to Day, May 8, 1933, Box 91, Folder 725, and Van Sickle to Day, June 5, 1933, Box 91, Folder 726, both RF RG2, RAC. See also Fehling to Day, May 13, 1933, Box

91, Folder 726; Officer's Diary, Lambert, July 3, 1933, Box 91, Folder 727; Lambert to Gregg, May 10, 1933, and Lambert to Gregg, April 26, 1933, Box 91, Folder 725, all RF RG2, RAC.

11. O'Brien to Gregg, April 11, 1933, Box 91, Folder 725, RF RG2, RAC.

12. Gerhard Ritter, *German Refugee Historians and Friedrich Meinecke* (Leiden: Brill, 2010), 79–91. Meinecke, paradoxically, justified his firing of Hintze by claiming that a politically tainted editor would tarnish the scientific character of the journal. *Historische Zeitschrift* soon began publishing articles on the "Jewish question" and the outcome of "Jew research," as well as favorable reviews of the works of anti–Jewish studies scholars. Karl Alexander Muller replaced Meinecke as editor in 1935. Horst Junginger, *The Scientification of "The Jewish Question" in Nazi Germany* (Leiden, Brill, 2017), 205–6; Hintze to Institute for Displaced German Scholars, March 14, 1939, Box 72, Folder 48, Emergency Committee Papers.

13. Klaus Taschwer, Johannes Feichtinger, Stefan Sienell, and Heidemarie Uhl, eds., *Experimental Biology in the Vienna Prater: On the History of the Institute for Experimental Biology 1902 to 1945* (Vienna: Austrian Academy of Sciences, 2016), 36–37; Klaus Taschwer, "Andenken an eine völlig vergessene Forcherim," *DerStandard*, September 23, 2012, https://derstandard.at/1348283731761/Andenken-an-eine-voellig-vergessene-Forscherin.

14. General Information, Allgemeine Auskunft, September 6, 1934, Box 46, Folder 34, Emergency Committee Papers; Brecher to Dunn, December 5, 1933, Leonore Brecher 1930–1938, L. C. Dunn Papers, R:D19, APS.

15. Rina Lapidus, *Jewish Women Writers in the Soviet Union* (London: Routledge, 2012), 50.

16. Memo, John Van Sickle, May 18, 1933, Box 91, Folder 726, RF RG2 RAC.

17. "Report Concerning the Present Situation at German Universities in So Far as Mathematics and Theoretical Physics Are Concerned," Rockefeller Foundation, June 26, 1933, Box 190, Folder 7, Emergency Committee Papers.

18. Karen J. Greenberg, "The Search for the Silver Lining: The American Academic Establishment and the 'Aryanization' of German Scholarship," *Simon Wiesenthal Center Annual* 2 (1985): Chapter 6, Museum of Tolerance, Multimedia Learning Center, http://motlc.wiesenthal.com/site/pp.asp?c=gvKVLcMVIuG&b=395009.

19. Junginger, *Scientification of "The Jewish Question,"* 135–42, 155–57, 164–65, 197.

20. "Mieczyslaw Kolinski," Universität Hamburg, Institut für Historische Musik wissenschaft, https://www.lexm.uni-hamburg.de/object/lexm_lexmperson_00001287.

21. Herskovits to Kolinski, February 13, 1932; April 6, 1932; November 10, 1932, all Melville Herskovits Papers, Mieczyslaw Kolinski Box 11, Folder 23.

22. Kolinski to Herskovits, April 24, 1933; Herskovits to Kolinski, May 11, 1933; Herskovits to Kolinski, April 2, 1934, ibid.

23. Herbert A. Strauss, "Jewish Emigration in the Nazi Period: Some Aspects of Acculturation," in Julius Carlebach, Gerhard Hirschfeld, Aubrey Newman, Arnold Paucker, and Peter Pulzer, eds., *Second Chance: Two Centuries of German-speaking Jews in the United Kingdom* (Tubingen: J. C. B. Mohr, 1991), 93. The overall number of those dismissed can vary quite a bit depending on the time frame and the definition of an aca-

demic, which sometimes does and sometimes does not include faculty members who did not teach or medical doctors with university affiliations. Marjorie Lamberti, "The Reception of Refugee Scholars from Nazi Germany in America: Philanthropy and Social Change in Higher Education," *Jewish Social Studies: History, Culture Society* 12 (Spring/ Summer 2006): 159, uses the number two thousand from Germany and Austria, including nonuniversity research scientists. Claus-Dieter Krohn, "American Foundations and Refugee Scholars Between the Two Wars," in Guiliana Gemelli, ed., *The "Unacceptables": American Foundations and Refugee Scholars Between the Two Wars and After* (Brussels: P.I.E.–Peter Lang, 2000), 35, estimates that four thousand scientists lost their positions for political or "racial" reasons; Officer's Diary, O'Brien, March 6–7, 1934, Box 115, Folder 1933–1934, RF RG12.1, RAC.

24. Arye Carmon, "The Impact of the Nazi Racial Decrees on the University of Heidelberg," *Yad Vashem Studies* 11 (1976): 131–41.

25. Officer's Diary, O'Brien, December 6, 1935, Box 115, Folder 1935–1938, RF RG 12.1, RAC.

26. Officer's Diary, O'Brien, September 14, 1936, ibid.

27. Demuth to Gregg, November 24, 1937, Box 4, Folder 13; Minutes, Emergency Committee Executive Committee Meeting, April 21, 1937, Box 6, Folder 20; Unidentified to Nason, March 9, 1938; Cohn to Duggan, April 1, 1938; Cohn to Drury, April 22, 1938, Box 4, Folder 14, all Alfred Cohn Papers.

28. Krohn, "American Foundations," 12.

29. Gortner to Stein, June 5, 1933, and Gortner to Weaver, May 10, 1933, both Box 118, Folder Minnesota University 1933, Emergency Committee Papers. Freundlich went first to University College, London, and then joined the University of Minnesota faculty in 1939. He died in 1941 at the age of sixty-one. Gortner continued to be interested in bringing top scholars to the United States, heading Minnesota's committee for German scholars. Gortner to Drury, February 15, 1938, Box 4, Folder 14, Alfred Cohn Papers. When the war started, Gortner also suggested trying to persuade the U.S. government to allow Europe's "outstanding natural scientists" to immigrate to help the government's defense efforts. Gortner to Duggan, June 9, 1941, Box 4, Folder 31, Alfred Cohn Papers.

30. Hansen to May, April 26, 1933, Box 91, Folder 725; and Spencer to Gregg, April 28, 1939, both Box 1, Folder 27, Alfred Cohn Papers.

31. Karen J. Greenberg, "The Mentor Within: The German Refugee Scholars of the Nazi Period and Their American Context," PhD diss., Yale University, 1987, 49–53; Notes, Dr. Kotschnig's Visit to U.S.A., January 6–March 10, 1936, Box 2, Folder 15; Minutes, Emergency Committee Executive Committee Meeting, February 26, 1936, Box 6, Folder 20, both Alfred Cohn Papers.

32. Report, Walter M. Kotschnig on his Visit to American Colleges and Universities, February 16–April 24, 1936; Notes, Dr. Kotschnig's Visit to U.S.A. Winter 1936; Notes, Dr. Kotschnig's Visit to the U.S.A., April 13 to April 16, all Box 2, Folder 15, Alfred Cohn Papers.

33. Boas to Butler, May 3, 1933, Box 318, Folder 7, Franz Boas Collection, UACL; See, for example, Hamburger to Johnson, December 17, 1940, Box 3, Folder 99; Jeffrey to

Johnson, October 19, 1940, Box 6, Folder 71; Sontag to Johnson, November 25, 1940, Box 6, Folder 143, all UASUNY; Carol Paul-Merritt, "The Reception of the German Writers in Exile by the American Liberal Press 1933–1945: Changes and Trends," in John M. Spalek and Robert F. Bell, eds., *Exile: The Writer's Experience* (Chapel Hill: University of North Carolina Press, 1982), 97, 105–6.

34. See C. A. Browne, "The Role of Refugees in the History of American Science," *Science* 91, no. 2357 (March 1, 1940), 203–8; Eduard Heimann, "The Refugee Speaks," *Annals of the American Academy of Political and Social Science* 203 (May 1939): 106–13; Richard H. Heindel, "The Alien Scientist and the War," *Annals of the American Academy of Political and Social Science* 223 (September 1942): 144–48; and Robert M. W. Kempner, "Who Is Expatriated by Hitler: An Evidence Problem in Administrative Law," *University of Pennsylvania Law Review and American Law Register* 90, no. 7 (May 1942): 824–29. Greenberg, "Search for the Silver Lining."

Chapter 2. Rescue Efforts

1. Brecher to Dunn, July 4, 1930, and Dunn to Brecher, November 21, 1930, both Leonore Brecher 1930–1938, L. C. Dunn Papers, R:D19, APS.

2. Brecher to Dunn, December 5, 1933, ibid.

3. Compton to Rosenwald, November 12, 1938, Box 4, Folder 15, Alfred Cohn Papers.

4. Interim Report, Faculty Fellowship Fund, November 27, 1933, Subject File, Folder Faculty, Faculty Fellow, and Boas to Fackenthal, June 30, 1935, Box 318, Folder 7, both Franz Boas Collection, UACL.

5. Shapley to Goldwasser, May 9, 1940, Box 1, Folder 25, Alfred Cohn Papers; Bessie Zaban Jones, "To the Rescue of the Learned: The Asylum Fellowship Plan at Harvard, 1938–1940," *Harvard Library Bulletin* 42, no. 3 (Summer 1984): 227.

6. Chamberlain to Cohn, January 10, 1939, Box 5, Folder 7, Alfred Cohn Papers.

7. Chamberlain to White, October 5, 1938, Folder 32, Joseph P. Chamberlain Papers, YIVO RG278, CJH; Riesman to Friedrich, February 7, 1940, Box 2, Folder David Riesman March–September 1940, Carl J. Friedrich Collection, HUG(FP)17.31, HUA; Riesman to Friedrich, January 8, 1940, and Riesman to Friedrich, January 19, 1940, both Box 10, Folder Friedrich Correspondence, David Riesman Jr. Collection UG9(FP)99.12, HUA; Boas to Butler, January 17, 1939; Butler to Boas, January 21, 1939; and Butler to Boas, January 6, 1941, all Box 7, Folder 7, Franz Boas Collection, UACL.

8. Reinhard Siegmund-Schultze, *Mathematicians Fleeing from Nazi Germany: Individual Fates and Global Impact* (Princeton, NJ: Princeton University Press, 2009); Fleischmann to Levene, n.d., and Levene to Fleischmann, n.d., both Rockefeller Institute for Medical Research, Manuscripts and Archives Division, NYPL; Victor Egon Fleischmann, TD #427367, International Tracing Service, USHMM. See also "List of Murdered Jews from Austria" found in Namentliche Erfassung der österreichischen Holocaustopfer, Dokumentationsarchiv des österreichischen Widerstandes (Documentation Centre for Austrian Resistance), Vienna; Kollmann to Levene, December 11, 1938;

Levene to Kollmann, January 3, 1939; and Kollmann to Levene, January 14, 1939, all Rockefeller Institute for Medical Research, Manuscripts and Archives Division, NYPL.

9. Kapeller-Adler to Levene, June 27, 1938; Levene to Kapeller-Adler, July 25, 1938; Kapeller-Adler to Levene, August 8, 1938; Levene to Kapeller-Adler, September 26, 1938; and Levene to Sachs, December 16, 1938, all Rockefeller Institute for Medical Research, Manuscripts and Archives Division, NYPL; Universität Wien, Gedenkbuch für die Opfer des Nationalsozialismus an der Universität Wien 1938, "Regine Kapeller-Adler," https:// translate.google.com/translate?hl=en&sl=de&u=https://gedenkbuch.univie.ac.at/%3Fid %3Dindex.php%3Fid%3D435%26no_cache%3D1%26person_single_id%3D11350&prev =search; Murlin to Levene, May 17, 1940, and Levene to Murlin, July 25, 1940, both Rocke-feller Institute for Medical Research, Manuscripts and Archives Division, NYPL.

10. Mitchell G. Ash, "Forced Migration and Scientific Change After 1933: A New Approach," conference paper, 2000, extended version published in Edward Timms and Jon Hughes, eds., *Intellectual Migration and Cultural Transformation: Refugees from National Socialism in the English-Speaking World* (Vienna: Springer, 2003), 241–63; American Philosophical Association newsletter, April 11, 1942, Record of the Emergency Committee, RG-19.061, USHMM; Memo, "Memorandum concerning a meeting on the placement of German refugee intellectuals," Fisher, Box 4, Folder 16, and Burks to Stoddard, April 27, 1939, Box 4, Folder 17, both Alfred Cohn Papers.

11. Nathan Reingold, "Refugee Mathematicians in the United States, 1933–1941: Reception and Reaction," in Jarrell C. Jackman and Carla M. Borden, eds., *The Muses Flee Hitler: Cultural Transfer and Adaptation 1930–1945* (Washington, DC: Smithsonian Institution Press, 1983), 210–11. See also Reinhard Siegmund-Schultze, "Rockefeller Support for Mathematicians Fleeing from the Nazi Purge," in Guiliana Gemelli, ed., *The "Unacceptables": American Foundations and Refugee Scholars Between the Two Wars and After* (Brussels: P.I.E.–Peter Lang, 2000), 88; Hans Böhm and Astrid Mehmel, "Introduction," in Alfred Philippson, *Wie ich zum Geographen wurde: aufgezeichnet im Konzentrations‐ lager Theresienstadt zwischen 1942 und 1945*, edited by Hans Böhm and Astrid Mehmel (Bonn: Bouvier, 1996), xvi–xxii; Karen J. Greenberg, "'Uphill Work': The German Refugee Historian and American Institutions of Higher Learning," in Harmutt Lehmann and James J. Sheehan, eds., *An Interrupted Past: German-Speaking Refugee Historians in the United States After 1933* (Cambridge: Cambridge University Press, 1991), 96–99.

12. Bagster-Collins to Duggan, November 3, 1933, Box 118, Folder Minnesota University 1933; Frankfurter to Cohn, March 15, 1934, Box 185, Folder 5; Sachs to Boas, August 10, 1933, and Sachs to Duggan, August 27, 1933, Box 164, Folder 6, all Emergency Committee Papers.

13. List, May 1933, Box 186, Folder 3, Emergency Committee Papers. A fall 1936 list of displaced German scholars included about 600 names under medicine, compared with 113 under law. List, Fall 1936, Box 5, Folder 13, Alfred Cohn Papers.

14. Although there was economic distress, it should be noted that not all universities and not all faculty were equally affected. Smaller schools had a harder time than larger, public ones, and non–tenure track faculty suffered more than those of at least the rank of assistant professor. Robin E. Rider, "Alarm and Opportunity: Emigration of

Mathematicians and Physicists to Britain and the United States, 1933–1945," *Historical Studies in the Physical Sciences* 15, no. 1 (1984): 124–25; Stein to Braude, October 5, 1933, Box 111, Folder Columbia University 1933, Emergency Committee Papers; Richardson to Birkhoff, February 25, 1932, Birkhoff 1–3 Nov (1931–1933), 4213.2.2, HUA; Kyle Graham, "The Refuge Jurist and American Law Schools, 1933–1941," *American Journal of Comparative Law* 50, no. 4 (Fall 2002): 777–818; Richard Hyland, Review, *The American Journal of Comparative Law* 51 (Spring 2003): 457–70, 783; Butler to Executive Officers, December 22, 1934, Box 22, Folder May 1934–December 1934, Nicholas Murray Butler Collection, UACL; Officer's Diary, O'Brien, January 11, 1935, Box 115, Folder 1935–1938, RF RG 12.1, RAC.

15. Drury to Guggenheimer, January 26, 1939, Box 164, Folder 3, Emergency Committee Papers; Hans Guggenheimer, International Tracing Service, USHMM.

16. Minutes, Emergency Committee Executive Committee Meeting, June 6, 1938, Box 6, Folder 21, and Memo, Promotional Policy, March 27, 1942, Box 1, Folder 26, both Alfred Cohn Papers; Seelye to Hildebrandt, August 21, 1942, and Seelye to Yoakum, July 24, 1942, Box 118, Folder Michigan University 1941–1942; Seelye to Johnson, April 11, 1942, Box 190, Folder 8, all Emergency Committee Papers.

17. Marjorie Lamberti, "The Reception of Refugee Scholars from Nazi Germany in America: Philanthropy and Social Change in Higher Education," *Jewish Social Studies* 12, no. 3 (Spring–Summer 2006): 157–92, 164; Duggan to Cohn, n.d., 1941, Box 186, Folder 12, Emergency Committee Papers; Drury to Cohn, June 24, 1936, Box 4, Folder 11, Alfred Cohn Papers; Duggan to Cohn, May 1, 1940, Box 186, Folder 11, and Drury to Duggan, May 5, 1941, Box 186, Folder 12, both Emergency Committee Papers. The committee did not like to publicize its Jewish support, which became an issue when a draft of the 1941 annual report included a paragraph acknowledging the group's Jewish donors and stating that most of the scholars placed were non-Aryans. One committee member, Alfred Cohn, objected strenuously to the paragraph's inclusion in the report; two others, Bernard Flexner and Charles Liebman, wanted it there. Cohn previously explained to Duggan that Jews' role in "this drama" was a "mere accident" and that it was "perhaps the greatest misfortune" to treat their role as "something separate and apart." (The original letter said "Libman," but this was most likely a typographical error.) The paragraph was included. Liebman to Cohn, May 19, 1941, Box 1, Folder 24, Alfred Cohn Papers. Drury to Duggan, May 5, 1941, and Duggan to Cohn, May 26, 1941, Box 186, Folder 12, both Emergency Committee Papers; Duggan to Keppel, April 15, 1939, Box 4, Folder 29, Alfred Cohn Papers.

18. Stephen Duggan and Betty Drury, *The Rescue of Science and Learning: The Story of the Emergency Committee in Aid of Displaced Foreign Scholars* (New York: Macmillan, 1948), 6; Report, Emergency Committee in Aid of Displaced Foreign Medical Scientists, January 27, 1942, Box 2, Folder 33, MSS I-92, American Jewish Historical Society, CJH. Another later accounting over the same time period recorded that the Emergency Committee made grants to place 150 medical scientists, primarily in teaching positions, with more than 80 percent finding permanent employment. It found research opportunities for at least another 200 refugee physicians. Report on Physicians' Com-

mittee, Biele to Beck, May 8, 1944, Box 4, Folder 7, National Refugee Service Collection, MSS I-92, American Jewish Historical Society, CJH.

19. Alvin Johnson, *Pioneer's Progress* (New York: Viking, 1952), 344–45.

20. "A Refuge for Scholars: Present Challenges in Historical Perspective," Institute for Advanced Study Working Group, 2017, https://library.ias.edu/sites/library.ias.edu /files/RefugeForScholars.pdf; see Stephen J. Whitfield, "Black Mountain and Brandeis: Two Experiments in Higher Education," *Southern Jewish History* 16 (2013): 127–68; Gabrielle Simon Edgcomb, *From Swastika to Jim Crow: Refugee Scholars at Black Colleges* (Malabar, FL: Krieger, 1993).

21. Kotschnig to Cohn, December 31, 1934, Box 2, Folder 12, Alfred Cohn Papers.

22. Claus-Dieter Krohn, "American Foundations and Refugee Scholars Between the Two Wars," in Guiliana Gemelli, ed., *The "Unacceptables": American Foundations and Refugee Scholars Between the Two Wars and After* (Brussels: P.I.E.–Peter Lang, 2000), 43–46.

23. Claus-Dieter Krohn, *Intellectuals in Exile: Refugee Scholars and the New School for Social Research* (Amherst: University of Massachusetts Press, 1993), 28; Officer's Diary, Makinsky, March 12–14, 1942, Box 96A, Folder 1942, RF RG 12.1, RAC.

24. See Christine von Oertzen, "Networks of an Academic World Community: The Exodus of German-Speaking Women Scientists and the Refugee Aid Program of the American Association of University Women," *GHI Bulletin* 27 (Fall 2000), https://www .ghi-dc.org/publications/ghi-bulletin/issue-27-fall-2000/bulletin-27-fall-2000.html?L =0#c20344; Bowie to Gildersleeve, March 18, 1940, Box 814, Folder War Relief Fund French University Women, 1940, Committee Records 8111, AAUWA.

25. Bernstein to AAUW, January 22, 1939, Box 839, Folder Martina Navarra Bernstein, Committee Records 8111, AAUWA; Iael Nidam-Orvieto, "Associazione Donne Ebree D'Italia (ADEI)," *Jewish Women: A Comprehensive Historical Encyclopedia,* March 1, 2009, Jewish Women's Archive, http://jwa.org/encyclopedia/article/associazione-donne -ebree-ditalia-adei.

26. Kock to Hermes, October 20, 1943, War Relief Fund, Polish Association of University Women, 1943, AAUWA.

27. Christine von Oertzen, *Science, Gender and Internationalism: Women's Academic Networks 1917–1955* (New York: Palgrave Macmillan, 2014), 145–46.

28. Parkins to Heineman, September 1938, Box 839, Folder Erna Barschak, and McHale, June 28, 1938, Box 814, both Folder General Correspondence and Information, 1933–1939, Committee Records 8111, AAUWA.

29. Bat-Ami Zucker, *In Search of Refuge: Jews and the American Consuls in Nazi Germany 1933–1941* (London: Vallentine Mitchell, 2001), 160.

30. Cohn to Demuth, April 13, 1936, and Minutes, Emergency Committee Executive Committee Meeting, September 26, 1940, both Box 13, Folder 3, Alfred Cohn Papers; Farrand to Whyte, March 11, 1936; Whyte to Farrand, March 12, 1936; Duggan to Whyte, March 16, 1936, all Box 2, Folder 5, Alfred Cohn Papers. Whyte also sought Murrow's opinion; Murrow agreed with Duggan. Whyte to Murrow, March 21, 1936, Box 191, Folder 6, Emergency Committee Papers.

31. Murrow to Cohn, November 30, 1934, and Murrow to Skepper, December 4,

1934, both Box 186, Folder 8, Emergency Committee Papers; Doron Niederland, "The Emigration of Jewish Academics and Professionals from Germany in the First Years of Nazi Rule," *Leo Baeck Institute Year Book* 30, no. 1 (January 1988): 285–300, 291.

32. Dunn to Cohn, November 25, 1938, Box 13, Folder 1, Alfred Cohn Papers; Krohn, *Intellectuals in Exile*, 27; von Oertzen, *Science, Gender and Internationalism*, 146, 128–42, 159–60.

33. See, for example, Kotschnig to Murrow, April 19, 1934, and Kotschnig to Murrow, May 15, 1934, both Box 4, Folder 2; Kaempffert to Duggan, February 10, 1939, Box 4, Folder 29; Minutes, Emergency Committee Executive Committee Meeting, February 21, 1939, Box 6, Folder 22; Kaempffert to Duggan, March 7, 1939; Kaempffert to Gregory, March 7, 1939; Gibson to Farrand, March 8, 1939; Minutes, "Excerpt from draft of March 23, 1939 Minutes," all Box 4, Folder 16; Cablegram, Duggan to Kenyon, Box 4, Folder 29; Resolution, February 20, 1939; Minutes, Emergency Committee Executive Committee Meeting, March 23, 1939, and Minutes, Emergency Committee Executive Committee Meeting, February 21, 1939, both Box 6, Folder 22; Draft Meeting, Emergency Committee Executive Committee Meeting, March 23, 1939, and Gibson to Farrand, March 9, 1939, both Box 4, Folder 16; Minutes, Emergency Committee Executive Committee Meeting, June 6, 1938, Box 6, Folder 21; Duggan to Drury, June 28, 1938, Box 4, Folder 15, all Alfred Cohn Papers. See also Minutes, Emergency Committee Executive Committee Meeting, May 9, 1939, Box 6, Folder 22, Alfred Cohn Papers.

34. Littauer to Thomas, October 27, 1938, Box 4, Folder 15; Minutes, Emergency Committee Executive Committee, April 3, 1939, Box 6, Folder 22; Cohn to Frankfurter, March 27, 1939, Box 13, Folder 26, all Alfred Cohn Papers.

35. Note, Academic Assistance Council, November 1934; Ladenburg to Murrow, January 4, 1934; "Career of Dr. Hedwig Kohn" and "Curriculum Vitae—Notes Regarding my Special Field of Work," all Box 81, Folder 61, Emergency Committee Papers.

36. See Box 131, Folder Curriculum Vitae Refugee Professors; Borchard to Hutchins, January 13, 1937, and Borchard to Lindbergh, October 30, 1940, both Edwin Borchard Papers, MS 670, YUA; Borchard to Johnson, August 16, 1939; Borchard to Johnson, September 26, 1940; Johnson to Borchard, September 27, 1940, all Box 4, Folder 52, UASUNY; Borchard to Duggan, February 10, 1939, Box 57, Folder 55, Emergency Committee Papers. Coyle to Johnson, February 28, 1940; Johnson to Coyle, February 29, 1940; Borchard to Johnson, March 2, 1940; Johnson to Borchard, March 5, 1940; Borchard to Johnson, March 7, 1940; Johnson to Borchard, March 13, 1940, all Box 2, Folder 96, UASUNY.

37. Dunn to Brecher, December 19, 1933, Leonore Brecher 1930–1938, L. C. Dunn Papers, R:D19, APS.

38. Brecher to Dunn, February 18, 1934, ibid.

39. Brecher to Dunn, April 15, 1934; Brecher to Dunn, December 10, 1930; Brecher to Dunn, September 24, 1931; Dunn to Brecher, May 7, 1934, ibid.

Chapter 3. Unsympathetic Administrators

1. Karen J. Greenberg, "The Mentor Within: The German Refugee Scholars of the Nazi Period and Their American Context," PhD diss., Yale University, 1987, 72; Thomas

Stockham Baker, "German Genius Comes to America," *Carnegie Magazine* 7, no. 4 (September 1933): 99–101; Yael Epstein, "When the Nobel Prize Was Not Enough: Jewish Chemists from the Nazi Regime as Refugees in the United States," in Richard Bodek and Simon Lewis, eds., *The Fruits of Exile: Central European Intellectual Immigration to America in the Age of Fascism* (Columbia: University of South Carolina Press, 2010), 135–36; Bowman "made life difficult for Jewish faculty," so much so that "even a Nobel laureate like James Franck felt he had to leave Johns Hopkins." Paul K. Hoch, "The Reception of Central European Refugee Physicists of the 1930s: U.S.S.R., U.K., U.S.A.," *Annals of Science* 40 (1983): 217–46, 241; Cohn to Johnson, January 25, 1936, Box 13, Folder 21, Alfred Cohn Papers.

2. Greenberg, "The Mentor Within," 76–82; Murrow to Cohn, December 17, 1934, Box 4, Folder 4, Alfred Cohn Papers; Hoch, "Reception of Central European Refugee Physicists," 241.

3. Report, "Excerpts from Informal Report of Field Study," Refugee Section, AFSC, May 28, 1940, Box 4, Folder 30, Alfred Cohn Papers.

4. Maurer to Committee, December 22, 1938, Box 4, Folder 15, Alfred Cohn Papers.

5. Johnson to Duggan, October 22, 1940, Box 190, Folder 8, Emergency Committee Papers.

6. Karen J. Greenberg, "Academic Neutrality: Nicholas Murray Butler, James B. Conant and Nazi Germany, 1933–1938," *Annals of Scholarship* 3 (1984): 72, 71, 75.

7. Butler to Fackenthal, September 6, 1940; Butler to Fackenthal, August 29, 1940; Butler to Fackenthal, September 5, 1940, all Box 487, Folder 5, Nicholas Murray Butler Collection, UACL. Butler to Fackenthal, September 10, 1940, Box 487, Folder 6, Nicholas Murray Butler Collection, UACL; Butler to Fosdick, October 31, 1940, Box 46, Folder 532, RF RG1.1, RAC; John Earl Haynes and Harvey Klehr, *Venona: Decoding Soviet Espionage in America* (New Haven: Yale University Press, 2000), 4, 211–12.

8. Butler to Fackenthal, August 16, 1934, Box 487, Folder 1, Nicholas Murray Butler Collection, UACL. Butler used infelicitous language in asking the university secretary in 1941 to come up with "the names of some of our really great Jews associated with the history of Columbia" and recollecting that one trustee had "been the outstanding New York Jew of his time." It is not clear what Butler needed the names for. Butler to Fackenthal, September 16, 1941, Box 30, Folder September 1941–July 1942; Butler to Bondy, May 27, 1937, Box 487, Folder 3, both Nicholas Murray Butler Collection, UACL.

9. Stephen H. Norwood, *The Third Reich in the Ivory Tower: Complicity and Conflict on American Campuses* (New York: Cambridge University Press, 2009), 79; Liebman to Flexner, July 16, 1938, Box 111, Folder Columbia University 1938–1940, Emergency Committee Papers.

10. Harold S. Wechsler, "Anti-Semitism in the Academy: Jewish Learning in American Universities, 1914–1939," *American Jewish Archives* 42, no. 1 (Spring/Summer, 1990): 7–21, 11–16; Jerome Karabel, *The Chosen: The Hidden History of Admission and Exclusion at Harvard, Yale and Princeton* (Boston: Houghton Mifflin, 2005), 87–103.

11. Zinsser to Edsall, May 15, 1933; Edsall to Lowell, May 17, 1933; Edsall to Zinsser,

June 16, 1933; Zinsser to Edsall, June 19, 1933, all Box 30, Folder 20:1356, Harvard Medical School, Office of the Dean, Subject Files, 1899–1954, RG N-DE01, FCLM; Shapley to Murrow, July 31, 1933, and Shapley to Duggan, September 27, 1933, both Box 141, Folder 24, Emergency Committee Papers; Memo, A. Lawrence Lowell, May 13, 1933, Box Call Temp, Folder German Scholars, James Conant Papers, HUA.

12. Jennet Conant, in her recent biography of her grandfather, argues that Conant approached the refugee issue as "a bureaucratic problem" and that his response "reflected 'a failure of compassion and political sensitivity.'" This minimizes both the overt antisemitism in his correspondence and the steps he took to block refugee hires. In addition, by suggesting that her grandfather's "single-minded focus on restoring Harvard's eminence" was why he was unwilling to hire more Jewish scholars, she overlooks the possibility that one reason he did not consider the scholars eminent was because they were Jewish. *Man of the Hour: James B. Conant Warrior Scholar* (New York: Simon and Schuster, 2017), 142–43; Conant to Bolton, September 13, 1933, Box Call Temp, Folder German Scholars, James Conant Papers, HUA. See also Norwood, *Third Reich in the Ivory Tower,* 38–39.

13. Hecht to Conant, October 13, 1933; Conant to Hecht, October 16, 1933; Laski to Conant, October 7, 1933; Conant to Laski, November 3, 1933; Conant to Clark, November 14, 1933, all Box Call Temp, Folder German Scholars, James Conant Papers, HUA.

14. Even after the war, Conant and the university he led discriminated against Jews in chemistry. Albert Sprague Coolidge, a Harvard chemist and physicist, testified before a Massachusetts legislative committee that "we know perfectly well that names ending in 'berg' or 'stein' have to be skipped by the board of selection of students for scholarships in chemistry" at Harvard. Coolidge explained that a "gentlemen's agreement" had been reached between university officials and the chemical industry that sponsored the scholarships and tended to exclude Jews. Carey McWilliams, *A Mask for Privilege: Anti-Semitism in America* (Boston: Little, Brown, 1949), 138; Conant to Clark, November 14, 1933, Box Call Temp, Folder German Scholars, James Conant Papers, HUA. In an otherwise fine article, "To the Rescue of the Learned: The Asylum Fellowship Plan at Harvard, 1938–1940," *Harvard Library Bulletin* 42, no. 3 (Summer 1984): 212, Bessie Zaban Jones quotes from the Clark letter but leaves out Conant's comments about Jews.

15. Baehr to Edsall, December 30, 1933, Box 30, Folder 20:1356, Harvard Medical School, Office of the Dean, Subject Files, RG M-DE01, FCLM. Harvard was one of twenty-seven medical schools that replied to the Emergency Committee's inquiry, and one of just fourteen that expressed a willingness to offer research positions to one or more refugees. The Emergency Committee's minutes did not record the medical schools that turned the group down. Minutes, Placement Committee, January 13, 1934, Box 164, Folder 5, Emergency Committee Papers. See Edsall to Doctor, January 3, 1934; Cobb to Edsall, January 18, 1934; Zinsser to Edsall, January, 9, 1934; Tolin to Edsall, January 6, 1934; and Cohn to Edsall, January 6, 1934, all Box 30, Folder 20:1356, Harvard Medical School, Office of the Dean, Subject Files, RG M-DE01, FCLM. A list of the refugees hired was not found in the files, but there are discussions of several hires, including Paul Kimmelsteil, an instructor in pathology; Richard Schatzki, instructor in roentgenology; and Fritz

Kant, a research fellow in psychiatry. Greene to Burwell, November 21, 1939, and Burwell to Greene, both Box 30, Folder 20:1356, Harvard Medical School, Office of the Dean, RG M-DE01, FCLM.

16. Conant to Clark, November 14, 1933, Box Call Temp, Folder German Scholars, James Conant Papers, HUA; Birkhoff to Debye, September 26, 1936, and Birkhoff 5–4 Dec (1936–1944), 4213.2.2, HUA. See Sybe Rispens, *Einstein in Nederland: Een intellectuele biografie* (Amsterdam: Ambo/Anthos, 2006); J. W. Williams, "Peter Joseph Wilhelm Debye," *Biographical Memoirs* 46 (1975), National Academies Press, https://www.nap.edu/read/569/chapter/3; and G. van Ginkel, "Prof. Peter J. W. Debye in 1935–1945: An Investigation of Historical Sources," December 2006, http://www.theochem.ru.nl/~pwormer/Historical%20sources%20Debye%201935-1945.pdf.

17. Assistant Director to Duggan, January 31, 1934, Box 186, Folder 4, Emergency Committee Papers.

18. Murrow to Friedrich, February 1, 1934, Box 178, Folder 9; Seligman to Stein, January 31, 1934, and Murrow to Seligman, February 5, 1934, both Box 178, Folder 7; Murrow to Duggan, February 7, 1934, and Murrow to Conant, February 7, 1934, both Box 199, Folder 6; Conant to Murrow, February 12, 1934, Box 191, Folder 4; Duggan to Murrow, February 12, 1934, Box 199, Folder 6, all Emergency Committee Papers.

19. Duggan to Frankfurter, July 18, 1933, Box 199, Folder 2; Frankfurter to Duggan, February 21, 1935, Box 178, Folder 7; Wunderlich to Frankfurter, March 2, 1935, and Frankfurter to Wunderlich, March 12, 1935, both Box 178, Folder 7, all Emergency Committee Papers.

20. Shapley to Veblen, May 2, 1940, Box 6A, Folder Niels Bohr, 4773.10, HUA; Salomon Bochner, "Harald Bohr," *Bulletin of the American Mathematical Society* 58, no. 1 (1952), 72–75, https://projecteuclid.org/download/pdf_1/euclid.bams/1183516518.

21. Burwell to Fitz, October 7, 1940; Burwell to Fitz, October 28, 1939; Memo, Discussion on Refugees, Faculty Council Meeting, November 3, 1939; Burwell to Dr. Lane, November 20, 1939, all Box 30, Folder 20:1356, Harvard Medical School, Office of the Dean, RG M-DE01, FCLM.

22. Cutler to Burwell, March 23, 1942; Burwell to Cutler, March 1, 1942; Burwell to Cutler, May 14, 1942; Burwell to Wislocki, February 9, 1942; "Regarding Refugees" Memo, February 25, 1943, all Box 30, Folder 20:1357; Fulton to Fine, February 18, 1939, Box 30, Folder 21:1362, all Harvard Medical School, Office of the Dean, RG M-DE01, FCLM; Kremace Terezin, 5070791-0-1, Ludwig Pick, TD #104458, International Tracing Service, USHMM; Cannon to Boas, November 4, 1939; Burwell to Fulton, May 26, 1939; Fulton to Burwell, June 1, 1939; Burwell to Cannon, November 14, 1939; Burwell to Castle, October 24, 1939; Castle to Burwell, December 4, 1939, all Box 30, Folder 21:1361, Harvard Medical School, Office of the Dean, RG M-DE01, FCLM; Nobel Prize in Physiology or Medicine 1936, Otto Loewi Biographical, The Nobel Prize, https://www.nobelprize.org/prizes/medicine/1936/loewi/biographical/.

23. Cannon to Lambert, October 24, 1940, Box 46, Folder 532, RF RG1.1, RAC; Greene to Duggan, October 4, 1940, Box 205, Folder 10; Johnson to Duggan, October 22, 1940, Box 190, Folder 8, both Emergency Committee Papers.

24. Chase to Duggan, January 19, 1942, Box 186, Folder 13, Emergency Committee Papers; Burwell to Greene, January 23, 1943; Wislocki to Burwell, January 28, 1943; Greene to Burwell, February 2, 1943; see also Greene to Burwell, January 26, 1943; Burwell to Wislocki, January 27, 1943, all Box 30, Folder 20:1357, Harvard Medical School, Office of the Dean, Subject Files, RG M-DE01, FCLM.

25. Duggan to Cohn, May 1, 1940, Box 1, Folder 25, Alfred Cohn Papers.

Chapter 4. World Class and Well Connected

1. Minutes, Staff Conference, October 23, 1940, Box 46, Folder 532, RF RG1.1, RAC; Robin E. Rider, "Alarm and Opportunity: Emigration of Mathematicians and Physicists to Britain and the United States, 1933–1945," *Historical Studies in the Physical Sciences* 15, no. 1 (1984): 124–25.

2. Johnson to Berl, November 20, 1940, Box 1, Ernst Berl Papers 2013.392.1, USHMM; "Situation of and Opportunities for Displaced German Scholars in the United States," Box 2, Folder 15, Alfred Cohn Papers; Richardson to Gumbel, December 26, 1940, Birkhoff 2–13 Nov (1938–1939), 4213.2.2, HUA.

3. Edsall to Cannon, April 13, 1934, Box 30, Folder 21:1360, Harvard Medical School, Office of the Dean Subject Files, 1899–1954, RG N-DE01, Series 00267, FCLM.

4. Borchard to Duggan, February 10, 1939, Box 57, Folder 55, Emergency Committee Papers.

5. Curriculum Vitae, Box 6, Folder 102, UASUNY.

6. Memo, Kittredge, October 9, 1940, Box 46, Folder 532, RF RG1.1, RAC.

7. Makinsky to Shapley, October 20, 1942, Box 6A, Folder Ferdinand Beer, Harlow Shapley Collection, 4773.10, HUA.

8. Hans Böhm and Astrid Mehmel, "Introduction," in Alfred Philippson, *Wie ich zum Geographen wurde: aufgezeichnet im Konzentrationslager Theresienstadt zwischen 1942 und 1945*, ed. Hans Böhm and Astrid Mehmel (Bonn: Bouvier, 1996), xvi–xxii, xiiiv; Johnson to Bowman, November 25, 1941, Box 5, Folder 136, UASUNY.

9. Memo, Institute for Advanced Study, February 6, 1942, Box 6A, Folder Bs, Harlow Shapley Collection, 4773.10, HUA; Weyl to Timbres, February 6, 1942, Case 2425, AFSC Case Files. Subsequent information indicated that the Berwalds lived in the ghetto in an unfinished, one-story schoolhouse that contained no beds. Fifty-five people slept on the floor in one room that measured twenty by twenty feet. J. J. O'Connor and E. F. Robertson, "Ludwig Berwald," http://www-groups.dcs.st-and.ac.uk/history/Biographies /Berwald.html; see also Ludwig Berwald, Ustredni Karkoteka—Transporty, 1.1.22.1 Lodz Death List, International Tracing Service, USHMM.

10. Weyl to Salmon, January 29, 1940, Case 2425, AFSC Case Files; Cable, February 6, 1942, Box 6A, Folder Arthur Beer, 4773.10, HUA; 1.1.22.1 Lodz Death List, International Tracing Service, USHMM; see also "Central Database of Shoah Victims' Names," Yad Vashem, http://db.yadvashem.org/names/nameDetails.html?itemId=4501 565&language=en.

11. Moon to Thieman, February 28, 1941, and Thieman to Moon, March 3, 1941, both Case 896, AFSC Case Files.

12. Brunauer to Beth, June 2, 1941, Box 839, Folder Marian Beth, International Relations Committee Records, Committee Records 8111, AAUWA; Jacob A. Belzen, "A Political End to a Pioneering Career: Marianne Beth and the Psychology of Religion," *Religions* 2, no. 3 (2011): 247–63.

13. Laura Fermi, *Illustrious Immigrants: The Intellectual Migration from Europe 1930–41*, 2nd ed. (Chicago: University of Chicago Press, 1971), 82–83; Alfons Sollner, "From Public Law to Political Science? The Emigration of German Scholars After 1933 and Their Influence on the Transformation of a Discipline," in Mitchell G. Ash and Alfons Sollner, eds., *Forced Migration and Scientific Change: Émigré German-Speaking Scientists and Scholars After 1933* (Washington, DC: German Historical Institute, Cambridge University Press, 1996), 257; Marjorie Lamberti, "The Reception of Refugee Scholars from Nazi Germany in America: Philanthropy and Social Change in Higher Education," *Jewish Social Studies: History, Culture Society* 12 (Spring/Summer 2006): 176; Paul K. Hoch, "The Reception of Central European Refugee Physicists of the 1930s: U.S.S.R., U.K., U.S.A.," *Annals of Science* 40 (1983): 230.

14. Watson to Johnson, n.d.; MacLeod to Johnson, October 30, 1940; Langfeld to Johnson, November 12, 1940; Johnson to Appleget, October 1, 1941; Appleget to Johnson, March 10, 1941, all Box 6, Folder 47, UASUNY; Jewish Virtual Library, A Project of AICE, "Edgar Rubin," https://www.jewishvirtuallibrary.org/jsource/judaica/ejud_0002_0017_0_17126.html.

15. Report, Kotschnig on his Visit to American Colleges and Universities, March 12–April 11, 1936, Box 2, Folder 15, Alfred Cohn Papers; Kallen to Johnson, April 1, 1941, Box 50, Folder 594, RF RG1.1, RAC; Goldberg to Staudinger, October 6, 1942, Box 2, Folder 175 Ginsberg to Adams, November 22, 1940, Box 1, Folder 4, both UASUNY.

16. Karen J. Greenberg, "'Uphill Work': The German Refugee Historian and American Institutions of Higher Learning," in Harmutt Lehmann and James J. Sheehan, eds., *An Interrupted Past: German-Speaking Refugee Historians in the United States After 1933* (Cambridge: Cambridge University Press, 1991), 95; Rhind to Murrow, August 22, 1933, Box 172, Folder 4, Emergency Committee Papers.

17. Murrow to Cohn, March 14, 1935, Box 4, Folder 7, Alfred Cohn Papers; Levene to Baehr, January 2, 1934, Rockefeller Institute for Medical Research, Manuscripts and Archives Division, NYPL; John E. Burton, *Southern Medicine and Surgery* 96 (1934): 78–144; Herman Kalckar, "Gerhard Schmidt" *Biographical Memoirs* (Washington, DC: National Academy of Sciences, 1987), http://www.nap.edu/openbook.php?record_id=1000&page=411.

18. List, Prof. W. Spielmeyer, September 6, 1933, Box 172, Folder 5, Emergency Committee Papers; Klaus-Jurgen Neumarker, "The Kramer-Pollnow Syndrome: A Contribution on the Life and Work of Franz Kramer and Hans Pollnow," *History of Psychiatry* 16, no. 4 (2005): 435–51. Berlin neuropsychiatrist Hans Pollnow (1902–1943), who fled to France to escape Nazi persecution in 1933, joined the French Army after the German invasion in 1940. Pollnow was demobilized after the French surrender and fled to southern France but was arrested by the Nazi secret police in 1943 and deported to the Mauthausen concentration camp in Austria, where he was murdered the same year.

19. List, Schumpeter, March 1, 1933, Box 91, Folder 724; Schumpeter to Day, May 2, 1933, Box 91, Folder 725, both RF RG2, RAC.

20. Shapley to Nock, December 8, 1939, and Nock to Shapley, December 12, 1939, both Box 6A, Folder Eberhard Bruck, 4773.10, HUA.

21. Johnson to Florence, August 1, 1941, Box 4, Folder 154, UASUNY.

22. Neuner to Johnson, October 18, 1940, Box 7, Folder 106, UASUNY; Christian Fleck, *A Transatlantic History of the Social Sciences: Robbers Barons, the Third Reich and the Invention of Empirical Social Research* (London: Bloomsburg Academic, 2011), 44–45.

23. Carnap to Johnson, September 9, 1940; Kaempffert to Johnson, April 21, 1938; Kaempffert to Johnson, August 1, 1940; Kaempffert to Johnson, August 16, 1940; Johnson to Kaempffert, August 19, 1940, all Box 5, Folder 86, UASUNY.

24. Berl to Merfeld, March 24, 1941, Box 1, Ernst Berl Papers 2013.392.1, USHMM. Berl's coldness to his former assistant was not unusual. He also blew off Felix Bauer, who had attended the Technical University as an architecture student when Berl was there and was trapped in Vienna after the Anschluss: "I will try to do my best but, in view of the great many cases like yours which came to my attention, I was doubtful that anything could be done by a single, weak individual as I am." Berl to Bauer, August 18, 1938, Box 1, ibid. After two years in a refugee camp in Switzerland, Bauer escaped to the Dominican Republic. He eventually became an art and music professor at Erskine College, dying in 2006 at the age of ninety-two. Berl would not provide a position to thirty-nine-year-old chemist Ernst Feigl in his "rather small research laboratory" and maintained that "all my efforts to get positions for relatives and friends in this country have failed." Nor would he provide affidavits to Feigl, or Paula Defris and her daughter, who were in Vienna in 1939, because he had already provided a "rather great number" to relatives. "Furthermore, I do not think the United States would be the right country for you and your daughter," he wrote, citing the unemployment rate. "I believe the question of immigration has to be regulated so that larger numbers of those unfortunate people could build up in a foreign country a life of honor and decency," he wrote. Berl to Feigl, February 23, 1939, and Berl to Defris, February 16, 1939, Box 1, ibid. Defris died in Auschwitz on July 17, 1942. It could not be determined what happened to her daughter or to Feigl.

25. Gropius to Johnson, October 15, 1940; Memo, Moholy-Nagy, October 17, 1940, both Box 7, Folder 20, UASUNY; Culture.pl, "Szymon and Helena Syrkus," Culture.pl Artists, https://culture.pl/en/artist/szymon-and-helena-syrkus.

26. Murrow to Flexner, April 2, 1935, Box 4, Folder 8, Alfred Cohn Papers.

27. Johnson to Kelsen, July 19, 1940, and Kelsen to Johnson, July 18, 1940, both Box 5, Folder 37, UASUNY; Cohn to Johnson, June 1, 1938; Johnson to Cohn, June 3, 1938; Biel to Johnson, May 19, 1938, all Box 1, Folder 139, UASUNY.

28. Schapiro to Johnson, December 1, 1940, and Johnson to Schapiro, December 6, 1940, both Box 2, Folder 76, UASUNY; Carlos Petit, *Max Radin, Cartas Romanisticas (1923–1950)* (Naples: Jovene, 2001), 129–34. Radin must have felt some guilt. After hearing from a University of California colleague and from David's brother-in-law, Radin wrote to the Jewish Theological Seminary of America recommending David for a position; Martin David, TD #549509, International Tracing Service, USHMM. See also

J. A. Ankum, "David, Martin (1898–1986)," in *Biografisch Woordenboek van Nederland,* http://www.historici.nl/Onderzoek/Projecten/BWN/lemmata/bwn4/david.

29. Memo, Drury, November 14, 1941, Box 4, Folder 22, Alfred Cohn Papers; Reinhard Siegmund-Schultze, *Mathematicians Fleeing from Nazi Germany: Individual Fates and Global Impact* (Princeton, NJ: Princeton University Press, 2009), 210–12.

30. Murrow to Friedrich, July 2, 1934, Box 172, Folder 7, Emergency Committee Papers; Aronson to Johnson, January 11, 1941; Ducasse to Johnson, January 13, 1940; Staudinger to Gurwitsch, January 30, 1941; Rice to Solow, January 28, 1941, all Box 6, Folder 68, UASUNY.

31. Babb to Johnson, January 7, 1941; Johnson to Radin, January 8, 1941; Radin to Johnson, January 20, 1941; Babb to Solow, February 19, 1941; Johnson to Babb, February 23, 1941, all Box 2, Folder 155, UASUNY; "Holocaust Survivors and Victims Database," USHMM, https://www.ushmm.org/online/hsv/person_advance_search.php?SourceId =20811&sort=name_primary_sort&MaxPageDocs=25&start_doc=1726; another Jerzy Finkelkraut, who was a physician, died during military service, "Central Database of Shoah Victims' Names," Yad Vashem, http://db.yadvashem.org/names/nameDetails.html ?itemId=7003448&language=en.

32. Hoch, "Reception of Central European Refugee Physicists of the 1930s"; Glueck to Johnson, October 14, 1940, Box 3, Folder 70, UASUNY.

33. Duggan exaggerated the problem somewhat. In another letter, he wrote that the committee had "the greatest difficulty in placing even one man in the whole of the United States in the field of law." The committee's executive secretary, Betty Drury, quickly corrected the record, noting that eight law teachers had received Emergency Committee grants and were teaching, one of whom had established himself "brilliantly." Duggan to Hunt, January 20, 1939, and Drury to Dowd, January 23, 1939, both Box 79, Folder 49, Emergency Committee Papers.

34. Kyle Graham, "The Refugee Jurist and American Law Schools, 1933–1941," *American Journal of Comparative Law* 50, no. 4 (Fall 2002): 778, 802–9; Powell to Duggan, November 21, 1938, Box 4, Folder 15, Alfred Cohn Papers; Bernard Grossfeld and Peter Winship, "The Law Professor Refugee," *Syracuse Journal of International Law and Commerce* 18, no. 3 (1992): 1–18.

35. Kaufmann to Colleague, June 27, 1940; Borchard to Johnson, August 16, 1939; Loewenstein to Johnson, August 24, 1940; Borchard to Johnson, September 26, 1940; Johnson to Borchard, September 27, 1940, all Box 4, Folder 52, UASUNY.

36. Beckerath to Duggan, October 15, 1940, Box 79, Folder 49, Emergency Committee Papers; James W. Whitman, *Hitler's American Model: The United States and the Making of Nazi Race Law* (Princeton, NJ: Princeton University Press, 2018), 41–42.

37. Baron to Staudinger, April 23, 1941, and Morgenstern to Johnson, May 5, 1941, both Box 6, Folder 84, UASUNY. See also Staudinger to Tillich, May 19, 1941, and Frank to Johnson, April 9, 1941, both ibid.

38. Notes, Johnson to Appleget, August 13, 1940; Spitzer to Johnson, October 12, 1940; Lewin to Johnson, October 16, 1940, all Box 7, Folder 102, UASUNY; Minutes,

Emergency Committee Executive Committee Meeting, September 26, 1940, Box 6, Folder 25, Alfred Cohn Papers.

39. Claus-Dieter Krohn, *Intellectuals in Exile: Refugee Scholars and the New School for Social Research* (Amherst: University of Massachusetts Press, 1993), 22. See also Stephen H. Norwood, *The Third Reich in the Ivory Tower: Complicity and Conflict on American Campuses* (New York: Cambridge University Press, 2009): 164–68; Report, "Situation of and Opportunities for Displaced German Scholars in the United States," Box 2, Folder 15, Alfred Cohn Papers. Duggan informed Emergency Committee members of the withdrawal during a meeting, Minutes, Emergency Committee Executive Committee Meeting, December 5, 1939, Box 6, Folder 21, Alfred Cohn Papers. Once ensconced in a German department himself, John Whyte, the Emergency Committee's assistant director in the early 1940s, challenged the notion that German departments were particularly antisemitic or hostile to refugees. "I think that on the whole we in German Departments are more free of [antisemitism] than other departments I might mention," wrote Whyte, who left the committee to join Brooklyn College's Department of German. While at the committee, Whyte had concluded that Rutgers University had fired a refugee for "his outspoken and determined criticism of Nazi Germany." But he now contended that the firing was not due to the department's antisemitism; the Rutgers professors "somewhat tainted by Nazi ideology" were not so "in the race sense but rather as nationalistic and patriotic Germans," Whyte wrote; Whyte to Duggan, November 7, 1945, Record of the Emergency Committee, RG-19.061, USHMM.

40. Cohn to Adams, March 8, 1935, Box 186, Folder 9, Emergency Committee Papers.

Chapter 5. Age, Politics, Gender, and Money

1. Borchard to Duggan, February 10, 1939, Box 57, Folder 55, Emergency Committee Papers.

2. Johnson to Fehr, September 26, 1940, Box 2, Folder 144; Johnson to Florence, August 1, 1941, Box 4, Folder 154; Note, Hugo Müller, Box 5, Folder 73, all UASUNY; Drury to Sigerist, January 25, 1939, Box 164, Folder 3, and Drury to Cohn, February 18, 1939, Box 186, Folder 10, both Emergency Committee Papers; Minutes, Emergency Committee Executive Committee Meeting, March 27, 1941, Box 6, Folder 26, Alfred Cohn Papers.

3. Staudinger to Brecht, March 14, 1941; Springer to Lederer, January 19, 1941; Brecht to Staudinger, March 11, 1941, all Box 5, Folder 121, UASUNY; Leopold Emil Perels, 45788585-0-1, International Tracing Service, USHMM.

4. Staudinger to Bierman, August 15, 1941; Johnson to Bowman, September 16, 1941; Johnson to Bowman, August 15, 1941; Bowman to Ambassador, October 3, 1941; Bowman to Johnson, December 23, 1941, all Box 2, Folder 6, UASUNY.

5. In 1936, Johnson chastised a Brooklyn woman, Charlotte Milbauer, who would not provide an affidavit for her cousin, a Berlin neurologist, at least partly because he would not be allowed to practice medicine right away. Johnson mentioned that he had

sponsored three people who were then in the United States. "If they get into a condition in which they cannot possibly live otherwise, I shall have to maintain them," he chided. "It would be a crushing burden to me. They are in no wise related to me except through the brotherhood of man. Of course, this may be entirely impossible for you. If it is, I fear there is nothing else you can do about it"; Milbauer to Johnson, January 16, 1936, and Johnson to Milbauer, January 23, 1936, both Box 5, Folder 51, UASUNY. Later, Johnson provided affidavits to the Wolken family from Austria. Johnson had collaborated with Marie Wolken's uncle, an Austrian scholar; Box 7, Folder 142, UASUNY. Jaszi to Johnson, December 5, 1938; Johnson to Jaszi, December 12, 1938; Goldmark to Johnson, March 29, 1939; Johnson to Goldmark, August 8, 1939, all Box 2, Folder 47, UASUNY.

6. Brunschvicg to Butler, October 25, 1940, and Focillon to Johnson, December 30, 1940, both Box 50, Folder 594, RF RG1.1, RAC.

7. Focillon to Johnson, December 30, 1940; Gurvitch to Johnson, October 2, 1940; Ducasse to Johnson, December 9, 1940; Aronson to Johnson, January 3, 1941; Salomon to Johnson, November 8, 1940; Maritain to Johnson, September 6, 1940; Bonnet to Johnson, January 23, 1941; Schneider to Johnson, October 16, 1940; Perry to Johnson, December 2, 1940, all Box 50, Folder 594, RF RG1.1, RAC; Marshall to Johnson, April 9, 1941, and Memo, John Marshall, March 5, 1941, both Box 50, Folder 595, RF RG1.1, RAC.

8. Murrow to Kotschnig, August 29, 1934, Box 186, Folder 7, Emergency Committee Papers.

9. Friedrich to Murrow, June 28, 1934; Murrow to Friedrich, July 2, 1934, Box 172, Folder 7; Memo, September 21, 1934, Box 186, Folder 7, all Emergency Committee Papers.

10. Kotschnig to Gregg, January 21, 1935, Box 172, Folder 9, Emergency Committee Papers; Minutes, Emergency Committee Executive Committee Meeting, October 6, 1939, Box 6, Folder 23, Alfred Cohn Papers; Cohn to Duggan, August 7, 1940, and Duggan to Cohn, August 12, 1940, Box 186, Folder 11, Emergency Committee Papers.

11. Report, Emergency Committee, April 1942, Record of the Emergency Committee, RG-19.061, USHMM.

12. Alfons Sollner, "From Public Law to Political Science? The Emigration of German Scholars After 1933 and Their Influence on the Transformation of a Discipline," in Mitchell G. Ash and Alfons Sollner, eds., *Forced Migration and Scientific Change: Émigré German-Speaking Scientists and Scholars After 1933* (Washington, DC: German Historical Institute, Cambridge University Press, 1996), 256–57; Reinhard Siegmund-Schultze, "Rockefeller Support for Mathematicians Fleeing from the Nazi Purge," in Guiliana Gemelli, ed., *The "Unacceptables": American Foundations and Refugee Scholars Between the Two Wars and After* (Brussels: P.I.E.–Peter Lang, 2000), 95; Touton to Murrow, June 16, 1934, Box 133, Folder Joseph P. Chamberlain, Emergency Committee Papers.

13. Cohn to Berle, August 9, 1940, Box 5, Folder 5, Alfred Cohn Papers.

14. Peter M. Rutkoff and William B. Scott, *New School: A History of the New School for Social Research* (New York: Free Press, 1986), 135–36; a different Hans Mayer was a prominent member of the conservative Austrian School of economists. See Hansjörg Klausinger, "Hans Mayer, Last Knight of the Austrian School, Vienna Branch," *History of*

Political Economy 47, no. 2 (2015): 271–305, https://doi.org/10.1215/00182702-2884333; Schwerin to Staudinger, October 6, 1942; Johnson to Hambro, May 6, 1941; Whitton to Johnson, August 10, 1941; Rappard to Johnson, October 7, 1941, all Box 5, Folder 17, UASUNY.

15. Note, September 12, 1940, Box 4, Folder 192, UASUNY; Staudinger to Heimann, November 26, 1940; Solow to Mankiewicz, May 1, 1941; Mankiewicz to Solow, May 14, 1941, all Box 4, Folder 200, UASUNY.

16. Johnson to Appleget, November 29, 1940, Box 7, Folder 1, UASUNY. Of women holding academic posts, two out of five lost their jobs for racial reasons; another 10 percent were let go because of left-wing politics or close association with Jews. Harriet Pass Freidenreich, *Female, Jewish and Educated: The Lives of Central European University Women* (Bloomington: Indiana University Press, 2002), 73, 42, 16–17, 165–68. Freidenreich does not discuss hiring at American universities or delve into the immigration process; Marilyn Ogilvie and Joy Harvey, eds., *Biographical Dictionary of Women in Science* (New York: Routledge 2000), 1393.

17. Johnson to Appleget, September 30, 1940, Box 4, Folder 76, UASUNY; File, "Dvoicenco, Dr.," Box 2, Folder 105, UASUNY. The file does not include her first name but lists that she is thirty-nine years old, Russian, and an assistant professor of Slavic history and culture in Bucharest; File, Maria Kokoszynska-Lutman, Box 4, Folder 76, UASUNY.

18. Miriam Intrator, "A Temporary Haven: Jewish World War II Refugee Scholars at the NYPL, 1933–1945," 23, https://www.studienverlag.at/bookimport/oezgArchiv/media /data0912/4898_oezg3_2010_s10_35_intrator.pdf.

19. Brigitte Bischof, "Women in Physics in Vienna," in *The Global and the Local: The History of Science and the Cultural Integration of Europe,* ed. M. Kokowski, Proceedings of the 2nd ICESHS, Kraków, Poland, September 6–9, 2006, 522–23, http://www .2iceshs.cyfronet.pl/2ICESHS_Proceedings/Chapter_18/R-10_Bischof.pdf; see also "Marie Anna Schirmann," http://lise.univie.ac.at/physikerinnen/historisch/marie_anna-schir mann.htm.

20. Bernstein to Murrow, April 15, 1935, Box 43, Folder 15, Emergency Committee Papers.

21. Mitchell G. Ash, "Forced Migration and Scientific Change After 1933: A New Approach," conference paper, 2000, extended version published in Edward Timms and Jon Hughes, eds., *Intellectual Migration and Cultural Transformation: Refugees from National Socialism in the English-Speaking World* (Vienna: Springer, 2003), 241–63; Brunauer to Hautermans, March 11, 1940, War Relief Files 839, Folder Charlotte Hautermans [Houtermans], Committee Records 8111, AAUWA; Judith P. Hallett, "'Saving Alive the Leading Scholar of the World in Her Line and Fostering an Ordinary Person Lucky in Her Chosen Career': The Endeavors and Example of the German Refugee Classicists Eva Lehman Fiesel and Ruth Fiesel," unpublished manuscript in the author's possession, pp. 2, 10.

22. *New York Times,* September 14, 1938, 23. Gildersleeve, at least early on, defended Nazi rule in Germany. Stephen H. Norwood, *The Third Reich in the Ivory Tower:*

Complicity and Conflict on American Campuses (New York: Cambridge University Press, 2009), 104–5, 108; Park to Seelye, March 4, 1941; Drury to Razovsky, November 9, 1939; Wheeler to Duggan, April 1, 1940; Park to Duggan, May 1, 1940; Weyl to Park, February 24, 1941; Memo, Drury, March 13, 1942; Seelye to Ford, May 13, 1942; Wheeler to Duggan, May 19 1942; Drury to Rechard, March 13, 1942, all Box 11, Folder 8-9, Emergency Committee Papers.

23. Interestingly, the NYPL hired eight refugee scholars in its Humanities Research Library, but only one of the eight, Käthe Meyer-Baer, was a woman. She also was the only one of the eight who did not work out. Intrator, "Temporary Haven," 25–26; Holt to Emergency Committee, October 5, 1939, Box 4, Folder 18, Alfred Cohn Papers.

24. Holt to Emergency Committee, October 5, 1939, and Singleton to Emergency Committee, October 4, 1939, both Box 4, Folder 18, Alfred Cohn Papers.

25. Giese to Parkins, November 19, 1938, Box 839, Folder Charlotte Giese, Committee Records 8111, AAUWA.

26. Mühsam to Coleman, January 17, 1939, Box 5, Folder 75, UASUNY; Lehmann-Hartleben to Brunauer, March 30, 1941, and Mühsam to Reid, June 28, 1944, both Box 839, Folder Alice Mühsam, Committee Records 8111, AAUWA.

27. Compton to Boschwitz, October 13, 1937, Box 4, Folder 12, Alfred Cohn Papers.

28. Colvin to Shapley, April 21, 1940, Box 6b, Folder Arthur Korn, 4773.10, HUA; Memo, Drury, January 20, 1939, Record of the Emergency Committee, RG-19.061, USHMM.

29. Coca to Johnson, November 18, 1940, Box 3, Folder 136, UASUNY; Coca to Morley, October 17, 1940, Box 73, Folder 24, Emergency Committee Papers.

30. Officer's Diary, Makinsky, February 18–25, 1942, Box 96A, Folder 1942, RF RG12.1, RAC.

31. Park to Seelye, March 4, 1941; Drury to Park, March 18, 1941; Geiringer to Duggan, May 4, 1944, all Box 11, Folder 8-9, Emergency Committee Papers.

32. Memo, Murrow, March 21, 1935, Box 172, Folder 10, Emergency Committee Papers. For the lengthy correspondence on Bryn Mawr's hiring of Noether, see Box 25, Folder 8-9, ibid.

33. Minutes, Emergency Committee Executive Committee Meeting, September 26, 1940, Box 6, Folder 25; Emergency Committee Meeting Minutes, September 22, 1943, Box 2, Folder 2; Drucker to Drury, February 23, 1944, Box 2, Folder 3, all Alfred Cohn Papers.

34. Johnson to Baer, January 18, 1939, Box 2, Folder 153, UASUNY; Edgar Feuchtwanger, "In Memoriam: Ludwig Feuchtwanger (28.11.1885–14.07.1947)," http://www.rijo.homepage.t-online.de/pdf/EN_MU_JU_feuchtwanger.pdf.

35. Interview Notes, Drury, December 17, 1940, and Telephone Conversation Notes, January 13, 1941, both Box 117, Folder 17, Emergency Committee Papers. The New School was willing to offer a position to Dr. Oscar Fehr, an ophthalmologist and eye surgeon, after his son, Robert, who was living in Schenectady, New York, agreed to guarantee he would pay his father's yearly salary of $1,500 for two years. (The New School did

not hire physicians or medical researchers except those in public health. Fehr studied conjunctivitis acquired from swimming pools, which seems to be his only connection to public health.) The New School ultimately concluded that Fehr would not be able to get a non-quota visa; his teaching experience at the Virchow Hospital would not count because the hospital was not affiliated with the University of Berlin's medical school. Fehr obtained a visa to Great Britain. Johnson to Fehr, September 26, 1940; Fehr to Johnson, October 2, 1940; Lewey to Johnson, December 26, 1940, all Box 2, Folder 144, UASUNY.

36. Warburg to Duggan, October 3, 1939; Duggan to Clothier, October 18, 1939; Marvin to Duggan, n.d.; Warburg to Duggan, October 28, 1939, all Box 55, Folder 31, Emergency Committee Papers; P. Eppstein to Johnson, December 19, 1939; Nussbaum to Johnson, September 11, 1940; Johnson to American Consul, Berlin, September 16, 1940; H. Eppstein to Johnson, December 10, 1940, all Box 2, Folder 127, UASUNY.

37. B. Polak to Johnson, July 15, 1941, Box 5, Folder 154, UASUNY.

38. Johnson to Thompson, May 19, 1939, Box 6, Folder 100, UASUNY; Thompson to Schwarzwald, May 31, 1939, Box 35, Folder 1939, Dorothy Thompson Papers, Syracuse University Library, Syracuse, N.Y.

Chapter 6. Too Jewish or Foreign

1. Jerome Karabel, *The Chosen: The Hidden History of Admission and Exclusion at Harvard, Yale, and Princeton* (Boston: Houghton Mifflin, 2005); Dan Oren, *Joining the Club: A History of Jews and Yale* (New Haven: Yale University Press, 1985); Nitza Rosovsky, *The Jewish Experience at Harvard and Radcliffe* (Harvard University Press, 1986); David Zimmerman ("'Narrow-Minded People': Canadian Universities and the Academic Refugee Crises, 1933–1941," *Canadian Historical Review* 88 [June 2007]) also found antisemitism to be a major factor in the dismal hiring record of Canadian universities. "Anti-Semitism appears to have been the single most significant factor in explaining why so few refugee scholars were placed at Canadian universities. The hatred of Jews, so prevalent in Canadian society, was the major influence within the Canadian academy, much more so than it was at universities in either Great Britain or the United States. . . . Canadian scholars did not rise to this challenge, and could not escape Hill's observation, that as a group they truly were 'narrow-minded people'" (294, 315); Paul K. Hoch, "The Reception of Central European Refugee Physicists of the 1930s: U.S.S.R., U.K., U.S.A.," *Annals of Science* 40 (1983): 217–46; Landis noted the antisemitism that restricted Jewish faculty in U.S. universities in a letter to Edmund Whitman. Kyle Graham, "The Refugee Jurist and American Law Schools, 1933–1941," *American Journal of Comparative Law* 50 (Fall 2002): 777–818, 783 n. 33; Peter M. Rutkoff and William B. Scott, *New School: A History of the New School for Social Research* (New York: Free Press, 1986), 96.

2. "Applications for Renewals," January 18, 1940, Box 6, Folder 14, Alfred Cohn Papers; Kraus to Meyer, July 21, 1939, Case 214, AFSC Case Files.

3. Officer's Diary, Makinsky, March 14, 1942, Box 96A, Folder 1942, RF RG12.1, RAC; Hoch, "Reception of Central European Refugee Physicists," 242.

4. Asked to estimate the number of Emergency Committee applicants who were

Aryan, Edward Murrow said 85 percent of the roughly one thousand cases on file in 1934 had been dismissed under the Aryan law—"That is to say, 15 percent are definitely 'pure Aryan.'" Murrow to Chamberlain, April 18, 1934, Box 133, Joseph P. Chamberlain Folder, Emergency Committee Papers; Cowley to Duggan, December 15, 1938, and Emergency Committee to Notschaft, December 27, 1938, both Box 141, Folder 17, Emergency Committee Papers. Around the same time as it wired the cable to the Notgemeinschaft, the committee sent Eureka College the names of four dismissed German mathematicians whom it "believed to be Aryan and Protestant"; Reinhard Siegmund-Schultze, *Mathematicians Fleeing from Nazi Germany: Individual Fates and Global Impact* (Princeton, NJ: Princeton University Press, 2009), 218.

　　5. The International Federation of University Women similarly acquiesced when McGill University refused to accept to its Royal Victoria College two scholarship students whom the federation had suggested. The residential college accepted only gentiles, as McGill's principal and vice chancellor F. Cyril James explained. The federation then suggested another candidate who seemed to fulfill "the race conditions prevailing at the Royal Victoria College"; James to Bowie, May 21, 1941; Hermes to James, July 12, 1941; Hermes to Brunauer, July 12, 1941, all Box 839, Folder Marthe Keller, Committee Records 8111, AAUWA; Officer's Diary, Makinsky, February 20, 1942, Box 96A, Folder 1942, RF RG12.1, RAC; Simpson to Birkhoff, July 27, 1931, Birkhoff 1–3 Nov (1931–1933), 4213.2.2, HUA.

　　6. The Emergency Committee had the same problem with recommending mathematicians to Eureka College. Of the four candidates it recommended to the college as "Aryan and Protestant," it had second thoughts about whether one of them fit Eureka's "racial and religious conditions." The committee turned out to be wrong about two of the others, who were actually non-Aryans; Siegmund-Schultze, *Mathematicians Fleeing from Nazi Germany,* 218. Duggan to Drury, January 5, 1939; Duggan to Cowley, January 12, 1939; Cowley to Duggan, January 24, 1939; Emergency Committee to Notschaft, February 1, 1939, all Box 141, Folder 17, Emergency Committee Papers; Drury to Cohn, February 1, 1939; Drury to Cohn, February 8, 1939; Drury to Cohn, March 20, 1939, all Box 186, Folder 10, Emergency Committee Papers.

　　7. Andrew Grant, "The Unlikely Haven for 1930s German Scientists," *Physics Today,* September 27, 2018, https://physicstoday.scitation.org/do/10.1063/PT.6.4.20180927a/full/; Seelye to Cowley, August, 4, 1942; Memo, O'Donnell, August 6, 1942; Cowley to Seelye, August 24, 1942, all Box 141, Folder 17, Emergency Committee Papers.

　　8. Todd Endelman, *Leaving the Jewish Fold: Conversion and Radical Assimilation in Modern Jewish History* (Princeton, NJ: Princeton University Press, 2015), 69; Enclosure to Mr. Sulzberger, February 16, 1939, Box 1, Folder Misc. Correspondence 1939, Carl J. Friedrich Collection HUG(FP) 17.31, HUA; Notes, "Dr. Kotschnig's Visit to U.S.A., January 6–March 10, 1936," Box 2, Folder 15, Alfred Cohn Papers.

　　9. Memo, Kittredge, October 25, 1940, Box 46, Folder 532, RF RG1.1, RAC. Around this time, President Hopkins acknowledged that Dartmouth had a Jewish quota and defended it. In a letter that was printed in the *New York Post* on August 7, 1945, Hopkins explained that Dartmouth's quota was actually better for Jews because without it the college would have to exclude Jews altogether. Hopkins wrote, "Dartmouth College is a

Christian college founded for the Christianization of its students," Carey McWilliams, *A Mask for Privilege: Anti-Semitism in America* (Boston: Little, Brown, 1949), 134.

10. Memo, Kittredge, October 25, 1940, Box 46, Folder 532, RF RG1.1, RAC; a separate evaluation of Bloch noted, "American scholars appraise Bloch's achievements unusually highly," Marc Bloch, Medieval History, n.d., Box 44, Folder 32, Emergency Committee Papers; Report, Knauth, Box 13, Folder 24, Box 13, Folder 24, Alfred Cohn Papers; Johnson to Park, April 24, 1941, Box 93, Folder 22, Emergency Committee Papers.

11. Chamberlain to Shantz, June 11, 1934, Box 133, Folder Joseph P. Chamberlain, Emergency Committee Papers. See also Britton to Murrow, August 4, 1934, Box 172, Folder 7; Flickinger to Rockefeller Foundation, December 6, 1933, Box 190, Folder 9, both Emergency Committee Papers.

12. Waldo to Shapley, February 7, 1939, Box 6A, Folder Eberhard Bruck, 4773.10, HUA; Babcock to Murrow, April 16, 1934, Box 172, Folder 6, Emergency Committee Papers; see Lederer to Murrow, February 27, 1934, Box 55, Folder 31, Emergency Committee Papers; David Lester, *Suicide and the Holocaust* (New York: Nova Science Publishers, 2005), 87; Judith P. Hallett, "'Saving Alive the Leading Scholar of the World in Her Line and Fostering an Ordinary Person Lucky in Her Chosen Career': The Endeavors and Example of the German Refugee Classicists Eva Lehman Fiesel and Ruth Fiesel," unpublished manuscript in author's possession, p. 4.

13. Brunauer to Keezer, July 14, 1938, Box 839, Folder Ruth Ehrmann de Albert and Henry Ehrmann, Committee Records 8111, AAUWA.

14. Memo, Hanstein, April 16, 1942, Case 292, AFSC Case Files.

15. Keppler to McHale, November 30, 1938, Box 839, Folder Margarete Merzbach-Kober, Committee Records 8111, AAUWA.

16. Noyes to Levene, January 5, 1939, Rockefeller Institute for Medical Research, Manuscripts and Archives Division, NYPL; Noyes to Duggan, October 26, 1933, Box 73, Folder 9, Emergency Committee Papers. There is some possibility that the transport went to Warsaw, but most sources consider Auschwitz the more likely destination; "Transport from Hamburg, Hansestadt Hamburg, Hansa City of Hamburg, Germany to Auschwitz Birkenau, Extermination Camp, Poland on 11/07/1942," International Institute for Holocaust Research, Yad Vashem, http://db.yadvashem.org/deportation/transportDetails.html?language=en&itemId=10675036; Else Hirschberg, 24750168-0-1, International Tracing Service, USHMM. Gedenkbuch—Opfer der Verfolgung der Juden unter der nationalsozialistischen Gewaltherrschaft in Deutschland 1933–1945, Bundesarchiv (German National Archives), Koblenz, 1986.

17. Wick to Duggan, May 18, 1938, Box 44, Folder 11; Statement, December 2, 1933, Box 27, Folder Nussbaum, both Emergency Committee Papers.

18. Curriculum Vitae, Ehrenzweig, Box 2, Folder Albert Ehrenzweig, UASUNY; Hirschberg to Brunauer, April 22, 1939, War Relief Files 839, Folder Margherita Hirschberg, Committee Records 8111, AAUWA; Rappaport to Buttenheim, December 12, 1938, Box 6, Folder 6, UASUNY; Siegmund-Schultze, *Mathematicians Fleeing from Nazi Germany*, 218.

19. Memo, Demuth, May 31, 1937, Box 13, Folder 2, Alfred Cohn Papers; Officer's

Diary, O'Brien, February 18, 1938, Box 115, Folder 1935–1938, RF RG12.1 RAC; Severo Ochoa, "David Nachmansohn, 1899–1983: A Biographical Memoir," *Biographical Memoirs* (Washington, DC: National Academy of Sciences, 1989), http://www.nasonline.org /publications/biographical-memoirs/memoir-pdfs/nachmansohn-david.pdf.

20. Boas to Butler, May 3, 1933, Box 318, Folder 7, Franz Boas Collection, UACL; Stieglitz to Cohn, February 21, 1936, Box 1, Folder 22, Alfred Cohn Papers.

21. S. S. Schweber, "The Empiricist Temper Regnant: Theoretical Physics in the United States 1920–1950," *Historical Studies in the Physical and Biological Sciences* 17, no. 1 (1986): 79–80. See also Hoch, "Reception of Central European Refugee Physicists," 242–43.

22. Murlin to Levene, May 17, 1940, and Levene to Murlin, July 25, 1940, both Rockefeller Institute for Medical Research, Manuscripts and Archives Division, NYPL; Rutkoff and Scott, *New School*, 86.

23. Uwe K. Faulhaber, "Intellectual Migration," *Simon Wiesenthal Center Annual* 3 (1997); Martin to Stein, January 7, 1939, Box 4, Folder 16; Drury to Executive Committee, July 11, 1939, and Cohn to Drury, November 17, 1939, both Box 4, Folder 18; Minutes, Emergency Committee Executive Committee Meeting, April 10, 1940, Box 6, Folder 25; Drury to Members of Executive Committee, November 13, 1939, Box 4, Folder 18, all Alfred Cohn Papers.

24. Story to Duggan, June 27, 1940, Box 4, Folder 30; Report, Knauth, Box 13, Folder 24; and Memo, Demuth, May 31, 1937, Box 13, Folder 2, all Alfred Cohn Papers; see also Cohn to Chamberlain, November 14, 1934; Razovsky to Sawyer, December 19, 1939; Sawyer to Chamberlain, December 29, 1939, all Box 133, Folder Joseph P. Chamberlain, Emergency Committee Papers.

25. National Refugee Service Quarterly Report, January–March 1940, and Report, Knauth, both Box 13, Folder 24, Alfred Cohn Papers.

26. Donald Peterson Kent, *The Refugee Intellectual: The Americanization of the Immigrants of 1933–1941* (New York: Columbia University Press, 1953), 42–45; Hintze to Parkins, January 8, 1939, War Relief Files 839, Folder Hedwig Hintze, Committee Records 8111, AAUWA.

27. Report, "Excerpts from Informal Report of Field Study, Refugee Section," AFSC, May 28, 1940, Box 4, Folder 30; Minutes, Emergency Committee Executive Committee Meeting, May 12, 1942, Box 6, Folder 26, both Alfred Cohn Papers; Inter-office correspondence, Kittredge, November 22, 1940, Box 46, Folder 533, RF RG1.1, RAC.

28. Lips to Duggan, May 1, 1939, Box 4, Folder 17; Minutes, Emergency Committee Executive Committee Meeting, September 21, 1939, Box 6, Folder 23; Thompson to O'Rourke, June 13, 1939, and Nathan to Drury, July 3, 1939, Box 4, Folder 18, all Alfred Cohn Papers.

29. Minutes, Emergency Committee Executive Committee Meeting, April 28, 1939, Box 6, Folder 22, Alfred Cohn Papers; Kent, *Refugee Intellectual*, 114.

30. His name was sometimes written as "Warner" and his last name as "Brock" or "Brook." Speech, Gumbel, and Speech, Heimann, both Box 1, Folder 29, UASUNY.

Chapter 7. State Department Barriers

1. See Barbara McDonald Stewart, *United States Government Policy on Refugees from Nazism 1933–1940* (New York: Garland, 1982): "The admission of scholars, artists and scientists marked the exception to the general reluctance to accept refugees. They encountered no popular opposition and the government did a great deal to be helpful" (572). Yet Stewart does not explain why only four hundred such professors had arrived in the United States by the spring of 1939 when there was no limit on the numbers who could come. The perception that professors had a relatively easy time immigrating persists. Yael Epstein, "When the Nobel Prize Was Not Enough: Jewish Chemists from the Nazi Regime as Refugees in the United States," in Richard Bodek and Simon Lewis, eds., *The Fruits of Exile: Central European Intellectual Immigration to America in the Age of Fascism* (Columbia: University of South Carolina Press, 2010), 135.

2. See Stewart, *United States Government Policy on Refugees;* Richard Breitman and Alan M. Kraut, *American Refugee Policy and European Jewry, 1933–1945* (Bloomington: Indiana University Press, 1988); David S. Wyman, *Paper Walls: America and the Refugee Crisis 1938–1941* (New York: Pantheon, 1985); Bat-Ami Zucker, *In Search of Refuge: Jews and US Consuls in Nazi Germany 1933–1941* (London: Vallentine Mitchell, 2001); and Laurel Leff, "Discretion as Discrimination: How the U.S. State Department Interpreted Immigration Laws to Bar Refugees from Nazi Europe," paper presented at Yad Vashem Biennial International Conference: "The Jewish Refugee Problem During the Shoah (1933–1945) Reconsidered," December 18–20, 2016, International School for Holocaust Studies Yad Vashem, Mount of Remembrance, Jerusalem.

3. Zucker, *In Search of Refuge,* 116–17. Messersmith also wrote in 1933: "We cannot fill our own universities with foreign professors who are alien to our thought and will influence our youth in a direction not in line with our national policy and our cultural life. The average Jew, for example, who desires to emigrate to the United States, will be very glad to be able to make a home for himself in our country and to fit himself into our picture; but these professors who feel that they have a mission in life, may potentially be a danger to us." Breitman and Kraut, *American Refugee Policy,* 44–45; Leff, "Discretion as Discrimination," includes a detailed discussion of antisemitism in the State Department and its impact on the government's refugee policy during the Nazi era.

4. Brod to Mann, November 30, 1938; Mann to Johnson, December 30, 1938; Johnson to Mann, January 4, 1939, all Box 1, Folder 28, UASUNY.

5. Sidney Kansas, *U.S. Immigration Exclusion and Deportation and Citizenship of the United States,* 2nd ed. (Albany, NY: Matthew Bender, 1941), 35; Reinhard Siegmund-Schultze, *Mathematicians Fleeing from Nazi Germany: Individual Fates and Global Impact* (Princeton, NJ: Princeton University Press, 2009), 105.

6. Michael A. Meyer, "The Refugee Scholars Project of the Hebrew Union," in Bertram Wallace Korn, ed., *A Bicentennial Festschrift for Jacob Radar Marcus* (New York: Ktav, 1976), 359–75, 364, 371.

7. Drury to Committee, January, 10, 1940, Box 4, Folder 19, Alfred Cohn Papers; Johnson to Florence, August 1, 1941, Box 4, Folder 154, UASUNY; Inter-office correspon-

dence, Kittredge, October 9, 1940, Box 46, Folder 532, RF RG11, RAC; Marilyn Ogilvie and Joy Harvey, eds., *Biographical Dictionary of Women in Science* (New York: Routledge, 2000), 1393.

8. State Department officials told Johnson in August 1940 that the restriction applied to "those who have been in research positions which did not include teaching." Inter-office correspondence, Appleget, August 8, 1940, Box 46, Folder 531, RF RG11, RAC; Coyle to Johnson, February 28, 1940; Johnson to Coyle, February 29, 1940; Borchard to Johnson, March 2, 1940; Johnson to Borchard, March 5, 1940; Borchard to Johnson, March 7, 1940; Johnson to Borchard, March 13, 1940, all Box 2, Folder 96, UASUNY.

9. The eight refugee scholars whom the NYPL hired to work in its Humanities Research Library did not immigrate as librarians with non-quota visas. Six were hired once they were in the United States, and two, Curt Sachs and Roman Jakobson, obtained faculty positions at New York University and the New School, respectively, while also working at the public library. Miriam Intrator, "A Temporary Haven: Jewish World War II Refugee Scholars at the NYPL, 1933–1945," 21–22, https://www.studienverlag .at/bookimport/oezgArchiv/media/data0912/4898_oezg3_2010_s10_35_intrator.pdf; Coulter to Brunauer, October 10, 1940, and Nathan to Brunauer, n.d., both Box 839, Folder Helen Nathan, Committee Records 8111, AAUWA.

10. Morgenstern to Drury, February 5, 1940, and Morgenstern to Drury, April 3, 1940, both Box 6, Folder 14, Alfred Cohn Papers. Arnold Reisman, "Walter Gottschalk: A Pioneer of Library Science and His Interactions with Albert Einstein During the Nazi Era," *Covenant* 3, no. 1 (August 2009), http://www.covenant.idc.ac.il/en/vol3/issue1/walter _gottschalk_a_pioneer_of_modern.html.

11. Memo, Concerning Appointment of Aliens, Greene, June 8, 1939, Box 30, Folder 20:1356, Harvard Medical School, Office of the Dean, RG M-DE01, FCLM; Meyer, "Refugee Scholars Project," 345.

12. Borchard to Johnson, January 24, 1941; Warren to Borchard, June 17, 1941; Borchard to Johnson, July 1, 1941; Johnson to Borchard, July 7, 1941, all Box 2, Folder 167, UASUNY; see also Meyer, "Refugee Scholars Project," 345.

13. Baron to Johnson, January 29, 1941, Box 6, Folder 158, UASUNY; see also Meyer, "Refugee Scholars Project," 370.

14. Emergency Committee Minutes, May 9, 1939, Box 6, Folder 22, Alfred Cohn Papers.

15. Waldo to Shapley, February 7, 1939, Box 6A, Folder Arthur Korn; Waldo to Shapley, March 2, 1939, Box 6A, Folder Eberhard Bruck; Waldo to Shapley, March 2, 1939, Box 6A, Folder Arthur Korn, all 4773.10, HUA.

16. In fiscal year 1939 the German quota—then a combined German and Austrian quota of 27,370—was filled for the first and only time during the Nazi era. The quotas were again unfilled in subsequent years, dropping to 4,883 in fiscal year 1942. Breitman and Kraut, *American Refugee Policy,* 64–66, 112; see Aden to Brunauer, August 29, 1939, Box 839, Folder Erna Opitz, Committee Records 8111, AAUWA; Meyer, "Refugee Scholars Project," 370; Baer to Sachar, February 15, 1939, Box 839, Folder Else Hirschberg; Notes,

Helen Parkins, January 28, January 29, and March 14, 1939, Box 839, Folder Auguste Jellinek, all Committee Records 8111, AAUWA.

17. Shapley to Korn, December 13, 1938, and Korn to Shapley, January 2, 1939, both Box 6B, Folder Korn, 4773.10, HUA.

18. Korn to Shapley, April 11, 1939, ibid.

19. Jellinek to Brunauer, September 7, 1938; Notes, Parkins, January 29, January 28, March 14, 1939; Jellinek to Parkins, n.d.; Parkins to Jellinek, January 30, 1939; Warren to Brunauer, June 29, 1939, all War Relief Files 839, Folder August Jellinek, Committee Records 8111, AAUWA; University Women's International Networks Database, "Dr. Auguste Jellinek," Max Planck Institute for the History of Science, http://uwind.mpiwg-berlin .mpg.de/de/fm13-dab-detail/56.

20. Officer's Diary, Makinsky, September 16, September 29, October 2, 1940, all Box 96A, Folder 1940, RF RG12.1, RAC.

21. Zucker, *In Search of Refuge,* 114–15.

22. Nathan to Brunauer, n.d., Box 839, Folder Helen Nathan, Committee Records 8111, AAUWA; Helen Nathan, 41769468-0-1.tif, International Tracing Service, USHMM.

23. Zucker, *In Search of Refuge,* 116; Breitman and Kraut, *American Refugee Policy,* 120, 135; Officer's Diary, Makinsky, June 13, 1941, Box 96, Folder 1941, RF RG12.1, RAC; Thieman to Cohn, August 19, 1941, Case 54, AFSC Case Files.

24. Hilb to Goldmann, etc., May 19, 1943, Box D16, Folder 9, World Jewish Congress MSS 361, American Jewish Archives, Cincinnati, Ohio; Johnson to Haensel, August 8, 1941; Haensel to Johnson, July 8, 1941; Haensel to Johnson, August 7, 1941; Haensel to Halle, February 7, 1941, all Box 5, Folder 47, UASUNY; Officer's Diary, Makinsky, Thursday, July 17, 1941, Box 96A, Folder 1941, RF RG12.1, RAC; Johnson to Haensel, July 10, 1941, and Josephson to Solow or Silberman, November 23, 1942, both Box 5, Folder 47, UASUNY; List, "Passengers on the 'Serpa Pinto'—November 29, 1942," Holocaust Victims and Survivors Database, USHMM, https://www.ushmm.org/media/images/vlp namelist/ACo355/ACo355.PDF.

25. Officer's Diary, Marshall, March 24, 1941, Box 96A, Folder 1941, RF RG12.1, RAC; the names and ages of Bloch's six children in July 1941 were: Alice (twenty-one), Etienne (nineteen), Louis (eighteen), Daniel (fifteen), Jean-Paul (eleven), and Suzanne (ten). Drury to Painter, October 14, 1941, Box 44, Folder 32, Emergency Committee Papers; see also Officer's Diary, Makinsky, May 26, 1941, Box 96A, Folder 1941, RF RG12.1, RAC; Carole Fink, *Marc Bloch: A Life in History* (Cambridge: Cambridge University Press, 1991); Peter M. Rutkoff and William B. Scott, *New School: A History of the New School for Social Research* (New York: Free Press, 1986), 133; along with the names and birthdates of his six children, Bloch also specified the names and location of his and his wife's siblings, who were all in France. Officer's Diary, Makinsky, July 14, 1941, Box 96A, Folder 1941, RF RG12.1, RAC.

26. Biele to Johnson, December 10, 1941; Johnson to Storch, December 18, 1941; Storch to Sir, January 6, 1942; Kristeller to Solow, January 21, 1942; Mayerson to Solow, July 3, 1942, all Box 7, Folder 1, UASUNY.

27. See Box 5, Folder 154, UASUNY. B. Polak to Johnson, July 15, 1941, Box 5,

Folder 153, UASUNY. See also Officer's Diary, Makinsky, July 2, 1941, Box 96A, Folder 1941, RF RG12.1, RAC; Staudinger to Wynmalen, March 24, 1942, and Staudinger to Wynmalen, March 25, 1942, Box 5, Folder 154, UASUNY; Leonard, Henriette, Bettina, Antoinette Polak, TD #959475, International Tracing Service, USHMM.

28. Officer's Diary, Makinsky, June 16, 1941, Box 96A, Folder 1940, RF RG12.1, RAC; Reinhard Siegmund-Schultze, "Rockefeller Support for Mathematicians Fleeing from the Nazi Purge," in Guiliana Gemelli, ed., *The "Unacceptables": American Foundations and Refugee Scholars Between the Two Wars and After* (Brussels: P.I.E.–Peter Lang, 2000), 103–4.

29. Johnson to Ehrlich, December 18, 1940; Johnson to Morris, December 18, 1940; Johnson to Appleget, March 11, 1941, all Box 2, Folder 117, UASUNY.

30. Lawton to Long, March 19, 1941, and Cunningham to Ferriere, May 12, 1941, ibid.

31. Ehrlich to Johnson, April 14, 1941, ibid.

32. Rockefeller Foundation official to Gardiner, November 21, 1941, and Note, Paine telephone call, August 23, 1943, ibid.; Warsaw Uprising Museum, "Andrzej Ehrlich," https://www.1944.pl/powstancze-biogramy/andrzej-ehrlich,9581.html.

33. Ehrlich to Johnson, May 27, 1945, and Johnson to Ehrlich, October 4, 1945, both Box 2, Folder 117, UASUNY; "Ehrlich, Ludwik," YIVO Encyclopedia of Jews in Eastern Europe, http://www.yivoencyclopedia.org/article.aspx/Ehrlich_Ludwik.

Chapter 8. An International Crisis

1. Herskovits to Kolinski, January 22, 1935; April 11, 1935; March 1, 1935; June 25, 1935; January 4, 1937, all Melville Herskovits Papers, Mieczyslaw Kolinski Box 11, Folder 23; Universität Hamburg, Institut für Historische Musikwissenschaft, "Mieczyslaw Kolinski," https://www.lexm.uni-hamburg.de/object/lexm_lexmperson_00001287.

2. Although Herskovits took a special interest in Kolinski, he cared about the refugee issue generally. When the former refugee high commissioner visited Northwestern in March 1936, Walter Kotschnig found Herskovits to be "the person most interested on the campus in German scholars." Herskovits asked for a complete, annotated list of displaced anthropologists. Notes, Kotschnig's Visit to U.S.A., March 11 to March 20, 1936, Box 2, Folder 15, Alfred Cohn Papers; Herskovits to Kolinski, January 13, 1937; February 17, 1937; April 14, 1937; June 4, 1937, all Melville Herskovits Papers, Mieczyslaw Kolinski Box 11, Folder 23.

3. Flexner to Levene, December 15, 1938, Rockefeller Institute for Medical Research, Manuscripts and Archives Division, NYPL.

4. Wieruszowski to Madam, September 25, 1938, War Relief Files 839, Folder Helene Wieruszowski, Committee Records 8111, AAUWA; Curriculum vitae, Helen Wieruszowski, and Singleton to Emergency Committee, October 4, 1939, both Box 4, Folder 18, Alfred Cohn Papers.

5. Cohn to Razovsky, March 3, 1939, Box 13, Folder 35, Alfred Cohn Papers.

6. Razovsky to Cohn, March 7, 1939, ibid.

7. Rappaport to Buttenheim, December 12, 1938, and Johnson to Buttenheim, December 28, 1938, both Box 6, Folder 6, UASUNY. As he was about to be deported to Theresienstadt via Hanover on February 9, 1945, the sixty-five-year-old Rappaport fled during the night. Philipp August Rappaport, IP 12531540-0-1, International Tracing Service, USHMM.

8. Drury to Barschak, October 24, 1938, Box 40, Folder 10–11, Emergency Committee Papers; Parkins to Blume, January 5, 1939, Box 839, Folder Erna Barschak, Committee Records 8111, AAUWA. Barschak then qualified for entry under the U.S. quota in August 1940. Barschak to Holitscher, August 5, 1940, Box 839, Folder Erna Barschak, Committee Records 8111, AAUWA. Upon arrival in the United States, Fritz Demuth of the Notgemeinschaft reconnected her with the Emergency Committee, which immediately set to work trying to find her an academic position with strong support from scholars Frieda Wunderlich and Alice Salomon. Demuth to Drury, September 5, 1940, Box 40, Folder 10–11, Emergency Committee Papers. Within a year, Barschak got a position at Wilson College in Chambersburg, PA, supported by a faculty fund. Seelye to Drury, July 3, 1941, and Memo, Allyn, June 24, 1942, both Box 40, Folder 10–11, Emergency Committee Papers. She then taught at Miami University in Ohio.

9. Kittredge to Paris office, May 16, 1938, Box 46, Folder 529, RF RG1.1, RAC.

10. Johnson to Menzies, July 14, 1938, and Menzies to Johnson, July 24, 1938, both Box 1, Folder 111, UASUNY.

11. Kittredge to SHW, April 25, 1938, and Graves to Stevens, May 27, 1938, both Box 46, Folder 529, RF RG1.1, RAC.

12. Klaus Taschwer, Johannes Feichtinger, Stafan Sienell, and Heidemarie Uhl, eds., *Experimental Biology in the Vienna Prater: On the History of the Institute for Experimental Biology 1902 to 1945* (Vienna: Austrian Academy of Sciences, 2016), 50.

13. Brecher to AAUW, April 9, 1938, War Relief Files 839, Folder Leonore Brecher, Committee Records 8111, AAUWA; Brecher to Dunn, April 7, 1938; Dunn to Brecher, April 22, 1938; Brecher to Dunn, June 6, 1938; Pond to Dunn, July 2, 1938, all Leonore Brecher 1930–1938, L. C. Dunn Papers, R:D19, APS.

14. Maltby to Drury, April 25, 1938, and Drury to Maltby, April 26, 1938, both Box 46, Folder 34, Emergency Committee Papers.

15. Brecher to Brunauer, February 29, 1940, War Relief Files 839, Folder Lenore Brecher, Committee Records 8111, AAUWA; Universität Kiel und Nationalsozialismus, "Dr. Leonore Brecher," Christian-Albrechts-Universität zu Kiel, https://www.uni-kiel.de/ns-zeit/bios/brecher-leonore.shtml.

16. Brecher to Dean, February 2, 1939; Drury to Hubbard, February 28, 1939; Assistant Director to Brunauer, March 2, 1939, all Box 46, Folder 34, Emergency Committee Papers.

17. It is not known how Sims knew Brecher or how she communicated her concerns to him. Sims to AAUW, November 1, 1939, War Relief Files 839, Folder Lenore Brecher, Committee Records 8111, AAUWA; Sims to Emergency Committee in Aid of Displaced Foreign Scholars, November 1, 1939, and Drury to Sims, November 10, 1939, both Box 46, Folder 34, Emergency Committee Papers.

18. Brecher to Brunauer, February 29, 1940, War Relief Files 839, Folder Lenore Brecher, Committee Records 8111, AAUWA.

19. Brecher to Drury, March 3, 1940; Drury to Dunn, March 29, 1940; Dunn to Drury, April 4, 1940; Drury to Brecher, April 12, 1940, all Box 46, Folder 34, Emergency Committee Papers.

20. Schirmann to Colleagues, September 21, 1940, Box 839, Folder Marie Anna Schirmann, Committee Records 8111, AAUWA.

21. Ibid.; Schirmann to Razovsky, January 19, 1939, Box 112, Folder 11, Emergency Committee Papers.

22. Schirmann to Drury, January 20, 1939, Box 112, Folder 11, Emergency Committee Papers.

23. Drury to Schirmann, May 13, 1939, and Schirmann to Drury, June 4, 1939, both ibid.; Schirmann to Colleagues, September 21, 1940, Box 839, Folder Marie Anna Schirmann, Committee Records 8111, AAUWA.

24. Schirmann to Razovsky, July 31, 1939; Schirmann to Razovsky, December 19, 1939; Schirmann to Drury, December 19, 1939, all Box 112, Folder 11, Emergency Committee Papers.

25. Carlos Petit, *Max Radin, Cartas Romanisticas (1923–1950)* (Naples: Jovene, 2001), 141–42. Schulz was not able to get a position in the United States. He fled first to the Netherlands and then to England.

26. Salmon to Munro, April 28, 1939, Case 1521, AFSC Case Files; Johnson to Borchard, January 17, 1941, Box 2, Folder 167, UASUNY.

27. Drury to Ladenburg, January 3, 1939, Box 81, Folder 61, Emergency Committee Papers; Christine von Oertzen, *Science, Gender, and Internationalism: Women's Academic Networks, 1917–1955* (New York: Palgrave Macmillan 2014), 147.

28. Kohn to Brunauer, March 29, 1939, Box 839, Folder Hedwig Kohn, Committee Records 8111, AAUWA.

29. Ibid.

30. Ibid.

31. Hollitscher to Brunauer, March 31, 1939, and Douglas to Holme, March 17, 1939, ibid.

32. Ladenburg to Brunauer, November 8, 1939, ibid.

33. See Horst Junginger, *The Scientification of "The Jewish Question" in Nazi Germany* (Leiden: Koninklijke Brill, 2017), 164.

34. Duggan to Borchard, March 23, 1939, Box 57, Folder 55, Emergency Committee Papers; Kraus to Hula, March 20, 1940, and Schaufuss to Kraus (quoting excerpt from Hula), April 4, 1940, both Case 3904, AFSC Case Files.

35. G. Field to Thieman, May 4, 1941, Case 3904, AFSC Case Files; Fleischmann to Borchard, March 2, 1939 (trans. from German by Eric Idsvoog), Box 57, Folder 55, Emergency Committee Papers.

36. Laurel Leff, *Buried by* The Times: *The Holocaust and America's Most Important Newspaper* (New York: Cambridge University Press, 2005), 71–72; Notes, Drury, March

14, 1940, Box 57, Folder 55, Emergency Committee Papers; Schaufuss to Kraus, April 11, 1940, Case 3904, AFSC Case Files.

37. Schaufuss to Kraus, April 11, 1940, Case 3904, AFSC Case Files; Horkheimer to Duggan, May 15, 1940, Box 4, Folder 30, Alfred Cohn Papers; Radin to Johnson, June 15, 1940, Box 2, Folder 167, UASUNY.

38. Autobiographical Data, Hintze, n.d., Box 72, Folder 48, Emergency Committee Papers; Bezirksamt Charlottenburg-Wilmersdorf, "Gedenktafeln für Otto und Hedwig Hintze," https://www.berlin.de/ba-charlottenburg-wilmersdorf/ueber-den-bezirk/geschichte/gedenktafeln/artikel.125744.php.

39. Hintze to Institute for Displaced German Scholars, March 14, 1939, Box 72, Folder 48, Emergency Committee Papers.

40. Ibid.

41. Kalmus to Duggan, October 15, 1938, Box 6, Folder 11, RF RG1.1, RAC; Andrew Gregory, "Hans Kalmus: Distinguished Geneticist and Biologist," Harpenden History, http://www.harpenden-history.org.uk/page_id__369.aspx.

42. Spiegel to AAUW, February 17, 1940; Spiegel to Brunauer, April 24, 1940; Brunauer to Hollitscher, March 27, 1940, all War Relief Files 839, Folder Käthe Spiegel, Committee Records 8111, AAUWA.

43. Spiegel to Brunauer, April 24, 1940, and Brunauer to Wilkins, May 15, 1940, ibid.

44. Spiegel to Duggan, May 7, 1940, and Spiegel to Sirs, March 28, 1941, both Box 118, Folder 25, Emergency Committee Papers; Spiegel to Friends, April 5, 1941, and Spiegel to Brunauer, November 21 1940, both War Relief Files 839, Folder Käthe Spiegel, Committee Records 8111, AAUWA.

45. Kolinski to Herskovits, February 20, 1938; Herskovits to Kolinski, February 22, 1938; Kolinski to Herskovits, December 18, 1938; Herskovits to Smets, August 18, 1938; Herskovits to Frans, August 18, 1938; Herskovits to Sliggs, August 18, 1938, all Melville Herskovits Papers, Mieczyslaw Kolinski Box 11, Folder 23.

46. Herskovits to Kolinski, October 17, 1938; Kolinski to Herskovits, November 14, 1938, December 18, 1938, all ibid.

47. Herskovits to Leland, December 16, 1938, ibid.; Herskovits to Kolinski, February 1, 1939; Herskovits to Goldsmith, March 23, 1939; Herskovits to Embree, March 27, 1939; Kolinski to Herskovits, March 31, 1939 (Kolinski uses a German idiom more like "from the rain into the gutter"), all Melville Herskovits Papers, Mieczyslaw Kolinski Box 12, Folder 1.

48. Herskovits to Drury, March 31, 1939; Boas to Emergency Committee, April 3, 1939; Herzog to Drury, April 24, 1939, all Box 82, Folder 1, Emergency Committee Papers.

49. Herskovits to Drury, May 15, 1939; Hibbard to Drury, September 11, 1939; Drury to Stein, September 23, 1939, all ibid.; Herskovits to Drury, April 17, 1939; Goodchild to Herskovits, April 26, 1939; Snyder to Broy, May 5, 1939; Herskovits to Kolinski, May 16, 1939; Herskovits to Kolinski, May 25, 1939, all Melville Herskovits Papers, Mieczyslaw Kolinski Box 12, Folder 1.

50. Kolinski to Herskovits, July 7, 1939, Melville Herskovits Papers, Mieczyslaw Kolinski Box 12, Folder 1.

51. Herskovits to Houghteling, September 29, 1939; Herskovits to Pattee, September 28, 1939; Smith to Sussdorf, September 28, 1939; Graves to Herskovits, October 14, 1939; Herskovits to Graves, October 18, 1939, all ibid.

52. Warren to Hibbard, October 13, 1939, and Sussdorf to Smith, October 27, 1939, both ibid. See also Drury to Committee, January 10, 1940, and Drury to Razovsky, January 2, 1940, both Box 4, Folder 19, Alfred Cohn Papers.

53. Kolinski to Herskovits, November 3, 1939; Herskovits to Kolinski, January 15, 1939 [sic]; Herskovits to Antoine, January 15, 1940; Antoine to Herskovits, January 19, 1940; Herskovits to Antoine, February 7, 1940; Herskovits to Kolinski, February 13, 1940, all Melville Herskovits Papers, Mieczyslaw Kolinski Box 12, Folder 1.

54. Herskovits to Drury, February 8, 1940; Snyder to Lucas, December 15, 1939; Herskovits to Hazard, December 16, 1939; Lucas to Snyder, December 27, 1939; Sussdorf to Lucas, January 23, 1940; Boas to Razovsky, January 15, 1940, all ibid.; Herskovits to Drury, February 8, 1940, Alfred Cohn Papers.

55. Herskovits to Kolinski, February 16, 1940; Herskovits to Keppel, May 1, 1940; Herskovits to Antoine, May 1, 1940; Herskovits to Goodchild, May 1, 1940; Keppel to Herskovits, May 3, 1940; Herskovits to Keppel, May 6, 1940, all Melville Herskovits Papers, Mieczyslaw Kolinski Box 12, Folder 1.

Chapter 9. More Need, Less Help

1. Report, "Excerpts from Informal Report of Field Study," Refugee Section, AFSC, May 28, 1940, Box 4, Folder 30, Alfred Cohn Papers.

2. Kotschnig to Gregg, January 31, 1935, Box 135, Folder Experts Committee 1934–1935; Chamberlain to Duggan, January 19, 1936, Box 133, Folder Joseph Chamberlain, both Emergency Committee Papers.

3. Chase to Duggan, September 4, 1940, July 2, 1941, both Box 120, Folder New York University 1938–1940, Emergency Committee Papers.

4. Report, Knauth, Box 13, Folder 24; Wolfe to Sirs, May 15, 1939, Box 4, Folder 17, both Alfred Cohn Papers.

5. Sigerist to Murrow, April 26, 1935, Box 172, Folder 11, Emergency Committee Papers.

6. Kyle Graham, "The Refugee Jurist and American Law Schools, 1933–1941," *American Journal of Comparative Law* 50 (Fall 2002): 777–818, 793–94; Waggoner to Biele, November 1, 1941, Box 7, Folder 1, UASUNY.

7. See Minutes, Emergency Committee Executive Committee Meeting, March 2, 1937, Box 6, Folder 20, Alfred Cohn Papers; Drury to Murrow, March 6, 1935, Box 172, Folder 10, Emergency Committee Papers.

8. Kahn to Razovsky, February 16, 1937, Box 5, Folder 32, Alfred Cohn Papers.

9. Whyte to Lambert, June 29, 1936, Box 190, Folder 9, Emergency Committee Papers; Dunn to Cohn, June 2, 1936, Box 13, Folder 1; Minutes, Emergency Committee

Executive Committee Meeting, January 20, 1937, Box 6, Folder 20, both Alfred Cohn Papers.

10. Kahn to Razovsky, March 2, 1937, Box 5, Folder 32; Memo, Drury to Whyte, November 18, 1936, Box 2, Folder 6, both Alfred Cohn Papers; Giuliana Gemelli, "Introduction: Scholars in Adversity and Science Policies (1933–1945)," in Guiliana Gemelli, ed., *The "Unacceptables": American Foundations and Refugee Scholars Between the Two Wars and After* (Brussels: P.I.E.–Peter Lang, 2000), 28–29; Dunn to Whyte, February 8, 1937, Box 3, Folder 6, Alfred Cohn Papers.

11. Kahn to Razovsky, March 2, 1937, Box 5, Folder 32; Dunn to Whyte, June 18, 1937, Box 2, Folder 7, both Alfred Cohn Papers.

12. Nathenson to Winter, March 14, 1940, and Cohn to Drury, March 27, 1940, both Box 4, Folder 19; Drury to Cohn, February 6, 1941, Box 4, Folder 21; Drury to Executive Committee, July 10, 1941, Box 4, Folder 22, all Alfred Cohn Papers. See also B. R. Erick Peirson, "Victor Jollos (1887–1941)," Embryo Project Encyclopedia, September 16, 2014, https://embryo.asu.edu/pages/victor-jollos-1887-1941.

13. Drury to Members of the Committee, April 6, 1938, Box 4, Folder 14; Comments on budget, December 8, 1937, Box 16, Folder 12; Gortner to Drury, February 15, 1938, Box 4, Folder 14; Application for renewals, n.d., Box 4, Folder 13, all Alfred Cohn Papers.

14. Read to Duggan, March 4, 1938, and Read to Salomon, March 4, 1938, both Box 4, Folder 14, Alfred Cohn Papers.

15. Claus-Dieter Krohn, *Intellectuals in Exile: Refugee Scholars and the New School for Social Research* (Amherst: University of Massachusetts Press, 1993), 29. When Duggan mentioned the reluctance to use already allocated student exchange funds to hire refugee scholars, other Emergency Committee members thought college presidents might respond differently if presented with a specific scholar; Minutes, Emergency Committee Executive Committee Meeting, September 4, 1940; Dunn to Cohn, August 1, 1940; Memo, Drury, July 26, 1939, all Box 4, Folder 18, Alfred Cohn Papers.

16. Minutes, Emergency Committee Executive Committee Meeting, April 28, 1939, Box 6, Folder 22, Alfred Cohn Papers.

17. Shapley to Hendrickson, April 25, 1940, Box 6B, Folder Frederick Lenz, 4773.10, HUA; List of contributors, February 1936, Box 4, Folder 11; Shapley to Ittleson February 5, 1940, Box 1, Folder 25, both Alfred Cohn Papers.

18. The colleague signed his letter "T.E.S.," so it was not possible to determine the author. In a letter to Jehle, Shapley mentions that he "had some correspondence with Dr. Struve," probably astrophysicist Otto Struve, yet the initials do not correspond; T.E.S. to Shapley, September 16, 1940, and Shapley to Jehle, September 17, 1940, both Box 6A, Folder U, 4773.10, HUA. Brought before a Gestapo tribunal in France, Jehle refused military service and was imprisoned in several internment camps in Vichy France, including Gurs. A Quaker friend facilitated Jehle's release, and he eventually came to the United States in September 1941, joining the Harvard faculty. Jehle had a long, distinguished career as a physics professor; his last position was at George Washington University. Bert Schroer, "Physicists in Times of War," last revised March 20, 2006, https://arxiv.org/abs

/physics/0603095. A friend of DeRoy's who lived in Cambridge, MA, had originally contacted Shapley in August 1940 after DeRoy had escaped to Toulouse ahead of the German Army and concluded he would not be able to live under Nazi rule. DeRoy later wrote himself from Toulouse: "Despite all the eventful happenings of the last few months, I am still astronomy-minded." He added that he had brought some of his papers with him to Toulouse and was in touch with observatory staff there and in Lyons. "I am doing some work, for there is a rather good library at Toulouse. This is a help to me in my present anxiety and trouble, for the stars are something of the Eternal." DeRoy decided to return to Antwerp but still hoped for a U.S. university post. "I would be very glad to avail myself of any suitable offer, in order to escape from the caricature of civilization which is bound to disfigure this part of the World," DeRoy wrote Shapley. DeRoy concluded: "If you were able to get me out of this European hell, words could hardly express my gratitude to you and your friends." Shapley was not able to do so; DeRoy remained in Antwerp. Despite limited food and constant terror, he returned to observing in September 1941. During that winter, he contracted pneumonia and never recovered. He died on May 15, 1942, at the age of fifty-eight. Jeremy Shears, "Félix de Roy: A Life of Variable Stars," *Journal of the British Astronomical Association* 121, no. 4 (2011), http://www.britastro.org/vss/JBAA%20121-4%20Shears%20de%20Roy.pdf.

19. Statement, "Summarized Statement of The Plan for Asylum Associateships," May 1940, Box 1, Folder 25, Alfred Cohn Papers.

20. Liebman to Ittleson, March 25, 1940, Box 1, Folder 25, Alfred Cohn Papers.

21. Minutes, Emergency Committee Executive Committee Meeting, April 10, 1940, Box 6, Folder 23, Alfred Cohn Papers; Bessie Zaban Jones, "To the Rescue of the Learned: The Asylum Fellowship Plan at Harvard, 1938–1940," *Harvard Library Bulletin* 32 (Summer 1984): 217–18. See also Cohn to Duggan, June 12, 1940, Box 186, Folder 11, Emergency Committee Papers; Memo, "Professor Shapley's Plan," April 19, 1940, and Cohn to Shapley, May 23, 1940, both Box 1, Folder 25, Alfred Cohn Papers.

22. Cohn to Stein, April 18, 1940; Duggan to Cohn, May 1, 1940; Shapley to Goldwasser, May 9, 1940; Cohn to Dugan, May 17, 1940; Shapley to Cohn, May 18, 1940; Cohn to Shapley, May 23, 1940, all Box 1, Folder 25, Alfred Cohn Papers; Emergency Committee Executive Meeting, September 26, 1940, Box 5, Folder 3, Alfred Cohn Papers. Eberhard Bruck was among them, even though his field (he had been a professor of Roman law at the University of Bonn until his dismissal in 1935) and his age (sixty-one in 1938) weighed against him. But ultimately Bruck had something more important in his favor— the intercession of Harvard secretary Jerome Greene. Greene, who knew Bruck's brother and Bruck's Harvard student son, wrote to UC Berkeley law professor Max Radin for help "rescuing the unfortunate man from his present precarious position." It took a while, but Bruck managed to get a research associate position at Harvard; Carlos Petit, *Max Radin, Cartas Romanisticas (1923–1950)* (Naples: Jovene, 2001), 139–40. See also Greene to Johnson, September 24, 1938; Johnson to Greene, September 26, 1938; Greene to Johnson, September 28, 1938, all Box 2, Folder 17, UASUNY.

23. Baker to Burwell, September 30, 1940, Box 30, Folder 20:1357, Harvard Medical School, Office of the Dean, Subject Files, RG M-DE01, FCLM; see, for example, Bur-

well to Castle, October 24, 1939, and Castle to Burwell, December 4, 1939, both Box 30, Folder 21:1362, Harvard Medical School, Office of the Dean, Subject Files, RG M-DE01, FCLM.

24. Cohn to Chamberlain, January 24, 1939, January 18, 1939, both Box 5, Folder 7, Alfred Cohn Papers; Cobb to Burwell, November 7, 1939; Burwell to Cobb, November 14, 1939; Burwell to Cobb, October 7, 1939, all Box 30, Folder 21:1362, Harvard Medical School, Office of the Dean, Subject Files, RG M-DE01, FCLM. Von Witzleben's fate could not be discovered. Wolbach to Burwell, July 24, 1940, and Nissen to Wolbach, July 19, 1940, both Box 30, Folder 21:1361, Harvard Medical School, Office of the Dean, Subject Files, RG M-DE01, FCLM. Jozsef Honti and Arin Namal, "Efforts in 1947 to Make Prof. Dr. Ernestus de Balogh (1890–1964) Work for the University of Istanbul," https://www.researchgate.net/publication/8017833_Efforts_in_1947_to_make_Prof_Dr_Ernestus_de_Balogh_1890-1964_work_for_the_University_of_Istanbul.

25. Lucas Ellerbroek and Andy Brown, *Planet Hunters: The Search for Extraterrestrial Life* (London: Reaktion, 2017), 89, 247; Shapley to Gentlemen, October 15, 1942, and Makinsky to Shapley, October 20, 1942, both Box 6A, Folder Ferdinand Beer, Harlow Shapley Collection, 4773.10, HUA.

26. Note, Shapley, n.d., and Shapley to Shane, October 27, 1942, both Box 6A, Folder Ferdinand Beer, Harlow Shapley Collection, 4773.10, HUA.

27. Minutes, Subcommittee on Applications Meeting, December 4, 1941, Box 5, Folder 1, Alfred Cohn Papers; Donald Peterson Kent, *The Refugee Intellectual: The Americanization of the Immigrants of 1933–1941* (New York: Columbia University Press, 1953), 124.

28. Reinhard Siegmund-Schultze, *Mathematicians Fleeing from Nazi Germany: Individual Fates and Global Impact* (Princeton, NJ: Princeton University Press, 2009), 225–26; Richardson to Fisher, March 10, 1939, Box 4, Folder 16, Alfred Cohn Papers.

29. Duggan to Keppel, April 15, 1939, Box 4, Folder 29, Alfred Cohn Papers; Drury to Duggan, December 28, 1938, Record of the Emergency Committee, RG-19.061, USHMM; Himstead to Duggan, April 28, 1939, Box 4, Folder 29, Alfred Cohn Papers; Himstead to Colleagues, October 14, 1939, Record of the Emergency Committee, RG-19.061, USHMM.

30. Robin E. Rider, "Alarm and Opportunity: Emigration of Mathematicians and Physicists to Britain and the United States, 1933–1945," *Historical Studies in the Physical Sciences* 15, no. 1 (1984): 124–25; Flexner to Birkhoff, September 30, 1938, Birkhoff 2–13 Nov (1938–1939), 4213.2.2, HUA; A. Flexner to Duggan, March 7, 1938, Box 4, Folder 14; Veblen to Duggan, March 13, 1939, Box 4, Folder 16, both Alfred Cohn Papers.

31. Freeman to Fosdick, July 18, 1940; Fosdick to Freeman, July 22, 1940, both Box 46, Folder 530; Staff Conference, October 23, 1940, Box 46, Folder 532, both Rockefeller Foundation RG1.1, RAC. See also Freeman to Fosdick, September 26, 1940, Box 46, Folder 531, Rockefeller Foundation RG1.1, RAC.

32. Steve Nadis and Shing-Tung Yau, *History in Sum: 150 Years of Mathematics at Harvard (1825–1975)* (Cambridge, MA: Harvard University Press, 2013), 81–85; Birkhoff to Evans, February 17, 1938; Evans to Birkhoff, February 21, 1938; Birkhoff to Evans,

March 12, 1938, Birkhoff 5–4 Dec (1936–1944), 4213.2.2, HUA. In 1936, Birkhoff recommended Harvard Ph.D. S. B. Myers, "who is, by the way, Jewish," and "very pleasant and attractive looking," to be a University of Michigan professor. Myers joined the Michigan faculty. The following year he also noted that Ralph P. Boas Jr., who had just obtained his Ph.D. from Harvard, was Jewish. Boas began teaching at Duke University in 1939; Birkhoff to Hildebrandt, March 30, 1936, and Birkhoff to Appointment Office, February 17, 1937, both Birkhoff 5–4 Dec (1936–1944), 4213.2.2, HUA.

33. Birkhoff to Richardson, November 15, 1935, Birkhoff 5–4 Dec (1936–1944), 4213.2.2, HUA.

34. Lengyel to Birkhoff, March 6, 1937; Lengyel to Birkhoff, April 1, 1937, both ibid.

35. Gale to Birkhoff, October 29, 1937; Gale to Birkhoff, November 6, 1937, both ibid.; Nadis and Yau, *History in Sum,* 82; Birkhoff to Gale, November 4, 1937, Birkhoff 5–4 Dec (1936–1944), 4213.2.2, HUA.

36. See Henry Fairchild, "Are Refugees a Liability? A Debate," *Forum* 101 (June 1939): 316–18, and Abbott Hamilton, "Refugee Scholars and American Education," *Scribner's Commentator* 11 (December 1941): 89–92.

37. The minutes for these meetings seem to be dated incorrectly. As indicated below, the minutes bear the dates October 9 and December 5, 1939, yet the conversation described in the minutes mentions *plans* to conduct a Gallup poll and to send a representative to U.S. universities. The Gallup poll was conducted in March 1939 and the tour began in October 1939. It is therefore likely that the minutes are from fall 1938 when those plans were in the works, not fall 1939 when they had already taken place; Minutes, Emergency Committee Executive Committee Meeting, October 9, 1939, Box 6, Folder 23, Alfred Cohn Papers. Stein maintained that position in 1944, encouraging the committee to close shop and stop helping "relief cases" whose "adjustment to this country would never come." Otherwise, he warned, American professors would return from war to find foreign scholars subsidized by outside money filling their positions; Minutes, Emergency Committee Executive Committee Meeting, September 21, 1944, Box 6, Folder 26; Minutes, Emergency Committee Executive Committee Meeting, December 5, 1939 [*sic*], Box 6, Folder 21, both Alfred Cohn Papers; Drury to Duggan, December 29, 1938, Record of the Emergency Committee, RG-19.061, USHMM.

38. Minutes, Emergency Committee Executive Committee Meeting, April 2, 1939, Box 6, Folder 22, Alfred Cohn Papers; Kenyon to Duggan, March 30, 1939, and Duggan to Keppel, April 15, 1939, both Box 4, Folder 29, Alfred Cohn Papers.

39. Gregg to Hill, April 15, 1939, Box 4, Folder 29; Dunn to Duggan, April 20, 1939, Box 4, Folder 17, both Alfred Cohn Papers.

40. Duggan to Keppel, April 15, 1939, and Cohn to Duggan, April 28, 1939, both Box 4, Folder 29, Alfred Cohn Papers.

41. Report, "Results Obtained from Questionnaires Sent to College Presidents in the United States and Territories by Mr. George Gallup," March 1, 1939, Box 202, Folder 21, Emergency Committee Papers.

42. Ibid.; Drury to Hiss, O'Donnell, March 10, 1939, ibid.

43. Minutes, Emergency Committee Executive Committee Meeting, October 9, 1939, Box 6, Folder 23, Alfred Cohn Papers.

44. Report, Knauth, Box 13, Folder 24, Alfred Cohn Papers.

45. Ibid.

46. Ibid.; Notes, "Dr. Kotschnig's Visit to U.S.A. Winter 1936," Box 2, Folder 15, Alfred Cohn Papers; Baer to Duggan, October 4, 1940, Box 205, Folder 10, Emergency Committee Papers.

47. Minutes, Emergency Committee Executive Committee Meeting, September 23, 1938, Box 6, Folder 21, Alfred Cohn Papers.

48. Giese to Brunauer, September 11, 1938, and Giese to Parkins, November 19, 1938, both War Relief Files 839, Folder Charlotte Giese, Committee Records 8111, AAUWA.

49. Cook to Brunauer, December 29, 1938, ibid.

50. Morley to McHale, January 12, 1939; Panofsky to McHale, January 12, 1939; Sachs to McHale, January 17 1938, all ibid.

51. Charlotte Giese, Gruppe P.P. Ordner 645, Briefbuch der Gestapo Lissa 1943/1944, International Tracing Service, USHMM.

Chapter 10. A Last Chance in France

1. Officer's Diary, O'Brien, September 12, 1940, Box 96A, Folder 1940, RF RG12.1, RAC; Susan Irving and Kristin Bollas, "Lives in the Balance: The Refugee Scholar Experience," *Rockefeller Archive Center Newsletter* (2008): 9–11; Officer's Diary, Makinsky, September 24, 1940, Box 96A, Folder 1940, RF RG12.1, RAC.

2. Memo, Willets, June 3, 1940, Box 46, Folder 530, RF RG1.1, RAC.

3. Willets to Fosdick, June 17, 1940, Armstrong to Long, June 21, 1940; Inter-office correspondence, Kittridge, June 28, 1940; Lefschetz to Weaver, June 27, 1940; Appleget to Friedrich, July 9, 1940, all Box 46, Folder 530, ibid.

4. Inter-office correspondence, Appleget, July 9, 1940, and Memo, Appleget, July 11, 1940, both ibid.

5. Fosdick to Makinsky, July 16, 1940, and Makinsky to Fosdick, July 25, 1940, both ibid.

6. Memo, Appleget, July 11, 1940, ibid.; Report, "Refugee Scholar Programs," Appleget, November 26, 1940, Record of the Emergency Committee, RG-19.061, USHMM.

7. Minutes, Emergency Committee Executive Committee Meeting, August 1, 1940, Box 6, Folder 25, Alfred Cohn Papers.

8. Staff conference, October 23, 1940, Box 46, Folder 532; Willets to Bowman, November 6, 1940, Box 46, Folder 533, both RF RG1.1, RAC.

9. Miller to Shapley, September 26, 1940, Box 6B, Folder K, Harlow Shapley Collection, 4773.10, HUA.

10. Handwritten note, n.d., Box 5, Folder 44, UASUNY; Koffka to Johnson, September 20, 1940; Kohler to Johnson, September 5, 1940; Langfeld to Johnson, September 24, 1940; Ogden to Emergency Committee, September 30, 1941; Drury to Burks, July 23, 1941; Gurwitsch to Emergency Committee, August 9, 1941; Kotschnig to Duggan,

September 26, 1941, all Box 95, Folder 53, Emergency Committee Papers; Note, n.d., Box 3, Folder 54, UASUNY.

11. Goodenough to Johnson, October 11, 1940; Baron to Johnson, January 29, 1941; Memo, Heschel, May 19, 1941, all Box 6, Folder 158, UASUNY; "Stein, Edmund," The YIVO Encyclopedia of Jews in Eastern Europe, http://www.yivoencyclopedia.org/article .aspx/Stein_Edmund.

12. Rina Lapidus, *Jewish Women Writers in the Soviet Union* (London: Routledge, 2012), 50–51; Lapidus's account of Gorlin's and Bloch-Gorlin's wartime travails, on pages 51–52, does not square with contemporaneous records of those trying to help Gorlin obtain a New School position and immigrate, nor with official records. Agnès Graceffa, "Raïssa Bloch-Gorlin (1898–1943). Parcours d'une histoirenne du Moyen Âge à travers l'Europe des années noires," *St. Petersburg Historical Journal,* no. 3 (2014): 200–223, http://www.spbiiran.nw.ru/wp-content/uploads/2015/03/selection-151.pdf.

13. Interviews, John Marshall, Professor Wacław Lednicki, Monday July 14, 1941, Box 233, Folder 2782; Marshall to Cross, July 14, 1941, Box 49, Folder 577, both RF RG1.1, RAC.

14. Cross to Marshall, July 16, 1941, Marshall to Cross, June 21, 1941, Box 49, Folder 577, ibid.

15. Marshall to Whitfield, July 17, 1941, and Whitfield to Marshall, July 18, 1941, ibid.

16. Whitfield to Marshall, July 19, 1941, and Lednicki to Marshall, July 21, 1941, ibid.

17. Stevens to Johnson, August 6, 1941, Box 49, Folder 577, RF RG1.1, RAC.

18. Bat-Ami Zucker, *In Search of Refuge: Jews and US Consuls in Nazi Germany 1933–1941* (London: Vallentine Mitchell, 2001), 126–32; David S. Wyman, *Paper Walls: America and the Refugee Crisis 1938–1941* (New York: Pantheon, 1985), 140–49; Robert A. Divine, *American Immigration Policy, 1924–1952* (New Haven: Yale University Press, 1957), 102–3; Richard Breitman and Alan M. Kraut, *American Refugee Policy and European Jewry, 1933–1945* (Bloomington: Indiana University Press, 1988), 128–35.

19. Kingdom to Friend, April 19, 1941, Box 4, Folder 11; Report, Emergency Committee, Box 7, Folder Sub Centre Secours, both Varian Fry Papers, Columbia Rare Book and Manuscript Library, New York; Langerhaus to Korsch, July 4, 1940, and Korsch to Solow, September 7, 1940, both Box 4, Folder 124, UASUNY. Langerhaus did survive, seemingly receiving an emergency visa to come to the United States in 1941. He may have been able to receive the visa by claiming to be a Social Democrat rather than a communist. Langerhaus taught at Gettysburg College until returning to a teaching career in Germany in 1956.

20. Clipping, Box 13, Folder 1, Alfred Cohn Papers.

21. Officer's Diary, Makinsky, 1941, Box 96A, Folder 1940, RF RG12.1, RAC; Walter Meyerhof became a Stanford University physicist; Officer's Diary, Makinsky, February 8, 9, and 10, 1941, Box 96A, Folder 1941, RAC. Ancel, who had been dismissed from the Sorbonne in 1940, was rounded up in December 1941 and imprisoned in Compiegne concentration camp. He died in 1943 at the age of fifty-one; Officer's Diary, Makinsky, February 17, 1941, ibid. Bayet survived the war.

22. Officer's Diary, Makinsky, February 27, 1941, Box 96A, Folder 1941, RAC.

23. Ibid.

24. Ibid.

25. Officer's Diary, Makinsky, September 24, 1940, Box 96A, Folder 1940; Officer's Diary, Makinsky, March 1, 1941; Officer's Diary, Makinsky, June 23, 1941, Box 96A, Folder 1941, RF RG12.1, RAC.

26. Lessy to AFSC, September 11, 1942, and Jones to Lessy, September 24, 1942, both Case 10, 936, AFSC Case Files; The Central Database of Shoah Victims' Names, Yad Vashem, https://yvng.yadvashem.org/index.html?language=en&s_lastName=Schweitzer&s _firstName=Ernst&s_place=&s_dateOfBirth=&s_inTransport=true.

27. Jones to Muenz, December 10, 1942, Case 12,297, AFSC Case Files; "Holocaust Survivors and Victims Database," USHMM https://www.ushmm.org/online/hsv/person _view.php?PersonId=5324835.

28. Email from Elie Belorizky, dated September 17, 2018, in the author's possession.

29. In one account, the Vichy government fired Belorizky in December 1940. This may be a discrepancy, or it may be that he was indeed fired but Bosler was able to have him reinstated. Observatoire de Haute-Provence, http://www.obs-hp.fr/dictionnaire/par _lettre/lettre_B1.pdf; Email from Elie Belorizky, dated September 17, 2018, in the author's possession; Shapley to Bosler, November 4, 1942, Box 6A, Folder Ferdinand Beer, Harlow Shapley Collection, 4773.10, HUA.

30. Email from Elie Belorizky, dated September 17, 2018, in the author's possession; Evry Schatzman, "The Desire to Understand the World," *Annual Review of Astronomy and Astrophysics* 34 (1996): 1–34, 18l; Danielle Briot and Jean Schneider, "Prehistory of Transit Searches," https://arxiv.org/pdf/1803.06896.pdf, and in H. Deeg and J. Belmonte, eds., *Handbook of Exoplanets* (Cham: Springer, 2018): 1–15, https://doi.org/10.1007/978 -3-319-30648-3_169-1.

31. Simons to Flynn, August 20, 1940, Box 6, Folder 126, UASUNY.

32. Flynn to Johnson, October 31, 1940, and Johnson to Flynn, November 14, 1940, ibid.

33. MacCreight to Hull, January 24, 1942, and Handwritten Note, February 19, 1942, ibid.

34. Bornstein to Johnson, May 21, 1942, ibid. After escaping to Switzerland, Simons worked at the Zurich Polytechnic Institute and warned U.S. intelligence that Germany was most likely developing biological weapons. Upon arriving in the United States, he joined the faculty of the Philadelphia College of Pharmacy and Science. Simons died in 1969. Neal H. Petersen, ed., *From Hitler's Doorstep: The Wartime Intelligence Reports of Allen Dulles, 1942–1945* (University Park: Pennsylvania State University Press, 1996), 173.

Chapter 11. Security Fears

1. Dunn to Cohn, August 1, 1940, Box 13, Folder 1, Alfred Cohn Papers.

2. Cohn to Berle, August 9, 1940, Box 5, Folder 5, Alfred Cohn Papers.

3. Berle to Cohn, August 26, 1940, ibid.; Richard Breitman and Alan M. Kraut,

American Refugee Policy and European Jewry, 1933–1945 (Bloomington: Indiana University Press, 1988), 124; Saul S. Friedman, *No Haven for the Oppressed: United States Policy Toward Jewish Refugees, 1938–1945* (Detroit: Wayne State University, 1973) 125–26.

4. Henry L. Feingold, *The Politics of Rescue: The Roosevelt Administration and the Holocaust, 1938–1945* (New York: Holocaust Library, 1970), 142; Rafael Medoff, *FDR and the Holocaust: A Breach of Faith* (Washington, DC: David S. Wyman Institute for Holocaust Studies, 2013), 35–36; Peter M. Rutkoff and William B. Scott, *New School: A History of the New School for Social Research* (New York: Free Press, 1986), 130–31, 134–35.

5. Kolinski to Herskovits, May 10, 1940, and Herskovits to Kolinski, May 14, 1940, both Melville Herskovits Papers, Mieczyslaw Kolinski Box 12, Folder 1.

6. Cable, Kolinski, via Alfred Rostow, Ilse Hess, to Herskovits, November 7, 1940; Herskovits to Goodchild, November 25, 1940, both Melville Herskovits Papers, Mieczyslaw Kolinski Box 12, Folder 1.

7. Cable, Kolinski, via Alfred Rostow, Ilse Hess, to Herskovits, November 7, 1940, ibid., and Kolinski to Herskovits, March 24, 1941, Box 82, Folder 1, Emergency Committee Papers.

8. Herskovits to Antoine, November 25, 1940; Herskovits to Coulter, December 19, 1940; Herskovits to Goodchild, January 20, 1941; Warren to Herskovits, February 11, 1941; Herskovits to Warren, February 15, 1941, all Melville Herskovits Papers, Mieczyslaw Kolinski Box 12, Folder 1.

9. Warren to Herskovits, March 3, 1941, and March 19, 1941; Herskovits to Warren, March 24, 1941; Herskovits to Antoine, March 24, 1941; Kolinski to Herskovits, March 23, 1941; Warren to Herskovits, April 5, 1941; Herskovits to Warren, April 9, 1941; Herskovits to Drury, April 14, 1941; Kolinski to Herskovits, March 24, 1941, all Box 82, Folder 1, Emergency Committee Papers.

10. Kolinski to Herskovits, March 24, 1941, Box 82, Folder 1, Emergency Committee Papers; Mayerson to Herskovits, May 13, 1941; Herskovits to Kolinski, April 14, 1941; Herskovits to Antoine, April 30, 1941; all Melville Herskovits Papers, Mieczyslaw Kolinski Box 12, Folder 1.

11. Herskovits to Drury, April 14, 1941; Drury to Herskovits, April 22, 1941; Boas to Herskovits, May 8, 1941, and June 4, 1941; Boas to Herskovits, June 9, 1941, all Melville Herskovits Papers, Mieczyslaw Kolinski Box 12, Folder 1.

12. Immigration forms, Box 139, Folder 1328, Edwin Borchard Papers, MS 670, YUA.

13. Ibid.

14. Makinsky to Shapley, October 20, 1942, Box 6A, Folder Ferdinand Beer, 4773.10, HUA.

15. David S. Wyman, *Paper Walls: America and the Refugee Crisis 1938–1941* (New York: Pantheon, 1985), 194–96. Two weeks before the law passed, State had sent instructions to the consuls to reject applicants if they had "'children, parents, spouse, brothers or sisters still residing in the ever-widening territories under Nazi domination'" (194); Feingold, *Politics of Rescue,* 159–63.

16. Makinsky to Shapley, October 20, 1942, Box 6A, Folder Ferdinand Beer, 4773.10,

HUA; Mayerson to Solow, July 3, 1942, Box 7, Folder 1, UASUNY; Lewi Stone, "Quantifying the Holocaust: Hyperintense Kill Rates During the Nazi Genocide," *Science Advances* 5, no. 1 (January 2, 2019), http://advances.sciencemag.org/content/5/1/eaau7292.

17. Breitman and Kraut, *American Refugee Policy*, 135–36; Feingold, *Politics of Rescue*, 200–203.

18. Marshall to Herskovits, June 19, 1941; Herskovits to Marshall, June 21, 1941; Herskovits to Snyder, June 12, 1941; Herskovits to Boas, July 5, 1941; Herskovits to Bryan, July 5, 1941, all Melville Herskovits Papers, Mieczyslaw Kolinski Box 12, Folder 1.

19. Makinsky to Marshall, July 31, 1941, ibid.

20. Officer's Diary, Makinsky, July 8, 1941, Box 96A, Folder 1941, RF RG12.1, RAC; Staudinger to Van Buuren, November 13, 1941, Box 7, Folder 60, UASUNY.

21. Herskovits to Snyder, August 7, 1941, and Marshall to Herskovits, August 19, 1941, Melville Herskovits Papers, Mieczyslaw Kolinski Box 12, Folder 1.

22. Hans Przibram, 0367171, International Tracing Service, USHMM; Luca Nogler, "In Memory of Hugo Sinzheimer (1875–1945): Remarks on the Methodenstreit in Labour Law," *Cardozo Law Bulletin* http://www.jus.unitn.it/cardozo/review/laborlaw /nogler-1996/nogler.htm. The University of Amsterdam named an institute and a moot court competition for Sinzheimer.

23. Herskovits to Drury, December 12, 1942, Box 82, Folder 1, Emergency Committee Papers; Subcommittee on Applications Agenda, December 8, 1942, Box 6, Folder 17, Alfred Cohn Papers; Herskovits to Drury, December 12, 1942.

24. Minutes, Rockefeller Foundation Meeting, October 20, 1941, Box 6, Folder 26, Alfred Cohn Papers; Officer's Diary, Makinsky, January 24, 1942, and January 24–February 5, 1942, Box 96A, Folder 1942, RF RG12.1, RAC.

25. Marshall to O'Brien, July 24, 1941, Box 50, Folder 668; "Detail of Information," Box 56, Folder 668, both RF RG1.1, RAC.

26. Wittek to Johnson, July 6, 1941; MacLeish to Marshall, July 25, 1941; Berle to MacLeish, July 23, 1941, all Box 50, Folder 668, ibid.

27. Marshall to O'Brien, July 24, 1941; Marshall to MacLeish, February 17, 1942; MacLeish to Marshall, February 20, 1942, all Box 56, Folder 668, ibid.

28. Officer's Diary, Makinsky, January 24, 1942, and January 24–February 5, 1942, Box 96A, Folder 1942, RF RG12.1, RAC; Boris's father-in-law, Leon Brillouin, a French physicist who was then teaching at Brown University, assumed that the Vichy government had denied Boris an exit visa because of his knowledge of North Africa. Alvin Johnson concurred. Johnson to Appleget, July 13, 1942, Box 48, Folder 557, RF RG1.1, RAC; see Box 101, Folder 55, Emergency Committee Papers.

29. Officer's Diary, Makinsky, January 24–February 5, 1942, Box 96A, Folder 1942, RF RG12.1, RAC.

30. Bickerman was misspelled Bikerman in the original. Officer's Diary, Makinsky, ibid.; for a detailed description of Bickerman's immigration problems, see Albert I. Baumgarten, *Elias Bickerman as a Historian of the Jews: A Twentieth Century Tale* (Tubingen: Mohr Siebeck, 2010), 130–38; see Box 48, Folder 556, 557, RF RG1.1, RAC. The State Department authorized the U.S. consul in North Africa to issue Boris a visa in April

1942. The Rockefeller Foundation terminated his grant in August 1942 upon learning he had been denied an exit visa. Memo, Makinsky, April 9, 1942, Box 48, Folder 556, 557, RF RG1.1, RAC; Guilbert Boris, 15970153-0-1.tif, International Tracing Service, USHMM; MEA to Fischer, June 4, 1942, Box 101, Folder 55, Emergency Committee Papers; *New York Times,* July 27, 1942, 16.

31. Warren to Gurvitch, March 18, 1942; Asofsky to Makinsky, April 1, 1942; Memo, Makinsky, June 7, 1943, all Box 50, Folder 595, RF RG1.1, RAC.

32. Officer's Diary, Makinsky, January 24, 1942, January 24–February 5, 1942, Box 96A, Folder 1942; Memo, Makinsky, April 15, 1942; L. Gorlin to Marshall, April 14, 1942; Marshall to L. Gorlin, April 16, 1942, Box 49, Folder 578, all RF RG1.1, RAC.

33. Rutkoff and Scott, *New School,* 129–36; in 1955, the Rockefeller Foundation, which helped just over three hundred scholars come to the United States, noted in a report that several "failed to reach America." A later accounting of fifty-eight scholars the foundation had tried to help included six who "failed to reach America." The list includes Boris, Hintze, Jankélévitch, Philip, Sinzheimer, and Wittek. It does not mention eight others who received Rockefeller grants and did not arrive in the United States: Gorlin, Warnier, Edgar Rubin, Alexander Michelson, Marc Bloch, Kurt Grelling, Stanislaw Saks, and Ludwik Ehrlich. There are almost certainly others. "The Rockefeller Foundation's Refugee Scholars Program, Emergency Placement, 1940–1945 Placement," Rockefeller Foundation Archives, https://rockarch.org/collections/rf/refugee.php. It may be that some of these scholars fell outside the "emergency placement" program. David S. Wyman, *The Abandonment of the Jews: America and the Holocaust 1941–1945* (New York: New Press, 1998), 136, 128. Wyman credits the State Department's cumbersome procedures for the low numbers. Wyman does not accept a common explanation, the unavailability of shipping, which he considers "a fraud." He cites as one example the willingness of military authorities in Casablanca to take refugees on ships that had brought troops to North Africa and were to return to the States empty. The consulate in Casablanca agreed to cooperate, and refugee organizations arranged for the refugees to depart. Then the State Department's visa division refused to provide quota numbers to refugees in North Africa until they had assurance of transportation, and the military would not assure they had transportation until the refugees had quota numbers.

Chapter 12. Final Appeals

1. Agnès Graceffa, "Raïssa Bloch-Gorlin (1898–1943). Parcours d'une histoirenne du Moyen Âge à travers l'Europe des années noires," *St. Petersburg Historical Journal,* no. 3 (2014): 200–223, http://www.spbiiran.nw.ru/wp-content/uploads/2015/03/selection-151.pdf.

2. "Transport 6 from Pithiviers, Camp, France to Auschwitz Birkenau, Extermination Camp, Poland on 17/07/1942," International Institute for Holocaust Research, Yad Vashem, http://db.yadvashem.org/deportation/transportDetails.html?language=en&itemId=5092631; Michel Gorlin, TD #2215085, International Tracing Service, USHMM.

3. Staudinger to Marshall, October 5, 1944, Box 49, Folder 578, RF RG1.1, RAC.

4. Graceffa, "Raïssa Bloch-Gorlin."

5. Ibid.; see also "Transport 62 from Drancy, Camp, France to Auschwitz Birkenau, Extermination Camp, Poland on 20/11/1943," International Institute for Holocaust Research, Yad Vashem, http://db.yadvashem.org/deportation/transportDetails.html?language=en&itemId=5092634.

6. Staudinger to Marshall, October 5, 1944, Box 49, Folder 578, RF RG1.1, RAC. Two decades later, Lalla Gorlin received her Ph.D. from Columbia University with a dissertation on "The Problem of Loneliness in the Narrative Works of Arthur Schnitzler." Seemingly without family, she lived on the Upper West Side and died in 1999 at the age of eighty-six.

7. Vincent Brown, "African America Survives the Shoah: Melville J. Herskovits, Mieczyslaw Kolinski, and the Reincarnation of Negro Music," paper presented at the Association for the Study of African American Life and History Annual Meeting, Raleigh, NC, October 2, 2010, manuscript in the author's possession. See also David F. Garcia, *Listening for Africa: Freedom, Modernity and the Logic of Black Music's African Origins* (Durham, NC: Duke University Press, 2017); Paul Helmer, *Growing with Canada: The Émigré Tradition in Canadian Music* (Montreal: McGill-Queens Press, 2009), 37; Kolinski to Herskovits, December 12, 1944, Melville Herskovits Papers, General Files 1943–1944, Mieczyslaw Kolinski Box 28, Folder 33, Northwestern University Archives, Evanston, IL.

8. Gerhard Ritter, *German Refugee Historians and Friedrich Meinecke* (Leiden: Koninklijke Brill NY, 2010), 79–91.

9. Anne Frank's family also tried to obtain visas to the United States from the consul in Rotterdam. Rebecca Erbelding and Gertjan Broek, "German Bombs and U.S. Bureaucrats: How Escape Lines from Europe Were Cut Off," *Medium*, July 5, 2018, https://medium.com/@HolocaustMuseum/german-bombs-and-us-bureaucrats-how-escape-lines-from-europe-were-cut-off-1b3e14137cc4. This account in *Medium*, although literally accurate, reads as if the rules the State Department and consular officials applied were clear and fixed, and they had no choice but to enforce them. This is not the case, however; Memo, January 16, 1941, Box 50, Folder 590, RF RG1.1, RAC. See also Schauffler to Warren, May 29, 1941; Cable, Amsterdam, March 24, 1941; Hanstein to Staudinger, January 13, 1941; Johnson to Hanstein, April 1, 1941; all Hedwig Hintze, Case 1058, AFSC Case Files.

10. Solow to Kittredge, April 1, 1941, Box 50, Folder 590, RF RG1.1, RAC; American Consulate, Rotterdam, to Hintze, February 28, 1941, Hedwig Hintze, Case 1058, AFSC Case Files.

11. Johnson to Hanstein, April 1, 1941, Hedwig Hintze, Case 1058, AFSC Case Files; Kittredge to Consul General, Rotterdam, April 9, 1941, Box 50, Folder 590, RF RG1.1, RAC.

12. Hintze to Johnson, August 8, 1941; DRF to TBA, September 9, 1941; Johnson to Appleget, August 14, 1941; Appleget to Johnson, August 25 and September 2, 1941; Marshall to Appleget, September 4, 1941; Marshall to Johnson, September 9, 1941; Johnson to Appleget, October 1, 1941; Solow to Marshall, October 28, 1941, all ibid.

13. Staudinger to Gillette, September 25, 1942, Box 50, Folder 591, RF RG1.1, RAC.

14. Harriet Pass Freidenreich, in *Female, Jewish and Educated: The Lives of Central European University Women* (Bloomington: Indiana University Press, 2002), demonstrates how overlooking refugees' immigration experience can distort history in powerful ways. Freidenreich described Hintze's 1941–1942 travails as follows: "Deeply depressed and unable to make the necessary arrangements to emigrate to New York to assume a position she had been offered at the New School for Social Research, Hedwig Hintze committed suicide in Holland" (176). Although "unable to make the necessary arrangements to emigrate to New York" is not an inaccurate characterization, it shifts the blame for Hintze's failure to emigrate from where it squarely belongs—the American consular officials who stood in her way for no apparent reason.

15. Jewish Refugee Committee to Schirmann, July 13, 1940, Box 112, Folder 11, Emergency Committee Papers; Schirmann to Colleagues, September 20, 1940, Box 839, Folder Marie Anna Schirmann, Committee Records 8111, AAUWA.

16. "Transport 4 from Wien, Vienna, Austria to Modliborzyce, Janow Lubelski, Lublin, Poland on 5/03/1941," International Institute for Holocaust Research, Yad Vashem, http://db.yadvashem.org/deportation/transportDetails.html?language=en&item Id=6996699.

17. Landsberg to Drury, April 4, 1941, and Drury to Landsberg, April 28, 1941, both Box 112, Folder 11, Emergency Committee Papers.

18. Kolischer to Drury, December 2, 1941, ibid.

19. Memo, Aslin to Drury, January 20, 1942, ibid.

20. Dokumentationsarchiv des osterreichischen Wilderstandes, http://www.doew .at/personensuche?gestapo=on&findall=&lang=de&shoah=on&politisch=on&spiegel grund=on&firstname=&lastname=Schirmann&birthdate=&birthdate_to=&birthplace =&residence=&phonetisch=on&newsearch=10&iSortCol_0=1&sSortDir_0=asc&lang =de&suchen=SuchenSchirmann Maria.

21. G. Fleischmann to Johnson, November 11, 1940, and Johnson to G. Fleischmann, November 15, 1940, both Box 2, Folder 167, UASUNY (trans. from German by Eric Idsvoog).

22. Borchard to Johnson, January 16, 1941; Johnson to Borchard, January 17, 1941; Borchard to Johnson, January 24, 1941; Johnson to Borchard, January 28, 1941; Warren to Borchard, June 17, 1941; Borchard to Johnson, July 1, 1941; Johnson to Borchard, July 7, 1941, all ibid.

23. G. Field to Thieman, May 4, 1941, Case 3904, AFSC Case Files.

24. G. Field to Thieman, May 15, 1941, and H. Field to Thieman, June 17, 1941, ibid.

25. Thieman to H. Field, June 27, 1941, ibid.

26. Philip Friedman, "Was There an 'Other Germany' During the Nazi Period?," in Michael R. Marrus, ed., *The Nazi Holocaust, Part 5: Public Opinion and Relations to the Jews in Nazi Europe, Volume 1* (Westport, CT: Meckler, 1989), 3–45, 24. Max Fleischmann, TD #773955, International Tracing Service, USHMM; Fleischmann's library was just one of thousands of libraries held by Jews throughout Europe that German univer-

sities and research institutions took with little or no compensation. The Reich Exchange Office of the Berlin State Library alone seized nearly a million books. Horst Junginger, *The Scientification of the "Jewish Question" in Nazi Germany* (Leiden: Koninklijke Brill NV, 2017), 257, 220–28, 255 n. 214.

27. Spiegel to friends, March 3, 1941, War Relief Files 839, Folder Käthe Spiegel, Committee Records 8111, AAUWA.

28. Ibid.

29. Ibid.

30. Spiegel to friends, April 5, 1941, ibid.; Spiegel to Duggan, May 7, 1940, and Spiegel to Sirs, March 28, 1941, both Box 118, Folder 25, Emergency Committee Papers.

31. Spiegel to friends, April 25, 1941, War Relief Files 839, Folder Käthe Spiegel, Committee Records 8111, AAUWA. Brunauer had provided an affidavit to photochemist Gertrud Kornfeld, whom she had met at a 1936 international federation conference in Kraków. Kornfeld immigrated to the United States. Christine von Oertzen, *Science, Gender and Internationalism: Women's Academic Networks 1917–1955* (New York: Palgrave Macmillan, 2014), 137–38.

32. Minutes, War Relief Committee Meeting, May 10, 1941, War Relief Committee— Meeting, Notes Minutes + Reports, 1941, AAUWA. The other women were Leonore Brecher, who had been an international fellow the 1920s, and Elly Elisabeth Schuck, a member of the Austrian association. Brunauer to Gildersleeve, November 14, 1941, and Crocker to Brunauer, November 28, 1941, both War Relief Files 839, Folder Elly Schuck, Committee Records 8111, AAUWA. The AAUW approved providing the funds to Brecher and Spiegel. It is not clear why Schuck's transportation was not approved at that meeting. Schuck was deported from Vienna to Theresienstadt on September 25, 1942, and then to Auschwitz on May 15, 1944, where she was murdered at the age of fifty. Dr. Elisabeth Schuck, International Tracing Service, USHMM; Lawson to Halberg, June 10, 1941; Brunauer to Halberg, June 13, 1941; Sayre to Woods, June 18, 1942, all War Relief Files 839, Folder Käthe Spiegel, Committee Records 8111, AAUWA.

33. Hamburg America Line to Brunauer, December 8, 1941, and Sayre to Woods, June 18, 1942, both War Relief Files 839, Folder Käthe Spiegel, Committee Records 8111, AAUWA.

34. "Transport B, Train Da 7 from Praha, Praha Hlavni Mesto, Bohemia, Czecho-slovakia to Lodz, Ghetto, Poland on 21/10/1941," International Institute for Holocaust Research, Yad Vashem, http://db.yadvashem.org/deportation/transportDetails.html ?language=en&itemId=5091969. See also Gerhard Oberkofle, "Käthe Spiegel: Aus dem Leben einer altösterreichischen Historikerin und Frauenrechtlerin in Prag," Studien Verlag, https://www.studienverlag.at/buecher/4137/kaethe-spiegel/.

35. Brecher to Brunauer, March 15, 1941, War Relief Files 839, Folder Leonore Brecher, Committee Records 8111, AAUWA.

36. Phillips to Brunauer, April 9, 1941, and Brunauer to Phillips, June 13, 1941, ibid.

37. Brunauer to Brecher, June 17, 1941, ibid.

38. Brecher to Brunauer, September 14, 1941, ibid.

39. Cable, Brunauer to Phillips, October 25, 1941; Brecher to Phillips, November 6, 1941; Brecher to Brunauer, November 7, 1941; Phillips to Brunauer, November 13, 1941, ibid.

40. Phillips to Brunauer, December 10, 1941; Cable, Brunauer to Phillips, December 10, 1941; Phillips to Brunauer, December 23, 1941, and January 12, 1942, ibid.

41. Sayre to Wiesenthal, June 3, 1942, ibid.; "Transport 41, Train Da 227 from Wien, Austria to Maly Trostenets Camp, Belorussia (USSR) on 14/09/1942," International Institute for Holocaust Research, Yad Vashem, http://db.yadvashem.org/deportation /transportDetails.html?language=en&itemId=7062103. Five other Institute for Experimental Biology colleagues died in the Holocaust, including Helene Jacobi who was murdered in Maly Trostinec four months before Brecher in May 1942. Klaus Taschwer, Johannes Feichtinger, Stafan Sienell, and Heidemarie Uhl, eds., *Experimental Biology in the Vienna Prater: On the History of the Institute for Experimental Biology 1902 to 1945* (Vienna: Austrian Academy of Sciences, 2016), 54.

42. Hollitscher to Brunauer, April 3, 1940, Box 839, Folder Hedwig Kohn, Committee Records 8111, AAUWA.

43. Ladenburg to Brunauer, May 7, 1940, ibid.

44. Ladenburg to Brunauer, May 25, 1940, and Brunauer to Ladenburg, May 25, 1940, both ibid.

45. Brunauer to Glass, May 25, 1940; Warren to Brunauer, May 30, 1940; Robertson to Brunauer, May 28, 1940, all ibid.

46. Glass to Brunauer, May 28, 1940, ibid.

47. Brunauer to Ladenburg, June 5, 1940, and McAfee to Brunauer, June 6, 1940, both ibid.

48. Cable, McAfee to Brunauer, June 17, 1940; Brunauer to McAfee, June 18, 1940; Brunauer to Hollitscher, June 25, 1940, all ibid.

49. Kohn to Brunauer, July 24, 1940; Cable, Kock to Brunauer, July 24, 1940; Sponer to Brunauer, August 18, 1940, all ibid.

50. Kohn to Brunauer, January 12, 1941, ibid.

Epilogue

1. Minutes, Emergency Committee Executive Committee Meeting, May 12, 1942, Box 6, Folder 26; Officer's Diary, Makinsky, January 24–February 5, 1942, and March 12, 1942, Box 96A, Folder 1942, all RF RG12.1, RAC.

2. Wiley to Duggan, March 4, 1942, Box 4, Folder 30, Alfred Cohn Papers.

3. Minutes, Emergency Committee Executive Committee Meeting, March 5, 1942, Box 6, Folder 18; Drury to Subcommittee on Applications, July 30, 1942, Box 4, Folder 24; Drury to Members of Executive Committee, June 30, 1942, Box 12, Folder 20, all Alfred Cohn Papers.

4. By the end of 1943, the Emergency Committee considered ending its operations. At the beginning of 1944, the committee decided to keep going, but on a modified basis. The issue arose again in September, with most members agreeing that the commit-

tee had outlived its usefulness. Minutes, Emergency Committee Executive Committee Meeting, December 1, 1943; January 27, 1944; and September 21, 1944, all Box 6, Folder 26, Alfred Cohn Papers. The Emergency Committee officially ended operations in 1946; Minutes, Emergency Committee Executive Committee Meeting, November 22, 1943, Box 2, Folder 3, Alfred Cohn Papers.

5. "Report on Work and Status of Committee," July 1, 1946, Box 1, Folder 8, UASUNY.

6. Ibid.; Johnson to Rockefeller, December 11, 1946, Box 7, Folder 15, UASUNY.

7. "Memorial Book for the Victims of National Socialism at the Austrian Academy of Sciences," Österreichische Akademie der Wissenschaften, https://translate.google.com /translate?hl=en&sl=de&u=https://www.oeaw.ac.at/gedenkbuch/personen/a-h/leonore -rachelle-brecher/&prev=search; Ilse Korotin and Nastasja Stupnicki, *Biographies of Important Austrian Scientists* (Vienna: Böhlau Verlag, 2018), pp. 753–54; https://lise.univie.ac .at/physikerinnen/historisch/marie_anna-schirmann.htm; Gerhard Oberkofler, "Kaethe Spiegel: Aus Dem Leben einer altosterreichischen Historikerin und Frauenrechtlerin in Prag," https://www.studienverlag.at/buecher/4137/kaethe-spiegel/; Alberto Melloni, "From a Catholic Identity to an American View: Historical Studies, Reviews, and Fundamentals in Articles on Late Modern and Contemporary Europe, 1914–2010," *Catholic Historical Review* 101, no. 2 (2015): 123–55, and https://www.academia.edu/12305818/From_a _Catholic_Identity_to_an_American_View_Historical_Studies_Reviews_and_Funda mentals_in_Articles_on_Late_Modern_and_Contemporary_Europe_1914_2010, 115 n. 71; M. I. Yupp, ed., *Inventory of Poetry Books from the Russian Diaspora of the Twentieth Century, 1917–2000* (Philadelphia: Space, 2004), 30; Maxim D. Shrayer, *An Anthology of Jewish Russian Literature: Two Centuries of Dual Identity in Prose and Poetry, Volumes 1–2: 1801–2001* (New York: Routledge, 2015), 462–66; Heroines of the Resistance, "Women of the Jewish Underground in France," September 15, 2015, http://resistanceheroines .blogspot.com/2015/09/jewish-women-of-french-underground.html; Agnès Graceffa, *Une femme face à l'Histoire-Itinéraire de Raïssa Bloch, Saint-Pétersbourg-Auschwitz, 1898–1943* (Paris: Éditions Belin, 2017).

8. Kohn to Brunauer, May 27, 1941; Brunauer to Kohn, May 29, 1941; Kohn to Brunauer, June 11, 1941, all Box 839, Folder Hedwig Kohn, Committee Records 8111, AAUWA; Brenda Winnewiser, "Hedwig Kohn, 1887–1964," Jewish Women's Archive, Encyclopedia, "Hedwig Kohn," https://jwa.org/encyclopedia/article/kohn-hedwig.

9. "Mieczyslaw Kolinski," Institut für Historische Musikwissenschaft, Universität Hamburg, https://www.lexm.uni-hamburg.de/object/lexm_lexmperson_00001287; Vincent Brown, "African America Survives the Shoah: Melville J. Herskovits, Mieczyslaw Kolinski and the Reincarnation of Negro Music," paper presented at the Association for the Study of African American Life and History Annual Meeting, Raleigh, NC, October 2, 2010, in the author's possession.

10. Stephen Duggan's son Laurence, a former State Department official, succeeded him at the Institute of International Education. Laurence Duggan died in late 1948 after falling or jumping from the institute's 45th Street offices, which also housed the Emergency Committee. Ten days earlier, the FBI had questioned him about his contacts with

the Soviet Union. At the time, Laurence Duggan seemed to have been accused unfairly, but decrypted Soviet cables suggested he had been in contact with Soviet agents. John Earl Haynes, Harvey Kiehr, and Alexander Vassiliev, *Spies: The Rise and Fall of the KGB in America* (Ann Arbor, MI: Sherida Books, 2009), 220–44.

11. Ludovic Tournès, "The Rockefeller Foundation and the Transition from the League of Nations to the UN (1939–1946)," *Journal of Modern European History* 12, no. 3 (August 2014): 323–41, doi: 10.17104/1611-8944_2014_3_323; E. J. Kahn Jr., "The Universal Drink," *New Yorker,* February 14, 1959, https://www.newyorker.com/magazine/1959/02 /14/the-universal-drink; Laureen Kuo, "Another Perspective on the Coca-Cola Affair in Postwar France," *Enterprise & Society* 18, no. 1 (March 2017): 108–45, https://doi.org /10.1017/eso.2016.44.

12. *Justice Denied* recently published a collection of Borchard's writings on wrongful convictions. Hans Sherrer, *Edwin M. Borchard: Convicting the Innocent and State Indemnity for Errors of Criminal Justice* (Seattle: Justice Institute, 2016), see justice denied.org/edwinborchard.html.

13. Rankin quoted in "Dr. Harlow Shapley Dies at 86; Dean of American Astronomers," *New York Times,* October 21, 1972, 1; Tony Ortega, "Red Scare: Astronomer Harlow Shapley Reshaped the Universe, but FBI Considered Him a Risk," *Astronomy,* January 2002, available at The Underground Bunker, https://tonyortega.org/red-scare -astronomer-harlow-shapley-reshaped-the-universe-but-the-fbi-considered-him-a-risk/.

14. "Mrs. Brunauer Tells of Death Threats," *Southeast Missourian/Associated Press,* March 28, 1950.

15. Barbara Sicherman and Carol Hurd Green, eds., *Notable American Women: The Modern Period: a Biographical Dictionary* (Cambridge, MA: Harvard University Press, 1980), 114–16; Richard M. Fried, *Nightmare in Red: The McCarthy Era in Perspective* (New York: Oxford University Press, 1990), 23–29.

16. Cohn to Johnson, January 25, 1936, Box 13, Folder 21, Alfred Cohn Papers.

Acknowledgments

Supportive colleagues throughout Northeastern University sustained me as I pursued this lengthy and demanding endeavor, including the faculty and staff in the School of Journalism, particularly director Jonathan Kaufman, who has made the school an exciting place to pursue our challenging and essential profession; Director Lori Lefkovitz and Associate Director Jenny Sartori (now of the Jewish Women's Archive) in Jewish Studies, who have a personal and existential commitment to Holocaust remembrance; Prof. Jeffrey Burds in the history department, who manages to confront the horrors of the Holocaust with scholarly distance and passionate devotion; and my Rediscovering Refugee Scholars collaborators, Profs. John Wihbey and Michelle Borkin and graduate student Michail Schwab, who helped me see data in a new and vital way.

Eric Idsvoog provided helpful translations, sometimes with very little notice. Satu Haase-Webb and Elizabeth Anthony led me through the intricacies of the International Tracing Service Collection at the U.S. Holocaust Memorial Museum. My remarkable graduate student, Alexa Mills, who is now a remarkable editor and reporter, waded into the Birkhoff papers at Harvard University Archives for me and emerged with gems.

At Yale University Press, Jennifer Banks saw I had a book before I did, Heather Gold helped to make it one, and Jessie Dolch ensured it was clear and consistent.

As world events turned dark, my many friends of many decades helped remind me of the energy, optimism, and ambitions of our youth, no more so than Peter Kougasian, who is as dedicated to ideas, honesty, and humor as he was when we met at Princeton in 1975. My mother, Ada Leff, embodied the Jewish spirit of resilience in the face of profound losses. My sons, Jason Paul and Russell Paul, and their partners, Eilish Brown and Leslie Diaz, never let me sink too deeply into the sorrows of my subject. My husband, Jeremy Paul, shared every discovery, discussed every concept, read every word, corrected every typo (well, almost), and made all things possible.

Index

Photographs are indicated by italicized page numbers.

Mirkine-Guetzévitch, Boris, 204–5
MIT. *See* Massachusetts Institute of
  Technology
Moholy-Nagy, L., 76
Morey, Charles, 190
Morgenstern, Julian, 82, 124, 125
Morgenthau, Henry, 99
Morley, Felix, 100
Mosse, Robert, 203, 224
motivation to save refugee scholars:
  conflict between goal of saving best
  scholars vs. saving most scholars, 66;
  exclusion of humanitarian consider-
  ations, 67; funding assistance as,
  98–104; Harvard on, 67. *See also*
  humanitarian desire to save lives;
  top scholars
Mühsam, Alice, 98
Müller, Hugo, 75, 84
Murlin, John, 115
Murrow, Edward R., 35–36, 53, 62, 77,
  77–78, 79, 88–89, 95, 290n30, 304n4;
  anti-McCarthyism of, 257; wartime
  and postwar career of, 257
Myers, S. B., 318n32
Myrdal, Gunnar, 42

Nabokov, Vladimir, 20
Nachmansohn, David, 113
Naples consul, 97, 121, 128
Nathan, Helen, 124, 130
Nathan, Otto, 118
Nathan Hofheimer Foundation, 39
Nathenson, William, 171
National Academy of Sciences, 73, 113, 255
National Coordinating Committee. *See*
  later name of National Refugee Service
national defense, as reason to grant visas
  to refugee scholars, 222
National Refugee Service, 32, 46, 49, 116,
  139–40, 146, 147, 166, 170, 251
National Socialists. *See Nazi headings*
National Society of Sigma Xi, 255

Navarra Bernstein, Marta, 43
Nazi ideology, 11, 108–9; German
  academic support for, 25; Mankiewicz
  as supporter of, 92; racial laws and
  Nuremberg laws, 24, 113, 128, 138–39,
  141, 157, 178, 206, 213; university curriculum changed to support, 20–23;
  U.S. academic support for, 83
Nazi sympathizers, 61, 83, 92
Nazi war criminals, trials of, 136
Nebraska Central College, 43
Némirovsky, Irène, 228
Netherlands: AAUW affiliations in, 43;
  as destination of refugee scholars, 74,
  76, 78, 81, 82, 123, 124, 156, 220, 284n4,
  312n25; extermination of Jews from,
  233; German invasion of (1940), 191,
  220, 231; professors losing jobs in, 30;
  Rockefeller Foundation's attempts to
  save scholars in, 42, 220
Neuberger, Max, 84–85
Neuner, Robert, 75
Neurath, Otto, 75
New Jersey College for Women, 2
New School for Social Research: American Council for Émigrés in the Professions, creation of, 195; Benoit-Levy
  and, 205; Bickerman and, 224; Bloch
  and, 131–32; Ehrlich and, 134–35;
  Emergency Committee coordination
  with, 40, 195–96; Eppstein and, 103;
  M. Fleischmann and, 50, 236; French
  antifascists and, 224; Gorlin and, 200,
  228, 320n12; Graduate Faculty of Political and Social Science, 39; Gumbel
  and, 90, 204; Hintze and, 232, 233;
  hiring criteria for refugee scholars, 78,
  115; Jakobson and, 308n9; Jankélévitch
  and, 88; Lederer and Löwe joining
  faculty of, 74; Mantoux and, 109;
  Mayer and, 91–92; Michelson and,
  131; Mirkine-Guetzévitch and, 204–5;
  Mosse and, 224; Müller and, 84; origins